BERLITZ®
TRAVEL GUIDE

ROME

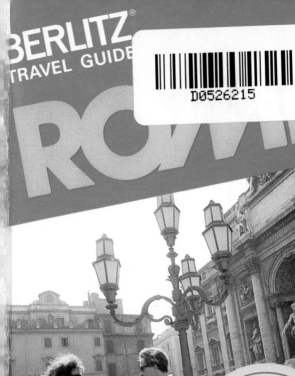

NEW!
with restaurant and hotel recommendations

World's Leading
of Pocket Travel

D0526215

Deluxe Guide
1988/1989 Edition

By the staff of Berlitz Guides

How best to use this guide

- All the practical information, hints and tips that you will need before or during your trip start on page 103.

- To capture the flavour of the city and its people, turn to the section Rome and the Romans, page 6.

- For a greater understanding of Rome's past, A Brief History, page 12, documents the major events, summed up by a chronological chart on page 21.

- Rome's principal sights and monuments are grouped between pages 22 and 73. There are also chapters on Rome's churches (p. 74) and museums (p. 79), with suggested day trips on pages 83 to 91.

- Those sights which we most highly recommend are pinpointed by the Berlitz traveller symbol.

- A rundown of entertainment possibilities and yearly events is to be found between pages 91 to 93.

- A section on shopping between pages 93 and 95 gives guidance on where to shop and items to look out for.

- Rome's culinary specialities are described between pages 96 to 102, with advice on tipping and meal times.

- If there is anything you can't find instantly, refer to the index at the back of the book, pp. 126–128.

- Finally, a special insert listing a selection of hotels and restaurants will help solve the dilemma of where to stay or eat.

Text: Christina Jackson and Jack Altman
Editor: Adrienne Farrell
Layout: Max Thommen
Photography: cover, pp. 9, 13, 18–19, 44–45, 87, 88–89, 94–95, Daniel Vittet; pp. 2–3, 6, 10, 16, 22–23, 31, 33, 35, 36–37, 38, 40, 43, 52–53, 55, 57, 60–61, PRISMA; pp. 7, 41, 69, Strawberry Media; pp. 47, 48, 65, 76, 77, 81, Herbert Fried; pp. 59, 67, 70–71, 73, 99, 100, Walter Imber.
We would like to thank Don Larrimore, and Francesco Casertano of the E.P.T. in Rome for invaluable assistance.
Cartography: 🔴 Falk-Verlag, Hamburg; p. 51, Max Thommen

Photos, cover: Trevi Fountain, pp. 2–3 Rome skyline

Contents

Rome and the Romans		6
A Brief History		12
Historical Landmarks		21
What to See		22
	Modern and Renaissance Rome	27
	Classical Rome	49
	The Vatican	59
	The Churches	74
	Museums	79
	Excursions	83
What to Do	Entertainment	91
	Festivals	92
	Shopping	93
Eating Out		96
Blueprint for a Perfect Trip		103
	How to Get There	103
	Planning Your Budget	105
	A–Z of Practical Information	106
Index		126

Maps	Rome	24–25
	The Forum	51
	Rome and Surroundings	85

Found an error or an omission in this Berlitz Guide? Or a change or new feature we should know about? Our editor would be happy to hear from you, and a postcard would do. Be sure to include your name and address, since in appreciation for a useful suggestion, we'd like to send you a free travel guide.

Although we make every effort to ensure the accuracy of all the information in this book, changes occur incessantly. We cannot therefore take responsibility for facts, prices, addresses and circumstances in general that are constantly subject to alteration.

Rome and the Romans

The Romans take it all for granted. They are used to sipping their *espressos* alongside a Baroque fountain in a piazza designed for chariot races. Each day on their way to work, they pass ruined temples, triumphal arches and aqueducts without so much as a second glance. They find it unsurprising that a Renaissance palace should sprout from an ancient amphitheatre, that the columns of Minerva should support a shrine to the Madonna, or that great basilicas should flower over the bones of martyrs dead nearly 2,000 years. And they toss their cigarette stubs into trash-bins embossed with the SPQR mark of municipal property with scarcely a thought that the initials of *Senatus Populusque Romanus* (the Senate and People of Rome) once adorned the legions' standards and represent one of the oldest democratic slogans in the world.

Yet in their heart of hearts they appreciate, even more than any of the millions of visitors, the marvel that is Rome.

The secret of the city lies in the ineffable blend of the spiritual and the temporal, of art

and architecture, of history, myth and legend, that binds the 27 centuries of the past into one harmonious present. You may deplore the sound and fury of the traffic, the cars triple-banked in the narrow streets and parked in a rising tide up the slopes of the Aventine. But this is a vibrant, living city and capital of a country of 57 million people. It refuses to consider itself just a museum piece or to allow the centre of power and decision to shift to the empty wide avenues and ultramodern ministries of the southern suburb of EUR.

The city fathers do their best to keep key sites as oases of peace. A few steps up from the tumult and you enter the Renaissance tranquillity of the Campidoglio, an enchantment especially at night, when subdued lighting illuminates the gracious façades of Michelangelo. And you can still find respite among the overgrown ruins of the Forum and Palatine, in the gardens of the Caelian Hill or Pincio and in the awed hush of the great churches and museums.

Sprawling on the rolling plain known as the Campagna,

Hot chestnuts to warm winter shoppers at Porta Portese.

about half-way down Italy's boot, Rome straddles the River Tiber as it winds and loops its way through vineyards and olive groves, pasture and scrub to disgorge into the Tyrrhenian Sea some 24 kilometres (15 mi.) to the south-west.

The municipality of Rome extends over 1,507 square kilometres (582 sq. mi.), with a population of 3 million. But the ancient walled city enclosing the seven hills of the historic kernel *(centro storico)* covers only four per cent of that area. Small as it is, it contains some 300 palaces and 280 churches, the ruins of republican and imperial Rome, numerous parks and gardens, the residence of the Italian president, the houses of parliament and government offices, not to mention countless banks, businesses, hotels, shops, restaurants and bars.

It *is* crowded. But the phlegmatic Romans take it all with characteristic good cheer and above all *pazienza* (patience), the local watchword. Nowhere is this more admirably demonstrated than on the buses. As the great orange monsters lurch through the traffic, passengers cling to the nearest available handle, all the time easing their way to the exit doors through the seemingly impenetrable mass of bodies with a *mi scusi*

here and a *permesso* there. Gesticulating constantly, hurling harmlessly barbed insults, religiously staying out of the sun, irreligiously whispering at mass, honking their horns over a football victory, parading in demonstrations, pampering their children, the Romans live and love life to the fullest.

Rome may at first seem chaotic, unmanageable, like the scattered pieces of a jigsaw. But as you explore the labyrinth of narrow cobbled streets on foot, the time will come when you will step out into a sunny piazza or into view of some historic monument and instantly know where you are. Another piece of the puzzle will have fallen neatly into place.

Architecturally speaking, Rome is also something of a jigsaw, an amalgam of different styles representing every phase of its history. The russet and ochre façades, fanciful fountains and exuberant churches are predominantly from the Renaissance and Baroque periods, but built onto— and out of—the ancient and medieval cities. It is said that were they to rebuild the hole in the side of the Colosseum with

All the grace of Classical Rome in a Vestal Virgin's poise.

its original material, many of Rome's beautiful Renaissance palaces would disintegrate.

In its 2,700 years of history, Rome has known unparalleled glory and utter degradation and humiliation. Its armies under Julius Caesar and Augustus went out and conquered an empire, but when the barbarians swarmed through the gates in successive waves, not a single heroic action was recorded. Under the popes, Rome triumphed again as a place of great beauty, source of learning and capital of the arts. The city remains to this day a memorial to its own supreme intellectual and artistic achievements and the inestimable role it played in shaping Western civilization.

As the spiritual and physical centre of the Catholic Church, Rome plays host to a never-ending tide of pilgrims who come to see the pope, visit the basilicas and pay their respects to the early Christian martyrs at the catacombs. Catholic seminaries and colleges have sprouted all over the city. Priests, monks and nuns, robed in every variety of ecclesiastical costume, are an integral part of the Roman scene.

Cars yield to pedestrians in streets around the Corso.

If for nothing else, follow the maxim "When in Rome..." when it comes to observing those excellent Roman institutions, the afternoon siesta and the evening *passeggiata*. In the torpid hours of the early afternoon, a distinct lull falls over the city, as shops and offices close down and the Romans return home for lunch and a rest. Everything comes to life again in the cool of the evening, as what seems to be the entire population of Rome descends into the streets to stroll along the crowded sidewalks, gaze in shop windows, or watch the world go by from pavement cafés or coffee bars. Join them. Then, like them, linger over several courses in a pleasant restaurant or trattoria and savour the hearty delights of Roman cuisine.

Rome wasn't built in a day, nor should it be visited in one. Take your time and allow the atmosphere to seep in slowly. It is not one building or monument that will leave a lasting imprint, it's that impression of the whole which will stay with you long after you have left. And when you do go, there's no need to say goodbye. You don't even need to throw a coin into the Trevi Fountain. Like everyone else you're bound to come back. *Arrivederci, Roma!* **11**

A Brief History

Cherished legend maintains that Rome was founded by Romulus, sired with twin brother Remus by Mars of a Vestal Virgin and abandoned on the Palatine Hill to be suckled by a she-wolf. Historians agree that the site and traditional founding date of 753 B.C. are just about right.

Archaeologists have further established that the site was occupied as early as the Bronze Age (c. 1500 B.C.) and that, by the 8th century B.C., independent villages had sprung up on the Palatine and Aventine hills and soon after on the Esquiline and Quirinal ridges. All proved favourable spots for settlement, since they were easily defensible and lay close to the midstream Isola Tiberina, which facilitated fording of the river.

After conquering their Sabine neighbours, the Romans merged the group of villages into a single city and surrounded it by a defensive wall, while the marshland below the Capitoline Hill was drained and became the Forum. Under the rule of seven kings, the last three Etruscan, Rome began to develop as a powerful force in central Italy.

The Republic

A revolt by Roman nobles in 510 B.C. overthrew the last Etruscan king and established a republic which was to last for the next five centuries. At first the young republic, under the leadership of two patrician consuls, was plagued by confrontations between patrician and plebeian factions. But the plebs put forward their own leaders, the tribunes, to protect their interests, and, thus strengthened internally, Rome began to expand its influence.

In 390 B.C. the Gauls laid siege to the city for seven months, destroying everything except the citadel on the Capitoline Hill. When the Gauls finally left, the hardy citizens set about reconstructing, this time enclosing their city in a wall of huge tufa blocks. For eight centuries, until the barbarians came, no foreign invader was to breach those walls. Rome now spread its control to the whole of Italy, consolidating its hold with six great military roads fanning out from the city—Appia, Latina, Salaria, Flaminia, Aurelia and Cassia. By 250 B.C. the city's population had grown to 100,000.

Victory over Carthage in the hundred years of Punic wars (264–146 B.C.) and conquests in Macedonia, Asia Minor,

Rome's emblem recalls legend of founder Romulus and twin Remus suckled by a she-wolf.

Spain and southern France extended Roman power around the Mediterranean. When Hannibal invaded Italy over the Alps in the Second Punic War, large areas of the peninsula were devastated and peasants sought refuge in Rome, swelling the population.

The acquisition of a largely unsought empire brought new social and economic problems to the Roman people. Unemployment, poor housing and an inadequate public works **13** programme fomented unrest in the city. Violent civil wars shook the republic, which ultimately yielded to dictatorship. Pro-consul Julius Caesar, who had achieved fame by subduing Gaul and Britain, crossed the tiny Rubicon river marking the boundary of his province and marched on Rome to seize power.

The Empire

Caesar's reforms, bypassing the Senate to combat unemployment and ease the tax burden, made dangerous enemies. His assassination on the Ides of March, 44 B.C., led to a bitter civil war and the despotic rule of his adopted son Augustus, who became the first emperor. Under Augustus, the Pax Romana reigned supreme over the far-flung empire. To make Rome a worthy capital, he added fine public buildings, baths, theatres, temples and warehouses, claiming he had "found Rome brick and left it marble". He also organized public services (including the first fire brigade). This was the Golden Age of Roman letters, distinguished by giants such as Horace, Ovid, Livy and Virgil.

In the first centuries of the empire, tens of thousands of foreigners flooded into Rome, among them the first Christians, including St. Peter and St. Paul. As the new religion gained ground, the emperors tried to suppress it by persecution, but the steadfastness of the martyrs only increased its appeal.

Each of Augustus' successors contributed his own embellishment to Rome. After a disastrous fire ravaged the city in A.D. 64, Nero rebuilt it and provided himself with an ostentatious palace, the Domus Aurea (Golden House) on the Esquiline Hill. Hadrian reconstructed the Pantheon, raised a monumental mausoleum for himself (Castel Sant'Angelo) and retired to his magnificent estate at Tivoli.

In the late 1st and 2nd centuries, Rome reached the peak of its grandeur, with a population numbering over a million. Inherent flaws in the imperial system, however, were to weaken the power of the emperors and lead eventually to the downfall of the empire.

After the death of Septimius Severus in 211, 25 emperors—all made and unmade by the armies—reigned in the short space of 74 years. Assassination was more often than not the cause of death. Fire and plague took their toll of the city's population. In 283 the Forum was almost totally destroyed by fire, never to recover its former magnificence.

As a result of a battlefield vision of the Cross, Emperor Constantine converted to Christianity, made it a state religion in 313 and built the first churches and basilicas in Rome. But in 331 he dealt a fatal blow to the empire's unity when he moved the imperial seat to Byzantium (Constantinople). Many of the nobility and wealthy, as well as talented artists and artisans, went with him, a "brain drain" from which the old capital never recovered. Constantine's move effectively split the empire in two.

The Dark and Middle Ages

As the Western Empire declined, the Romans recruited barbarians into the legions to help defend it against other outsiders. But the hired defenders soon joined the attackers, and the weary and disenchanted Roman populace could not summon up the same enthusiasm to defend the city that they had shown in going out to conquer an empire.

Wave after wave came the dreaded barbarians to sack, rape, murder and pillage— Alaric the Visigoth in 410, Attila the Hun, the Vandals and the Ostrogoths. Finally the barbarian chieftain Odovacar forced the last Roman emperor, Romulus Augustulus, to abdicate in 476. The crumbling Western Empire was at an end. (The Eastern or Byzantine Empire continued to prosper until Constantinople was captured by the Seljuks in 1453.)

In the 6th century Justinian reannexed Italy to his Byzantine Empire and codified Roman law as the state's legal system. But, as later Byzantine emperors lost interest, a new power arose out of the chaos in Rome: the Papacy. Pope Leo I (440–461) had already asserted the position of Bishop of Rome as Primate of the Western Church, tracing the succession back to St. Peter; and Pope Gregory the Great had shown statesmanship in 573 in warding off the Lombards, a Germanic tribe already established in the north of Italy. In the 8th century, citing a document, the *Donation of Constantine* (later found to be forged), the popes began to claim political authority over all Italy.

Rome by this time had been reduced to a village, its small population subsisting in the Tiber marsh on the Campus Martius, deserting the seven hills when barbarian invaders cut the imperial aqueducts. Seeking the powerful support **15**

of the Franks, Pope Leo III crowned their king, Charlemagne, ruler of the Holy Roman (in fact mostly Germanic) Empire, in St. Peter's Basilica on Christmas Day, 800. But the pope had in turn to kneel in allegiance, and this exchange of spiritual blessing for military protection laid the seeds of future conflict between popes and emperors.

Over the next 400 years Italy saw invasions by Saracens and Magyars, Saxons and Normans (they sacked Rome in 1084), with papal Rome struggling along as only one of many feudal city-states on the tormented peninsula. The papacy, and with it Rome, was controlled by various powerful families from the landed nobility. As the situation in Rome degenerated into chaos—deplored by Dante in his *Divine Comedy*—the popes moved to comfortable exile in Avignon in 1309, remaining under the protection of the French king for 68 years. Rome was left to the brutal rule of the Orsini and Colonna families. Self-educated visionary Cola di Rienzo headed a popular revolution in 1347 and, styling

Ancient Roman, Renaissance, Baroque and modern—Rome's history permeates Piazza Navona.

himself Tribune of Rome, governed for a brief seven months before the nobles drove him out.

The Renaissance

Re-established in Rome in 1377, the popes harshly put down any resistance to their rule and remained dominant in the city for the next 400 years. Yet, during the 15th and 16th centuries, the papacy also became a notable patron of the Renaissance, that remarkable effusion of art and intellectual endeavour which gloriously transformed medieval Rome from a squalid, crumbling and fever-ridden backwater into the foremost city of the Christian world.

It was Giorgio Vasari, facile artist but first-rate chronicler of this cultural explosion, who dubbed it a *rinascita* or rebirth of the glories of Italy's Greco-Roman past. But even more, it proved, with the humanism of Leonardo da Vinci and Michelangelo and the political realism of Machiavelli, to be the birth of our modern age.

True father of Rome's High Renaissance, Pope Julius II (1503-13) began the new St. Peter's, commissioned Michelangelo to paint the ceiling of the Vatican's Sistine Chapel and Raphael to decorate the 17

Stanze. Architect Donato Bramante was nicknamed *maestro ruinante* because of all the ancient monuments he dismantled to make way for the pope's megalomaniac building plans. With the treasures uncovered in the process, Julius founded the Vatican's magnificent collection of ancient sculpture.

The exuberant life of Renaissance Rome was brutally snuffed out in May, 1527, by mutinous troops of the invading German emperor (and Spanish king), Charles V. It was to be the last—and worst—sack of the city.

Counter-Reformation

Meanwhile the position of the papacy and the doctrines of the Church of Rome were being challenged by Luther, Calvin and other leaders of the Protestant Reformation. The Church's Counter-Reformation, formally proclaimed in 1563, reinforced the Holy Office's Inquisition to combat heresy and the Index to censor the arts. Italian Protestants fled and Jews in Rome were shut up in a ghetto.

Art proved a major instrument of Counter-Reformation propaganda. As the Church regained ground, it replaced the pagan influences of Classicism with a more triumphant image,

epitomized by Bernini's grandiose Baroque altar in St. Peter's.

In the 18th century, Spain's authority over many of the states in Italy passed to the Habsburgs of Austria, who were determined to curb the power of the popes in Rome. The papacy lost prestige with the enforced dissolution of the Jesuits and the crippling loss of revenue from the Habsburg church reforms and now sank to its lowest ebb.

In 1798 Napoleon's troops

Vittorio Emanuele Monument honours Italy's unity.

entered Rome and later seized the Papal States and proclaimed a republic. They treated old Pius VI with contempt and carried him off a virtual prisoner to France. His successor Pius VII was forced to anoint Napoleon as Emperor and in turn was also made prisoner, returning to Rome only after Napoleon's defeat in 1814. But, during the French occupation, a national self-awareness had begun to develop among Italians, who challenged the re-establishment of Austrian rule.

Many people looked to Pope Pius IX to lead this nationalist movement, but he feared the spread of liberalism and held back. In 1848, when a republic **19** was set up in Rome by Giuseppe Mazzini in the name of Italian nationalism, the pope fled the city. He returned only the following year after the republic had been crushed by the French army.

National unity for most of Italy was achieved in 1860 through the shrewd diplomacy of Cavour, the first prime minister, the heroics of adventurer Giuseppe Garibaldi and the leadership of King Vittorio Emanuele of Piedmont. The nationalists captured Rome in 1870 and made it capital of the Kingdom of Italy the following year. Pope Pius IX retreated to the Vatican and declared himself a "prisoner of the monarchy".

The Modern Era

World War I saw Italy on the winning side against Austria and Germany. But, after the peace conference of 1919, general disarray on the political scene led to an economic crisis, with stagnant productivity, bank closures and rising unemployment. Threatened by the Fascists' March on Rome in 1922, King Vittorio Emanuele III meekly invited their leader, *il Duce* Benito Mussolini, to form a government.

Once firmly established in power, Mussolini made peace with the pope by the Lateran Treaty of 1929, which created a separate Vatican state and perpetuated Catholicism as Italy's national religion. He diverted attention from the worsening economic climate at home with an invasion of Ethiopia in 1936 and proclamation of the Italian Empire. Two years later he introduced German-style racist legislation against Italy's 57,000 Jews. After France's collapse in 1940, Italy plunged on Germany's side into World War II.

The Allies landed in Sicily in June 1943 and fought their way up the peninsula. Rome was declared an open city to spare it from bombing and was liberated in 1944 with its treasures intact. Mussolini was caught fleeing to the Swiss border by Italian partisans and executed.

In June 1946, Italy voted in a referendum to abolish the monarchy and establish a democratic republic. Adherence to the grouping of states which became the European Economic Community opened up wider opportunities for trade and the hope of squeezing some of the benefits of Italy's post-war "economic miracle" down from the north into the more deprived southern half of the mainland and the islands of Sicily and Sardinia.

Historical Landmarks

Earliest Beginnings	753 B.C.	Legendary founding of Rome.
	510	Establishment of Republic.
	390	Gauls sack the city.
	264–146	Punic Wars against Carthage.
	49	Julius Caesar seizes power.
	44	Caesar assassinated in Rome.
Empire	27 B.C.	Augustus becomes first Roman emperor.
	c. 64 A.D.	Persecution of Christians begins.
	312	Constantine turns Christian.
	331	Imperial capital moved to Byzantium.
Dark and Middle Ages	410	Visigoths sack Rome.
	440–461	Leo I asserts papal authority.
	476	End of Western Roman Empire
	800	Pope crowns Charlemagne in St. Peter's.
	1084	Normans sack Rome.
	1309–77	Popes exiled to Avignon.
Renaissance and Counter-Reformation	1508–12	Michelangelo paints Sistine Chapel ceiling.
	1527	Sack of Rome by Imperial troops.
	1798–1809	Napoleon's troops enter Rome, establish republic.
Risorgimento	1814	Pope restored with Austrian rule.
	1848	Italian Nationalists revolt.
	1861	Italy unified.
	1871	Rome capital of Italy.
Modern Era	1915	Italy enters World War I.
	1922	Mussolini begins Fascist regime with March on Rome.
	1929	Lateran Treaty creates separate Vatican state.
	1940	Italy joins Germany in World War II.
	1944	Allies liberate Rome.
	1946	Monarchy abolished in favour of republic.

What to See

Within and beyond its seven hills and along the winding banks of the River Tiber, Rome has four or five different personalities: ancient Rome of the imperial ruins; Catholic Rome of the Vatican and churches; the Renaissance city of Michelangelo and Raphael or the Baroque of Bernini and Borromini; and a modern metropolis of interminable traffic jams, fashionable boutiques and cafés, but also factories and high-rises in the industrial suburbs. None is easily separable from the others. The secret

The Essentials
For those making only a brief visit to Rome, here are the very highest of the highlights:
Roman Forum
Campidoglio
Colosseum
St. Peter's Basilica
Vatican Museums
Spanish Steps
Trevi Fountain
Piazza Navona
Pantheon

Even the tourists desert the
22 *Colosseum at siesta time.*

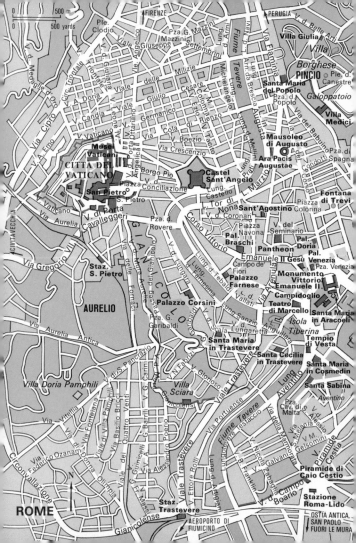

of the Eternal City is that it has lived all its ages simultaneously.

But it's a big city and on a first visit, you are well advised to begin with an orientation tour by bus. All large travel agencies conduct daily tours with informative commentaries on major sights by guides who speak a variety of languages. The tours usually last about three hours and can be booked by any hotel desk-clerk.

For the rest, you should see Rome on foot. Virtually all the major sights lie within comfortable walking distance of each other, though you will need several days to cover the most outstanding sights. In this guide, we have grouped together places which can be most conveniently visited on the same walking tour.

A word about opening hours of museums and historic sites: keeping track of all the variations is a nightmare. The best advice we can give is to check at the tourist office, your hotel or in the papers to avoid disappointment. Keep as a general rule of thumb that most museums close on Mondays and that many open only until 1 or 2 p.m. Churches close at midday and reopen in the afternoon. In high season, longer hours are the rule.

Preserving for Posterity

Exposure to weather, earthquakes and fire has scarcely inflicted more damage on Rome's historic and artistic heritage over 2,000 years than the effects of car exhausts over a matter of decades. The level of pollution in the city centre is reckoned to be the highest in Europe. Alarmed, the city has begun an intensive restoration programme, combined with a ban on traffic in sensitive spots.

Piazzas now declared pedestrian-only zones have become havens of peace. Blackened buildings are being systematically cleaned. Ancient columns and statues have disappeared under scaffolding and swathes of green net.

Some museums are closed temporarily, for days, months, even years, for restoration *(restauro)*. This is a blanket term covering budgetary problems, lack of staff or modern security systems or genuine, long-overdue renovation of the building and restoration of the paintings.

Don't be too disappointed if some of Rome's treasures are not visible at the time of your visit. With a little luck, they will be next time.

Modern and Renaissance Rome

The Rome of Michelangelo and Bernini is also the modern Italians' Rome. It grew up on what was, in Roman times, the Campus Martius, lying in a loop in the Tiber. Ironically, today's most crowded quarter was considered uninhabitable by the ancient Romans because of frequent flooding. Lying outside the earlier city walls, the "Field of Mars" was where the legions exercised, ambassadors were received and emperors cremated, and during the republic it became a site of public entertainment. Of the temples, baths, theatres and stadiums, few vestiges remain, and your lingering impression will be of piazzas designed like stage sets, glorious fountains and peach-coloured Renaissance palaces from the heyday of the popes.

Around the Piazza Venezia

Unlike many Italian cities, Rome has no main square as its heart. In Roman times, life centred on the Forum, but as the medieval and then Renaissance city evolved, innumerable piazzas emerged scattered throughout the city, each one laying some claim to eminence.

The nerve centre, at least for traffic, has to be the **Piazza Venezia**. Four major thoroughfares, Via del Corso, Via dei Fori Imperiali, Via Nazionale and Via del Teatro di Marcello converge on this open space dominated by the massive bulk of the **Vittorio Emanuele Monument** *(il Vittoriano)*. Celebrating the first king of unified Italy with inimitable 19th-century pomposity, the dazzling white marble edifice with bombastic colonnade was met with almost universal hostility and derisive nicknames such as the "Wedding Cake" and "Rome's False Teeth". But as a giant landmark, it proves tremendously helpful in finding the way around the city. The nation's Unknown Soldier of World War I lies buried here.

Turn with relief to the early Renaissance **Palazzo Venezia,** termed the finest palace of Christian Rome. Crowned with battlements and pierced by arched windows, the severe but elegant edifice was built for Cardinal Pietro Barbo, later Pope Paul II, supposedly so that he could watch the horse races along the Corso in comfort. Subsequently it served as the embassy of the Republic of Venice and more recently as the private office of Mussolini. His desk stood in the far corner of the vast Sala del Mappamondo to intimidate visitors who had to cross the full length of the marble floor to approach him. A tiny balcony from which *Il Duce* harangued his followers overlooks the square. The palace now contains a museum of medieval and Renaissance arms, furniture, tapestries, ceramics and sculpture.

Two flights of steps lead up from behind the Vittorio Emmanuele Monument. The more gradual and graceful, known as La Cordonata, takes you up between larger-than-life Roman statues of the heavenly twins, Castor and Pollux, to the quiet elegance of the **Campidoglio** atop the Capitoline Hill, once the Capitol and most sacred site of ancient Rome.

Symbolically, Michelangelo's beautifully cambered square turns its back on the Forum and pagan Rome to face the "new" Christian Rome and St. Peter's. A gilt bronze equestrian **statue of Marcus Aurelius** normally graces the centre. The handsome bearded and curly-headed figure escaped destruction over the centuries because it was believed to be Constantine, first Christian emperor. After undergoing prolonged restoration to repair the "bronze can-

cer" corroding its metal, the statue is expected to be replaced by a copy and the original displayed in the Capitoline Museums. At the back of the square stands the 16th-century **Palazzo Senatorio** (now the City Hall).

The Palazzo Nuovo and the Palazzo dei Conservatori, flanking the square, house sections of the **Capitoline Museums.** Gorgeously decorated rooms, with gilt and coffered ceilings and frescoed walls, feature a display of sculpture excavated from ancient Rome. Look out for the poignant statue of the **Dying Gaul** and the beautifully poised bronze of a boy taking a thorn from his foot. In an octagonal recess off the sculpture gallery is the sensual **Capitoline Venus**, a Roman copy of a Greek original dating from the 2nd century B.C. She survives today thanks to a by-gone art-lover who walled her up in a hiding place to preserve her from destruction by early Christians. The museums' most celebrated piece is undoubtedly the **Capitoline She-Wolf**, an Etruscan bronze from the 5th-century B.C., which has become the symbol of Rome. The infant Romulus and Remus that she is suckling are Renaissance additions by Pollaiuolo. The giant

Artists Galore

A host of artists and architects contributed to Rome's splendour. Here are some names that will crop up repeatedly during your visit, with examples of their most famous works in Rome:

Arnolfo di Cambio (c. 1245–1302). Gothic architect and sculptor from Pisa. *Statue of St. Peter in St. Peter's Basilica, tabernacle in St. Paul's.*

Bernini, Gianlorenzo (1598–1680). As painter, sculptor and architect, the foremost exponent of Baroque art. *St. Peter's Square, Fountain of the Four Rivers, Palazzo Barberini*... the list is endless.

Borromini, Francesco (1599–1667). Baroque architect, assistant to and later great rival of Bernini. *Sant'Agnese in Agone, Palazzo Barberini.*

Bramante, Donato (1444–1514) Architect and painter from Urbino. Foremost architect of High Renaissance. *St. Peter's, Belvedere Courtyard in the Vatican.*

Canova, Antonio (1757–1822). Most celebrated sculptor of Neoclassical movement. *Statue of Napoleon's sister Pauline in Borghese Gallery.*

Caravaggio, Michelangelo Merisi da (1571–1610). Greatest Italian painter of 16th century. *Crucifixion of St. Peter and Conversion of St. Paul in Santa Maria del Popolo.*

Maderno, Carlo (1556–1629). Architect from northern Italy. *Façade of St. Peter's, pope's palace at Castel Gandolfo.*

Michelangelo Buanarroti (1475–1564). Florentine painter, sculptor and architect, one of the most influential men in history of art. *Dome of St. Peter's Basilica, Pietà, Sistine Chapel ceiling, Moses in San Pietro in Vincoli, Campidoglio.*

Pinturicchio, Bernardino (c.1454–1513). Painter from Perugia. *Frescoes in Sistine Chapel, Borgia Apartments, Santa Maria del Popolo and Santa Maria in Aracoeli.*

Raphael (Raffaello Sanzio, 1483–1520). Painter and architect of High Renaissance. *Stanze in Vatican, Chigi Chapel in Santa Maria del Popolo, La Fornarina in Palazzo Barberini.*

Valadier, Giuseppe (1762–1839). Archaeologist, town-planner and architect for Napoleon. *Piazza del Popolo, Pincio gardens.*

The First Capitol Hill

To the Romans, the Capitol was both citadel and sanctuary, the symbolic centre of government, where the consuls took their oath and where the Republic's coinage was minted. Its name, now applied to many legislatures across the world (notably Congress in Washington), originated in a legend that the skull of a mythical hero was unearthed here during excavations for the temple of Juno. Augurs interpreted this as a sign that Rome would one day be head *(caput)* of the world.

When the Gauls sacked Rome in 390 B.C., the Capitol was saved by the timely cackling of the sanctuary's sacred geese which warned that attackers were scaling the rocks.

Later, victorious Caesars ended their triumphal processions here. They rode up from the Forum in chariots drawn by white steeds to pay homage at the magnificent gilded temple of Jupiter, which dominated the southern summit of the Capitoline.

In the Middle Ages, the collapsed temples were pillaged and the hill was abandoned to goats until Pope Paul III in the 16th century commissioned Michelangelo to give it new glory.

head, hand and foot in one of the courtyards come from a statue of Emperor Constantine. Visit the museums' **Picture Gallery** *(Pinacoteca Capitolina)* for important Venetian works by Bellini, Titian, Tintoretto, Lotto, Veronese and Caravaggio.

Alongside the Palazzo Senatorio, a cobbled road opens onto a terrace which gives you the first glimpse of the ruins of the Roman Forum (p. 49), stretching from the Arch of Septimius Severus to the Arch of Titus, with the Colosseum beyond. Gory detail—from the Tarpeian Rock on your right the Romans hurled traitors to their death.

The steeper flight of steps up the Campidoglio climbs to the austere 13th-century church of **Santa Maria in Aracoeli**, on the site of the great temple of Juno Moneta, where the Sybil of the Tiber announced the coming of Christ to Augustus. The church harbours the curious and much-revered **Bambino**, kept in a separate little chapel. Some Romans attribute miraculous healing powers to this statue of the infant Jesus. Stacks of unopened letters from all over

Harmony reigns in the Piazza del Campidoglio, Rome's quiet heart.

the world addressed to Il Bambino surround the stumpy jewel-bedecked figure. At Christmas it becomes the centrepiece of the manger scene. Pinturicchio's frescoes in the first chapel on the right of the nave recount the story of his namesake St. Bernardino of Siena.

The Corso

This mile-long thoroughfare, more properly the Via del Corso, runs straight as an arrow from the Piazza Venezia to the Piazza del Popolo. It took its name from the wild races of riderless Barbary horses, "Corsa dei Barberi", once the main attraction of the Roman carnival. Most fun at the hour of the evening stroll or *passeggiata*, the street is lined with shops, palaces and churches.

In **Piazza Colonna**, the column of Marcus Aurelius, decorated with spiralling reliefs of the emperor's military triumphs, rises in front of the Italian prime minister's offices in the Chigi Palace. Some 200 steps lead up inside the hollow column to the 16th-century statue of St. Paul at the top, which replaced the original bronze of the philosopher-emperor.

On adjacent **Piazza Montecitorio**, dominated by an Egyptian obelisk from the 6th century B.C., stands the Chamber of Deputies *(Camera dei Deputati)*, Italy's legislative lower house, designed by Bernini as a palace for the Ludovisi family.

Turn off the Corso to the banks of the Tiber, to visit the **Ara Pacis Augustae,** disappointingly boxed in an unprepossessing white and plate glass building. When fragments of this "Altar of Peace", commissioned to celebrate Augustus' victorious campaigns in Gaul and Spain, first came to light in 1568 they were dispersed among several museums, but were returned when reconstruction began. Along the friezes you can make out Augustus himself, with his wife Livia and daughter Julia, friend Agrippa and a host of priests, nobles and dignitaries.

Alongside it, the green hillock encircled by cypresses is the **Mausoleum of Augustus,** repository of the ashes of the Caesars until Hadrian built his own mausoleum (now the Castel Sant'Angelo, p. 61) across the Tiber.

At its northern end the Corso culminates in the harmonious curving **Piazza del Popolo**, an exemplary piece of open-air urban theatre designed in 1818 by Giuseppe Valadier, former architect to Napoleon. The cen-

Not even the traffic distracts an ancient Roman from his news.

tral obelisk, dating back to the Egypt of Rameses II (13th century B.C.), was brought to Rome by Augustus and erected in the Circus Maximus. Pope Sixtus V had it moved here in 1589.

The square takes its name from the Renaissance church of **Santa Maria del Popolo**, built on the site of Nero's tomb to exorcize his ghost, reputed to haunt the area. It's interior, remodelled in the Baroque era, is famous for its works of art.

They include an exquisite fresco of the Nativity by Pinturicchio and Raphael's Chigi Chapel, built as a mausoleum for the family of the immensely rich Florentine banker and patron of the arts, Agostino Chigi. In the Cerasi Chapel left of the choir hang two powerful canvases by Caravaggio, the *Conversion of St. Paul* and the *Crucifixion of St. Peter*, notable for the dramatic use of light and shade and the masterly foreshortening of the figures.

Next to the church, the arched 16th-century **Porta del Popolo** marks the gateway to ancient Rome at the end of the 33

Via Flaminia, which led from Rimini on the Adriatic Coast. Pilgrims arriving in Rome by the gate were greeted by the imposing twin Baroque churches of Santa Maria dei Miracoli and Santa Maria in Montesanto, guarding the entrance to the Corso on the south side of the square.

Above the piazza to the east, reached by a monumental complex of terraces, the **Pincio** gardens offer a magical view of the city, especially at sunset, when the rooftops are tinged with purple and gold. Also the work of Valadier, the gardens occupy the site of the 1st-century B.C. villa of Lucullus. This provincial governor returned enriched by the spoils of Asia to impress his contemporaries by his extravagant life style.

The gardens stretch on into the less formal park of the **Villa Borghese**, once the estate of Cardinal Scipione Borghese, nephew of Pope Paul V. The extensive grounds contain the Borghese Gallery (see p. 79) in the cardinal's former palace and a zoo to the north. Lined with pine trees and open-air cafés, the Pincio promenade takes you past the **Villa Medici**, built in 1544 and bought by Napoleon to house the French National Academy.

Around the Piazza di Spagna

At one time Rome's bohemian quarter, the **Piazza di Spagna** is now the heart of the city's most fashionable shopping area, extending over to the Corso.

The boat-shaped marble fountain, **Fontana della Barcaccia**, forever foundering in the centre of the piazza, was designed by the great Bernini's father. From the square, the **Spanish Steps** *(Scalinata della Trinità dei Monti)* ascend grandly in three tiers, with the twin-belfried French church of Trinità dei Monti soaring above. From the top of the steps you have a splendid view across Rome, over myriad roof gardens, dripping with greenery and flowers, which constitute outdoor living-rooms for the fortunate owners of top-floor apartments.

The steps have nothing Spanish about them (other than that the Spanish Embassy to the Holy See stands nearby), but were the idea of a *French* diplomat, Stéphane Gouffier, and realized half a century later in 1721 by the architects Francesco de Sanctis and Ales-

View from the Pincio stretches from Piazza del Popolo across the Tiber to St. Peter's.

sandro Specchi. Now they are the eternal hangout of guitar-playing youths, lovers, hippies and pedlars of trinkets and flowers.

Ordinary tourists and Italians, too, enjoy basking in this pleasant daze, which the poet John Keats celebrated as a "blissful cloud of summer indolence". He should know; the window of the room where he died in 1821 looks out onto the steps. The second floor of his house has been preserved as the **Keats-Shelley Memorial**.

The venerable **Babington's Tea Rooms**, a relic of the days when English lords rolled up in carriages in the 18th and 19th centuries on their grand tour of Europe, offer genteel afternoon tea and hearty American breakfasts.

More quintessentially Roman, on nearby Via Condotti, is the city's oldest coffee house (1760), the **Caffè Greco**. The walls of this mini-museum are covered with autographed portraits, busts and statues, bearing witness to its famous clientele, among them Goethe, Byron, Baudelaire, Liszt, Gogol and Fellini.

Free seats for all on the Spanish Steps to watch the world go by. **37**

The **Trevi Fountain** *(Fontana di Trevi)*, tucked away behind narrow alleys, is an extravaganza out of all proportion to its tiny piazza. Nicola Salvi's astounding 18th-century fountain is in fact a triumphal arch and palace façade (to the old Palazzo Poli), framing mythic creatures in a riot of rocks and

There's still magic in the toss of a coin at Trevi Fountain.

pools. The massive figure of Neptune rides on a sea-shell drawn by sea horses, the rearing steed symbolizing the ocean's turmoil and a calmer one its tranquillity. You may have to compete with the crowds, even late at night when the fountain is illuminated, to throw a coin in over your shoulder and ensure your return to Rome. Urchins think up all manner of devious means to snatch some of the considerable revenues, which are otherwise collected by the municipality of Rome.

The fortress-like **Palazzo del Quirinale** crowns the highest of Rome's original seven hills, once summer residence to popes escaping the malarial swamps of the Vatican down by the Tiber. From this palace, Napoleon's men kidnapped one pope (Pius VI) and arrested another (Pius VII), while a third (Pius IX) fled from revolutionary crowds in 1848. After 1870 it housed the King of Italy and is now the presidential palace.

The piazza, with magnificent statues of Castor and Pollux flanking an ancient obelisk, affords a panoramic view—somewhat marred by the forest of television aerials—over the city towards St. Peter's.

That symbol of the *dolce vita*, the **Via Veneto**, has been more or less deserted by its starlets and *paparazzi*, but the cafés, shops and hotels remain just as expensive.

Around the Piazza Navona

Pause at a café in that serenest of city squares, the **Piazza Navona**. Nowhere in Rome is the spectacle of Italian street life so pleasantly indulged, thanks to an inspired collaboration of Roman genius across the ages. The elongated piazza was laid out around A.D. 90 by Emperor Domitian as an athletics stadium, *Circus Agonalis*—a sporting tradition continued in the Middle Ages with jousting tournaments. The 17th century contributed its sublime décor.

Until 1867 it was the scene of curious water pageants in July and August, when the fountains were allowed to overflow until the piazza was flooded. As bands played, the aristocracy drove through the water in their gilded coaches, to the delight of the onlookers. Today, sages on the city council safeguard it as a pedestrian zone.

Reigning over the square, on a base of craggy rock and topped by an obelisk, Bernini's **Fountain of the Four Rivers** *(Fontana dei Fiumi)* celebrates the world's great rivers, Rio de la Plata (the Americas), Danube (Europe), Ganges (Asia) and Nile (Africa). Romans who delight in Bernini's scorn for his rivals suggest that **39** the Nile god covers his head rather than look at Borromini's church of **Sant'Agnese in Agone** and that the river god of the Americas is shielding himself in case it collapses. In fact the fountain was completed several years *before* Borromini's splendid—and structurally impeccable—façade and dome.

Via dei Coronari, the old Street of the Rosary Makers, is now the Street of Very Expensive Antique Shops. The narrow cobbled lane draws collectors from around the world. Along the street stands the huge and sombre Lancellotti Palace, seat of a great aristocratic family. In 1870, when Italian troops occupied papal Rome, the prince was so angered that he locked his main door, which remained unopened until the 1929 Lateran Pact reconciled Church and State.

The **Pantheon**, in Piazza della Rotonda, stands out as the best preserved monument

of ancient Rome—it was converted into a church in the 7th century—and rivals the Colosseum in its combination of quiet elegance and massive power. Emperor Hadrian, its builder (around A.D. 120), achieved a marvel of engineering with the magnificent coffered dome (larger than St. Peter's), measuring 43 metres (142 ft.) across the interior diameter, exactly equal to its height. The dome is supported by 16 monolithic pink and grey granite columns. With typical modesty, Hadrian left the inscription of the original builder in 27 B.C., Marcus Agrippa, but the stamp on every brick proclaims that it was constructed in the time of Hadrian.

The bronze beams that once embellished the entrance were taken away by the Barberini

Enduring Bernini statue on the fountain; ephemeral portrait on the pavement.

Pope Urban VIII to make Bernini's canopy for the high altar in St. Peter's. His action prompted the saying: "Quod non fecerunt barbari, fecerunt Barberini." ("What even the barbarians did not do was done by the Barberinis."). A shaft of light illuminates the windowless vault through the circular hole *(oculus)* in the dome, which also (be warned) lets in the rain.

This "Temple of all the Gods" today contains the Renaissance tombs of Raphael and architect Baldassare Peruzzi, and those of modern kings Vittorio Emanuele II and Umberto I. The massive bronze doors remain, but the veneer of precious marbles has long been stripped from the outside walls, and the gilded bronze tiles were carried off by the Byzantine emperor Constans II when he visited Rome in 655.

South of the Piazza Navona, the **Campo de' Fiori** (Field of Flowers) supports a lively and boisterous market, with a jumble of fish, fruit, vegetable, meat and flower stalls, the luscious produce temptingly displayed. In the afternoons, when the stands and brightly coloured awnings have been taken away, political militants hold sway below the statue of the philosopher-monk Giordano Bruno. The Inquisition

burned him alive here in 1600 for his preposterous idea that the universe was infinite, with many more galaxies than ours.

An even more famous death occurred at the adjacent Piazza del Biscione. The restaurant Da Pancrazio stands over the foundations of Pompey's Theatre where Julius Caesar was stabbed to death by the conspirators in 44 B.C.

For security reasons, the general public can no longer visit the **Palazzo Farnese**, which has housed the French Embassy since 1871. Antonio da Sangallo the Younger, Michelangelo and Giacomo Della Porta all contributed to this magnificent Renaissance palace, begun in 1515 for Cardinal Alessandro Farnese, later Pope Paul III. Only a privileged few get in to see the ceremonial dining room's fabulous frescoes by Annibale Carracci. The French pay a rent of one lira every year and provide a palace in Paris as Italy's embassy—very nice, too, but not exactly Michelangelo.

Piazza Farnese has been turned into one of Rome's traffic-free squares; at night, the only sound you'll hear is the water splashing into the Egyptian granite basins brought from the Baths of Caracalla for the twin Farnese fountains.

The Pantheon is aglow by night.

Between the Sant'Angelo Bridge and the Farnese Palace, ancient houses crowd along lanes with intriguing names such as Via dei Cappellari (Street of the Hat-Makers), Via dei Bales- trari (Crossbow-Makers), Via dei Chiavari (Locksmiths) and Via del Pellegrino, along which Holy Year pilgrims used to pass on their way to St. Peter's.

Narrow streets south-east of the Campo de' Fiori take you into the old **Jewish Ghetto**. This district bubbles with life at any time, but particularly so **43** during the evening *passeggiata*. Some of Rome's best restaurants and shopping bargains are found here. Jews were a permanent feature of Roman life for more than 2,500 years but were forced into a ghetto in the 16th century by Pope Paul IV. A small Jewish community still lives around the Via del Portico d'Ottavia. The hefty neo-Babylonian synagogue (1904) down by the river is linked to a museum of Jewish history.

Probably the most captivating fountain in Rome, the 16th-century **Turtle Fountain** *(Fontana delle Tartarughe)* in Piazza Mattei presents a perfect little scene. Four bronze boys perched on dolphins lift four turtles into the marble basin above with gracefully outstretched arms.

A crumbling arched façade more than 2,000 years old, the Portico d'Ottavia, dedicated to Augustus' sister, dominates the ghetto. Beyond extends the

Theatre of Marcellus *(Teatro di Marcello)*, begun by Julius Caesar and architectural model for the Colosseum. The semi-circle of superimposed arches was incorporated into the Palazzo Savelli-Orsini in the 16th century.

The Ponte Fabricio, Rome's oldest bridge (62 B.C.), links the left bank to the **Isola Tiberina**, a tiny island in the river. Three centuries before Christ the island was sacred to Aesculapius, god of healing, to whom a temple and hospital were dedicated. A hospital still stands here to this day, tended by the Brothers of St. John of God. A second bridge, Ponte Cestio, remodelled in the 19th century, leads over to the right bank of the Tiber and Trastevere (see p. 46).

Choosy housewives shop daily for fresh fruit and vegetables in Campo de' Fiori market.

The Aventine

One of Rome's original seven hills, the Aventine remains a quiet sanctuary above the clamour of the city, a favoured residential zone, with villas and apartments set in gardens of flowers and palms.

On the western edge stands the Dominican basilica of **Santa Sabina**, a favourite among the city's many churches for its dignity and purity of line and the grace of its Roman columns. It was built on the site of the palace of a Roman matron, who was converted to Christianity by her Greek slave and martyred in the time of Hadrian. The beautifully carved old cypress-wood doors in the portico are protected from vandalism and graffiti by glass. Through a circular window opposite them **45** you can see the descendant of an orange tree planted by St. Dominic 700 years ago.

A few steps away, take a peep through the **keyhole** in the garden door of the Villa of the Knights of Malta *(Cavalieri di Malta)*, for an unusual view in the distance of the dome of St. Peter's, perfectly framed at the end of an avenue of trees. When busloads arrive, you may have to queue for a look!

Lying at the foot of the Aventine near the Tiber, **Santa Maria in Cosmedin** is a jewel of a church serving Rome's Greek community. Its Romanesque exterior and unadorned interior favour a devout simplicity, in contrast to the Baroque grandeur of many of Rome's churches. The portico contains an ancient marble carving of a fierce face known as the **Bocca della Verità** (Mouth of Truth), possibly once a well cover. Pilgrims of the Middle Ages believed that anyone who told a lie with his hand in the gaping mouth would have his fingers bitten off. Copies of all sizes are on sale at the church.

On the opposite side of the road, two of Rome's most charming and well-preserved temples grace an open green space by the Tiber, once part of the city's ancient cattle-market. The circular marble temple with fluted columns, known erroneously as the **Temple of Vesta** because of its resemblance to the one in the Forum, was probably dedicated to Hercules. Next to it, the rectangular so-called **Temple of Fortune** is now believed to be that of Portunus, god of harbours.

Glance over the Tiber embankment here to see the mouth of the Cloaca Maxima, ancient Rome's main drain, still opening into the river near the Palatine Bridge.

South of the Aventine, near the Porta San Paolo, you should visit the serenely beautiful **Protestant Cemetery**, where Keats lies buried (see p. 37) and Shelley's ashes are interred. Rome's only pyramid, incorporated into the city walls, towers over the cemetery. A Roman praetor, Caius Cestius, commissioned it for his tomb in 12 B.C. on his return from a spell of duty in Egypt.

Trastevere

A crowded, noisy and cheerful neighbourhood south of the Vatican, Trastevere (literally "across the Tiber") has long been renowned as the most popular quarter of Rome. Here, ordinary people—who like the cockneys of London consider themselves to be de-

Will those turtles in Piazza Mattei ever reach the water?

scendants of the original citizens—uphold ancient traditions and customs. Make a point of wandering through the narrow cobbled streets, past quaint tumbledown houses with flowered balconies, to take the pulse of the authentic life of the city, highlighted by the July *Noiantri* ("We Others") street festival of music and fireworks down by the river.

Inevitably, "popular" and "authentic" became chic, and the ambience is now somewhat diluted by a certain smart set moving in—and raising the rents. But the true Trasteverini hang on, mainly in the area immediately around **Santa Maria in Trastevere**, one of the oldest churches in the city. Its foundation (on the spot where oil is said to have gushed to presage the birth of Christ) may date **47**

back to the 3rd century, but the present structure is the work of Pope Innocent II, himself a Trasteverino, around 1140. A wonderful Byzantine-influenced mosaic of Mary enthroned with Jesus decorates the domed ceiling of the apse. The façade's gilded mosaics and the square's gently playing fountain are illuminated at night, providing a perfect backdrop to a meal in one of the restaurants and bars around the square.

Santa Maria in Trastevere's square comes to life at night.

Before entering the church of **Santa Cecilia in Trastevere**, pause in the courtyard to admire the russet Baroque façade and endearingly leaning Romanesque tower. The main altar encloses the serene marble sculpture of St. Cecilia as she lay in her coffin, her body undecomposed, when the sculptor Stefano Maderno saw her in

1599. To the right of the nave is her chapel, over the site of the Roman *caldarium* where this patron saint of music was imprisoned and tortured by scalding. You pay to go down into the crypt, a warren of vaulted rooms and passageways with fragments of old Roman columns and the sarcophagus of St. Cecilia.

Classical Rome

The nucleus of Classical Rome lies around the Colosseum, with the Forum to the northwest and the Baths of Caracalla to the south. Don't be daunted—even the best-informed scholars find the monumental relics hard to decipher. The mystery itself is half the charm of these vestiges of a vanished world. Even if you're not an archaeology buff who wants to understand the meaning of every stone, it's worth at least an hour or two to dream among the debris of empire and wonder whether Fifth Avenue, Piccadilly, the Champs-Elysées or Red Square will look any better 2,000 years from now.

⚓ The Roman Forum
(Foro Romano)
With an exhilarating leap of the imagination, you can stand

The Seven Hills
The original Seven Hills of Republican Rome were:
Palatine: Cradle of the city, once covered by palaces, now a garden of ruins.
Capitoline: Ancient citadel, remodelled as Renaissance square by Michelangelo.
Esquiline: Once Sabine stronghold, site of Nero's Golden House on southern crest, dominated by basilica of Santa Maria Maggiore in north.
Caelian: Area of patrician homes, now occupied by ruins, gardens and churches.
Quirinal: Highest of the Seven Hills, crowned by residence of president, once palace of popes and kings.
Viminal: Built-up area near Diocletian's Baths.
Aventine: In imperial times, and still, a smart residential quarter.

among the columns, arches and porticoes of the Roman Forum and picture the hub of the great imperial city, the first in Europe to house a million inhabitants.

Ringed by the Palatine, Capitoline and Esquiline hills and drained by an underground channel, the Cloaca Maxima, the flat valley of the Forum developed as the civic, commer- 49 cial and religious centre of the growing city. Under the emperors, it attained unprecedented splendour, the white marble and golden roofs of temples, law courts and market halls glittering in the sun. After the barbarian invasions, the area was abandoned. Earthquake, fire, flood and the plunder of barbarians and Renaissance architects reduced it to a muddy cow pasture until excavations in the 19th century brought many of the ancient edifices again to light. But grass still grows between the cracked paving stones of the Sacred Way, poppies bloom among the piles of toppled marble, and tangles of red roses entwine the brick columns, softening the harshness of the ruins.

Portable sound-guides are available for hire at the entrance (on Via dei Fori Imperiali) or you can find your own way round the Forum. But first sit down on a chunk of fallen marble in the midst of the ruins and orient yourself with the help of a detailed plan, to trace the layout of the buildings and make sense of the apparent confusion.

Start your tour at the western end, just below the Campidoglio's Palazzo Senatorio (see p. 28). Here you can look up and see how the arches of the Roman record office *(Tabularium)* have been incorporated into the rear of the Renaissance palace. And from here you can look down the full length of the **Sacra Via** (Sacred Way), along which the victorious generals rode in triumphal procession— followed by the standards of the legions, the massed ranks of prisoners and carts piled with the spoils of conquest—to the foot of the Capitoline Hill.

Then, to counterbalance this image of the Romans as ruthless military conquerors, turn to the severe brick-built rectangular **Curia** (Senate House) in the north-west corner of the Forum. Here you can gaze through the bronze doors (copies of the originals which are now in St. John Lateran, see p. 75) at the "venerable great-grandmother of all parliaments", where the senators, robed in simple white togas, argued the affairs of Republic and Empire. It is worth remembering that the tenets of Roman law, which underpin most western legal systems, were first debated in this modest chamber.

Believed to mark the site of the very first assembly hall of the Roman elders, the Curia was constructed in its present form by Diocletian in A.D. 303 and once faced with marble.

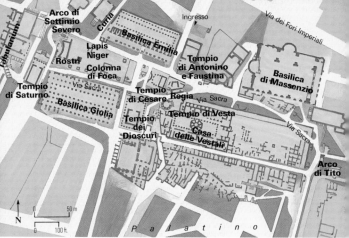

The church that covered it was dismantled in 1937 to reveal the ancient floor set with geometrical patterns in red and green marble, the tiers on either side where the Roman senators sat, and the brick base of the golden statue of Victory at the rear. The Curia shelters two large basreliefs, possibly from the Rostra, outlining in marble the ancient buildings of the Forum.

In front of the Curia, a concrete shelter protects the underground site of the **Lapis Niger** (generally not on view), a black marble paving stone over the traditional grave of Romulus, founder of the city. Beside it, a broken stele engraved with the oldest Latin inscription ever found, dates back some six centuries before Christ; no one has completely deciphered it yet.

The triple **Arch of Septimius Severus** *(Arco di Settimio Severo)* dominates this end of the Forum, depicting the military triumphs in the east of the 3rd-century emperor who later campaigned as far as Scotland and died in York. Nearby, the broad orators' platform or **Rostra**, from which Cicero and Mark Antony harangued the crowds, stretches across the Forum. Its name comes from the iron prows *(rostra)* which once adorned it, taken from the **51** enemy ships at the Battle of Antium in 338 B.C. Two points at each end of the Rostra have special significance: the Umbilicus Urbis Romae, marking the traditional centre of Rome; and the Miliarium Aureum (Golden Milestone), which once recorded in gold letters the distances in miles from Rome to the provinces of the empire.

In front of the Rostra, public meetings and ceremonies took place in the social forum, kept bare save for samples of three plants essential to Mediterranean prosperity—the vine, the olive and the fig. Still prominent above this open space is the **Column of Phocas** *(Colonna di Foca)*, built to honour the Byzantine emperor who presented the Pantheon to Pope Boniface IV.

Eight tall columns standing on a podium at the foot of the Capitol belong to the **Temple of Saturn** *(Tempio di Saturno)*, one of the earliest temples in Rome. It doubled as state treasury and centre of the merry December debauchery known as the Saturnalia, pagan precursor of Christmas.

Of the **Basilica Julia**, once the busy law courts, only the

Broken temple columns line the
52 *Forum's ancient Sacred Way.*

paving and some of the arches and travertine pillars survive. Even less remains of the Basilica Aemilia on the opposite side of the Sacra Via, destroyed by the Goths in A.D. 410.

Three slender columns, the podium and a portion of the entablature denote the **Temple of Castor and Pollux** *(Tempio dei Dioscuri)*. It was dedicated to these twin sons of Jupiter (the Dioscuri) after they appeared on the battlefield at Lake Regillus to rally the Romans against the Latins and Etruscans.

You'll have to look for the **altar of Julius Caesar**, tucked away in a semicircular recess of the Temple of the Divine Julius *(Tempio di Cesare)*. On March 19, 44 B.C., the grieving crowds, following Caesar's funeral procession to the cremation spot in the Campus Martius, made an impromptu pyre of chairs and tables and burned the body here in the Forum.

Pause for a pleasant idyll in the **Hall of the Vestal Virgins** *(Casa delle Vestali)*, surrounded by graceful statues in the serene setting of a rose garden and old rectangular fountain basins, once more filled with water. In the circular white marble **Temple of Vesta** *(Tempio di Vesta)*, the sacred

flame perpetuating the Roman state was tended by six Vestal Virgins who, from childhood, observed a 30-year vow of chastity on pain of being buried alive if they broke it. They were under the supervision of the high priest, the Pontifex Maximus (the popes have appropriated this title). His official residence was in the nearby Regia, of which only overgrown brick vestiges remain.

Further along the Sacra Via, the imposing **Temple of Antoninus and Faustina** has survived because, like the Curia, it was converted to a church, acquiring a Baroque façade in 1602.

Few ancient buildings reach the massive proportions of the **Basilica of Maxentius**, completed by Constantine (whose name it also bears), of which three giant vaults still stand.

The Sacra Via culminates in the **Arch of Titus**, built to commemorate the sack of Jerusalem in A.D. 70. Restored by Giuseppe Valadier in 1821, it shows in magnificently carved relief the triumphal procession of the emperor bearing the spoils of Jerusalem, among them the temple's seven-branched golden candlestick and silver trumpets which later vanished, possibly in the sack of Rome by the Vandals. Even today, many Jews will avoid walking through the arch, built to glorify their tragedy.

From this end of the Forum, a slope leads up to the **Palatine Hill**, Rome's legendary birthplace and today its most romantic garden. At the time of the Republic, this was a desirable residential district for the wealthy and aristocratic; Cicero and Crassus were among its distinguished inhabitants. Augustus began the imperial trend by building onto the house where he was born,

and later emperors added and expanded, each vying to outdo the last in magnificence and luxury, until the whole was one immense palace (the very word takes its name from the hill). From the pavilions and terraces of the botanical gardens laid out up here by the 16th-century Farnese family, you have an excellent view of the whole Forum.

The so-called **House of Livia** is now reckoned to be that of her husband, Emperor Augustus, where he lived in characteristic modesty, but good taste. Small but graceful rooms retain remnants of the mosaic floors and a well-preserved wall

Roses bloom again in the Hall of the Vestal Virgins.

painting depicting the love of Zeus for a young priestess. Nearby, a circular Iron-Age dwelling characteristic of the time of Rome's legendary beginnings (see p. 12) is known as **Romulus' Hut**.

Through the Palatine threads the **Cryptoporticus of Nero**, an underground passageway linking the palaces. In the dim light you can make out stucco decorations on the ceilings and walls.

The vast assemblage of ruins of the Domus Flavia include a basilica, throne room, banqueting hall, baths, porticoes and a fountain in the form of a maze. Together with the Domus Augustana alongside, the complex is known as the **Palace of Domitian**. From one side of it you can look down into the **Stadium of Domitian**, more of a vast exercise yard for the imperial family than a ground for public athletics.

Last emperor to build on the Palatine, Septimius Severus carried the imperial palace to the very south-eastern end of the hill, so that his seven-storied **Domus Severiana** was the impressive first glimpse of the capital for new arrivals. It was dismantled to build Renaissance Rome, and only the huge arcaded foundations remain.

From this edge of the Palatine you have a splendid view down onto the immense grassy stretch of the **Circus Maximus**, where crowds of up to 200,000 watched the chariot races from tiers of marble seats. Beyond lies the Aventine Hill (see p. 45).

The separate **Imperial Forums**, along the Via dei Fori Imperiali, were built as an adjunct to the Roman Forum as the capital grew ever larger and were named after Julius Caesar, Augustus, Trajan, Vespasian and Nerva. Most impressive monument is the 30-metre-high (98-ft.) **Trajan's Column** (A.D. 113). Celebrating Trajan's campaigns against the Dacians in what is today Rumania, the minutely detailed friezes spiralling around the column constitute a veritable textbook of Roman warfare, featuring embarkation on ships, the clash of armies and the surrender of barbarian chieftains. St. Peter's statue replaced the emperor's in 1587.

The Colosseum

It says something about Rome's essential earthiness that, more than any inspira-

Time—and man—have gutted the Colosseum.

tional church or opulent palace, it's the Colosseum —what Byron called "the gladiator's bloody circus"— that is the symbol of the city's eternity. Built in A.D. 80 by 20,000 slaves and prisoners, the four-tiered elliptical arena seated 50,000 spectators on stone benches according to social status. Flowing in and out of arched passageways, nobles and plebs alike came to see blood: bears, lions, tigers and leopards starved into fighting each other and against criminals and Christians. Gladiators butchered one another to the cries of *Jugula!* ("Slit his throat!"). In one spectacle in A.D. 249, 2,000 gladiators took part and 32 elephants, 60 lions, 10 tigers and 10 giraffes were slaughtered.

For their churches and palaces, popes and princes have stripped the Colosseum of its precious marble, travertine and metal. They have left in the arena's basin a ruined maze of cells and corridors that funnelled man and beast to the slaughter. The horror has disappeared beneath the moss, and what remains is the thrill of the monument's endurance. As an old Anglo-Saxon prophecy goes: "While stands the Colosseum, Rome shall stand; when falls the Colosseum, Rome shall fall; and when Rome falls, with it shall fall the world."

The nearby **Arch of Constantine** honours the ruler's 4th-century battlefield conversion to Christianity and victory over the rival emperor Maxentius at Ponte Milvio north of Rome. Unperturbed by the depiction of pagan rituals and sacrifices, a cost-conscious Senate took fragments from monuments of earlier rulers. Only a few reliefs show the newly Christian Constantine.

A kilometre (half a mile) south of the Colosseum, the huge 3rd-century **Baths of Caracalla** *(Terme di Caracalla)* provided room for 1,600 people to bathe in style and luxury. Imagine the still impressive brick walls covered in coloured marble. The baths and gymnasia were of alabaster and granite, profusely decorated with statues and frescoes. Public bathing was a prolonged social event, as merchants and senators passed from the *caldarium* hot room to cool down in the *tepidarium* and *frigidarium*. The baths ran dry in the 6th century, when barbarians cut the aqueducts. Now the stage for spectacular open-air operas in summer, the *caldarium* is vast enough for processions of elephants, camels and four-horse chariots.

The Vatican

The power of Rome endures in the spirituality evoked by every stone of St. Peter's Basilica and in the almost physical awe inspired by the splendours of the Vatican Palace. At their best, the popes and cardinals replaced military conquest by moral leadership and persuasion; at their worst, they could show the same hunger for political power and worldly wealth as any Caesar. A visit to the Vatican is an object lesson for faithful and sceptic alike.

Constantine, first Christian emperor, erected the original St. Peter's Basilica near (probably over) the site of the Apostle's tomb in A.D. 324. After it was sacked in 846 by marauding Saracens, Pope Leo IV ordered massive walls built around the sacred church, and

A present for the pope?

the enclosed area became known as the Leonine City—later as the Vatican City, after the Etruscan name of its hill.

The Vatican has been a papal residence for more than 600 years, but a sovereign state independent of Italy only since the Lateran Pact signed with Mussolini in 1929. Since 1506, the pope has been guarded by an elite corps of Swiss Guards whose old-style blue, scarlet and orange uniforms are said to have been designed by Michelangelo. The papal domain is served by an independent Vatican radio, a tiny railway station (rarely used) and a separate post office issuing its own stamps, which have become collector's items. Apart from the 440,000 square metres (less than half a square mile) comprising St. Peter's Square, St. Peter's Basilica and the papal palace and gardens, the Vatican has jurisdiction over several extraterritorial enclaves, including the basilicas of Santa Maria Maggiore, St. John Lateran and St. Paul, as well as the Pope's summer residence outside Rome at Castel Gandolfo.

You won't need a passport to cross the border; you will hardly even notice when you do—though it is marked by a band of white travertine stones

Castel Sant'Angelo was in turn tomb, fort, palace and prison.

running from the ends of the two colonnades at the rim of St. Peter's Square. But for a public papal audience, security men will check your bags for weapons before allowing you past the control barriers.

The Vatican Pilgrim and

Tourist Information Bureau on St. Peter's Square arranges guided tours and issues tickets to the grounds of the Vatican City, including the gardens. From here also buses leave regularly to the entrance of the Vatican Museums.

A visit to St. Peter's ideally combines with a tour of the Castel Sant'Angelo, culminating in a picnic and siesta on the nearby Janiculum Hill. It is best to save the Vatican Museums for a separate day.

Castel Sant'Angelo

Cross the Tiber from the left bank by the pedestrians-only **Ponte Sant'Angelo**, incorporating arches of Hadrian's original bridge, the Pons Aelius. The balustrades are adorned by ten windswept angels designed by Bernini, each bearing a symbol of the Passion of Christ.

From the bridge you have the best view of the cylindrical bulk of the Castel Sant'Angelo, its mighty brick walls stripped of **61**

Oh, Tiber! Father Tiber!

The muddy yellow Tiber rolls through Rome almost unobserved, sunk below its high embankments. In imperial times, barges carried obelisks from Egypt and marble from Tuscany right into the heart of Rome. Nowadays, only a few floating restaurants and sunbathing barges lie moored to the banks.

Twenty-six bridges link Renaissance, Classical and business Rome with the Vatican City, Janiculum and Trastevere.

In the early days of the republic, a single wooden bridge straddled the Tiber. When the Etruscans tried to capture the city, the Roman hero Horatius held back an entire army on the narrow bridge, while his fellow citizens cut down the timbers behind him. As the last plank fell, Horatius leaped fully armed into the raging flood and swam safely to the Roman shore, crying (as every schoolchild, with a little help from poet Macaulay, used to know):

Oh, Tiber! Father Tiber!
To whom the Romans pray,
A Roman's life, a Roman's
arms
Take thou in hand this day!

Modern Romans can hardly emulate him. Swimming is out because of pollution.

their travertine and pitted by cannonballs, but nevertheless well withstanding the onslaught of time. Conceived by Hadrian around A.D. 130 as a mausoleum for himself and his family, it became part of the defensive Aurelian Wall a century later. It gained its present name in 590 after Pope Gregory the Great had a vision of the Archangel Michael alighting on one of the turrets and sheathing his sword to signal the end of a plague. It remained for centuries Rome's mightiest military bastion and hideout of popes in times of trouble; Clement VII holed up here during the sack of Rome by Habsburg troops in 1527. Here also were kept the Vatican's most precious possessions in treasure chests, still on view.

A spiral ramp, showing traces of the original black and white mosaic paving, leads up to the funerary chamber where the imperial ashes were kept in urns. You emerge into daylight in the **Court of the Angel** *(Cortile dell'Angelo or d'Onore)*, stacked with neat piles of cannonballs and watched over by a marble angel. A museum of arms and armour opens off the courtyard.

After the grimness of the exterior, it comes as a surprise

to step into the luxurious surroundings of the old **Papal Apartments**. At times effectively besieged in this fortress, the popes saw to it that they did not lack comforts. Lavish frescoes cover the walls and ceilings of rooms hung with masterpieces by Dosso Dossi, Nicolas Poussin and Lorenzo Lotto. Set away by itself off the Courtyard of Alexander VI is possibly the most exquisite **bathroom** in history. The tiny room, just wide enough for the marble bathtub at the far end, is painted with delicate designs over every inch of its walls and along the side of the bath.

A harsh jolt brings you back to reality as you enter the **dungeons,** scene of torture and executions. You have to bend double to pass through low doors into bare stone cells where famous prisoners languished—among them philosopher Giordano Bruno and sculptor-goldsmith Benvenuto Cellini.

The **Gallery of Pius IV,** surrounding the entire building, affords tremendous views in every direction, as does the terrace on the summit, at the foot of the 18th-century bronze **statue of St. Michael** by Verschaffelt. You may be suitably awed by the thought that this is the stage for the final act of Puccini's opera *Tosca*, in which the heroine hurls herself to her death from the battlements.

St. Peter's

From the Castel Sant'Angelo, a wide straight avenue, **Via della Conciliazione**, leads triumphantly up to St. Peter's. A maze of higgledy-piggledy streets, in which stood Raphael's studio, was destroyed in the 1930s to provide an unobstructed view of St. Peter's all the way from the banks of the Tiber. A thick wall running parallel to the avenue conceals a passageway *(il Passetto)* linking the Vatican to the Castel Sant'Angelo, by which the fleeing popes reached their bastion in safety.

In **St. Peter's Square** *(Piazza San Pietro)*, his greatest creation, Bernini has performed one of the world's most exciting pieces of architectural orchestration. The sweeping curves of the colonnades reach out to Rome and the whole world, *urbi et orbi*, to draw the flood of pilgrims into the bosom of the church beyond. On Easter Sunday as many as 300,000 people cram into the space. The square is on or near the site of Nero's circus where many early Christians were martyred.

Bernini completed the 284

Seeing the Pope

When he's not in Bogotà or Bangkok, it is possible to see the pope in person at the Vatican. He normally holds a public audience every Wednesday at 11 a.m. (5 p.m. in summer). An invitation to the Papal Audience Hall may be obtained from the Pontifical Prefect's Office (open Tuesday and Wednesday mornings) through the bronze gates off St. Peter's Square. A visitor's bishop at home can arrange a private audience.

On Sundays at noon, the pope appears at the window of his apartments in the Apostolic Palace (right of the basilica, overlooking the square), delivers a brief homily, says the Angelus and blesses the crowd below. On a few major holy days, the pontiff celebrates high mass in St. Peter's.

travertine columns and 88 pilasters topped by 140 statues of the saints in just 11 years, from 1656 to 1667. In the centre of the ellipse rises a red granite obelisk (84 feet, 25.5 m. high) brought here from Egypt by Caligula in A.D. 37. Stand on one of two circular paving stones set between the obelisk and the square's twin 17th-century fountains to see the quadruple rows of perfectly aligned

Doric columns appear magically as one. Above the northern colonnade are the windows of the Apostolic Palace where the pope lives and works.

By any standards a grandiose achievement, **St. Peter's Basilica** *(Basilica di San Pietro)* inevitably suffers from the competing visions of all the architects called in to collaborate—Bramante, Giuliano da Sangallo, Raphael, Baldassare Peruzzi, Michelangelo, Giacomo Della Porta, Domenico Fontana and Carlo Maderno, each adding, subtracting, modifying, often with a pope looking over his shoulder.

From 1506 when the new basilica was begun under Julius II to 1626 when it was consecrated, it changed form several times. It started as a simple Greek cross, with four arms of equal length (favoured by Bramante and Michelangelo) and ended as Maderno's Latin cross extended by a long nave, as demanded by the popes of the Counter-Reformation. One result is that Maderno's porticoed façade and nave obstruct a clear view of Michelangelo's dome from the square.

Entering the basilica, you are less inspired by religious fervour than by awe at its magnificence and immensity—it is, after all, the world's largest

Catholic church, 212 metres (695 ft.) in exterior length, 187 metres (613 ft.) long on the inside; 132.5 metres (435 ft.) to the tip of the dome (the dimensions of "lesser" churches such as St. Paul's in London are marked out on the floor of the central aisle).

Set in the floor by the centre door is the large round slab of red porphyry where Charlemagne knelt for his coronation as Holy Roman Emperor (see p. 17).

Crowds throng St. Peter's Square for the pope's blessing.

To the right of the entrance doors, in its own chapel, you'll find the basilica's most treasured work of art, Michelangelo's sublime **Pietà**—Mary with the dead Jesus in her lap—sculpted when the artist was only 24. The life-size figures express with the utmost simplicity the grieving mother's profound love for her son. This is the only one of his sculptures that Michelangelo signed, his name clearly visible on Mary's sash. Since it was attacked by a religious fanatic with a hammer, it has been protected by bulletproof glass.

Reverence can cause damage, too: on the 13th-century bronze seated **statue of St. Peter,** attributed to Florentine architect-sculptor Arnolfo di Cambio, the toes have been worn away by the lips of countless pilgrims.

Beneath the dome, Bernini's great **baldacchino** (canopy) soars above the high altar, at which only the pope celebrates mass. The canopy and four spiralling columns were cast from bronze beams taken from the Pantheon. Notice at the bottom of each column the coat of arms bearing the three bees of the Barberini Pope Urban VIII who commissioned the work.

In the apse beyond, Bernini gives full vent to his exuberance with his bronze and marble **Cathedra of St. Peter,** throne of the Apostle's successors, into which is supposedly incorporated the wooden chair of St. Peter.

For his imposing **dome,** Michelangelo drew inspiration from the Pantheon and the cathedral in Florence. A lift will take you as far as the gallery above the nave. From here you have a dizzying view down into the interior of the basilica, as well as close-ups of the inside of the dome. Spiral stairs and ramps lead on and up to the outdoor balcony which circles the top of the dome for stunning views of the Vatican City and all Rome.

The **Vatican Grottoes** beneath the basilica harbour numerous little chapels, some decorated by such masters as Melozzo da Forlì, Giotto and Pollaiuolo, and the tombs of popes. The necropolis, even deeper underground, shelters pre-Christian tombs, as well as a simple monument which may have marked St. Peter's burial place. The excavated area is not open to general viewing and visits must be arranged in

Gilded magnificence for a papal mass in St. Peter's.

advance through the Vatican Tourist Office.

St. Peter's is open without interruption every day from 7 a.m. until sunset. Masses are said frequently in the side chapels, in various languages. Visitors wearing shorts, bare-backed dresses, miniskirts or other scanty attire are politely turned away.

Vatican Museums

The 7 kilometres (4 mi.) of rooms and galleries of the Vatican Museums offer a microcosm of Western civilization. It is all there in almost bewildering profusion, from Egyptian mummies, exquisite Etruscan gold jewellery and Greek and Roman sculpture, right through medieval and Renaissance masterpieces to modern religious art. On a single ticket you can visit eight museums, five galleries, the Apostolic Library, the Borgia Apartments and Raphael Rooms and, of course, the Sistine Chapel.

Once past the entrance doors, you ascend a wide spiral ramp, which somehow manages to suck in all the crowds and disperse them up through the galleries. There is a choice of tours, ranging from 5 hours (A) to 1½ hours (D). Here are some of the highlights:

With the booty from the ruthless dismantling of ancient monuments to make way for the Renaissance city in the 16th century, the **Pio-Clementino Museum** has assembled a wonderful collection of classical art. The most celebrated piece is the 1st-century B.C. *Laocoön* group of the Trojan priest and his sons strangled by serpents for offending Apollo. Famous in imperial times, it was unearthed from a vineyard near Rome in 1506, to the delight of Michelangelo, who rushed to view it. It now stands in a recess of the charming octagonal Belvedere courtyard. Roman copies of other Greek sculptures, such as the *Aphrodite of Cnidos* of Praxiteles and the superb *Apollo*, achieved a fame as great as the originals, now lost. Take special note of the powerful muscular *Torso* by Apollonius which had such a profound influence on Renaissance artists and sculptors, in particular Michelangelo.

Some of archaeology's most exciting finds from a 7th-century B.C. Etruscan burial mound at Cerveteri (see p. 90) are displayed in the **Gregorian-Etruscan Museum**. The tomb yielded an abundance of treasures. Among the finely worked jewellery is an ornate gold brooch surprisingly decorated with lions and ducklings. Look out for the unusual bronze statue of a sprightly Etruscan warrior, the *Mars of Todi*, from the 4th century B.C.

Judging by the number of obelisks scattered throughout Rome, Egyptian art was much admired and sought after by the ancient Romans. The basis of the collection in the **Egyptian Museum** rests on finds from Rome and its surroundings,

particularly from the Gardens of Sallust between the Pincian and Quirinal hills, the Temple of Isis on the Campus Martius and Hadrian's Villa at Tivoli (see p. 86). The black granite throne of Rameses II is displayed, as well as a colossal statue of his mother, Queen Tuia.

Pope Julius II took a calculated risk in 1508 when he called in a relatively untried 25-year-old to decorate his new apartments. The result was the four **Raphael Rooms** *(Stanze di Raffaello)*. In the central Stanza della Segnatura are the two masterly frescoes, *Disputation over the Holy Sacrament*

Graceful ramp leads to labyrinth of Vatican Museums.

and the *School of Athens*, confronting theological and philosophical wisdom. The *Disputation* unites biblical figures with historical pillars of the faith such as Pope Gregory and Thomas Aquinas, as well as painter Fra Angelico and the divine Dante. At the centre of the *School,* Raphael is believed to have given the red-robed Plato the features of Leonardo da Vinci, while portraying Michelangelo as the thoughtful Heraclitus, seated in the foreground.

For a stark contrast to Raphael's grand manner, seek out the gentle, luminous beauty of Fra Angelico's frescoes in the **Chapel of Nicholas V**. The lives of St. Lawrence and St. Stephen are depicted here in delicately subdued pinks and blues, highlighted with gold.

The lavishly decorated **Borgia Apartments** contain Pinturicchio's sublime frescoes, with portraits of lusty Pope Alexander VI and his notorious son Cesare and daughter Lucrezia, and lead into the modern religious art collection of Paul VI. This includes Rodin bronzes, Picasso ceramics, Matisse's Madonna sketches and designs for ecclesiastical robes and, somewhat unexpectedly, a grotesque Francis Bacon pope.

Rare literary treasures are on view in the Apostolic Library.

One of Europe's finest collections of rare books and ancient manuscripts is kept in the hallowed precincts of the **Apostolic Library**. In the great vaulted reading room, or Sistine Hall, designed by Domenico Fontana in 1588, ceilings and walls are covered in paintings of ancient libraries, conclaves, thinkers and writers. Showcases displaying precious illuminated manuscripts have replaced the old lecterns. A 1,600-year-old copy of Virgil's works, the poems of Petrarch, a 6th-century gospel of St. Matthew, and Henry VIII's love letters to Anne Boleyn are among the prize possessions.

Nothing can prepare you for the visual shock of the **Sistine Chapel** *(Capella Sistina)*, built for Sixtus IV in the 15th century. Even the discomfort of the throngs of visitors (silence requested) seems to yield to the power of Michelangelo's ceiling, his *Last Judgment* and the other wall frescoes by Botticelli, Pinturicchio, Perugino, Ghirlandaio, Rosselli and Signorelli. In this private chapel of popes, where the cardinals hold their conclave to elect a new pope, the glory of the Catholic Church achieves its finest artistic expression.

The chapel portrays nothing less than the biblical history of man, in three parts: from Adam to Noah; the giving of the Law to Moses; and from the birth of Jesus to the Last Judgment. Towards the centre of Michelangelo's **ceiling,** you'll make out the celebrated outstretched finger of the *Creation of Adam*. Most overwhelming of all is the impression of the whole—best appreciated looking back from the bench at the chapel's exit.

A controversial programme of restoration, which involves 71

cleaning the frescoes of the dust and grime of the centuries, has revealed an unsuspected brilliance of colour.

On the chapel's altar wall is Michelangelo's **Last Judgment**, begun 23 years after the ceiling, when he was 52 and imbued with deep religious soul-searching. An almost naked Jesus dispenses justice more like a stern, even fierce classical god-hero than the conventionally gentle biblical figure. The artist's agonizing self-portrait can be made out in the flayed skin of St. Bartholomew, to the right below Jesus.

Amid all the Vatican treasures, the 15 rooms of the **Picture Gallery** *(Pinacoteca Vaticana)* sometimes get short shrift. This collection of ten centuries of paintings began with 73 canvases returned from Paris (where Napoleon had taken them). A separate wing of the palace was built in 1922 by Milanese architect Luca Beltrami to house the expanded collection. Among the most important exhibits are works by Giotto, Fra Angelico, Perugino, Raphael's *Transfiguration* (his last great work), Leonardo da Vinci's unfinished *St. Jerome* in sombre tones of sepia, Melozzo da Forlì's ethereal *Musician Angels* frescoes, Bellini's *Pietà* from a large

Man at Work

As might be imagined, painting the Sistine ceiling wasn't easy. Michelangelo, sculptor in marble with only a little oil painting behind him, had never before done a fresco (wall-painting on damp plaster). Preferring his inexperience to their incompetence, he fired his seven assistants in the first couple of weeks and continued alone for four years, from 1508 to 1512. He worked on tiptoe, bent backwards (he said) "like a Syrian bow"—not, as has been suggested, lying on his back. Pope Julius II kept a close eye on progress, climbing the scaffolding himself and threatening to throw Michelangelo off his platform if he didn't hurry up.

"I'm not in a good place," wrote Michelangelo to a friend, "and I'm no painter."

altarpiece, and Caravaggio's dramatic *Descent from the Cross.*

As you wander the galleries, glance out of the windows from time to time to view St. Peter's dome over the clipped hedges of the Vatican gardens (best views from the Gallery of the Maps). Take a rest in the **Cortile della Pigna,** dominated by the enormous bronze pinecone fountain (1st century A.D.) which gives the courtyard its name. And stop for a snack or refreshment at the self-service cafeteria.

The Janiculum
(Gianicolo)

After absorbing the riches of the Vatican, you can be forgiven for suffering a severe case of cultural overload. Rising above the Vatican, the Janiculum Hill provides the prescribed respite in the welcome shade of its parks. From the crest, you have a breathtaking view of Rome from the **Piazzale Garibaldi**. In the centre of the square stands an imposing bronze equestrian statue of the hero of the Risorgimento, who fought one of his fiercest battles here in 1849. From the crest, the road winds down into Trastevere (see p. 46).

The Sistine Chapel's frescoes have undergone a clean-up.

The Churches

You can't see them all. Don't try. There's one for every day of the year! On the other hand, what a pity to leave Rome without visiting at least some, for quite apart from their religious significance, many contain magnificent works of art.

Catholic pilgrims aim to visit all four great patriarchal basilicas: St. Peter's (see p. 64), Santa Maria Maggiore, St. John Lateran and St. Paul's Outside the Walls. And these top the list for most visitors. But numerous other churches can claim your attention for their architectural or artistic splendours or their historic interiors. We touch on only a representative selection of the best.

Santa Maria Maggiore

This largest and most splendid of all the churches dedicated to the Virgin Mary was first built in the 4th century by Pope Liberius over the site of a Roman temple to the goddess Juno on the Esquiline Hill. A century later it was expanded and embellished by Sixtus III.

Glittering **mosaics** enhance the perfect proportions of the interior. Above the 40 ancient Ionic columns of the triple nave, a mosaic frieze portrays Old Testament scenes leading up to the coming of Christ. The theme continues in the gilded Byzantine-style mosaics on the triumphal arch, detailing the birth and childhood of Jesus, and culminates in the magnificent portrayal of Mary and Jesus enthroned, in the apse behind the high altar.

Inlaid red and green precious marbles pattern the floor in the cosmatesque style, first pioneered by Rome's Cosmati family of craftsmen in the 12th century. Note the opulence of the coffered Renaissance ceiling, gilded with the first shipment of gold from the Americas.

A casket of gold, silver and crystal below the high altar contains fragments reputed to come from the **holy crib**, brought back from the Holy Land by St. Helena, Constantine's mother.

The incomparably rich **Pauline Chapel** *(Capella Paolina)* has an altar inlaid with lapis lazuli, amethyst and agate below a revered 9th-century painting of the Madonna and Child. Every August 5th, white flower petals are showered onto the altar to mark the date when a miraculous fall of snow, prophesied by the Virgin, showed Pope Liberius where to build her church.

St. John Lateran

(San Giovanni in Laterano)

Regarded as the mother church of the Catholic world (it's the seat of the pope as Bishop of Rome), the original Lateran church predated even St. Peter's by a few years; Constantine built both basilicas in the early 4th century. Popes lived in the Lateran Palace for a thousand years until they moved to Avignon and then to the Vatican in the 14th century. On a wooden table, incorporated in the high altar, St. Peter himself is believed to have celebrated mass.

Fire, earthquake and looting by the Vandals reduced the church to ruins over the centuries. The present basilica, little more than 300 years old, is at least the fifth on this site. But the bronze central doors go all the way back to ancient Rome when they graced the entrance to the Curia in the Forum (see p. 49). High above the basilica's façade, 15 giant white statues of Jesus, John the Baptist and the sages of the Church stand out against the sky.

Transformed by Borromini in the 17th century, the interior gives a predominant impression of sombre white and grey, more restrained than is usual for Baroque architects, and enlivened only by the coloured marble inlays of the paving. In recesses along the nave stand majestic statues of the Apostles sculpted by pupils of Bernini.

The octagonal **baptistery** preserves some truly splendid 5th- and 7th-century mosaics. It was built over the baths of Constantine's second wife Fausta, where Rome's first baptisms took place. The beautiful bronze doors of St. John the Baptist's Chapel, removed from the Baths of Caracalla, sing musically on their hinges when opened.

Foremost exponents of the cosmatesque style of inlaid marble, brothers Jacopo and Pietro Vassalletto have excelled themselves in the **cloisters**, where alternating straight and twisted columns, set mosaic-style with coloured stone, create a perfect setting for meditation.

An ancient edifice opposite the basilica—almost all that's left of the old Lateran Palace—shelters the **Scala Santa**, the holy stairway brought back by St. Helena from Jerusalem and said to have been trodden by Jesus in the house of Pontius Pilate. The devout climb the 28 marble steps on their knees.

Outside the basilica stands an Egyptian **obelisk** brought from the Temple of Ammon in Thebes. It's the tallest in the world—31 metres (102 ft.)—

and the oldest (1449 B.C.) of the 13 still standing in Rome.

St. Paul's
Outside the Walls
(San Paolo fuori le Mura)
The basilica, largest in Rome after St. Peter's, was built by Constantine in 314 and later enlarged by Valentinian II and Theodosius. It survived aston-

San Pietro in Vincoli harbours Michelangelo's majestic Moses.

ishingly until destroyed by a tragic fire in 1823, but has been faithfully restored to its original splendour.

A tabernacle designed by the 13th-century sculptor Arnolfo di Cambio and retrieved from the ashes of the great fire decorates the high altar under which lies the burial place of St. Paul. After Paul was beheaded, a Roman matron, Lucina, placed the body here in her family vault. Constantine later encased it in a sarcophagus of marble and bronze, looted by Saracen invaders in 846.

Above the 86 Venetian marble columns runs a row of mosaic medallions representing all the popes from St. Peter to the present.

Pause in the peaceful Benedictine **cloisters**, designed by Pietro Vassalletto and surpassing even his work at St. John Lateran. Slender spiralled columns in the cosmatesque tradition glitter with green, red and gold mosaic, enclosing a garden of roses and gently rippling fountain.

San Clemente
This gem of a church hides a fascinating history which can be traced down through each of its three levels. The present **church,** dating back to the 12th

century, is built in basilica form with three naves divided by antique columns and embellished by a pavement of cosmatesque geometric designs. A richly symbolic mosaic in the apse features the Cross as the Tree of Life nourishing all living things—birds, animals and plants.

To the right of the nave a staircase leads down to the 4th-century **basilica,** which underpins the present church. Sadly, the Romanesque frescoes—copies show they were in near-perfect condition when uncovered earlier this century—have now drastically faded.

An ancient stairway leads further underground to a maze of corridors and chambers, believed to be the 1st-century home of St. Clement himself, third successor to St. Peter as pope. Down here is also the

The cloister at St. Paul's offers an oasis of peace.

earliest religious structure on this site, a pagan **temple** *(Mithraeum)* dedicated to the Eastern cult of the god Mithras. A well-preserved sculpture shows Mithras slaying a bull. The sound of trickling water from nearby streams echoes eerily through these subterranean chambers as it drains off into the Cloaca Maxima.

Santa Prassede

Though unremarkable from the outside, this little church is enchanting in the intimacy of its interior. St. Praxedes and her sister Pudenziana (her church is nearby) were the daughters of a Roman senator, who as one of the first converts to Christianity gave shelter to St. Peter.

Delicate 9th-century mosaics glittering with gold cover the walls and ceiling of the **Chapel of St. Zeno**, making it the city's most important Byzantine monument. It was designed as a tomb for Theodora, mother of Pope Paschal I. Medieval Romans called it the "Garden of Paradise" because of its beauty.

San Pietro in Vincoli

The church of St. Peter in Chains might not attract a second look (and might even prefer it that way, given the hordes of visitors), if it did not contain one of the greatest of Michelangelo's sculptures, his formidable **Moses**. Intended for St. Peter's Basilica as part of Michelangelo's botched project for Julius II's tomb, the statue of the great biblical figure sits in awesome majesty at the centre of the monument. The horns on his head continue a medieval mistranslation of the Hebrew word for halo-like rays of light. On each side, the comparatively passive figures of Jacob's wives—a prayerful Rachel and melancholy Leah—were Michelangelo's last completed sculptures.

The Empress Eudoxia founded the church in the 5th century, on the site of the Roman law court where St. Peter was tried and sentenced. It was built as a sanctuary for the chains with which Herod bound St. Peter in Palestine, together with those used when he was imprisoned in Rome. They are kept in a bronze reliquary under the high altar.

The Gesù

Severe and relatively discreet on its own piazza west of the Piazza Venezia, the Gesù is the mother church of the Jesuits and was a major element in their Counter-Reformation campaign. Begun as their Roman "headquarters" in 1568, its open ground plan was the model for the congregational churches that were to regain popular support from the Protestants. While its façade is more sober than the exultant Baroque churches put up as the movement gained momentum, the interior glorifies the new militancy in gleaming bronze, gold, marble and precious stones.

St. Ignatius Loyola, the Spanish soldier who founded the order, has a fittingly magnificent **tomb** under a richly decorated, almost overwhelming altar in the left transept, with a profusion of lapis lazuli. The globe at the top is said to be the largest piece of this stone in the world.

Sant'Ignazio

In gentler contrast, the church of Sant'Ignazio stands in an enchanting stage-set of russet and ochre Rococo houses. Inside, Andrea Pozzo (himself a Jesuit priest and designer of the saint's tomb in the Gesù) has painted a superb *trompe-l'œil* **ceiling fresco** (1685) depicting St. Ignatius' entry into paradise. Stand on a buff stone disk in the nave's central aisle and you will have the extraordinary impression of the whole building rising hundreds of feet above you through the ingenious architectural effect of the painting. From any other point, the columns appear to collapse. From another disk further up the aisle you can admire the celestial **dome** above the high altar, but as you advance, it begins to take on strange proportions: it is just another illusionist painting.

Museums

You could spend your entire visit to Rome just in museums. The city has yielded so much over the centuries that there is barely enough room to put it all on display. And invariably the collections are enhanced by the incomparable setting of an old palazzo or villa or ancient Roman building. Here are just a few among the very best (the Vatican Museums are described on p. 68, the Capitoline Museums on p. 28):

Borghese Gallery
(Galleria Borghese)
The avid and ruthless art patron Cardinal Scipione Borghese conceived this handsome Baroque villa in the Villa Borghese park as a home for his small but outstanding collection, using his prestige as nephew of Pope Paul V to ex-

tort coveted masterpieces from their owners.

The ground floor is devoted to **sculpture**, with works from antiquity, as well as by the young Bernini, in splendidly decorated rooms of marble and frescoes. As the cardinal's protégé, Bernini contributed busts of his patron, a vigorous *David* (said to be a youthful self-portrait), and a graceful sculpture of *Apollo and Daphne*, with the water-nymph turning into a laurel just as the god is about to seize her. In a later addition and star attraction, Canova portrays Napoleon's sister Pauline, who married into the Borghese family, as a naked reclining Venus.

On the first floor, the **picture gallery** boasts some exceptional paintings, with Raphael's *Descent from the Cross*, Titian's *Sacred and Profane Love*, Caravaggio's *David with the Head of Goliath* and *Madonna of the Serpent,* along with works by Rubens, Correggio, Veronese and Botticelli.

Villa Giulia

This pleasure palace of a pope, north-west of the Villa Borghese, is now the lovely setting for Italy's finest museum of **Etruscan art.** Although much about this pre-Roman civilization is still a mystery, the Etrus-cans left a wealth of detail about their customs and every-day life by burying the personal possessions of the dead with them in their tombs.

Replicas show the round stone burial mounds, built like huts. Room after room is filled with objects from the tombs—bronze statuettes of warriors in full battle dress; shields, weapons and chariots (even the skeletons of two horses); gold, silver and ivory jewellery; a large variety of decorative vases mass-imported by the Etruscans from Greece; and a host of everyday cooking utensils, mirrors and combs. Note the large bronze toilet box adorned with figurines of the Argonauts. The highlight is a life-size terracotta sculpture for a sarcophagus lid of a blissful young couple reclining on a banquet couch.

Museo Nazionale Romano

You'll find your best introduction to the city's Greek and Roman antiquities in this superb collection housed in the Roman Baths of Diocletian.

Larger even than those of Caracalla, Diocletian's baths covered some 120 hectares (300 acres), part of which is now occupied by the Piazza della Repubblica and Michelangelo's church of Santa Maria degli Angeli, near Termini station.

The small cloister *(Piccolo Chiostro)* of the old Carthusian monastery, adapted from part of the baths, provides an attractive setting for the magnificent **Ludovisi Collection**, assembled by Cardinal Ludovico Ludovisi in the 17th century. Among the most important pieces, look for the marble altar-top known as the *Ludovisi Throne,* an orig-inal Greek work of the 5th century B.C., with exquisitely carved reliefs of Aphrodite and a maiden playing the flute; and the tragic statue of a barbarian warrior in the act of killing himself and his wife rather than submit to slavery.

In the so-called **"New Rooms"**, you'll find the *Apollo of the Tiber,* a copy of a bronze group by the young Phidias discovered in 1891 during excavations near the Palatine Bridge; a copy, probably the

The Borghese is the perfect home for these sublime sculptures.

best ever made, of Myron's famed *Discobolos* (Discus-Thrower); the *Daughter of Niobe*, a Greek original of the 5th century B.C.; the *Venus of Cyrene*; a bronze of a young man leaning on a lance; another of a seated boxer signed by Apollonius; and a variety of portrait sculptures, including one of Augustus. On the first floor, the **landscape frescoes** from the imperial villa of Livia show nature at its most bountiful, with flowers, trees, birds and luscious fruits painted with realistic attention to detail.

Galleria Nazionale d'Arte Antica

The Palazzo Barberini (Via delle Quattro Fontane) provided another architectural battleground for arch-rivals Borromini and Bernini, each of whom built one of its grand staircases and contributed to the superb façade. It is worth a visit as much for its Baroque décor as for its collection of paintings. Art and architecture converge in the palace's **Great Hall** with Pietro da Cortona's dazzling illusionist ceiling fresco, *Triumph of Divine Providence*.

The major part of the national art collection is hung in the first-floor gallery (the rest is housed in the Palazzo Corsini across the Tiber in Trastevere). Works include a Fra Angelico triptych, the celebrated portrait of *Henry VIII* by Hans Holbein, and paintings by Titian, Tintoretto, Perugino, Lorenzo Lotto and El Greco. Look out especially for Raphael's *La Fornarina*, the most famous of the many he painted of the baker's daughter who was his mistress.

Galleria Doria Pamphili

The vast Palazzo Doria in the Corso is still the private residence of the Doria family, but the public are allowed in several days a week to view their richly endowed private collection of paintings, assembled over hundreds of years.

Here's a case where you can't do without a catalogue, as the paintings are identifiable only by number. They hang three deep on either side of four galleries enclosing a Renaissance courtyard.

In this stunning collection, virtually every one of the paintings, mostly from the 15th to the 17th centuries, is a masterpiece. It covers works by Titian, Raphael, Veronese, Caravaggio, as well as painters of the Dutch and Flemish schools —Rembrandt and Van Dyck. Look out for the serene and evocative landscape of the

Flight into Egypt by Annibale Carracci, and the windswept *Naval Battle in the Bay of Naples* by Breughel the Elder.

You'll find a nice stylistic contrast in a little room off the galleries, which juxtaposes a brilliant worldly portrait by Velazquez of **Innocent X**, the family pope elected in 1644, alongside a more serene marble bust of him by Bernini.

Excursions

The main excursions into the Lazio (Latium) countryside around Rome today are still those that ancient Romans took to vacation homes by the sea or nearby hills and lakes. But first you should take an important short trip just outside the city walls to the Old Appian Way.

Old Appian Way
(Via Appia Antica)
As you head south-east through the Porta San Sebastiano, look back for a good view of the old **Aurelian Wall**, which still encloses part of Rome. Its massive defensive ramparts stretch into the distance, topped by towers and bastions built to resist the onslaught of barbarian invasions in the 3rd century.

Ahead lies a narrow lane, hemmed in at first by hedges

The Third City
The historic centre of Rome has been kept mercifully free of antagonistic 20th-century innovations. But there is an ultra-modern "Third Rome", 5 kilometres (3 mi.) south along the Ostian Way—Mussolini's dream, intended to rival the glories of the Imperial and Renaissance cities.

Known simply by its initials EUR (pronounced Ay-oor), this complex of massive white marble buildings, with wide avenues and green open spaces grouped around an artificial lake, was designed for a world fair in 1942 to mark 20 years of fascism. The war interrupted construction and the fair never took place.

In recent years, EUR has developed into a thriving township of government ministries, offices, conference centres and fashionable apartments. Several buildings remain from Mussolini's time, including the formidable cube of arches of the Palace of Workers *(Palazzo della Civiltà del Lavoro)*, known as the "Square Colosseum". For the 1960 Olympics, engineer Pier Luigi Nervi designed the huge domed Palazzo dello Sport. The Museum of Roman Civilization *(Museo della Civiltà Romana)* contains a fascinating model of ancient Rome.

and the high walls of film stars' and millionaires' homes—the **Old Appian Way**. When Appius Claudius the Censor opened it and gave it his name in 312 B.C., this was the grandest road the western world had ever known. You can still see some of the original basalt paving stones, over which the Roman legions marched on their way to Brindisi to set sail for the Levant and North Africa.

Since by law no burial could take place within the city walls, the tombs of the dead were built along this road. On either side lie the ruins of sepulchres of 20 generations of patrician families, some marked by simple tablets, others by impressive mausoleums. For the same reason, the Christians built their cemeteries in the catacombs here.

At a fork in the road, the chapel of **Domine Quo Vadis** marks the spot where St. Peter, fleeing from Nero's persecution in Rome, is said to have encountered Christ. "Whither goest thou, Lord?" asked Peter. ("Domine quo vadis?"). Christ replied: "I go to Rome to be crucified again." Ashamed of his fear, Peter turned back to Rome and his own crucifixion. The little chapel contains a copy of a stone with a footprint said to have been left by Christ (the original is in the Basilica of San Sebastiano).

Further along the Appia Antica, within a short distance of each other, are four of Rome's most celebrated catacombs, St. Calixtus, St. Sebastian, Domitilla and Priscilla. About 6 million early Christians, many of them martyrs and saints, were buried in some 50 of these vast underground cemeteries. Knowledgeable guides accompany you in groups into the labyrinth of damp and musty-smelling tunnels and chambers burrowed into the soft volcanic tufa rock, sometimes six levels deep (claustrophobes should abstain). Paintings and carvings adorn the catacombs with precious examples of early Christian art.

The entrance to the **Catacombs of St. Calixtus** lies at the end of an avenue of cypresses. An official tour takes you down to the second level of excavations, where you will see the burial niches, called *loculi*, cut into the rock one above the other on either side of the dark galleries. Occasionally the narrow passageways open out into larger chambers or *cubicula*, where a whole family would be buried together. One such crypt sheltered the remains of 3rd-century popes; another held the body of St. Cecilia until it was transferred to the church of Santa Cecilia in Trastevere (the statue of the saint lying in a recess is a copy of the one by Stefano Maderno in the church, see p. 48).

In the **Catacombs of St. Sebastian**, the bodies of the Apostles Peter and Paul are said to have been hidden for several years during 3rd-century persecutions. You can still see graffiti in Latin and Greek invoking the two saints.

The cylindrical **tomb of Cecilia Metella** dominates the Appian landscape. This little-known noblewoman was a relative of the immensely rich Crassus who financed Julius Caesar's early campaigns. A Roman family of the 14th century added the castellated parapet when they turned it into a fortress.

Alongside extends the well-preserved **Circus of Maxentius** built for chariot races in A.D. 309 under the last pagan emperor, who carried out the final wave of Christian persecutions in Rome.

Turn off the Via Appia to visit the **Fosse Ardeatine**, a modern place of pilgrimage for Italians. In March 1944, in retaliation for the killing of 32 German soldiers by the Italian Resistance, the Nazis rounded

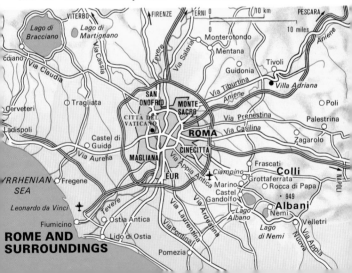

ROME AND SURROUNDINGS

up at random 335 Italian men (10 for each killed and an extra 15 for good measure) and machine-gunned them down in the sandpits of the Via Ardeatina. As soon as the Germans left Rome, a poignant memorial was raised here to the dead, among them a boy of 14.

Tivoli

The picturesque town of Tivoli perches on a steep slope amid the woods, streams and twisted silvery olive trees of the Sabine Hills. Inhabited even in ancient times, when it was known as Tibur, Tivoli continued to prosper throughout the Middle Ages and thus preserves interesting Roman remains and medieval churches, as well as the famous Renaissance villa and gardens.

Public buses leave Rome regularly from Via Gaeta, opposite the Stazione Termini; the drive, 30 kilometres (19 mi.) along the old Roman chariot road (repaved) of the Via Tiburtina, takes about an hour and a quarter.

The **Villa d'Este**, sprawls along the hillside. From its windows and balconies, you look down on the **gardens**, falling away in a series of steep terraces—a paradise of dark cypresses, fountains (a reputed 500), grottoes, pools and statues.

Cardinal Ippolito II d'Este conceived this pleasure garden in the 16th century. Architect Pirro Ligorio, with that genius for playing with water that has characterized the Romans since ancient times, created it. On the Terrace of 100 Fountains jets of water splash into a long basin guarded by eagle statues. The grand Organ Fountain, originally accompanied by organ music, cascades steeply down the rocks. You can walk up behind it to view the gardens through a haze of spray. On the lowest level, three large deep pools contrast in their stillness with the rush and roar of the water elsewhere.

The architect took particular delight in strange fantasies, such as the row of sphinxes spurting water from their nipples, or hidden joke jets which sprayed the unsuspecting passer-by. Don't worry, you won't be in for any unpleasant shocks; the "water tricks" are no more.

Tucked away at the foot of the hills lie the haunting ruins of **Hadrian's Villa** *(Villa Adriana)*. Spread across 70 hectares (173 acres), this retirement hideaway of the great emperor-builder (the Pantheon in Rome, Hadrian's Wall across Britain) was designed to recapture some of the architectural marvels of his empire, especially the Greece he loved above all else—a travel memoir for his old age, filled with treasures that have since found their way to museums around the world.

Those arriving at the villa by public bus are dropped off at the main gate and ticket office. Tourist coaches and private cars continue up the drive to the car park within the grounds. An excellent scale model here will give you an overview of the whole. As you will see, this was more a miniature city than a villa, even if it was an emperor's. The monumental baths, separate Greek and Latin libraries, Greek theatre, temples and pavilions together make up the home of a man who drew no distinction between the pleasures of mind and body.

You enter the ruins through the colonnades of the Greek-style **Stoa Poikile** (Painted Portico), which leads to the main imperial residence. Adjoining the palace are guest rooms, their black and white mosaic floors still visible, and an underground passageway for the servants to move about unseen.

A curtain of water screens the view at Tivoli's Villa D'Este.

The enchanting **Villa dell'-Isola,** a pavilion surrounded by a little reflecting pool and circular portico, epitomizes all the magic of the place.

To the south, remnants of arches and copies of Greek-style caryatids (female statues used as pillars) surround the **Pool of Canopus** leading to the sanctuary of the Egyptian god Serapis.

Barbarians and museum collectors have removed most of the villa's treasures, but a stroll among the remaining pillars, arches and mosaic fragments in gardens running wild among the olive trees, cypresses and umbrella pines can be marvellously evocative of a lost world.

Ostia Antica

Excavations continue to uncover fascinating sections of what was once the seaport and naval base of ancient Rome. The long-buried city of Ostia stands at the mouth *(ostium)* of the Tiber, 23 kilometres (14 mi.) south-west of the capital on the shores of the Tyrrhenian Sea.

Sea-going vessels were unable to travel inland along the shallow Tiber, so river barges plied back and forth from the port, carrying Rome's food and building materials. In its
88 palmiest days, Ostia had

Strawberries for lunch and a wide panorama, away from Rome's heat in the Alban Hills.

100,000 residents and boasted splendid baths, temples, a theatre and imposing houses.

Ostia's well-preserved ruins, set among cypress and pine, reveal more about the daily life and building methods of the ancient Romans than do those

of the capital. Excavations since the 19th century have unearthed warehouses, offices, apartment blocks known as *insulae* (islands) and private houses with gardens, built facing the sea and decorated with mosaics and murals.

The porticoed **Piazzale delle Corporazioni** (Corporations' Square) held 70 commercial offices round a central temple to Ceres, goddess of agriculture. Mottoes and emblems in mosaic in the pavement tell of the grain factors, caulkers, ropemakers and shipowners from many parts of the world who traded here.

The neighbouring **theatre** from the time of Augustus now hosts performances of classical plays translated into Italian. It is worth climbing the tiered seats for a view over the whole ruined city.

As in Rome, the **Forum** was the focus of city life, dominated at one end by the Capitol, a temple dedicated to Jupiter,

Juno and Minerva and at the other end by the Temple of Rome and Augustus, with the Curia, seat of the municipal authorities, and the basilica or law courts lying between.

To see a typical private dwelling, visit the **House of Cupid and Psyche**, with rooms paved in marble built round a central garden courtyard. Nearby, a small **museum** traces the history of Ostia with statues, busts and frescoes excavated in the region.

The modern seaside resort of Ostia attracts crowds of weekend Romans, who flock to the beaches of grey sand. Swimming is not recommended on account of the pollution. Dine instead in one of the cheerful open-air restaurants.

Rome's metro runs to Ostia, as well as city buses and guided excursions. The trip takes about 45 minutes.

The Alban Hills and Castel Gandolfo

Immediately south-east of Rome, the scattered hill villages known locally as the *Castelli Romani* (Roman Castles) began as fortified refuges during the medieval civil wars. Today it's just the summer heat that drives the Romans out on day-trips to the vineyards of the Alban hills and lakes.

The pope has his summer home at **Castel Gandolfo**, above Lake Albano, where he relaxes in the huge late-Renaissance palace designed by Carlo Maderno, set in beautiful landscaped gardens. He holds audience on Wednesdays from mid-July to early September and blesses the thousands of pilgrims on Sunday at noon. The palace, gardens and Vatican Observatory in the grounds are closed to visitors.

A terrace near the papal palace looks down on the dark blue waters of **Lake Albano**, lying in an old forested volcanic crater hundreds of feet below.

The villages of Frascati, Grottaferrata, Marino and Rocca di Papa make delightful stops, not least of all for a cool glass of their estimable white wine, especially during the autumn grape-harvest festivals. In the mellow microclimate of **Lake Nemi**, strawberries are grown all year round, served— with cream or lemon juice—in Nemi's village park.

Cerveteri

If the Villa Giulia in Rome (see p. 80) and the Gregorian-Etruscan Museum in the Vatican (see p. 68) have whetted your curiosity about the Etruscans, it is worth making a trip to the ancient necropolis at Cerveteri,

43 kilometres (27 mi.) north-west of Rome.

Known in ancient times as Caere, it was one of the original 12 towns of the powerful Etruscan League (at one time Etruscan kings even ruled Rome). But the city declined in the 3rd century B.C., after it became a Roman dependency.

The scores of **tombs** discovered represent every kind of burial from the early shaft and pit graves to tumuli, dating from the 7th–1st centuries B.C. These later mounds often contain several chambers, carved into the volcanic tufa in the shape of wooden Etruscan homes. Stucco decorations and rock carvings represent the weapons, hunting equipment, domestic animals and even household pots and pans that the Etruscans felt they would still need in the after-life. Most famous is the Regolini-Galassi tomb, whose riches are now on display in the Vatican's Gregorian-Etruscan Museum.

Unfortunately many tombs have been plundered—and are still being plundered—by grave-robbers. But the **Museo Nazionale di Cerveteri** in a 16th-century castle displays in chronological order a rich array of objects from the tombs, including sarcophagi, sculptures, wall-paintings and vases.

What to Do

Entertainment

Like every big city, Rome has its share of nightclubs and discotheques, but the most popular custom is to linger well past midnight over dinner in one of the attractive outdoor restaurants, serenaded by minstrels and guitarists (see p. 96).

Music. Almost every evening in July and August, there's outdoor opera (with *Aïda* a long-standing favourite) in the spectacular setting of the ruined Baths of Caracalla (see p. 58). The official opera season runs from November to June at the Teatro dell'Opera.

Summer concerts of classical music take place in picturesque and historic settings, such as the Campidoglio, Santa Maria Sopra Minerva and the Villa Medici.

Open-air festivals of jazz, pop and rock are held in the parks and gardens of Rome for the *Estate Romana* (Roman Summer).

Theatre. Several theatres stage classical and modern plays and musical comedies, almost always in Italian. Italian translations of classical plays are performed in the ancient

Calendar of Events

January 5–6	*Befana* (Epiphany) Festival on Piazza Navona.
March 9	*Festa di Santa Francesca Romana*; Romans drive their cars to the Piazzale del Colosseo near the church of Santa Francesco Romano (also known as Santa Maria Nova) in the Forum, for blessing.
March–April	Good Friday; Pope leads the Procession of the Cross at 9 p.m. from the candlelit Colosseum to the Forum. Easter Sunday; Pope blesses the crowds from the balcony at St. Peter's at noon.
April	*Festa della Primavera* (Spring Festival); the Spanish Steps are decked with pink azaleas.
April 21	Anniversary of Rome's founding.
April/May	International Horse Show, with Nations' Cup, in Villa Borghese park.
May	Open-air art exhibition in Via Margutta. Antiques fair in Via dei Coronari. International tennis championship in Foro Italico.
June (first week)	*Festa della Repubblica*; military parade along Via dei Fori Imperiali.
June 29	*Festa di San Pietro e San Paolo*; solemn rites in St. Peter's and St. Paul's Outside the Walls.
July	*Noiantri* street festival in Trastevere.
August 5	*Festa della Madonna della Neve* in Santa Maria Maggiore.
August 15	*Ferragosto* or Feast of the Assumption; most Romans leave the city for the sea or hills.
September	Open-air art exhibition in Via Margutta.
December	Children's toy and Christmas decoration market on Piazza Navona.
December 8	*Festa della Madonna Immacolata* (Immaculate Conception); the pope or his envoys place flowers at the column of the Virgin in Piazza di Spagna.
December 24	Midnight mass at St. Peter's and at Santa Maria Maggiore with veneration of Holy Crib.
December 25	Nativity crib with revered Bambino in Santa Maria in Aracoeli.

amphitheatre at Ostia (see p. 88).

Cinema. Rome has about 100 cinemas, but few show films in their original language; foreign films are dubbed in Italian. The *Pasquino* in Trastevere offers the original sound track. Rome's cinemas are almost always filled to capacity.

Shopping

Rome's international reputation as a marvellous shopping city is unquestionably deserved. Nowhere is the Italian flair for display more striking than in the chic boutiques, and the shop assistants, even if they don't speak English, will bend over backwards to be helpful.

Where to Shop

Rome's most fashionable shopping district is found between the Spanish Steps and Via del Corso, notably along Via Condotti, Via Frattina and Via Borgognona. Some of Europe's finest shops and boutiques are here, but while bargains can occasionally be found, Roman shoppers who know go elsewhere—and pay considerably less.

A favoured shopping street is the Via Cola di Rienzo on the right bank of the Tiber. Prices are also reasonable around Via del Tritone, near the Trevi Fountain, and in the twisting streets near the Campo de' Fiori and the Pantheon.

For quality goods, Italians prefer shopping in small boutiques with a long tradition, very often a family business guaranteeing generations of craftsmanship. As a result, you won't find upmarket department stores, but popular, low-price chain stores, such as Rinascente or Upim.

Rome's incredible flea market, the Porta Portese, extends for about 4 kilometres (2½ mi.) of streets and alleys. It begins at a battered archway, the Porta Portese, just across the Tiber at the Ponte Sublicio. Invariably jammed, Porta Portese operates on Sundays from dawn to about 1 p.m. The cluttered stalls offer everything from refrigerators to kittens, with the emphasis on clothing. Look out especially for the Abruzzi peasant rugs and bedspreads. Traveller's cheques are accepted at many of the market stalls. But leave any unnecessary money or documents behind; pickpockets love this place. Other outdoor markets during the week are on Via Sannio and Piazza Vittorio Emanuele II. **93**

What to Buy

Antiques. If you are looking for genuine, authenticated antiques—silver, paintings, jewellery or furniture—stick to reputable dealers rather than the open-air markets. Quality shops will provide a certificate of guarantee *(certificato di garanzia)* and will arrange international shipping, while taking care of all the formalities. The best antique shops are to be found in the streets around the Piazza di Spagna (especially in Via del Babuino) and in the area west of the Corso Vittorio Emanuele, not to mention the Via dei Coronari (see p. 40).

Ceramics. Carafes, jugs, plates, bowls, etc., with attractive and colourful designs make decorative as well as useful gifts.

Fashion. From ultra-chic to sports clothes and ready-to-wear, Italian design is unsurpassed. Women's fashions include the major French designers, as well as the natives (such as Valentino, Armani, Gianni Versace and Missoni). The men's clothes meccas are Cucci (with a C) and Battistoni. Children's clothing is not neglected, and no less expensive either, with some superb items in Tablò's two shops.

Food and wine. Possibilities are inevitably limited because of the problems of transportation, but you can take home without too much risk a block of parmesan, which travels and keeps well, salamis, the Parma and San Daniele ham *(prosciutto crudo)*, and to accompany them, Rome's local vintages from the Alban Hills (see p. 90).

Jewellery. Italian gold- and silversmiths are among the best and most prolific in Europe. For sheer exclusivity, if you can afford the price, brave the

94

imposing marble façade of Bulgari on Via Condotti. Costume jewellery is also a good buy.

Leather. Especially shoes, but also gloves, bags, wallets, jackets, belts, desk sets and luggage are of impeccable quality and design. Some of the finest leather goods can be found at Gucci, Fendi or Pier Caranti.

Souvenirs. When it comes to mass-produced souvenirs, you will find endless invention in the realm of the cheap—and not so cheap—and nasty:

Trevi Fountain water squirters, Colosseum with plaster Christians fed to plastic lions, glass balls of the pope blessing the faithful in a snow storm...

Textiles. You'll find a wide range of quality silks—blouses, shirts, suits, scarves and ties—and knitwear with colourful and distinctive patterns.

Window-shopping along the Corso is one of the joys of the evening stroll.

Eating Out

Do as the Romans do so enthusiastically and turn your eating out into an evening out. They like to spend hours over a leisurely meal of innumerable courses in the genial company of family or friends in one of the pleasant *trattorie* or restaurants which abound in the city. And with the banning of traffic in sections of Rome's historic centre, not to mention a benevolent climate, outdoor dining is once more a delight.

Choice spots are Trastevere (see p. 46), which boasts hundreds of little *trattorie*, and the Jewish Ghetto (see p. 43), with its own specialities. Still in the tracks of the Romans, drive out at least once into the countryside beyond the walls to lunch or dine in one of the restaurants along the Via Appia Antica or the roads to the Alban Hills or Ostia.

Where to Eat

Only in a few hotels catering to tourists will you find an English or American-style breakfast. Otherwise head for a good *caffè* on the piazza and settle happily for the *prima colazione* of superb coffee, espresso black or *cappuccino* with foaming hot milk (sprinkled in the best establishments with powdered chocolate), and toast or sweet roll. Italian tea is somewhat anemic, but the hot chocolate is excellent.

For those adopting a healthy "sightseer's diet" of one main meal a day, preferably in the evening, the ideal place for a lunch-time snack is a stand-up bar serving *tavola calda* ("hot table"). All through the day, without interruption, you can choose from a variety of hot and cold dishes—sandwiches, pasta, fish and chips, spit-roasted chicken, and slices of pizzas with different rich toppings—to take away or eat on the spot.

In theory, a *ristorante* is a fancier and larger establishment than a family-style *trattoria*. But in Rome the distinction is blurred beyond recognition; they're both ways of saying restaurant, as is the less frequent *osteria*. A *trattoria-pizzeria* will serve pizza in addition to the standard *trattoria* fare.

Price should not be taken as an indication of the quality of the cooking; an expensive restaurant may offer a superb meal with service to match, but you may also be paying for the location. Only a few steps away from such famous tourist spots as the Piazza del Popolo and the Piazza Navona, you'll find numerous little *trattorie*, with considerably lower prices, where the ambience, half the value of an Italian meal, is infinitely more enjoyable and the food has more real character. Don't expect to find too much character in the hotel dining room.

Many restaurants display the menu with prices in a glass case outside, so you will have an idea of what's on offer, without any obligation to go inside.

When to Eat

Roman restaurants serve lunch from 12.30 to 3 p.m. and dinner from 7.30 to midnight. Each is closed one day a week, which will vary from restaurant to restaurant. If you are set on a particular restaurant, it's wise to book a table by telephone, especially at peak hours (around 1.30 and 9 p.m.).

What to Eat

Any *trattoria* worth its olive oil will set out on a long table near the entrance a truly painterly display of its **antipasti** (hors d'oeuvre). The best way to get to know the delicacies is to make up your own assortment *(antipasto misto)*. Both attractive and tasty are the cold *peperoni*: red, yellow and green peppers grilled, skinned and marinated in olive oil and lemon juice. Mushrooms *(funghi)*, baby marrows *(zucchini)*, aubergines *(melanzane)*, artichokes *(carciofi)* and sliced fennel *(finocchio)* are also served cold, with a dressing *(pinzimonio)*. One of the most refreshing *antipasti* is the *mozzarella alla caprese*, slices of soft white buffalo cheese and tomato in a dressing of fresh basil and olive oil. Ham from Parma comes paper thin with melon *(prosciutto con melone)* or, better still, fresh figs.

Popular **soups** are mixed vegetable *(minestrone)* and clear soup *(brodo)*, with a beaten egg in it *(stracciatella)*.

Pasta is usually the first of at least three courses. While you are not strictly obliged to emulate the Italians, waiters will raise a sad eyebrow if you make a whole meal out of a plate of spaghetti. But foreigners will be foreigners.

It is said that there are as many forms of pasta as there are French cheeses—some 360 at last count, with new forms being created every year. Each sauce—tomato, cream, cheese, meat or fish—needs its own kind of noodle. As well as spaghetti and macaroni, other names will be familiar: baked *lasagne* with layers of minced meat, cheese and tomato, rolled *cannelloni*, stuffed *ravioli*, and *fettucine* or *tagliatelle* ribbon noodles. From there you launch into the lusty poetry of *tortellini, cappelletti* and *agnolotti* (all variations of *ravioli*), or curved *linguine*, flat *pappardelle*, feather-like *penne*, corrugated *rigatoni* and potato or semolina *gnocchi*. Discover the other 346 for yourselves.

And there are almost as many sauces. The most famous is, of course, *bolognese*, also called *ragù*; the best includes not only minced beef, tomato puree and onions, but chopped chicken livers, ham, carrot, celery, white wine and nutmeg. Other popular sauces range from the simple (but flavourful) *pomodoro* (tomato, garlic and basil), *aglio e olio* (garlic, olive oil and chilli peppers), *carbonara* (diced bacon and egg), *matriciana* (salt pork and tomatoes), *pesto* (basil and garlic ground up in olive oil with pine nuts and pecorino cheese) to *vongole* (clams and tomatoes).

Another Italian invention familiar around the world, the **pizza** is a much more elaborate affair than you may be used to. Toppings may include the following ingredients: tomato, ham, cheese, mushrooms, peppers, anchovies, artichoke hearts, egg, clams, tuna fish,

garlic—or any other ingredient that takes the cook's fancy. It is a popular midnight snack, especially after the opera or theatre.

The main course will be a hearty **meat** dish. Veal has pride of place, with Rome's great speciality *saltimbocca* (literally "jump in the mouth", a veal roll with ham, sage and Marsala wine. Try the pan-fried cutlet *(costoletta)* in breadcrumbs, or *scaloppine al limone* (veal fillets with lemon). *Osso buco* is veal shinbone cooked in butter, with tomatoes, onions and mushrooms.

Beef *(manzo)* and pork *(maiale)* are most often served plain, charcoal-grilled or roast *(arrosto* or *al forno)*. Grilled Florentine T-bone *(bistecca alla fiorentina)* is the emperor of steaks and costs a royal ransom, but you should splash out and try it once. After that, the lesser proportions of the *bistecca* or *filetto* are something of an anticlimax. Romans claim the best roast kid *(capretto)*, sucking pig *(porchetta)* —roasted whole on a spit—or spring lamb *(abbacchio)*, flavoured with garlic, sage and rosemary, dusted with flour, and seasoned just before serving with anchovy paste. The most common chicken dishes are grilled *(pollo alla diavola)* or filleted with ham and cheese *(petti di pollo alla bolognese).*

Fish is prepared simply—grilled, steamed or fried. You may find scampi, prawns *(gamberi)*, mussels *(cozze)*, fresh sardines *(sarde)*, but also chewily delicious squid *(calamari)* and octopus *(polpi).* You should also look out for sea bass *(spigola)*, red mullet *(triglia)* and swordfish *(pesce spada)*. The *fritto misto di pesce* is mixed fried fish, mostly shrimp and octopus.

Vegetable accompaniments must be ordered separately, as they do not automatically come with the meat dish. What is available will depend on the season, but you are most likely to find spinach *(spinaci)*, endives *(cicoria)*, green beans *(fagioli)* done in butter and garlic, peas *(piselli)* and baby marrow *(zucchini)*. Aristocrats among the vegetables are the big boletus mushrooms *(funghi porcini)*, which sometimes come stuffed *(ripieni)* with bacon, garlic, parsley and cheese. The white truffle is an autumn delicacy. Try red peppers stewed with tomatoes *(peperonata)* or

This waiter happily shows that pasta is a well-balanced diet.

aubergine stuffed with anchovies, olives and capers. The Jewish Ghetto originated the spectacular *carciofi alla giudea*, whole artichokes, crisply fried, stem, heart, leaves and all.

Of the **cheeses**, the famous parmesan *(parmigiano)*, far better than the exported product, is also eaten separately, not just grated over soup or pasta. The cheese board may also offer blue *gorgonzola*, *provolone* buffalo cheese, creamy *fontina*, the pungent cow's milk *taleggio* or ewe's milk *pecorino*. *Ricotta* can be sweetened with sugar and cinnamon.

Dessert means first and foremost *gelati*, the creamiest ice-cream in the world. But it's generally better in an ice-cream parlour *(gelateria)*, of which there is an abundance in Rome, than in the average *trattoria*. *Zuppa inglese* (literally "English soup"), the Italian version of trifle, can be anything from an extremely thick and sumptuous mixture of fruit, cream, cake and Marsala to a disappointing sickly slice of cake. You may prefer the coffee-flavoured trifle *(tirami sù)*. The *zabaglione* of whipped egg yolks, sugar and Marsala

Old-time surroundings and music add charm to an evening out.

should be served warm or sent back.

The fruits of the season *(frutta della stagione)* can be a succulent alternative: strawberries *(fragole)* or the tiny, sweet wild strawberries *(fragolini del bosco)*, served with whipped cream or lemon juice; grapes *(uva)*, apricots *(albicocche)*, and fresh figs *(fichi)*, both black and green.

Drinks

All restaurants, no matter how small, will offer the open wine of the house, red or white, in one-quarter, half-litre or litre carafes, as well as a good selection of bottled vintages.

Rome's "local" wine comes from the surrounding province of Lazio, where the rich volcanic soil gives a special aroma. The whites from the Alban Hills, called Castelli Romani, are light and pleasant and can be sweet or dry. The most famous is Frascati.

From further afield, the Chiantis of Tuscany and Umbria are available everywhere; as are the lovely velvety Valpolicella, Barolo and Gattinara. Falerno, a wine which was popular already in the time of the Caesars, is still a favourite today. Look out for the unusually named Est! Est! Est! from Montefiascone.

Italian beer is increasing in popularity; it is not as strong as north European brands. Italians will also order mineral water *(acqua minerale)* with their meal. You can ask for it fizzy *(gasata)* or still *(naturale)*.

Among aperitifs, bitters such as Campari and Punt e Mes are refreshing with soda and lemon. Many vermouths tend to be sweet rather than dry. For after-dinner drinks, try the anis-flavoured *sambuca* with a *mosca* ("fly") coffee bean swimming in it, or *grappa* eau-de-vie distilled from grapes.

Prices and Tips

While some restaurants offer fixed-price, three-course meals *(menu turistico* or *prezzo fisso)* which will save money, you'll almost always get better food by ordering dishes individually.

Warning: by law all restaurants must now issue a formal receipt indicating the value added tax (I.V.A.). A customer may be stopped outside the premises and fined if unable to produce a receipt to show the tax has been paid. The bill usually includes cover *(coperto)* and service *(servizio)*.

It's customary to leave the waiter about 5—10 per cent of the bill. Never tip the owner, no matter how much he fusses over you—he'd be offended. **101**

To Help You Order...

What do you recommend? **Cosa consiglia?**
Do you have a set menu? **Avete un menù a prezzo fisso?**

I'd like a/an/some... **Vorrei...**

beer	**una birra**	napkin	**un tovagliolo**
bread	**del pane**	pepper	**del pepe**
butter	**del burro**	potatoes	**delle patate**
coffee	**un caffè**	salad	**dell'insalata**
cream	**della panna**	salt	**del sale**
fish	**del pesce**	soup	**una minestra**
fruit	**della frutta**	sugar	**dello zucchero**
ice-cream	**un gelato**	tea	**un tè**
meat	**della carne**	(iced) water	**dell'acqua (fredda)**
milk	**del latte**	wine	**del vino**

...and Read the Menu

aglio	garlic	**manzo**	beef
agnello	lamb	**mela**	apple
albicocche	apricots	**melanzana**	aubergine
aragosta	spiny lobster	**merluzzo**	cod
arancia	orange	**ostrica**	oyster
bistecca	beef steak	**pancetta**	bacon
braciola	chop	**peperoni**	peppers, pimentos
brodetto	fish soup		
bue	beef	**pesca**	peach
calamari	squid	**pesce**	fish
carciofi	artichokes	**piselli**	peas
cavolo	cabbage	**pollo**	chicken
cicoria	endive	**pomodoro**	tomato
cipolle	onions	**prosciutto**	ham
coniglio	rabbit	**rognoni**	kidneys
cozze	mussels	**salsa**	sauce
crostacei	shellfish	**sarde**	sardines
fagioli	beans	**sogliola**	sole
fegato	liver	**stufato**	stew
fichi	figs	**tonno**	tunny (tuna)
formaggio	cheese	**uova**	eggs
funghi	mushrooms	**uva**	grapes
gamberi	scampi, prawns	**vitello**	veal
lamponi	raspberries	**vongole**	clams

BLUEPRINT for a Perfect Trip

How to Get There

If the choice of ways to go is bewildering, the complexity of fares and regulations can be downright stupefying. A reliable travel agent will have full details of all the latest flight possibilities, fares and regulations.

BY AIR

Rome's Fiumicino (Leonardo da Vinci) airport is on intercontinental air routes and is linked by frequent services to cities in Europe, North America, the Middle East and Africa.

Flying times: New York–Rome 8 hours; Los Angeles–Rome 15 hours; London–Rome 2½ hours; Sydney–Rome 26 hours.

BY CAR

Cross-Channel car-ferries link the U.K. with France, Belgium and Holland. Once on the continent, you can put your car on a train to Milan (starting points include Boulogne, Paris, Cologne). Or you can drive from the Channel coast to Rome without ever leaving a motorway. The main north-south (Milan–Florence–Regio-Calabria) and east-west (L'Aquila–Civitavecchia) motorways connect with Rome via a huge ring motorway *(grande raccordo anulare)*.

BY RAIL

Inter-Rail and Rail Europ Senior cards are valid in Italy, as is the Eurailpass for non-European residents (sign up before you leave home). Within Italy, you can obtain an Italian Tourist Ticket *(Biglietto Turistico di Libera Circolazione)* for unlimited first- or second-class rail travel for 8, 15, 21, or 30 days. The Kilometric Ticket *(Biglietto Chilometrico)* can be used by up to 5 people, even if not related, and is good for 20 trips or 3,000 kilometres, first or second class, over two months.

When to Go

Rome can be a city of extremes. From mid-June to mid-September, temperatures range from hot to very hot. Winters are cool, even cold, and at times rainy, with occasional snow, but often with days of warm sunshine. Spring and autumn are pleasantly mild.

		J	F	M	A	M	J	J	A	S	O	N	D
Maximum	°F	52	55	59	66	74	82	87	86	79	71	61	55
	°C	11	13	15	19	23	28	30	30	26	22	16	13
Minimum	°F	40	42	45	50	56	63	67	67	62	55	49	44
	°C	5	5	7	10	13	17	20	20	17	13	9	6

*Minimum temperatures are measured just before sunrise, maximum temperatures in the afternoon.

Planning Your Budget

To give you an idea of what to expect, here's a list of average prices in lire (L.). However, remember that all prices must be regarded as *approximate*.

Airport transfer. Bus between Fiumicino airport and Termini railway station L. 5,000, from Ciampino airport to Cinecittà metro station L. 800. Taxi from Fiumicino to city centre L. 45,000–50,000 (from airport to centre L. 5,500 in addition to meter charge, from centre to airport L. 12,500 in addition).

Baby-sitters. L. 14,000–20,000 per hour, plus transport.

Buses (city) **and metro.** Standard fare L. 700. Book of 10 tickets L. 6,000.

Camping. L. 6,000 per person per night, caravan (trailer) or camper L. 5,000–10,000, tent L. 2,500–3,000, car L. 2,500–3,000, motorbike L. 1,200–2,500.

Car hire. *Fiat Panda 45* L. 38,300 per day, L. 599 per km., L. 592,000 per week with unlimited mileage. *Alfa 33* L. 67,800 per day, L. 816 per km., L. 939,000 per week with unlimited mileage. Add 18% tax.

Cigarettes (packet of 20). Italian brands L. 1,600 and up, imported brands L. 2,500–3,000.

Entertainment. Cinema L. 6,000–7,000, discotheque (entry and first drink) L. 20,000–30,000, outdoor opera L. 15,000–35,000.

Hairdressers. *Woman's* shampoo and set or blow-dry L. 18,000–27,000, permanent wave L. 45,000–70,000. *Man's* haircut L. 12,000–15,000, L. 20,000 with shampoo.

Hotels (double room with bath, including tax and service). ***** L. 400,000–600,000, **** L. 130,000–380,000, *** L. 70,000–240,000, ** L. 45,000–190,000, * L. 30,000–100,000.

Meals and drinks. Continental breakfast L. 7,000–15,000, lunch/dinner in fairly good establishment L. 35,000–80,000, coffee served at a table L. 2,500–4,500, served at the bar L. 600–800, bottle of beer L. 4,000, soft drinks L. 1,500–3,000, aperitif L. 2,500 and up.

Museums. L. 3,000–7,000.

Shopping bag. 500 g. of bread L. 1,000–1,900, 250 g. of butter L. 1,800 and up, 6 eggs L. 1,200 and up, 500 g. of beefsteak L. 8,000 and up, 200 g. of coffee L. 2,800 and up, bottle of wine L. 3,000 and up.

Taxis. L. 2,800 for first 250 metres or period of 1 minute, L. 200 for each successive 300 metres or 60 seconds. Night charge L. 2,500, suitcases L. 500 each, holiday surcharge L. 1,000.

An A–Z Summary of Practical Information and Facts

> Listed after some entries is the appropriate Italian translation, usually in the singular, plus a number of phrases that may come in handy during your stay in Italy.

A

ACCOMMODATION (see also CAMPING). Rome's array of lodgings ranges from small, family-style boarding-houses *(pensione)* to de-luxe hotels *(albergo* or *hotel)*. In summer, booking ahead is important, but for the rest of the year you can normally find accommodation in your preferred category without difficulty. The Italian Tourist Office has up-to-date hotel information at the air terminal in Termini railway station.

If you plan to walk to most of Rome's sights, as you should, choose a hotel in the *centro storico* (historic centre), rather than in the suburbs. The saving in transport costs should compensate for the slightly higher rates in the centre of town.

As much as 20 % in taxes and service charges may be added to the hotel rates listed on p. 105.

On its periphery, Rome has several motels. Some Roman Catholic institutions also take guests at reasonable rates.

Youth hostels *(ostello della gioventù)* are open to holders of membership cards issued by the International Youth Hostels Federation, or by the A.I.G. *(Associazione Italiana Alberghi per la Gioventù)*, the Italian Youth Hostels Association, at:

Lungotevere Maresciallo Cadorna, 31; tel. 3 96 00 09

Day hotels *(albergo diurno)*. Rome has three of these "day-time" hotels, one of them at Termini railway station. They provide bathrooms, hairdresser and left-luggage facilities.

I'd like a single/double room.	**Vorrei una camera singola/matrimoniale.**
with bath/shower	**con bagno/doccia**
What's the rate per night?	**Qual è il prezzo per notte?**

AIRPORTS *(aeroporto)*. Rome is served by two airports, **Leonardo da Vinci**, commonly referred to as Fiumicino, near the seaside, 30 km. (22 mi.) south-west of the city, and **Ciampino,** 16 km. (10 mi.) south-east on the Via Appia Nuova. Fiumicino handles mainly scheduled air traffic, while Ciampino is used by most charter companies. Fiumicino has two terminals, one for domestic and one for international flights, a five-minute walk apart.

Airport information: Fiumicino, tel. 6 01 21
                         Ciampino, tel. 46 94

Ground transport. A frequent public bus service links Fiumicino to the city air terminal at Termini railway station in the centre of town. Buses leave Ciampino every 30 minutes for Cinecittà, where you can pick up the metrò to Rome. City air terminal:

Via Giolitti, 36; tel. 46 46 13

Check-in time is one hour and a half before departure for international flights, 30 minutes before domestic flights. Luggage may be checked in only at the airport. A few hours before your flight is due to leave, have your hotel receptionist telephone both the airport and city air terminal to enquire about any delay.

Porter!	**Facchino!**
Take these bags to the	**Mi porti queste valige fino**
bus/taxi, please.	**all'autobus/al taxi, per favore.**

ANIMAL WELFARE. An animal welfare association will take care of any animals found cruelly treated or in distress:

Associazione Italiana Difesa Animali, Via Marche, 84; tel. 49 18 77

BABY-SITTERS. Hotels can usually arrange for a reliable baby-sitter. Italian newspapers carry baby-sitter advertisements under the heading "Bambinaia". Agencies are also listed in English in the telephone directory under "Baby Sitters"; you will probably need to phone a couple of days in advance.

Can you get me a baby-sitter	**Può trovarmi una bambinaia per**
for tonight?	**questa sera?**

BICYCLE AND MOTORSCOOTER HIRE. You can rent bicycles and motorscooters from several locations, including the Piazza del Popolo. A telephone hire service for bicycles offers delivery at your hotel. To hire a scooter, you have to be over 21 years old.

C

CAMPING. Rome and the surrounding countryside have some 20 official campsites, mostly equipped with electricity, water and toilet facilities. They are listed in the yellow pages of the telephone directory under "Campeggio Ostelli Villaggi Turistici". You can also contact the tourist office (see Tourist Information Offices) for a comprehensive list of sites and rates. The Touring Club Italiano (TCI) and the Automobile Club d'Italia (ACI) publish lists of campsites and tourist villages, available at bookstores or the tourist office.

It is inadvisable to camp outside official sites. If you must, at least choose sites where there are other campers and always obtain permission from the owner of the property or the local authorities.

If you enter Italy with a caravan (trailer), you must be able to show an inventory (with two copies) of the material and equipment in the caravan: dishes, linen, etc.

May we camp here?	**Possiamo campeggiare qui?**
Is there a campsite near here?	**C'è un campeggio qui vicino?**
We have a tent/caravan (trailer).	**Abbiamo la tenda/la roulotte.**

CAR HIRE *(autonoleggio).* Major international car rental firms are represented in Rome and have offices at the airports; they are listed in the yellow pages of the telephone directory. Your hotel receptionist may be able to recommend a less expensive local firm.

You will need a valid driving licence. Minimum age varies from 21 to 25 according to the company. A deposit is often required if you are not paying with a credit card. It is possible to rent a car in one Italian city and turn it in another.

I'd like to rent a car (tomorrow).	**Vorrei noleggiare una macchina (per domani).**
for one day	**per un giorno**
for one week	**per una settimana**

CIGARETTES, CIGARS, TOBACCO *(sigarette, sigari, tabacco).* Tobacco products are a state monopoly and price-controlled in Italy and can only be sold in official tobacconists—recognizable by a large white *T* on a dark background over the door—or at authorized hotel newsstands and café counters. Foreign brands cost as much as 50% more than domestic makes.

Smoking is prohibited on public transport and in taxis, in most cinemas and theatres, and in some shops.

I'd like a packet of...	**Vorrei un pacchetto di...**	**C**
with/without filter	**con/senza filtro**	
I'd like a box of matches.	**Per favore, mi dia una scatola di fiammiferi.**	

COMMUNICATIONS (see also HOURS)

Post offices *(posta* or *ufficio postale)* handle telegrams, mail and money transfers. Postage stamps are also sold at tobacconists and at some hotel desks. Post boxes are red. The slot marked *Per la città* is for local mail only; the one marked *Altre destinazioni* is for all other destinations. Post to and from Italy can be slow; the Vatican operates well for outgoing mail, but you must buy the Vatican stamps.

Poste Restante/General Delivery *(fermo posta)*. For a short stay it is not worth arranging to receive mail. However, there is a poste restante service at the main post office in Piazza San Silvestro. Don't forget your passport for identification when you go to pick up mail. You will have to pay a small fee.

Telegrams *(telegramma)*. Night letters, or night-rate telegrams *(lettera telegramma)*, delivered the next morning, are cheaper than ordinary cables, but can only be sent outside Italy.

Telephone *(telefono)*. Public telephone booths are scattered at strategic locations throughout the city, as well as in almost every bar and café, indicated by a yellow sign showing a telephone dial and receiver, where you pay at the counter after making your call. The main public telephone office, in the Palazzo delle Poste in Piazza San Silvestro, is open 24 hours a day.

Older types of public payphones require tokens *(gettoni)* with a value of 200 lire (available at bars, hotels, post offices and tobacconists); modern ones, with two separate slots, take both *gettoni* and coins.

From telephones labelled *Teleselezione* you can make direct international calls, but be sure to have a great many coins or tokens. Some telephones will take magnetic cards with a value of 6,000 or 9,000 lire, available at SIP (Italian Telephone Service) offices.

The normal dialling tone is a series of long dash sounds. A dot-dot-dot series means the central computer is overloaded; hang up and try again.

English-speaking operators of the ACI's telephone assistance service provide tourists with information and advice of all kinds. Dial 116.

Some useful numbers:

Local directory and other Italian enquiries	12
European international operator	15
Intercontinental operator	170
Telegrams	186

Give me... gettoni, please.	**Per favore, mi dia... gettoni.**
Can you get me this number in...?	**Può passarmi questo numero a...?**
I'd like a stamp for this letter/postcard.	**Desidero un francobollo per questa lettera/cartolina.**

COMPLAINTS *(reclamo).* Observe the cardinal rule of commerce in Italy: come to an agreement in advance—the price, the supplements, the taxes and the services to be received, preferably in writing. In hotels, shops and restaurants, complaints should be made to the manager *(direttore)* or the proprietor *(proprietario).*

Any complaint about a taxi fare should be settled by referring to the notice, in four languages, affixed by law in each taxi, specifying charges in excess of the meter rate.

For theft and other serious complaints, contact the police (see POLICE).

CONSULATES and EMBASSIES *(consolato; ambasciata).* The telephone directory lists all diplomatic representatives. The main ones for English-speaking visitors are:

Australia	Via Alessandria, 215; tel. 84 12 41
Canada	Via G. Battista de Rossi, 27; tel. 85 53 41/4
Eire	Largo del Nazareno, 3; tel. 6 78 25 41
South Africa	Piazza Monte Grappa, 4; tel. 3 60 84 41
United Kingdom	Via XX Settembre, 80; tel. 4 75 54 41
U.S.A.	Via Vittorio Veneto, 119; tel. 46 741

CONVERSION CHARTS. For fluid and distance measures, see p. 114–115. Italy uses the metric system.

Temperature

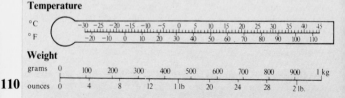

Weight

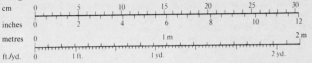

cm	0	5	10	15	20	25	30
inches	0	2	4	6	8	10	12
metres	0			1 m			2 m
ft./yd.	0	1 ft.		1 yd.		2 yd.	

COURTESIES. On entering and leaving a shop, restaurant or office, the expected greeting is *buon giorno* (good morning) or *buona sera* (good evening). When approaching anyone with an enquiry, the correct form is *per favore* (please), and for any service say *grazie* (thanks), to which the reply is *prego* (don't mention it; you're welcome).

Introductions are usually accompanied by handshaking and the phrase *piacere* (it's a pleasure). With people you know well, *ciao* is the casual form of greeting or farewell. When wished *buon appetito* before starting a meal, reply *grazie, altrettanto* (thank you, and the same to you).

How are you?	**Come sta?**
Very well, thanks.	**Molto bene, grazie**

CRIME and THEFT. Petty theft is an endless annoyance, but cases of violence against tourists are rare. It's wise to leave unneeded documents and excess cash in the hotel safe and keep what you take in an inside pocket. Handbags are particularly vulnerable; agile thieves, often operating in pairs on motorscooters, whisk past and snatch them from your shoulder, sometimes even cutting or breaking the straps to do so. Be particularly attentive on crowded public transport or in secluded streets and districts. It's a good idea to make photocopies of your tickets, passport and other vital documents, to facilitate reporting any theft and obtaining replacements.

If you park your car, lock it and empty it of everything, leaving the glove compartments open to discourage prospective thieves.

I want to report a theft.	**Voglio denunciare un furto.**
My wallet/handbag/passport/	**Mi hanno rubato il portafoglio/**
ticket has been stolen.	**la borsa/il passaporto/**
	il biglietto.

CUSTOMS *(dogana)* **and ENTRY REGULATIONS.** For a stay of up to three months, a valid passport is sufficient for citizens of Australia, 111

C Canada, New Zealand and U.S.A. Visitors from Eire and and the United Kingdom need only an identity card to enter Italy. Tourists from South Africa must have a visa.

Here are some main items you can take into Italy duty-free and, when returning home, into your own country:

Entering Italy from:	Cigarettes		Cigars		Tobacco	Spirits		Wine
1)	200	or	50	or	250 g.	¾ l.	or	2 l.
2)	300	or	75	or	400 g.	1.5 l.	and	4 l.
3)	400	or	100	or	500 g.	¾ l.	or	2 l.
Into:								
Australia	200	or	250 g.	or	250 g.	1 l.	or	1 l.
Canada	200	and	50	and	900 g.	1.1 l.	or	1.1 l.
Eire	200	or	50	or	250 g.	1 l.	and	2 l.
N. Zealand	200	or	50	or	250 g.	1.1 l.	and	4.5 l.
S. Africa	400	and	50	and	250 g.	1 l.	and	2 l.
U.K.	200	or	50	or	250 g.	1 l.	and	2 l.
U.S.A.	200	and	100	and	4)	1 l.	or	1 l.

1) within Europe from non-EEC countries
2) within Europe from EEC countries
3) countries outside Europe
4) a reasonable quantity

Currency restrictions. Non-residents may import or export up to L. 500,000 in local currency. In foreign currencies, you may import unlimited amounts, but to take the equivalent of more than L. 5,000,000 in or out of the country, you must fill out a V2 declaration form at the border upon entry.

If you're exporting archaeological relics, works of art or gems, you should obtain a bill of sale and a permit from the government (normally handled by the dealer).

I've nothing to declare.   **Non ho nullo da dichiarare.**
It's for my personal use.   **È per mio uso personale.**

DRIVING IN ITALY

Entering Italy: To bring your car into Italy, you will need:

- an International Driving Permit or a valid national licence
- car registration papers
- Green Card (an extension to your regular insurance policy, making it valid specifically for Italy)
- a red warning triangle in case of breakdown
- national identity sticker for your car

Drivers of cars that are not their own must have the owner's written permission.

Before leaving home, check with your automobile association about the latest regulations concerning *petrol coupons* (giving tourists access to cheaper fuel) in Italy, as these are constantly changing.

Speed limits. Speed limits in Italy are based on the car engine size. The following chart gives the engine size in cubic centimetres and the limits (in kilometres per hour) on the open road (limit in built-up areas is usually 50 kph).

Engine size	less than 600 cc.	600 to 900 cc.	900 to 1,300 cc. (and motorcycles more than 150 cc.)	more than 1,300 cc.
Main roads	80 kph.	90 kph.	100 kph.	110 kph.
Motorways (Expressways)	90 kph.	110 kph.	130 kph.	140 kph.

Driving conditions. Drive on the right, pass on the left. Traffic on major roads has right of way over that entering from side roads; this, like other traffic regulations, is frequently ignored, so be very careful. At intersections of roads of similar importance, the car on the right has the priority. When passing other vehicles, or remaining in the left-hand (passing) lane, keep your directional indicator flashing.

The motorways *(autostrada)* are designed for fast and safe driving; a toll is collected for each section. Take a card from an automatic machine or from the booth attendant and pay at the other end according to the distance travelled.

D **Driving in Rome.** Only the most intrepid motorist stays cool in the face of the Romans' hair-raising driving techniques. But, Roman drivers are not reckless—simply attuned to a different concept of driving. If you observe the following ground rules and venture with prudence into the urban traffic whirlpool, you stand a good chance of coming out unscathed.

Glance round to right and left and in your rear-view mirror all the time; other drivers are doing the same, and they've developed quick reflexes.

Treat traffic lights which are theoretically in your favour and white lines across merging side streets with caution—don't take your priority for granted.

To make progress in a traffic jam in one of Rome's squares, inch gently but confidently forward into the snarl-up. To wave on another driver, courteously letting him or her cut in ahead of you, is tantamount to abdicating your rights as a motorist.

Traffic-free zones are being tried out in various parts of town; these areas are constantly changing (but growing), and as at present, much of the city centre is "under trial".

Traffic police *(polizia stradale)*. All cities and many towns and villages have signs posted at the outskirts indicating the telephone number of the local traffic police or *carabinieri*.

The traffic police patrol the highways and byways on motorcycles or in Alfa Romeos, usually light blue. Speeding fines often have to be paid on the spot; ask for a receipt *(ricevuta)*.

Breakdowns. Call boxes are located at regular intervals on the *autostrade* in case of breakdowns or other emergencies. You can dial 116 for breakdown service from the ACI.

Fuel and oil. Service stations abound in Italy, usually with at least one mechanic on duty. Most close on Sundays, and every day from noon to 3 p.m. Fuel *(benzina)*, sold at government-set prices, comes in super (98–100 octane), unleaded—still rare—(95 octane) and normal (86–88 octane). Diesel fuel is usually also available.

Fluid measures

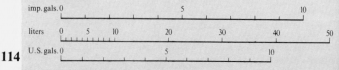

km   0   1   2   3   4   5   6   8   10   12   14   16
miles 0   ½   1   1½   2   3   4   5   6   7   8   9   10

Parking (see also CRIME AND THEFT). For motorized tourists as well residents, parking is one of Rome's greatest challenges. Your wisest course is to find a legal parking place near your hotel for the duration of your stay and see the city on foot or by public transport.

There are formal guarded parking areas operated by the ACI; they are not watched overnight. And Rome has a raft of freelance parking attendants who will offer to "guard" your car, even if illegally parked, for a fee.

Beware particularly of tow-away zones; if you park your car there, it may be towed to the municipal garages or parking lots. You will be able to retrieve it only after paying a hefty fine at the post office. On Sundays and holidays the municipal garages are closed and cars cannot be recovered.

Road signs. Most road signs employed in Italy are international pictographs, but there are some written ones you may come across:

Accendere le luci	Use headlights
Deviazione	Diversion (Detour)
Divieto di sorpasso	No overtaking (passing)
Divieto di sosta	No stopping
Lavori in corso	Road works (Men working)
Passaggio a livello	Level railway crossing
Pericolo	Danger
Rallentare	Slow down
Senso unico	One-way street
Senso vietato/Vietato l'ingresso	No entry
Zona pedonale	Pedestrian zone

driving licence	**patente**
car registration papers	**libretto di circolazione**
green card	**carta verde**
Fill the tank, please.	**Per favore, faccia il pieno.**
super/normal	**super/normale**
unleaded/diesel	**senza piombo/gasolio**
I've had a breakdown.	**Ho avuto un guasto.**
There's been an accident.	**C'è stato un incidente.**

E **ELECTRICITY.** Generally 220 volts, 50 Hz AC, but sometimes 125-volt outlets, with different plugs and sockets for each. The voltage might be indicated on the socket in hotels, but it's best to ask, to avoid ruining your shaver or hair dryer.

EMERGENCIES. In an emergency you can phone the following numbers 24 hours a day:

Police, all purpose emergency number	113
Carabinieri (see POLICE) for urgent police problems	112
Fire	444441
Ambulance and Red Cross	51 00
Night and day medical service	4756741
Road assistance (ACI) and advice for tourists	116

Careful!	**Attenzione!**
Fire!	**Incendio!**
Help!	**Aiuto!**
Stop thief!	**Al ladro!**

G **GUIDES and TOURS.** Most hotels in Rome can arrange for multilingual guides or interpreters. A selection is found in the yellow pages of the telephone directory under the entry "Traduzione", and local newspapers carry advertisements offering such services. There are also guides near most of the major tourist attractions, and portable recorders with commentaries in English can often be hired.

The Italian State Tourist Agency, CIT, and many private firms offer tours of all the major sights, plus excursions to other points of interest. Often tourists are picked up and dropped off at their hotels. Your hotel receptionist will have a list of available guided group tours.

H **HAIRDRESSERS and BARBERS** *(parrucchiere; barbiere)*. Women should telephone in advance for an appointment. As in most countries, the owner of a salon should never be tipped; the shampooist, manicurist or stylist should be tipped up to 15% of the bill.

I'd like a shampoo and set.	**Vorrei shampo e messa in piega.**
I want a...	**Voglio...**
haircut	**il taglio**
shave	**la rasatura**
blow-dry (brushing)	**asciugatura al fon**
permanent wave	**la permanente**

HEALTH and MEDICAL CARE. If your health-insurance policy does not cover foreign countries, take out a short-term policy before leaving home. Visitors from Great Britain and Ireland, as members of the EEC, can claim public health services available to Italians. Before departure obtain a copy of the proper form (E 111) from the U.K. Department of Health and Social Security.

If you need medical care, ask your hotel receptionist to help you find a doctor (or dentist) who speaks English. Local Health Units of the Italian National Health Service are listed in the telephone directory under "Unità Sanitaria Locale". The first-aid *(pronto soccorso)* section of hospitals handles medical emergencies.

Pharmacies. The Italian *farmacia* is open during shopping hours (see Hours). Usually one operates at night and on weekends for each district on a rota basis. The opening schedule for duty pharmacies is posted on every pharmacy door and in the local papers.

Bring along an adequate supply of any prescribed medication.

I need a doctor/dentist.	**Ho bisogno di un medico/ dentista.**
Where's the nearest (all-night) chemist?	**Dov'è la farmacia (di turno) più vicina?**

HOURS. Even within Rome opening hours vary. In true Mediterranean fashion, much of the city shuts or slows down after lunch. However, for some offices the modern non-stop business day is gradually creeping in. The following therefore is just a guideline.

Shops. Open 9 a.m.–12.30 or 1 p.m. and 4–7.30 p.m., Monday to Saturday (half-day closing is usually Monday mornings); food stores open 8.30 a.m.–12.30 or 1 p.m. and 5–7.30 p.m. (half-day closing usually Thursday afternoons). Tourist resort shops stay open all day, every day, in high season.

Post offices. Normally open 8.15 a.m.–2.30 p.m., Monday to Friday, until noon on Saturdays. The main post office in Piazza San Silvestro and the branch at Stazione Termini stay open till 9 p.m.

Banks. 8.30 a.m.–1.30 p.m. and sometimes again for an hour or so in the afternoon, Monday to Friday.

Principal businesses. 8 or 9 a.m.–1 or 1.30 p.m. and 4, 4.30 or 5–7, 7.30 or 8 p.m., Monday to Saturday. Sometimes closed Saturday afternoons.

Pharmacies. Open 8.30 a.m.–1 p.m. and 4–8 p.m.

H **Museums and historic sites.** These are usually open Tuesday to Sunday, 9 a.m.–2 p.m., and, in some cases, again 5–8 p.m. Closing day is usually Monday; if Monday is a holiday, the museums are closed the following day.

L **LANGUAGE.** Italians appreciate foreigners making an effort to speak their language, even if only a few words. In the major tourist hotels and shops, staff usually speak some English.

Remember that the letter "c" is pronounced like "ch" when it is followed by an "e" or an "i", while the letters "ch" together sound like the "c" in cat.

The Berlitz phrase book ITALIAN FOR TRAVELLERS covers most situations you are likely to encounter; also useful is the Italian-English/English-Italian pocket dictionary, with a special menu-reader supplement.

Do you speak English?	**Parla inglese?**
I don't speak Italian.	**Non parlo italiano.**

LAUNDRY and DRY-CLEANING. Most hotels handle laundry and dry-cleaning. For lower rates you can do your own washing at a *lavanderia* (or leave it with the attendant) or hand it in at a *tintoria,* which usually offers a normal or express service. Most hotels will handle laundry and dry-cleaning, but rates are much higher.

When will it be ready?	**Quando sarà pronto?**
I must have this for to-morrow morning.	**Mi serve per domani mattina.**

LOST PROPERTY. Cynics say anything lost in Italy is lost forever, but that's not necessarily true in Rome. Restaurants more often than not will have your forgotten briefcase, guide book or camera waiting for you at the cashier's desk. If you've lost something away from your hotel, have the receptionist call the lost property office *(Ufficio Oggetti Rinvenuti)*
tel. 58 16 040, or go to Via Bettoni, 1.

There are lost property offices at the Termini railway station and at ATAC in Via Volturno, 65; tel. 46 95.

Report lost documents to the police or your consulate.

I've lost my passport/wallet/handbag.	**Ho perso il passaporto/portafoglio/la borsetta.**

MAPS *(pianta; carta topografica)*. Newsstands and tourist offices have a large selection of maps at a wide range of prices. Some are old (look for the publication date in a corner of the map), and others may have pretty symbols of the Colosseum and St. Peter's, but hopelessly distort urban proportions. The maps in this guide were prepared by Falk-Verlag, Hamburg, which also publishes a complete map to Italy and to Rome.

MONEY MATTERS (see also HOURS)

Currency. The *lira* (plural: *lire*, abbreviated *L.* or *Lit.*) is Italy's monetary unit.
   Coins: L. 5, 10, 20, 50, 100, 200 and 500.
   Notes: L. 1,000, 2,000, 5,000, 10,000, 50,000 and 100,000.
   For currency restrictions, see CUSTOMS AND ENTRY REGULATIONS.

Currency exchange offices *(cambio)* are open in the morning and usually reopen after the siesta, until at least 6.30 p.m.; some are open on Saturday. Exchange rates are less advantageous than in banks. A flat rate of commission is common, so it is not worth changing small amounts many times. Passports are sometimes required when changing money.

Credit cards and traveller's cheques. Most hotels, many shops and some restaurants take credit cards. Traveller's cheques are accepted almost everywhere, but you will get better value if you exchange your cheques for lire at a bank or *cambio*. Passports are required when cashing cheques. Eurocheques are easily cashed in Italy.

I want to change some pounds/ dollars.	**Desidero cambiare delle sterline/ dei dollari.**
Do you accept traveller's cheques?	**Accetta traveller's cheques?**
Can I pay with this credit card?	**Posso pagare con la carta di credito?**

NEWSPAPERS AND MAGAZINES. Some British and continental newspapers and magazines are on sale, sometimes a day late, at the airport and stations and in the kiosks. The *International Herald Tribune* is printed in Rome and is available early in the morning. Prices are high for all foreign publications.

Have you any English-language newspapers?	**Avete giornali in inglese?**

P

POLICE. The municipal police *(Vigili Urbani)*, dressed in navy blue with white helmets or all-white with shiny buttons, handle city traffic and other city police tasks. They are courteous and helpful to tourists, though they rarely speak a foreign language. Those who act as interpreters carry a badge.

The *Carabinieri,* who wear brown or black uniforms, deal with serious crimes and demonstrations, and the national police *(Polizia di Stato)* handle usual police matters. (For traffic police see DRIVING IN ITALY.)

The all-purpose emergency number, 113, will get you police assistance.

Where's the nearest police station?	**Dov'è il più vicino posto di polizia?**

PUBLIC HOLIDAYS *(festa).* When a national holiday falls on a Thursday or a Tuesday, Italians may make a *ponte* (bridge) to the weekend, meaning that Friday or Monday is taken off as well.

January 1	*Capodanno* or *Primo dell'Anno*	New Year's Day
January 6	*Epifania*	Epiphany
April 25	*Festa della Liberazione*	Liberation Day
May 1	*Festa del Lavoro*	Labour Day
August 15	*Ferragosto*	Assumption Day
November 1	*Ognissanti*	All Saints' Day
December 8	*L'Immacolata Concezione*	Immaculate Conception
December 25	*Natale*	Christmas Day
December 26	*Santo Stefano*	St. Stephen's Day
Movable date:	*Lunedì di Pasqua*	Easter Monday

Note: On all national holidays, banks, government offices, most shops and some museums and galleries are closed.

R

RADIO AND TV *(radio; televisione).* During the tourist season, RAI, the Italian state radio and TV network, occasionally broadcasts news in English. Vatican Radio carries foreign-language religious news programmes. British (BBC), American (VOA) and Canadian (CBC)

programmes are easily obtained on short-wave transistor radios. RAI
television and private channels broadcast only in Italian.

RELIGIOUS SERVICES. Roman Catholic mass is celebrated daily
and several times on Sunday in Italian. Some services are in English.
Major non-Catholic denominations and Jews have congregations
in Rome, often with services in English. Local newspapers publish
details.

Mass is celebrated in St. Peter's Basilica at no set times on week-
days, except on Thursdays, when there is a pilgrims' mass at 9.30 a.m.
On Sundays, high mass is at 10 a.m., on the last two Sundays of the
month at 1 p.m. and 5 p.m., in winter at 4 p.m. Services in languages
other than Italian are held at times in side chapels within the basilica.
Check on the spot for timings.

TIME DIFFERENCES. Italy follows Central European Time (GMT
+ 1), and from late March to September clocks are put one hour
ahead (GMT + 2).

Summer time chart:

New York	London	**Italy**	Jo'burg	Sydney	Auckland
6 a.m.	11 a.m.	**noon**	noon	8 p.m.	10 p.m.

What time is it?   **Che ore sono?**

TIPPING. A service charge is added to most restaurant bills, but it is
customary to leave an additional tip. It is also in order to tip bellboys,
doormen, hat check attendants, garage attendants, etc. The chart
below will give you some guidelines:

Hotel porter, per bag	L. 1,000
Hotel maid, per day	L. 1,000–2,000
Lavatory attendant	L. 300
Waiter	5–10 %
Taxi driver	10 %
Hairdresser/Barber	up to 15 %
Tour guide	10 %

T **TOILETS.** Most museums and art galleries have public toilets. Restaurants, bars, cafés, large stores, the airports, railway stations and car parks all have facilities. On the whole they are clean and in good order, but carry your own tissues.

Toilets may be labelled with a symbol of a man or a woman or the initials W.C. Sometimes the wording will be in Italian, but beware, as you might be misled: *Uomini* is for men, *Donne* is for women. Equally, *Signori*—with a final *i*—is for men, *Signore*—with a final *e*—is for women.

Where are the toilets?	**Dove sono i gabinetti?**

TOURIST INFORMATION OFFICES. The Italian Tourist Office (*Ente Nazionale Italiano per il Turismo,* abbreviated ENIT) is represented in Italy and abroad. They publish detailed brochures with up-to-date information on accommodation, means of transport and other general tips and useful addresses for the whole country.

Australia and New Zealand	c/o Alitalia, 118 Alfred Street, Milson Point 2061, Sydney; tel. 2921555.
Canada	3, Place Ville-Marie, Store 56, Montreal 113, Que.; tel. (514) 866.76.67.
Eire	47, Merrion Square, Dublin, tel. (01) 766397.
South Africa	London House, 21 Loveday Street, P.O. Box 6507, Johannesburg 2000, tel. 838-3247.
United Kingdom	1, Princes Street, London W1R 8AY; tel. (01) 408 1254.
U.S.A.	500 N. Michigan Avenue, Chicago, Il 60611; tel. (312) 644 0990/1. 630 Fifth Avenue, New York, NY 10111; tel. (212) 795 5500. St. Francis Hotel, 360 Post Street, San Francisco, CA 94108; tel. (415) 392 6206.

The tourist office headquarters in Rome are at
Via Parigi, 11; tel. 461851
Via Parigi, 5 (Tourist Assistance); tel. 463748, with branches at Stazione Termini and Fiumicino airport.

Where's the tourist office?   **Dov'è l'ufficio turistico?**

TRANSPORT

Underground/Subway *(metropolitana,* or *metrò)*. Rome has two underground railway lines. Line A runs from Via Ottaviano near the Vatican south-east to Via Anagnina, stopping at more than 20 stations and passing under most of Rome's popular tourist sights. The intersecting Line B runs from Termini railway station, with stops at the Colosseum, EUR, Ostia Antica and Ostia Lido. Entrances are marked by a large red *M*. Tickets are sold at newsstands and tobacconists, or can be purchased from machines at the stations.

Buses *(autobus)*. Rome's fleet of orange buses serves every corner of the city. Although crowded on certain routes and at rush hours, they are an inexpensive way of crossing the city. Newsstands sell maps showing the major bus routes. Each bus stop *(fermata)*, marked by green and white signs, indicates the numbers of the buses stopping there and the routes they serve. Tickets for buses must be bought in advance from newsstands or tobacco shops. Enter by the rear doors and frank your ticket in a machine; exit by the middle doors. You can buy booklets of ten tickets; weekly and one-day tickets are available from offices of Rome's public transport organization (ATAC) at Largo Giovanni Montemartini and Piazza dei Cinquecento, both near Stazione Termini. There are also special tourist tickets valid for specific periods of unlimited travel. ACOTRAL operates bus services to the environs of Rome.

Taxis *(tassì* or *taxi)*. The distinctive yellow taxis may be hailed in the street (but vacant ones are hard to find), picked up at a taxi rank or obtained by telephone. The yellow pages of the telephone directory list all the ranks under "Taxi".

Taxis remain cheap by North European and American standards, but make sure that the meter is running. Extra charges for luggage and for night, holiday or airport trips are posted in four languages inside all taxis. A tip of at least 10% is customary. Beware of the non-metered unlicensed taxis *("abusivi")*, which charge much more than the normal taxi rates for trips in private cars.

Radio-Taxi, phone 35 70/49 94/84 33

Horse-cabs *(carrozza)*. A familiar sight in Rome for centuries, horse-drawn carriages now, sadly, number only a few dozen. Found at tourist haunts such as St. Peter's Square, the Spanish Steps, the Trevi Fountain and the Via Veneto, the horse-cabs theoretically have meters, but it's best to agree a price with the driver before setting off.

T **Train.** The Italian State Railway *(Ferrovie dello Stato)* operates an extensive network all over the country. The fares are among the lowest in Europe. Choose your train carefully, as journey times vary a good deal. The following list describes the various types of train:

TEE	The Trans-Europ-Express, first class only with surcharge; seat reservations essential.
EuroCity (EC)	International express; first and second class.
Intercity (IC)	Intercity express with few stops; luxury service with first and second class.
Rapido (R)	Long-distance express stopping at major cities only; first and second class.
Espresso (EXP)/ Direttissimo	Long-distance train, stopping at main stations.
Diretto (D)	Slower than the *Espresso,* it makes a number of local stops.
Locale (L)/ Accelerato (A)	Local train which stops at almost every station.
Littorina	Small diesel train used on short runs.

Tickets (see also p. 104) can be purchased and reservations made at a local travel agency or at the railway station. Better-class trains have dining-cars or self-service cars which offer food and beverages at reasonable prices. If you don't have a reservation, you should arrive at the station at least 20 minutes before departure; Italy's trains are often crowded.

Where's the nearest bus stop/ underground station?	**Dov'è la fermata d'autobus/la stazione della metropolitana più vicina?**
When's the next bus/ train to...?	**Quando parte il prossimo autobus/treno per...?**
I'd like a ticket to...	**Vorrei un biglietto per...**
single (one-way)	**andata**
return (round-trip)	**andata e ritorno**

WATER. Rome's drinking water, not least from its outdoor fountains, is famous for its flavour and is perfectly safe. Nonetheless, with meals it is customary to drink bottled mineral water. If tap water is not drinkable it will usually carry a sign reading *acqua non potabile*.

I'd like a bottle of mineral water.	**Vorrei una bottiglia di acqua minerale.**
fizzy (carbonated)/still	**gasata/naturale**

SOME USEFUL EXPRESSIONS

yes/no	**sì/no**
please/thank you	**per favore/grazie**
excuse me/you're welcome	**mi scusi/prego**
where/when/how	**dove/quando/come**
how long/how far	**quanto tempo/quanto dista**
yesterday/today/tomorrow	**ieri/oggi/domani**
day/week/month/year	**giorno/settimana/mese/anno**
left/right	**sinistra/destra**
up/down	**su/giù**
good/bad	**buono/cattivo**
big/small	**grande/piccolo**
cheap/expensive	**buon mercato/caro**
hot/cold	**caldo/freddo**
open/closed	**aperto/chiuso**
free (vacant)/occupied	**libero/occupato**
near/far	**vicino/lontano**
early/late	**presto/tardi**
right/wrong	**giusto/sbagliato**
I don't understand.	**Non capisco.**
Waiter/Waitress, please.	**Cameriere!/Cameriera!** (or **Senta!** = "listen")
I'd like …	**Vorrei …**
How much is that?	**Quant'è?**

Index

An asterisk (*) next to a page number indicates a map reference. Where there is more than one set of page references, the one in bold type refers to the main entry.

Alban Hills   85*, **90**, 94, 101
Albano, Lake   90
Appia Antica, Via   12, **83–86**, 85*
Ara Pacis Augustae   24*, 32
Arch of Constantine   25*, 58
Arnolfo di Cambio   29, 66, 76
Augustus   11, 14, 21, 30, 32, 33, 55
Aurelian Wall   83
Aventine Hill   7, 12, 24*, **45–46**, 49

Babington's Tea Rooms   37
Baths of Caracalla   25*, 42, 49, **58**, 75, 91
Bernini, Gianlorenzo   18, 22, 29, 32, 39, 61, 63, 66, 80, 82, 83
Bocca della Verità   46
Borromini, Francesco   22, 29, 40, 75, 82
Bramante, Donato   18, 29, 64

Caelian Hill   7, 49
Caesar, Julius   11, 14, 21, 42, 45, 54, 85
Caffè Greco   37
Campidoglio   7, 12, 22, 24*, **28–32**, 49, 50, 91
Campo de' Fiori   24*, 42
Campus Martius   15, 27, 54
Canova, Antonio   29, 80

Capitoline Hill, see Campidoglio
Caravaggio, Michelangelo Merisi da   29, 30, 33, 72, 80, 82
Castel Gandolfo   25*, 29, 60, 85*, **90**
Castel Sant'Angelo   14, 24*, 32, **61–63**
Castelli Romani, see Alban Hills
Catacombs   11, **84–85**
Cerveteri   68, 85*, **90–91**
Charlemagne   17, 21, 65
Churches
   Gesù, the   24*, **78–79**
   St. John Lateran   25*, 60, 74, **75–76**
   St. Paul's Outside the Walls   24*, 29, 60, 74, **76**, 92
   St. Peter's Basilica   17, 18, 21, 22, 24*, 28, 29, 60, 63, **64–68**, 78, 92
   San Clemente   25*, **76–78**
   San Pietro in Vincoli   25*, 29, **78**
   Sant'Agnese in Agone   29, **40**
   Santa Cecilia in Trastevere   24*, **48–49**, 85
   Santa Maria in Aracoeli   24*, 29, **30–32**, 92
   Santa Maria in Cosmedin   24*, 46
   Santa Maria Maggiore   25*, 49, 60, **74**, 92
   Santa Maria del Popolo   24*, 29, **33**

Churches *(contd.)*
  Santa Maria in Trastevere
    24*, 47–48
  Santa Prassede *25*, 78*
  Santa Sabina *24*, 45–46*
  Sant'Ignazio *79*
Circus Maximus *24*, 33,* **56**
Circus of Maxentius *85*
Cloaca Maxima *46, 49, 78*
Colosseum *8, 22, 25*, 30, 49,*
    56–58, *92*
Conciliazione, Via della *24*, 63*
Constantine *15, 21, 28, 54, 58,*
    59, 75, 76
Coronari, Via dei *24*,* **40,** *92,*
    94
Corso, Via del *24*, 27,* **32–34**
Counter-Reformation *18, 21,*
    64, 78–79

Domine Quo Vadis, Chapel of
    84

Eating Out *11, 96–102*
Entertainment *91–93*
Esquiline Hill *12, 14, 49, 74*
EUR *7,* **83,** *85**

Festivals *92*
Food, see Eating Out
Forum *7, 12, 14, 22, 25*, 27,*
    28, 30, **49–54,** *51*, 56, 92*
Fosse Ardeatine *85–86*
Fountain (Fontana)
  ~ della Barcaccia *34*
  ~ of the Four Rivers *29,*
    39–40
  Trevi ~ *11, 22, 24*,* **38–39**
  Turtle ~ *44*

Garibaldi, Giuseppe *20, 73*
Garibaldi, Piazzale *24*, 73*

Hadrian *14, 32, 41, 61, 62,*
    86–87
Hadrian's Villa *14, 85*,* **86–88**

Imperial Forums *25*, 56*
Isola Tiberina *12, 24*,* **45**

Janiculum Hill *24*, 61,* **73**
Jewish Ghetto *18, 24*,* **43–44,**
    96, 100
Julius Caesar, see under Caesar

Keats, John *37, 46*
Keats-Shelley Memorial *37*

Lateran Treaty *20, 21, 40, 60*

Maderno, Carlo *29, 64, 90*
Mausoleum of Augustus *24*,*
    32
Michelangelo Buanaroti *7, 17,*
    21, 22, 28, 29, 30, 42, 49, 60,
    64, 66, 68, 70, 71, 72, 78, 80
Museums (Museo)
  Borghese Gallery *25*, 29, 34,*
    79–80
  Capitoline ~ *28–30*
  Galleria Doria Pamphili *24*,*
    82–83
  Galleria Nazionale d'Arte
    Antica *25*, 82*
  ~ Nazionale Romano *24*,*
    80–82
  Vatican ~ *22, 24*, 61,* **68–73**
Mussolini, Benito *20, 21,*
    27–28, 60, 83

Napoleon *19, 21, 32, 34, 39, 72*
Nemi, Lake *85*, 90*

Ostia Antica *24*, 88–90, 85**

Palatine Hill   7, 12, 24–25*, 49, **54–56**
Palazzo
~ Barberini   25*, **29**, 82
~ Farnese   24*, 42
~ del Quirinale   **39**, 49
~ Senatorio   **28**, 30, 50
~ Venezia   27–28
Pantheon   14, 22, 24*, **40–42**, 52, 66
Paul, St.   14, 76, 85
Peter, St.   14, 15, 66, 75, 76, 78, 84, 85
Piazza
~ Colonna   24*, 32
~ Montecitorio   24*, 32
~ Navona   22, 24*, **39–40**, 92
~ del Popolo   24*, **29**, 32–34
~ San Pietro   24*, **29**, 60, **63–64**
~ di Spagna   24*, **34–37**, 92
~ Venezia   24*, **27–28**, 32
Pietà   29, **66**
Pincio   7, 24*, 29, **34**
Pinturicchio, Bernardino   29, 32, 33, 71
Pope, the   11, 64, 66, 75, 90, 92
Porta del Popolo   33–34
Porta Portese   93
Protestant Cemetery   24*, 46

Quirinal Hill   12, 39, 49

Raphael   17, 22, 29, 33, 42, 63, 64, 69, 70, 72, 80, 82
Renaissance, the   8, 17–18, 21

Roman Forum, see Forum
Romulus   12, 51

St. Peter's Square, see Piazza San Pietro
Sant'Angelo, Ponte   61
Shopping   93–95
Sistine Chapel   17, 21, 29, 68, **71–72**
Spanish Steps   22, **34–37**, 92

Temple of Vesta   24*, 46
Temple of Fortune   46
Theatre of Marcellus   24*, 45
Tiber, River   8, 22, 24*, 27, 62, 85*, 88
Tivoli   85*, 86
Tomb of Cecilia Metella   85
Trajan's Column   56
Trastevere   **46–49**, 82, 92, 96

Valadier, Giuseppe   29, 32, 34, 54
Vatican   20, 21, 22, 24*, 39, **59–73**, 75, 85*
Vatican Grottoes   66–68
Veneto, Via   24–25*, 39
Villa Borghese   24*, **34**, 79, 92
Villa d'Este   86
Villa Giulia   24*, 80
Villa Medici   24*, **34**, 91
Viminal Hill   49
Vittorio Emanuele Monument   24*, **27**, 28

Wine   90, 94, 101

INDEX

128

Selection of Rome Hotels and Restaurants

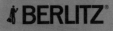

Where do you start? Choosing a hotel or restaurant in a place you're not familiar with can be daunting. To help you find your way amid the bewildering variety, we have made a selection from the *Red Guide to Italy 1987* published by Michelin, the recognized authority on gastronomy and accommodation throughout Europe.

Our own Berlitz criteria have been price and location. In the hotel section, for a double room with bath and breakfast, Higher-priced means above L. 250,000, Medium-priced L. 120,000–250,000, Lower-priced below L. 120,000. As to restaurants, for a meal consisting of a starter, a main course and a dessert, Higher-priced means above L. 45,000, Medium-priced L. 30,000–45,000, Lower-priced below L. 30,000. Special features where applicable, plus regular closing days are also given. As a general rule many Rome restaurants are closed in August. For hotels and restaurants, both a check to make certain that they are open and advance reservations are advisable.

For a wider choice of hotels and restaurants, we strongly recommend you obtain the authoritative Michelin *Red Guide to Italy,* which gives a comprehensive and reliable picture of the situation throughout the country.

HOTELS

HIGHER-PRICED
(above L. 250,000)

Ambasciatori Palace
via Vittorio Veneto 125
00187 Rome
Tel. 474931
Tlx. 610241
149 rooms
Grill Bar ABC restaurant.

Atlante Star
via Vitelleschi 34
00193 Rome
Tel. 6564196
Tlx. 622355
61 rooms
Roof-garden restaurant with view over St. Peter's Basilica.

Cavalieri Hilton
via Cadlolo 101
00136 Rome
Tel. 3151
Tlx. 610296
387 rooms
Quiet hotel. View of the city. Terrace and park. Outdoor swimming pool. Hotel tennis court. La Pergola restaurant.

D'Inghilterra
via Bocca di Leone 14
00187 Rome
Tel. 672161
Tlx. 614552
102 rooms
No restaurant.

Eden
via Ludovisi 49
00187 Rome
Tel. 4743551
Tlx. 610567
110 rooms
Roof-garden restaurant with view over city.

Forum
via Tor de' Conti 25
00184 Rome
Tel. 6792446
Tlx. 622549
81 rooms
Roof-garden restaurant with view of Imperial Forums.

Hassler
piazza Trinità dei Monti 6
00187 Rome
Tel. 6792651
Tlx. 610208
101 rooms
View over city from roof-garden restaurant.

Le Grand Hotel
via Vittorio Emanuele Orlando 3
00185 Rome
Tel. 4709
Tlx. 610210
168 rooms

Lord Byron
via De Notaris 5
00197 Rome
Tel. 3609541
Tlx. 611217
50 rooms
Quiet, pleasant hotel. Garden.

3

Parco dei Principi
via Frescobaldi 5
00198 Rome
Tel. 841071
Tlx. 610517
203 rooms
Small park with outdoor swimming pool.

Victoria
via Campania 41
00187 Rome
Tel. 473931
Tlx. 610212
110 rooms

Outskirts of Rome

Sheraton
viale del Pattinaggio
00144 Rome
Tel. 5453
Tlx. 614223
615 rooms
Outdoor swimming pool. Hotel tennis court.

MEDIUM-PRICED
(L. 120,000–250,000)

Accademia
piazza Accademia
di San Luca 75
00187 Rome
Tel. 6786705
44 rooms
No restaurant.

Aldrovandi Palace Hotel
via Aldrovandi 15
00197 Rome
Tel. 841091
Tlx. 616141
139 rooms
Outdoor swimming pool. Garden.

Atlantico
via Cavour 23
00184 Rome
Tel. 485951
83 rooms
No restaurant.

Borromini
via Lisbona 7
00198 Rome
Tel. 841321
Tlx. 680485
75 rooms
No restaurant.

Britannia
via Napoli 64
00184 Rome
Tel. 463153
Tlx. 611292
32 rooms
No restaurant.

Claridge
viale Liegi 62
00198 Rome
Tel. 868556
Tlx. 610340
88 rooms
Lo Chef restaurant.

Clodio
via di Santa Lucia 10
00195 Rome
Tel. 317541
115 rooms
No restaurant.

Colonna Palace
piazza Montecitorio 12
00186 Rome
Tel. 6781341
Tlx. 621467
100 rooms
No restaurant.

Columbus
via della Conciliazione 33
00193 Rome
Tel. 6565435
Tlx. 620096
107 rooms
Beautiful decor in 15th-century-style building.

Commodore
via Torino 1
00184 Rome
Tel. 485656
Tlx. 612170
62 rooms
No restaurant.

Degli Aranci
via Oriani 11
00197 Rome
Tel. 870202
42 rooms
Outdoor dining.

Diana
via Principe Amedeo 4
00185 Rome
Tel. 4751541
Tlx. 611198
187 rooms

Diplomatic
via Vittorio Colonna 28
00193 Rome
Tel. 6542084

Tlx. 610506
36 rooms
Outdoor dining.

Edera
via Poliziano 75
00184 Rome
Tel. 7316341
Tlx. 621472
38 rooms
Quiet hotel with garden.
No restaurant.

Eliseo
via di Porta Pinciana 30
00187 Rome
Tel. 460556
Tlx. 610693
53 rooms
Roof-garden restaurant with view of Villa Borghese.

Fenix
viale Gorizia 5
00198 Rome
Tel. 850741
67 rooms
Garden.

Giulio Cesare
via degli Scipioni 287
00192 Rome
Tel. 310244
Tlx. 613010
86 rooms
Garden. No restaurant.

Gregoriana
via Gregoriana 18
00187 Rome
Tel. 6794269
19 rooms
No restaurant.

Imperiale
via Vittorio Veneto 24
00187 Rome
Tel. 4756351
Tlx. 621071
85 rooms

Jolly Leonardo da Vinci
via dei Gracchi 324
00192 Rome
Tel. 39680
Tlx. 611182
245 rooms

Jolly Vittorio Veneto
corso d'Italia 1
00198 Rome
Tel. 8495
Tlx. 612293
200 rooms

Madrid
via Mario de' Fiori 95
00187 Rome
Tel. 6791243
24 rooms
No restaurant.

Massimo D'Azeglio
via Cavour 18
00184 Rome
Tel. 460646
Tlx. 610556
210 rooms

Mediterraneo
via Cavour 15
00184 Rome
Tel. 464051
272 rooms

Mozart
via dei Greci 23/b
00187 Rome
Tel. 6787422
31 rooms
No restaurant.

Napoleon
piazza Vittorio Emanuele 105
00185 Rome
Tel. 737646
Tlx. 611069
82 rooms

Nord-Nuova Roma
via Amendola 3
00185 Rome
Tel. 465441
156 rooms
No restaurant.

P.L.M. Etap Boston
via Lombardia 47
00187 Rome
Tel. 473951
Tlx. 622247
121 rooms

Quirinale
via Nazionale 7
00184 Rome
Tel. 4707
Tlx. 610332
193 rooms
Outdoor dining. Garden.

Regency
via Romagna 42
00187 Rome
Tel. 4759281
Tlx. 622321
50 rooms
No restaurant.

San Giorgio
via Amendola 61
00185 Rome
Tel. 4751341
186 rooms
No restaurant.

Siena
via Sant'Andrea delle Frate 33
00187 Rome
Tel. 6796121
21 rooms
No restaurant.

Sitea
via Vittorio Emanuele
Orlando 90
00185 Rome
Tel. 4751560
Tlx. 614163
37 rooms
No restaurant.

Villa del Parco
via Nomentana 110
00161 Rome
Tel. 864115
23 rooms
Garden. No restaurant.

Villa Florence
via Nomentana 28
00161 Rome
Tel. 8442841
Tlx. 624626
32 rooms
Garden. No restaurant.

Visconti Palace
via Cesi 37
00193 Rome
Tel. 3684
Tlx. 680407
247 rooms
No restaurant.

<u>Outskirts of Rome</u>

Dei Congressi
viale Shakespeare 29
00144 Rome
Tel. 5926021
Tlx. 614140
96 rooms
No restaurant.

Holiday Inn St. Peter's
via Aurelia Antica 415
00165 Rome
Tel. 5872
Tlx. 625434
330 rooms
Outdoor swimming pool. Garden. Hotel tennis court.

Holiday Inn-Eur Parco dei Medici
viale Castello della Magliana 65
00148 Rome
Tel. 5475
Tlx. 613302
324 rooms
Outdoor swimming pool. Garden. Hotel tennis court.

Villa Pamphili
via della Nocetta 105
00164 Rome
Tel. 5862
Tlx. 611675
253 rooms
Outdoor swimming pool (covered in winter). Garden. Hotel tennis court.

LOWER-PRICED
(below L. 120,000)

Adriano
via di Pallacorda 2
00186 Rome
Tel. 6542451
82 rooms
No restaurant.

Alba
via Leonina 12
00184 Rome
Tel. 484471
26 rooms
No restaurant.

Alpi
via Castelfidardo 84/a
00185 Rome
Tel. 464618; Tlx. 611677
46 rooms
No restaurant.

Arcangelo
via Boezio 15
00192 Rome
Tel. 318851
33 rooms
No restaurant.

Ariston
via Turati 16
00185 Rome
Tel. 7310341; Tlx. 614479
96 rooms
No restaurant.

Canada
via Vicenza 58
00185 Rome
Tel. 4957385; Tlx. 613037
62 rooms
No restaurant.

Cesàri
via di Pietra 89
00186 Rome
Tel. 6792386
50 rooms
No restaurant.

Della Conciliazione
borgo Pio 165
00193 Rome
Tel. 6567910
55 rooms
No restaurant.

Della Torre Argentina
corso Vittorio Emanuele 102
00186 Rome
Tel. 6548251
32 rooms
No restaurant.

Domus Maximi
via Santa Prisca 11/b
00153 Rome
Tel. 5782565
23 rooms
Quiet hotel. No restaurant.

Eurogarden
raccordo anulare Salaria-
Flaminia
00138 Rome
Tel. 6910117
40 rooms
*Outdoor swimming pool. Garden.
No restaurant.*

Galileo
via Palestro 33
00185 Rome
Tel. 464910
36 rooms
No restaurant.

Gerber
via degli Scipioni 241
00192 Rome
Tel. 3595148
28 rooms
No restaurant.

King
via Sistina 131
00187 Rome
Tel. 4741515
Tlx. 626246
79 rooms
No restaurant.

Lloyd
via Alessandria 110
00198 Rome
Tel. 850432
Tlx. 612598
48 rooms
No restaurant.

Margutta
via Laurina 34
00187 Rome
Tel. 3614193
21 rooms
No restaurant.

Milani
via Magenta 12
00185 Rome
Tel. 4940051
Tlx. 614356
78 rooms
No restaurant.

Portoghesi
via dei Portoghesi 1
00186 Rome
Tel. 6564231
27 rooms
No restaurant.

Rivoli
via Torquato Taramelli 7
00197 Rome
Tel. 870141
Tlx. 614615
49 rooms

Sant' Anselmo
piazza Sant'Anselmo 2
00153 Rome
Tel. 573547
45 rooms
Garden. No restaurant.

Senato
piazza della Rotonda 73
00186 Rome
Tel. 6793231
51 rooms
View of the Pantheon. No restaurant.

Siviglia
via Gaeta 12
00185 Rome
Tel. 4750004
Tlx. 612225
41 rooms
No restaurant.

Terminal
via Principe Amedeo 103
00185 Rome
Tel. 734041
35 rooms
No restaurant.

Villa San Pio
via di Sant'Anselmo 19
00153 Rome
Tel. 5755231
59 rooms
Garden. No restaurant.

RESTAURANTS

HIGHER-PRICED
(above L. 45,000)

Al Moro
vicolo delle Bollete 13
00187 Rome
Tel. 6783495
*Trattoria. Reservation essential.
Closed Sunday.*

Alberto Ciarla
piazza San Cosimato 40
00153 Rome
Tel. 5818668
*Notably good cuisine. Outdoor
dining. Reservation essential.
Closed at lunchtime and Sunday.*

4 Colonne
via della Posta 4
00186 Rome
Tel. 6547152
*Reservation essential. Closed
Sunday.*

Coriolano
via Ancona 14
00198 Rome
Tel. 861122
*Reservation essential. Closed
Sunday.*

El Toulà
via della Lupa 29
00186 Rome
Tel. 6781196
*Elegant restaurant. Reservation
essential. Closed Saturday lunchtime and Sunday.*

Girarrosto Toscano
via Campania 29
00187 Rome
Tel. 493759
*Modern taverna. Closed
Wednesday.*

Harry's Bar
via Vittorio Veneto 150
00187 Rome
Tel. 4745832
*Reservation essential. Closed
Sunday.*

La Maiella
piazza Sant'Apollinare 45/46
00186 Rome
Tel. 6564174
*Abruzzi specialities. Outdoor
dining. Closed Sunday.*

La Rosetta
via della Rosetta 9
00187 Rome
Tel. 6561002
*Trattoria with seafood specialities.
Notably good cuisine. Closed
Sunday and Monday lunchtime.*

Loreto
via Valenziani 19
00187 Rome
Tel. 4742454
*Seafood specialities. Closed
Sunday.*

Mastrostefano
piazza Navona 94
00186 Rome
Tel. 6541669
*Restaurant with American-style
bar. Outdoor dining in summer
with view of Bernini fountain.
Closed Monday.*

Piccolo Mondo
via Aurora 39/d
00187 Rome
Tel. 4754595
*Elegant little taverna. Closed
Sunday.*

Piperno
Monte de' Cenci 9
00186 Rome
Tel. 6540629
*Notably good cuisine. Roman
specialities. Closed Sunday
evening and Monday.*

Ranieri
via Mario de' Fiori 26
00187 Rome
Tel. 6791592
*Reservation essential. Closed
Sunday.*

Relais le Jardin
via De Notaris 5
00197 Rome
Tel. 3609541
Tlx. 611217
*Excellent cuisine. Elegant restau-
rant. Reservation essential. Closed
Sunday.*

Sabatini
vicolo Santa Maria
in Trastevere 18
00153 Rome
Tel. 5818307
*Outdoor dining. Typical Roman
inn. Closed Tuesday.*

**Sabatini a Santa Maria
in Trastevere**
piazza di Santa Maria
in Trastevere 10
00153 Rome
Tel. 582026

*Outdoor dining. Seafood and
Roman specialities. Closed
Wednesday.*

Sans Souci
via Sicilia 20/24
00187 Rome
Tel. 493504
*Notably good cuisine. Elegant
restaurant. Reservation essential.
Late-night dinners. Closed at
lunchtime and Monday.*

Squalo Bianco
via Federico Cesi 36
00193 Rome
Tel. 312524
*Seafood specialities. Closed
Sunday.*

MEDIUM-PRICED
(L. 30,000–45,000)

Al 59
via Brunetti 59
00186 Rome
Tel. 3619019
*Bolognese specialities. Closed
Sunday and in July and August
also on Saturday.*

Al Bersagliere-da Raffone
via Ancona 43
00198 Rome
Tel. 861003
*Typical country-style restaurant.
Closed Saturday.*

11

Al Ceppo
via Panama 2
00198 Rome
Tel. 8449696
*Typical restaurant. Outdoor
dining. Closed Monday.*

Al Chianti
via Ancona 17
00198 Rome
Tel. 861083
*Tuscan trattoria with taverna.
Reservation essential. Closed
Sunday.*

Al Fogher
via Tevere 13/b
00198 Rome
Tel. 857032
*Typical restaurant with Venetian
specialities. Closed Sunday.*

Angelino ai Fori
largo Corrado Ricci 40
00184 Rome
Tel. 6791121
Outdoor dining. Closed Tuesday.

Apuleius
via Tempio di Diana 15
00153 Rome
Tel. 572160
*Ancient-Roman-style taverna.
Closed Sunday.*

Cesarina
via Piemonte 109
00187 Rome
Tel. 460828
*Bolognese specialities. Closed
Sunday.*

Checco er Carettiere
via Benedetta 10
00153 Rome
Tel. 5817018
*Outdoor dining. Typical restau-
rant with seafood and Roman
specialities. Closed Sunday
evening and Monday.*

Colline Emiliane
via degli Avignonesi 22
00187 Rome
Tel. 4757538
Reserve. Closed Friday.

Corsetti-il Galeone
piazza San Cosimato 27
00153 Rome
Tel. 5816311
*Seafood specialities. Typical
atmosphere. Closed Wednesday.*

Da Benito
via Flaminia Nuova 230/232
00191 Rome
Tel. 3272752
*Trattoria-pizzeria. Closed
Monday.*

Da Giggetto
via del Portico d'Ottavia 21/a
00186 Rome
Tel. 6561105
*Typical trattoria with Roman
specialities. Closed Monday.*

Da Mario
via della Vite 55
00187 Rome
Tel. 6783818
*Tuscan specialities. Closed
Sunday.*

Da Pancrazio
piazza del Biscione 92
00186 Rome
Tel. 6561246
Ancient-Roman-style taverna.
Closed Wednesday.

Dai Toscani
via Forli 41
00161 Rome
Tel. 862477
Tuscan specialities. Closed
Sunday.

Dal Bolognese
piazza del Popolo 1
00187 Rome
Tel. 3611426
Bolognese specialities. Art collec-
tion. Closed Sunday evening and
Monday.

Delle Vittorie
via di Monte Santo 62/64
00195 Rome
Tel. 386847
Closed Sunday.

Eau Vive
via Monterone 85
00186 Rome
Tel. 6541095
16th-century building. Catholic
missionaries. International cuisine.
Reservation essential in evening.
Closed Sunday.

Ecce Bomboo
via di Tor Millina 22
00186 Rome
Tel. 6543469
Pleasant atmosphere. Reservation
essential. Closed at lunchtime and
on Sundays.

Galeassi
piazza di Santa Maria
in Trastevere 3
00153 Rome
Tel. 5803775
Outdoor dining. Seafood
and Roman specialities. Closed
Monday.

Giovanni
via Marche 64
00187 Rome
Tel. 493576
Typical habitués' restaurant.
Closed Friday evening and
Saturday.

Hostaria Costa Balena
via Messina 5/7
00198 Rome
Tel. 857686
Trattoria with seafood specialities.
Closed Sunday.

Hostaria da Cesare
via Crescenzio 13
00193 Rome
Tel. 6561227
Trattoria-pizzeria with seafood
specialities. Closed Sunday
evening and Monday.

Il Buco
via Sant'Ignazio 8
00186 Rome
Tel. 6793298
Tuscan specialities. Closed
Monday.

Il Caminetto
viale dei Parioli 89
00197 Rome
Tel. 803946
Closed Thursday.

Il Drappo
vicolo del Malpasso 9
00186 Rome
Tel. 6877365
Sardinian specialities. Reservation essential. Closed Sunday.

Il Falchetto
via Montecatini 12/14
00186 Rome
Tel. 6791160
Country-style trattoria. Closed Friday.

Il Tinello
via di Porta Pinciana 16
00187 Rome
Tel. 4745378
Typical taverna. Closed Sunday.

La Sacrestia
via del Seminario 89
00186 Rome
Tel. 6797581
Typically decorated pizzeria-restaurant. Closed Wednesday.

La Scala
viale dei Parioli 79/d
00197 Rome
Tel. 803978
Outdoor dining. Closed Wednesday.

La Vallata del Sangro
via Urbana 11/a
00184 Rome
Tel. 4743310
Trattoria with Abruzzi specialities. Closed Sunday.

Mario's Hostaria
piazza del Grillo 9
00184 Rome
Tel. 6793725
Reserve. Closed Sunday.

Piccola Roma
via Uffici del Vicario 36
00186 Rome
Tel. 6798606
Closed Sunday.

Romolo
via di Porta Settimiana 8
00153 Rome
Tel. 5818284
Typical trattoria with summer service in cool courtyard. Closed Monday.

Scoglio di Frisio
via Merulana 256
00185 Rome
Tel. 734619
Typically Neapolitan, with seafood specialities. Closed at lunchtime, Monday from November to April and on Sundays in the other months.

Taverna Giulia
vicolo dell'Oro 23
00186 Rome
Tel. 6569768
Restaurant with Ligurian specialities. Reservation essential. Closed Sunday.

Tempio di Bacco
via Lombardia 36/38
00187 Rome
Tel. 4754625
Dining room with frescoes. Closed Sunday.

Tullio
via di San Nicola
da Tolentino 26
00187 Rome
Tel. 4758564
Tuscan trattoria. Closed Sunday.

Vecchia Roma
piazza Campitelli 18
00186 Rome
Tel. 6564604
*Typical restaurant with seafood
and Roman specialities. Closed
Wednesday.*

Outskirts of Rome

La Fattoria
via Flaminia al km 14
00188 Rome
Tel. 6910033
Outdoor dining. Closed Tuesday.

La Maielletta
via Aurelia Antica 270
00165 Rome
Tel. 6374957
*Abruzzi specialities. Outdoor
dining. Closed Monday.*

Quo Vadis
via Appia Antica 38
00179 Rome
Tel. 5136795
*Outdoor dining. Closed evenings
and Tuesday.*

Vecchia America-Corsetti
piazza Marconi 32
00144 Rome
Tel. 5926601
*Typical restaurant and "birreria",
ale house. Closed Tuesday.*

LOWER-PRICED
(below L. 30,000)

Abruzzi
via del Vaccaro 1
00187 Rome
Tel. 6793897
Closed Saturday.

Cannavota
piazza San Giovanni
in Laterano 20
00184 Rome
Tel. 775007
Closed Wednesday.

Crisciotti-al Boschetto
via del Boschetto 30
00184 Rome
Tel. 4744770
*Rustic trattoria. Outdoor dining.
Closed Saturday.*

Da Domenico
via di San Giovanni
in Laterano 134
00184 Rome
Tel. 734774
*Typical habitués' trattoria. Closed
Monday.*

Elettra
via Principe Amedeo 72
00185 Rome
Tel. 4745397
*Typical habitués' trattoria. Closed
Friday evening and Saturday.*

Grappolo d'Oro
via Palestro 4/8
00185 Rome
Tel. 465283
Closed Sunday.

Hostaria da Vincenzo
via Castelfidardo 6
00185 Rome
Tel. 484596
Closed Sunday.

Hostaria Tempio de Mecenate
largo Leopardi 16
00185 Rome
Tel. 732310
Closed Sunday.

La Buca di Ripetta
via di Ripetta 36
00186 Rome
Tel. 3619391
Typical habitués' trattoria. Closed Sunday evening and Monday.

La Giada
via 4 Novembre 137/i
00187 Rome
Tel. 6798334
Chinese cuisine. Closed Monday.

La Pariolina
viale del Parioli 93/d
00197 Rome
Tel. 879734
Outdoor dining. Closed Monday.

La Tavernetta
via del Nazareno 3/4
00187 Rome
Tel. 6793124
Closed Monday.

Monte Arci
via Castelfidardo 33
00185 Rome
Tel. 4742562
Trattoria with Sardinian specialities. Closed Wednesday.

Peppino
via Principe Amedeo 70/a
00185 Rome
Tel. 4745387
Station trattoria. Closed Sunday.

Taverna Trilussa
via del Politeama 23
00153 Rome
Tel. 5818918
Outdoor dining. Typical establishment with Roman specialities. Closed Sunday evening and Monday.

Zi' Gaetana
via Cola di Rienzo 263
00192 Rome
Tel. 3595342
Typical taverna-pizzeria. Closed Monday.

Outskirts of Rome

Da Giacobbe
via Appia Nuova 1681
00043 Ciampino
Tel. 600131
Outdoor dining. Closed Monday.

La Cuccagna
via Flaminia al km 16,500
00188 Rome
Tel. 6912827
Country restaurant with outdoor dining and garden. Closed Monday.

La Giustiniana
via Cassia 1298
00123 Rome
Tel. 3765203
Summer dining in garden. Closed Tuesday.

Say BERLITZ®

... and most people think of outstanding language schools. But Berlitz has also become the world's leading publisher of books for travellers – Travel Guides, Phrase Books, Dictionaries – plus Cassettes and Self-teaching courses.

Informative, accurate, up-to-date, Books from Berlitz are written with freshness and style. They also slip easily into pocket or purse – no need for bulky, old-fashioned volumes.

Join the millions who know how to travel. Whether for fun or business, put Berlitz in your pocket.

BERLITZ®

Leader in
Books and Cassettes
for Travellers

A Macmillan Company

BERLITZ® Books for travellers

TRAVEL GUIDES
They fit your pocket in both size and price. Modern, up-to-date,
Berlitz gets all the information you need into 128 lively pages
with colour maps and photos throughout. What to see and do,
where to shop, what to eat and drink, how to save.

ASIA, MIDDLE EAST	China (256 pages)
	Hong Kong
	India (256 pages)
	Japan (256 pages)
	Nepal*
	Singapore
	Sri Lanka
	Thailand
	Egypt
	Jerusalem and the Holy Land
	Saudi Arabia
AUSTRAL-ASIA	Australia (256 pages)
	New Zealand
BRITISH ISLES	Channel Islands
	London
	Ireland
	Oxford and Stratford
	Scotland
BELGIUM	Brussels

AFRICA	Kenya
	Morocco
	South Africa
	Tunisia

*in preparation

PHRASE BOOKS
World's bestselling phrase books feature all the expressions and
vocabulary you'll need, and pronunciation throughout. 192 pages,
2 colours.

Arabic	Hebrew	Russian
Chinese	Hungarian	Serbo-Croatian
Danish	Italian	Spanish (Castilian)
Dutch	Japanese	Spanish (Lat. Am.)
Finnish	Korean	Swahili
French	Norwegian	Swedish
German	Polish	Turkish
Greek	Portuguese	European Phrase Book
		European Menu Reader

FRANCE	Brittany France (256 pages) French Riviera Loire Valley Normandy Paris		Costa Brava Costa del Sol and Andalusia Ibiza and Formentera Madrid Majorca and Minorca
GERMANY	Berlin Munich The Rhine Valley	EASTERN EUROPE	Budapest Dubrovnik and Southern Dalmatia Hungary (192 pages) Istria and Croatian Coast Moscow & Leningrad Split and Dalmatia Yugoslavia (256 pages)
AUSTRIA and SWITZER- LAND	Tyrol Vienna Switzerland (192 pages)		
GREECE, CYPRUS & TURKEY	Athens Corfu Crete Rhodes Greek Islands of the Aegean Peloponnese Salonica and Northern Greece Cyprus Istanbul/Aegean Coast Turkey (192 pages)	NORTH AMERICA	U.S.A. (256 pages) California Florida Hawaii Miami New York Canada (256 pages) Toronto Montreal
ITALY and MALTA	Florence Italian Adriatic Italian Riviera Italy (256 pages) Rome Sicily Venice Malta	CARIBBEAN, LATIN AMERICA	Puerto Rico Virgin Islands Bahamas Bermuda French West Indies Jamaica Southern Caribbean Mexico City Brazil (Highlights of) Rio de Janeiro

NETHER-
LANDS and
SCANDI-
NAVIA
	Amsterdam
	Copenhagen
	Helsinki
	Oslo and Bergen
	Stockholm
		EUROPE	Business Travel Guide –
			   Europe (368 pages)
			Pocket guide to Europe
			   (480 pages)
			Cities of Europe (504 pages)

PORTUGAL	Algarve Lisbon Madeira	CRUISE GUIDES	Caribbean cruise guide (368 pages) Alaska cruise guide (168 p.) Handbook to Cruising (240 p.)
SPAIN	Barcelona and Costa Dorada Canary Islands Costa Blanca		

Most titles with British and U.S. destinations are available in French, German, Spanish and as many as 7 other languages.

BERLITZ

german
english
englisch
deutsch

DICTIONARIES

Bilingual with 12,500 concepts each way. Highly practical for travellers, with pronunciation shown plus menu reader, basic expressions and useful information. Over 330 pages.

Danish	Finnish	German	Norwegian	Spanish
Dutch	French	Italian	Portuguese	Swedish

Berlitz Books, a world of information in your pocket!
At all leading bookshops and airport newsstands.

BERLITZ CASSETTEPAKS

Together in one set, a phrase book and a hi-fi cassette.
Here are just those expressions you need for your trip,
plus a chance to improve your accent. Simply listen and
repeat! Available in 24 different languages.
Each cassettepak includes a script giving tips on pronunciation and the complete text of the dual-language
recording.

The most popular Berlitz cassettepaks have been completely revised and brought up to date with a 90-minute
cassette and a newly revised phrase book containing a
2000 word dictionary, plus expanded colour coding
and menu reader.

BERLITZ® GOES VIDEO – *FOR LANGUAGES*

Here's a brand new 90-minute video from Berlitz for learning key words and phrases for your trip. It's easy and fun. Berlitz language video combines computer graphics with live action and freeze frames. You see on your own TV screen the type of dialogue you will encounter abroad. You practice conversation by responding to questions put to you in the privacy of your own living room.

Shot on location for accuracy and realism, Berlitz gently leads you through travel situations towards language proficiency. Available from video stores and selected bookstores and Berlitz Language Centers everywhere.

To order by credit card, call 1-800-228-2028 Ext. 35. Coming soon to the U.K.

Quick reference page *Espressioni indispensabili*

Good morning/ Good afternoon.	Buon giorno.	bwon joarnoa
Please ...	Per favore ...	pair fahvoaray
Thank you.	Grazie.	graatseeay
Yes/No.	Sì/No.	see/no
Excuse me.	Mi scusi.	mee skoozee
Do you speak English?	Parla inglese?	pahrlah eengglaysay
Where can I find/ buy/hire (rent) ...?	Dove posso trovare/ comprare/noleg- giare ...?	doavay possoa trovaaray/ koampraaray/noalaydjaaray
Where is ...?	Dov'è ...?	doavai
How far?	Quanto dista?	kwahntoa deestah
How long?	Quanto tempo?	kwahntoa tehmpoa
How much is it?	Quant'è?	kwahntai
Waiter/Waitress, please.	Cameriere/ Cameriera!	kahmayreeairay/ kahmayreeairah
I'd like ...	Vorrei ...	vorraiee
What does this mean?	Che cosa significa questo?	kay kawsah seeñeefeekah kooaystoa
I don't understand.	Non capisco.	noan kahpeeskoa
When does ... open/ close?	Quando apre/ chiude ...?	kwahndoa ahpray/ keeoooday
What time is it?	Che ore sono?	kay oaray soanoa
Do you mind if I smoke?	Le dispiace se fumo?	lay deespeeaachay say foomoa
Would you mind not smoking, please. It's not permitted here.	Le dispiace non fumare per favore? Non è permesso qui.	lay deespeeaachay noan foomaaray pair fahvoaray? noan ai pehrmehssoa kooee
Where are the toilets?	Dove sono i gabi- netti?	doavay soanoa ee gahbee- nehttee
Help me, please.	Mi aiuti, per favore.	mee aheeootee pair fah- voaray
Where is the ... consulate?	Dov'è il conso- lato ...?	doavai eel koansoalaatoa
American British Canadian	americano britannico canadese	ahmayreekaanoa breetahnneekoa kahnahdaysay

BERLITZ®

ITALIAN
for travellers

By the staff of Berlitz Guides

How best to use this phrase book

● We suggest that you start with the **Guide to pronunciation** (pp. 6–8), then go on to **Some basic expressions** (pp. 9–15). This gives you not only a minimum vocabulary, but also helps you get used to pronouncing the language. The phonetic transcription throughout the book enables you to pronounce every word correctly.

● Consult the **Contents** pages (3–5) for the section you need. In each chapter you'll find travel facts, hints and useful information. Simple phrases are followed by a list of words applicable to the situation.

● Separate, detailed contents lists are included at the beginning of the extensive **Eating out** and **Shopping guide** sections (Menus, p. 39, Shops and services, p. 97).

● If you want to find out how to say something in Italian, your fastest look-up is via the **Dictionary** section (pp. 164–189). This not only gives you the word, but is also cross-referenced to its use in a phrase on a specific page.

● If you wish to learn more about constructing sentences, check the **Basic grammar** (pp. 159–163).

● Note the **colour margins** are indexed in Italian and English to help both listener and speaker. And, in addition, there is also an **index in Italian** for the use of your listener.

● Throughout the book, this symbol 🖝 suggests phrases your listener can use to answer you. If you still can't understand, hand this phrase book to the Italian-speaker to encourage pointing to an appropriate answer. The English translation for you is just alongside the Italian.

Contents

Guide to pronunciation	**6**
Some basic expressions	**9**
Arrival	**16**

16	Passport control	19	Where is...?
16	Customs	19	Hotel reservation
18	Baggage—Porter	20	Car hire (rental)
18	Changing money	21	Taxi

Hotel—Accommodation	**22**

23	Checking in—Reception	28	Difficulties
25	Registration	29	Laundry—Dry cleaner's
26	Hotel staff	30	Hairdresser—Barber
27	General requirements	31	Checking out
28	Telephone—Post (mail)	32	Camping

Eating out	**33**

34	Meal times	50	Game and poultry
35	Italian cuisine	52	Vegetables and salads
36	Asking and ordering	53	Spices and herbs
38	Breakfast	53	Cheese
39	What's on the menu?	54	Fruit
41	Starters (appetizers)	55	Dessert
42	Pizza	56	Drinks
42	Omelets	56	Wine
43	Soups	59	Beer
44	Pasta	59	Spirits and liquors
44	Sauces	60	Nonalcoholic drinks
45	Rice	61	Complaints
46	Fish and seafood	62	The bill (check)
48	Meat	63	Snacks—Picnic

4

Travelling around 65

65	Plane	73	Underground (subway)
66	Train	74	Boat service
68	Inquiries	74	Bicycle hire
69	Tickets	75	Car
69	Reservation	76	Asking the way
70	On the train	77	Parking
71	Baggage and porters	78	Breakdown—Road
72	Coach (long-distance bus)		assistance
72	Bus—Tram (streetcar)	79	Road signs

Sightseeing 80

81	Where is...?	84	Religious services
82	Admission	85	Countryside
83	Who—What—When?	85	Landmarks

Relaxing 86

86	Cinema (movies)—Theatre	89	Sports
88	Opera—Ballet—Concert	90	On the beach
88	Nightclubs—Discos	91	Winter sports

Making friends 92

92	Introductions	94	Invitations
94	The weather	95	Dating

Shopping guide 97

98	Shops and services	119	Electrical appliances
100	General expressions	120	Grocery
104	Bookshop—Stationer's	121	Jeweller's—Watch-
106	Camping equipment		maker's
108	Chemist's (drugstore)	123	Optician
112	Clothing	124	Photography
112	Colour	126	Tobacconist's
113	Material	127	Souvenirs
114	Size	127	Records—Cassettes
116	Clothes and accessories	128	Toys
118	Shoes		

Your money: banks—currency 129

| 130 | At the bank | 131 | Business terms |

At the post office 132

| 133 | Telegrams | 134 | Telephoning |

Doctor 137

137	General	143	Prescription—Treat-
138	Parts of the body		ment
139	Accident—Injury	144	Fee
140	Illness	144	Hospital
141	Women's complaints	145	Dentist

Reference section 146

146	Countries	152	Greetings and wishes
147	Numbers	153	Time
149	Year and age	154	Abbreviations
150	Seasons	155	Signs and notices
150	Months	156	Emergency
151	Days and date	156	Lost property
152	Public holidays	157	Conversion tables

Basic Grammar 159

Dictionary and index (English-Italian) 164

Italian index 190

Map of Italy 192

Acknowledgments
We are particularly grateful to Francesca Grazzi Rahimi for her
help in the preparation of this book, and to Dr. T.J.A. Bennett who
devised the phonetic transcription.

Guide to pronunciation

An outline of the spelling and sounds of Italian

You'll find the pronunciation of the Italian letters and sounds explained below, as well as the symbols we're using for them in the transcriptions. Note that Italian has some diacritical letters—letters with accent marks—which we don't use in English.

The imitated pronunciation should be read as if it were English except for any special rules set out below. It is based on Standard British pronunciation, though we have tried to take account of General American pronunciation also. Of course, the sounds of any two languages are never exactly the same; but if you follow carefully the indications supplied here, you'll have no difficulty in reading our transcriptions in such a way as to make yourself understood.

Letters written in **bold** should be stressed (pronounced louder).

Consonants

Letter	Approximate pronunciation	Symbol	Example	
b, d, f, k, l, m, n, p, q t, v	as in English			
c	1) before e and i, like ch in chip	ch	cerco	chayrkoa
	2) elsewhere, like c in cat	k	conto	koantoa
ch	like c in cat	k	che	kay
g	1) before e and i, like j in jet	j	valigia	vahleejah
	2) elsewhere, like g in go	g	grande	grahnday

gh	like g in go	g	ghiaccio	geeahtchoa
gl	like lli in million	ly	gli	lyee
gn	like ni in onion	ñ	bagno	bahñoa
h	always silent		ha	ah
r	trilled like a Scottish r	r	deriva	dehreevah
s	1) generally like s in sit	s	questo	kooaystoa
	2) sometimes like z in zoo	z	viso	veezoa
sc	1) before e and i, like sh in shut	sh	uscita	oosheetah
	2) elsewhere, like sk in skin	sk	scarpa	skahrpah
z/zz	1) generally like ts in hits	ts	grazie	graatseeay
	2) sometimes like ds in roads	dz	romanzo	roamahndzoa

Vowels

a	1) short, like a in car, but shorter	ah	gatto	gahttoa
	2) long, like a in car	aa	casa	kaasah
e	1) can always be pronounced like ay in way, but without moving tongue or lips	ay	sera	sayrah
	2) in correct speech, it is sometimes pronounced like e in get or, when long, more like ai in hair	eh	bello	behlloa
		ai	bene	bainay
i	like ee in meet	ee	vini	veenee
o	1) can always be pronounced like oa in goat, but without moving tongue or lips	oa	sole	soalay
	2) in correct speech, it is sometimes pronounced like o in got, or when long, more like aw in law	o	notte	nottay
		aw	rosa	rawzah
u	like oo in foot	oo	fumo	foomoa

PRONUNCIATION

Two or more vowels

In groups of vowels **a**, **e**, and **o** are strong vowels, and **i** and **u** are weak vowels. When two strong vowels are next to each other, they are pronounced as two separate syllables, e.g., *beato* = bay**ah**toa. When a strong and weak vowel are next to each other, the weak one is pronounced more quickly and with less stress (less loudly) than the strong one, e.g., *piede* = pee**ay**day; such sounds are diphthongs and constitute only one syllable. If the weak vowel is stressed, then it is pronounced as a separate syllable, e.g., *due* = doo**ay**. Two weak vowels together are pronounced as a diphthong, and it is generally the second one that is more strongly stressed, e.g., *guida* = goo**ee**dah.

Stressing of words

Generally, the vowel of the next to last syllable is stressed. When a final vowel is stressed, it has an accent written over it *(caffè)*. Normally, when the stress falls on the syllable before the next to last one, it is not indicated by an accent.

Pronunciation of the Italian alphabet

A	ah	H	**ahk**kah	O	o	V	vee
B	bee	I	ee	P	pee	W	vee **doap**peeah
C	chee	J	ee **loong**gah	Q	koo	X	eeks
D	dee	K	**kahp**pah	R	**ehr**ray	Y	ee **gray**kah
E	ay	L	**ehl**lay	S	**ehs**say	Z	**dzay**tah
F	**ehf**fay	M	**ehm**may	T	tee		
G	jee	N	**ehn**nay	U	oo		

Pronuncia

Some basic expressions

Yes.	Sì.	see
No.	No.	no
Please.	Per favore/ Per piacere.	pair fahvoaray/ pair peeahchayray
Thank you.	Grazie.	graatseeay
Thank you very much.	Molte grazie/ Tante grazie.	moaltay graatseeay/ tahntay graatseeay
That's all right/ You're welcome.	Prego.	praygoa

Greetings *Saluti*

Good morning.	Buon giorno.	bwon joarnoa
Good afternoon.	Buon giorno.	bwon joarnoa
Good evening.	Buona sera.	bwonah sayrah
Good night.	Buona notte.	bwonah nottay
Good-bye.	Arrivederci.	ahrreevaydairchee
So long!	Ciao!	chaaoa
See you later.	A più tardi.	ah peeoo tahrdee
This is Mr./Mrs./ Miss ...	Le presento il Signor/la Signora/la Signorina ...	lay prayzayntoa eel seeñoar/lah seeñoarah/ lah seeñoareenah
How do you do? (Pleased to meet you.)	Molto lieto(a).*	moaltoa leeaytoa(ah)
How are you?	Come sta?	koamay stah
Very well, thanks. And you?	Molto bene, grazie. E lei?	moaltoa bainay graatseeay. ay laiee

---

* In the case where there are masculine and feminine forms of a word, we give the masculine first, with the feminine in brackets afterwards; in this example, a woman would say **Molto lieta**.

How's life?	**Come va?**	**koa**may vah
Fine.	**Bene.**	**bai**nay
I beg your pardon?	**Prego?**	**pray**goa
Excuse me.	**Mi scusi.**	mee **skoo**zee
Excuse me. (May I get past?)	**Permesso?**	pairmaissoa
Sorry!	**Mi dispiace.**	mee deespeeahchay

Questions *Domande*

Where?	**Dove?**	**doa**vay
How?	**Come?**	**koa**may
When?	**Quando?**	**kwahn**doa
What?	**Che cosa/Che?**	kay **kaw**sah/kay
Why?	**Perchè?**	pehr**kay**
Who?	**Chi?**	kee
Which?	**Quale?**	**kwaa**lay
Where is ...?	**Dov'è/Dove si trova ...?**	doa**vai**/**doa**vay see **traw**vah
Where are ...?	**Dove sono/ Dove si trovano ...?**	**doa**vay **soa**noa/**doa**vay see **traw**vahnoa
Where can I find/ get ...?	**Dove posso trovare ...?**	**doa**vay **poss**oa trovaaray
How far?	**Quanto dista?**	**kwahn**toa **dee**stah
How long?	**Quanto tempo?**	**kwahn**toa **tehm**poa
How much/How many?	**Quanto/Quanti?**	**kwahn**toa/**kwahn**tee
How much does this cost?	**Quanto costa questo?**	**kwahn**toa **kost**ah **kooy**stoa
When does ... open/ close?	**A che ora apre/ chiude ...?**	ah kay **oar**ah **aa**pray/ **keeooo**day
What do you call this/that in Italian?	**Come si chiama questo/quello in italiano?**	**koa**may see **keeaa**mah **kooy**stoa/**kooyl**loa een eetahleeaanoa
What does this/that mean?	**Che cosa significa questo/quello?**	kay **kaw**sah see**ñee**feekah **kooy**stoa/**kooyl**loa

Do you speak ...? *Parla ...?*

Do you speak English?	**Parla inglese?**	pahrlah eengglaysay
Is there anyone here who speaks ...?	**C'è qualcuno qui che parla ...?**	chai kwahlkoonoa kooee kay pahrlah
I don't speak (much) Italian.	**Non parlo (bene) l'italiano.**	noan pahrloa (bainay) leetahleeaanoa
Could you speak more slowly?	**Può parlare più lentamente, per favore?**	pwo pahrlaaray peeoo layntahmayntay pair fahvoaray
Could you repeat that?	**Vuol ripetere, per favore?**	vwol reepaitayray pair fahvoaray
Could you spell it?	**Può sillabarlo?**	pwo seellahbaarloa
Please write it down.	**Per favore, me lo scriva.**	pair fahvoaray may loa skreevah
Can you translate this for me?	**Può tradurmi questo?**	pwo trahdoormee kooaystoa
Please point to the word/phrase/ sentence in the book.	**Per favore, mi indichi la parola/ l'espressione/ la frase nel libro.**	pair fahvoaray mee eendeekee lah pahrolah/ laysprehsseeoanay/ lah fraazay nehl leebroa
Just a minute. I'll see if I can find it in this book.	**Un attimo. Guardo se posso trovarla in questo libro.**	oon ahtteemoa. gwahrdoa say possoa troavaarlah een kooaystoa leebroa
It's on page ...	**È a pagina ...**	ai ah paajeenah
I understand.	**Capisco.**	kahpeeskoa
I don't understand.	**Non capisco.**	noan kahpeeskoa
Do you understand?	**Capisce?**	kahpeeshay

Can/May ...? *Posso ...?*

Can I have ...?	**Posso avere ...?**	possoa ahvayray
Can we have ...?	**Possiamo avere ...?**	posseeaamoa ahvayray
Can you show me ...?	**Può mostrarmi ...?**	pwo moastraarmee
I can't.	**Non posso.**	noan possoa
Can you tell me ...?	**Può dirmi ...?**	pwo deermee

Can you help me?	**Può aiutarmi?**	pwo aheeootaarmee
Can I help you?	**Posso aiutarla?**	possoa aheeootaarlah
Can you direct me to ...?	**Può indicarmi la direzione per ...?**	pwo eendeekahrmee lah deeraytseeoanay pair

Wanting ...   *Vorrei ...*

I'd like ...	**Vorrei ...**	vorraiee
We'd like ...	**Vorremmo ...**	vorrehmmoa
What do you want?	**Che cosa desidera?**	kay kawsah dayzeedayrah
Give me ...	**Mi dia ...**	mee deeah
Give it to me.	**Me lo dia.**	may loa deeah
Bring me ...	**Mi porti ...**	mee portee
Bring it to me.	**Me lo porti.**	may loa portee
Show me ...	**Mi mostri ...**	mee moastree
Show it to me.	**Me lo mostri.**	may loa moastree
I'm looking for ...	**Cerco ...**	chayrkoa
I'm hungry.	**Ho fame.**	oa faamay
I'm thirsty.	**Ho sete.**	oa saytay
I'm tired.	**Sono stanco(a).**	soanoa stahngkoa(ah)
I'm lost.	**Mi sono perduto(a).**	mee soanoa pehrdootoa(ah)
It's important.	**È importante.**	ai eemportahntay
It's urgent.	**È urgente.**	ai oorjehntay
Hurry up!	**Presto!**	prehstoa

It is / There is ...   *È / C'è ...*

It is/It's ...	**È ...**	ai
Is it ...?	**È ...?**	ai
It isn't ...	**Non è ...**	noan ai
Here it is. (masc./fem.)	**Eccolo/Eccola.**	ehkkoaloa/ehkkoalah
Here they are. (masc./fem.)	**Eccoli/Eccole.**	ehkkoalee/ehkkoalay

There it is.	Eccolo/Eccola.	ehkkoaloa/ehkkoalah
There they are.	Eccoli/Eccole.	ehkkoalee/ehkkoalay
There is/There are ...	C'è/Ci sono ...	chai/chee soanoa
Is there/Are there ...?	C'è/Ci sono ...?	chai/chee soanoa
There isn't/aren't ...	Non c'è/Non ci sono ...	noan chai/noan chee soanoa
There isn't/aren't any.	Non ce n'è/Non ce ne sono.	noan chay nai/noan chay nay soanoa

It's ... È ...

big/small	grande/piccolo*	grahnday/peekkoaloa
quick/slow	rapido/lento	raapeedoa/lehntoa
hot/cold	caldo/freddo	kahldoa/frayddoa
full/empty	pieno/vuoto	peeaynoa/vwawtoa
easy/difficult	facile/difficile	faacheelay/deeffeecheelay
heavy/light	pesante/leggero	paysahntay/laydjairoa
open/shut	aperto/chiuso	ahpehrtoa/keeoosoa
right/wrong	giusto/sbagliato	joostoa/zbahlyaatoa
old/new	vecchio/nuovo	vehkkeeoa/nwawvoa
old/young	anziano/giovane	ahntseeaanoa/joavahnay
beautiful/ugly	bello/brutto	bailloa/broottoa
free (vacant)/occupied	libero/occupato	leebayroa/okkoopaatoa
good/bad	buono/cattivo	bwawnoa/kahtteevoa
better/worse	migliore/peggiore	meelyoaray/paydjoaray
here/there	qui/là	kooee/lah
early/late	presto/tardi	prehstoa/tahrdee
cheap/expensive	buon mercato/caro	bwawn mayrkahtoa/kaaroa
near/far	vicino/lontano	veecheenoa/lontaanoa
first/last	primo/ultimo	preemoa/oolteemoa

---

*For feminine and plural forms, see grammar section page 160 (adjectives).

Quantities *Quantità*

a little/a lot	un po'/molto	oon po/**molta**oa
few/a few	pochi/alcuni	pokee/ahl**koo**nee
much	molto	**molt**oa
many	molti	**molt**ee
more/less	più/meno	peeoo/**main**oa
more than/less than	più di/meno di	peeoo dee/**main**oa dee
enough/too	abbastanza/troppo	ahbbah**stahnt**sah/**tropp**oa
some/any	del, della, dei, degli, delle	dayl **dayl**lah daiee **dayl**yee **dayl**lay

Some prepositions ... *Alcune preposizioni ...*

at	a*	ah
on	su	soo
in	in	een
to	a	ah
after	dopo	**daw**poa
before (time)	prima di	**pree**mah dee
before (place)	davanti a	dah**vahn**tee ah
for	per	pair
from	da	dah
with	con	kon
without	senza	**saynt**sah
through	per, attraverso	pair ahttrah**vehr**soa
towards	verso	**vehr**soa
until	fino a	**fee**noa ah
during	durante	doo**rahn**tay
next to	accanto a	ahk**kahn**toa ah
near	vicino a	vee**chee**noa ah
behind	dietro	dee**ay**troa

---

* See also grammar section page 163 (prepositions).

between	**tra, fra**	trah frah
since	**da**	dah
above	**sopra**	soaprah
below	**al di sotto**	ahl dee sottoa
under	**sotto**	sottoa
inside	**dentro**	dayntroa
outside	**fuori**	fwawree
up	**su, in alto**	soo een ahltoa
upstairs	**di sopra**	dee soaprah
down	**giù**	joo
downstairs	**di sotto**	dee sottoa

... and a few more useful words ... e qualche altra parola utile

and	**e**	ay
or	**o**	oa
not	**non**	noan
never	**mai**	mahee
nothing	**nulla/niente**	noollah/neeayntay
something	**qualcosa**	kwahlkawsah
none	**nessuno**	nayssoonoa
very	**molto**	moaltoa
too, also	**anche**	ahngkay
yet	**ancora**	ahngkoarah
but	**ma, però**	mah payroa
at once	**subito**	soobeetoa
soon	**presto**	prehstoa
now	**adesso**	ahdehssoa
then	**poi, in seguito**	poaee een saygooeetoa
again	**ancora**	ahngkoarah
perhaps	**forse**	forsay
only	**soltanto**	soltahntoa

Arrival

Here's my passport.	Ecco il passaporto.	ehkkoa eel pahssahportoa
I'll be staying ...	Resterò ...	raystayroa
a few days	qualche giorno	kwahlkay joarnoa
a week	una settimana	oonah saytteemaanah
a month	un mese	oon maizay
I don't know yet.	Non so ancora.	noan soa ahngkoarah
I'm here on holiday.	Sono qui in vacanza.	soanoa kooee een vahkahntsah
I'm here on business.	Sono qui per affari.	soanoa kooee pair ahffaaree
I'm just passing through.	Sono di passaggio.	soanoa dee pahssadjoa

If things become difficult:

I'm sorry, I don't understand.	Mi dispiace, non capisco.	mee deespeeahchay noan kahpeeskoa
Is there anyone here who speaks English?	C'è qualcuno qui che parla inglese?	chai kwahlkoonoa kooee kay pahrlah eengglaysay

After collecting your baggage at the airport *(l'aeroporto)* you have a choice: follow the green arrow if you have nothing to declare. Or leave via a doorway marked with a red arrow if you have items to declare (in excess of those allowed).

The chart below shows what you can bring in duty-free.*

	Cigarettes	Cigars	Tobacco	Spirits	Wine
Italy 1)	400 or	100 or	500 g.	¾ l. or	2 l.
2)	300 or	75 or	400 g.	1½ l. or	5 l.
3)	200 or	50 or	250 g.	¾ l. or	2 l.
Switzerland	200 or	50 or	250 g.	1 l. and 2 l.	

1) residents of countries outside Europe
2) residents of countries within Europe and entering from an EEC country
3) residents of countries within Europe and entering from another country

I've nothing to declare.	**Non ho nulla da dichiarare.**	noan oa **noo**llah dah deekeeah**raa**ray
I've a carton of cigarettes/bottle of whisky.	**Ho una stecca di sigarette/bottiglia di whisky.**	oa **oo**nah **stay**kkah dee seegah**rayt**tay/ bot**tee**lyah dee "whisky"
Must I pay on this?	**Devo pagare per questo?**	**day**voa pah**gaa**ray pair koo**ay**stoa
It's for my personal use.	**È per mio uso personale.**	ai pair **mee**oa **oo**zoa pairsoa**naa**lay

🖐   ✍

Il passaporto, per favore.	Your passport, please.
Ha qualcosa da dichiarare?	Do you have anything to declare?
Per favore, apra questa borsa.	Please open this bag.
Deve pagare il dazio per questo.	You'll have to pay duty on this.
Ha altri bagagli?	Do you have any more luggage?

* All allowances subject to change without notice.

Baggage—Porter *Bagagli—Facchino*

These days porters are only available at airports or the railway stations of large cities. Where no porters are available you'll find luggage trolleys for the use of the passengers.

Porter!	**Facchino!**	fahkkeenoa
Please take my ...	**Per favore, prenda ...**	pair fahvoaray prehndah
bag	**la mia borsa**	lah meeah borsah
luggage	**i miei bagagli**	ee meeaiee bahgaalyee
suitcase	**la mia valigia**	lah meeah vahleejah
That's mine.	**Quella è mia.**	kooayllah ai meeah
Take this luggage ...	**Porti questi bagagli ...**	portee kooaystee bahgaalyee
to the bus	**all'autobus**	ahllowtoabooss
to the luggage lockers	**alla custodia automatica dei bagagli**	ahllah koostawdeeah owtoamaateekah daiee bahgaalyee
How much is that?	**Quant'è?**	kwahntai
There's one piece missing.	**Manca un collo.**	mahngkah oon kolloa
Where are the luggage trolleys (carts)?	**Dove sono i carrelli portabagagli?**	doavay soanoa ee kahrrehllee portahbahgaalyee

Changing money *Cambio*

Where's the currency exchange office?	**Dove si trova l'ufficio cambio?**	doavay see trawvah looffeechoa kahmbeeoa
Can you change these traveller's cheques (checks)?	**Può cambiare questi traveller's cheques?**	pwo kahmbeeaaray kooaystee "traveller's cheques"
I want to change some dollars/pounds.	**Vorrei cambiare dei dollari/delle sterline.**	vorraiee kahmbeeaaray daiee dollahree/dayllay stayrleenay
Can you change this into lire/Swiss francs?	**Può cambiare questo in lire/franchi svizzeri?**	pwo kahmbeeaaray kooaystoa een leeray/frahngkee sveettssayree
What's the exchange rate?	**Qual è il corso del cambio?**	kwahl ai eel korsoa dayl kahmbeeoa

BANK—CURRENCY, see page 129

Where is ...? *Dov'è ...?*

Where is the ...?	Dov'è ...?	doavai
booking office	l'ufficio preno-tazioni	looffeechoa praynoatah-tseeoanee
car hire	l'autonoleggio	lowtoanoalaydjoa
duty-free shop	il negozio duty-free	eel naygotseeoa "duty-free"
newsstand	l'edicola	laydeekolah
restaurant	il ristorante	eel reestoarahntay
shopping area	la zona dei negozi	lah dzoanah daiee naygotsee
How do I get to ...?	Come posso andare a ...?	koamay possoa ahndaaray ah
Is there a bus into town?	C'è un autobus per la città?	chai oon owtoabooss pair lah cheettah
Where can I get a taxi?	Dove posso prendere un taxi?	doavay possoa prehndayray oon "taxi"
Where can I hire a car?	Dove posso noleg-giare una macchina?	doavay possoa noalayd-jaaray oonah mahkkeenah

Hotel reservation *Prenotazione d'albergo*

Do you have a hotel guide?	Ha una guida degli alberghi?	ah oonah gweedah dailyee ahlbayrgee
Could you reserve a room for me at a hotel/boarding-house?	Potrebbe prenotarmi una camera in un albergo/una pensione?	poatrehbbay praynoa-taarmee oonah kaamayrah een oon ahlbayrgoa/oonah paynseeoanay
in the centre	in centro	een chayntroa
near the railway station	vicino alla stazione	veecheenoa ahllah stahtseeoanay
a single room	una camera singola	oonah kaamayrah seenggoalah
a double room	una camera doppia	oonah kaamayrah doappeeah
not too expensive	non troppo cara	noan troappoa kaarah
Where is the hotel/boarding house?	Dov'è l'albergo/la pensione?	doavai lahlbayrgoa/lah paynseeoanay
Do you have a street map?	Ha una pianta della città?	ah oonah peeahntah dayllah cheettah

HOTEL/ACCOMMODATION, see page 22

Arrivo

Car hire (rental) *Autonoleggio*

To hire a car you must produce a valid driving licence (held for at least one year) and your passport. Some firms set a minimum age at 21, other 25. Holders of major credit cards are normally exempt from deposit payments, otherwise you must pay a substantial (refundable) deposit for a car. Third-party insurance is usually automatically included.

I'd like to hire (rent) a car.	**Vorrei noleggiare una macchina.**	vorraiee noalaydjaaray oonah mahkkeenah
small	**piccola**	peekkoalah
medium-sized	**di media grandezza**	dee maydeeah grahndayttsah
large	**grande**	grahnday
automatic	**automatica**	owtoamahteekah
I'd like it for a day/a week.	**La vorrei per un giorno/una settimana.**	lah vorraiee pair oon joarnoa/oonah saytteemaanah
Are there any week-end arrangements?	**Vi sono condizioni speciali per il week-end?**	vee soanoa koandeetseeoanee spaychaalee pair eel "week-end"
Do you have any special rates?	**Avete tariffe parti-colari?**	ahvaytay tahreeffay pahr-teekoalaaree
What's the charge per day/week?	**Qual è la tariffa giornaliera/setti-manale?**	kwahl ai lah tahreeffah joarnahleeayrah/sayttee-mahnaalay
Is mileage included?	**È compreso il chilometraggio?**	ai koampraysoa eel keelomaytrahdjoa
What's the charge per kilometre?	**Qual è la tariffa al chilometro?**	kwahl ai lah tahreeffah ahl keelawmaytroa
I want to hire the car here and leave it in ...	**Vorrei noleggiare la macchina qui e renderla a ...**	vorraiee noalaydjaaray lah mahkkeenah kooee ay rayndayrlah ah
I want full insurance.	**Voglio l'assicura-zione completa.**	volyoa lahsseekooraht-seeoanay koamplaytah
What's the deposit?	**Quanto è la cauzione?**	kwahntoa ai lah kowtseeoanay
I've a credit card.	**Ho una carta di credito.**	oa oonah kahrtah dee kraydeetoa
Here's my driving licence.	**Ecco la mia patente.**	ehkkoa lah meeah pahtehntay

CAR, see page 75

Taxi *Taxi*

Taxis are clearly marked and available in all the larger towns. If the cab is unmetered, or you have a fair distance to go, ask the fare beforehand. Special rates for night journeys, baggage, etc. should be posted on an official fare chart.

Where can I get a taxi?	Dove posso trovare un taxi?	doavay possoa trawvaaray oon "taxi"
Please get me a taxi.	Per favore, mi trovi un taxi.	pair fahvoaray mee trawvee oon "taxi"
What's the fare to ...?	Qual è il prezzo della corsa fino a ...?	kwahl ai eel prehttsoa dayllah korsah feenoa ah
How far is it to ...?	Quanto dista ...?	kwahntoa deestah
Take me to ...	Mi conduca ...	mee koandookah
this address	a questo indirizzo	ah kooaystoa eendeereettsoa
the airport	all'aeroporto	ahllahayroportoa
the town centre	in centro città	een chayntroa cheettah
the ... Hotel	all'albergo ...	ahllahlbayrgoa
the railway station	alla stazione	ahllah stahtseeoanay
Turn ... at the next corner.	Al prossimo angolo giri ...	ahl prosseemoa ahnggoloa jeeree
left/right	a sinistra/a destra	ah seeneestrah/ah dehstrah
Go straight ahead.	Vada sempre diritto.	vahdah sehmpray deereettoa
Please stop here.	Per favore, si fermi qui.	pair fahvoaray see fayrmee kooee
I'm in a hurry.	Ho fretta.	oa frayttah
Could you drive more slowly?	Può andare più lentamente?	pwo ahndaaray peeoo layntahmayntay
Could you help me carry my luggage?	Può aiutarmi a portare i miei bagagli?	pwo aheeootaarmee ah portaaray ee meeaiee bahgaalyee
Could you wait for me?	Può aspettarmi?	pwo ahspehttaarmee
I'll be back in 10 minutes.	Tornerò fra 10 minuti.	tornayro frah 10 meenootee

TIPPING, see inside back-cover

Hotel—Other accommodation

Early reservation (and confirmation) is essential in most major tourist centres during the high season. Most towns and arrival points have a tourist information office (*azienda di soggiorno e turismo*—ahdzee**ehn**dah dee sod**joar**noa ay too**ree**smoa), or *ufficio turistico* (oof**fee**choa too**ree**steekoa), and that's the place to go if you're stuck without a room.

The Italian tourist organization, E.N.I.T., publishes an annual directory of all hotels in Italy with details of minimum and maximum prices and facilities.

albergo/hotel (ahl**bayr**goa/oa**tehl**)	Hotels in Italy are classified as *di lusso* (international luxury class), or *prima, seconda, terza, quarta categoria* (first, second, third, fourth class). *Note:* Especially near railway stations, one often finds *alberghi diurni* (ahl**bayr**gee dee**oor**nee—"daytime hotels"). These have no sleeping accommodation, but provide bathrooms, rest rooms, hairdressers, and other similar services. Most close at midnight.
motel (mo**tehl**)	Increasing in number, improving in service, the Automobile Association of Italy has a list of recommended motels.
locanda (lo**kahn**dah)	A country inn.
pensione (paynsee**oa**nay)	Corresponds to a boarding house; it usually offers *pensione completa* (full board) or *mezza pensione* (half board). Meals are likely to be from a set menu. *Pensioni* are classified first, second or third class.
ostello della gioventù (oa**stehl**loa day**llah** joavay**ntoo**)	Youth hostel. They are open to holders of membership cards issued by the International Youth Hostel Association.
appartamento ammobiliato (ahppahrtah**mayn**toa ahmmoabeelee**ah**toa)	Furnished flat (apartment). Contact a specialized travel agent if this is the type of arrangement you're looking for.

CAMPING, see page 32

Albergo

Checking in—Reception *Ufficio ricevimento*

My name is ...	**Mi chiamo ...**	mee keeaamoa
I've a reservation.	**Ho fatto una prenotazione.**	oa fahttoa oonah praynoatahtseeoanay
We've reserved two rooms.	**Abbiamo prenotato due camere.**	ahbbeeaamoa praynoatah-toa dooay kaamayray
Here's the confirmation.	**Ecco la conferma.**	ehkkoa lah konfehrmah
Do you have any vacancies?	**Avete camere libere?**	ahvaytay kaamayray leebayray
I'd like a...room...	**Vorrei una camera ...**	vorraiee oonah kaamayrah
single	**singola**	seenggoalah
double	**doppia**	doappeeah
with twin beds	**con due letti**	kon dooay lehttee
with a double bed	**con un letto matrimoniale**	kon oon lehttoa mahtreemoaneeaalay
with a bath	**con bagno**	kon baañoa
with a shower	**con doccia**	kon dotchah
with a balcony	**con balcone**	kon bahlkoanay
with a view	**con vista**	kon veestah
We'd like a room ...	**Vorremmo una camera ...**	vorrehmmoa oonah kaamayrah
in the front	**sul davanti**	sool dahvahntee
at the back	**sul retro**	sool raitroa
facing the sea	**sul mare**	sool maaray
It must be quiet.	**Deve essere tranquilla.**	dayvay ehssaray trahngkooeellah
Is there ...?	**C'è ...?**	chai
air conditioning	**l'aria condizionata**	laareeah kondeetseeoanaatah
heating	**il riscaldamento**	eel reeskahldahmayntoa
a radio/television in the room	**la radio/il televisore nella stanza**	lah raadeeoa/eel taylayvee-zoaray nayllah stahntsah
laundry service	**il servizio di lavanderia**	eel sayrveetseeoa dee lahvahndayreeah
room service	**il servizio nella stanza**	eel sayrveetseeoa nayllah stahntsah
hot water	**l'acqua calda**	lahkkwah kahldah
running water	**l'acqua corrente**	lahkkwah korraintay
a private toilet	**il gabinetto privato**	eel gahbeenayttoa preevaatoa

CHECKING OUT, see page 31

Albergo

Could you put an extra bed in the room?	**Può mettere un altro letto nella camera?**	pwo mayttehray oon ahltroa lehttoa nayllah kaamayrah

How much? *Quanto?*

What's the price ...?	**Qual è il prezzo ...?**	kwahl ai eel prehttsoa
per night	**per una notte**	pair oonah nottay
per week	**per una settimana**	pair oonah saytteemaanah
for bed and breakfast	**per la camera e la colazione**	pair lah kaamayrah ay lah koalahtseeoanay
excluding meals	**pasti esclusi**	paastee ayskloozee
for full board (A.P.)	**per la pensione completa**	pair lah paynseeoanay koamplaytah
for half board (M.A.P.)	**per mezza pensione**	pair mehdzah paynseeoanay
Does that include ...?	**Il prezzo comprende ...?**	eel prehttsoa koampraynday
breakfast	**la colazione**	lah koalahtseeoanay
service	**il servizio**	eel sayrveetseeoa
value-added tax (VAT)*	**l'I.V.A.**	leevah
Is there any reduction for children?	**C'è una riduzione per i bambini?**	chai oonah reedootseeoanay pair ee bahmbeenee
Do you charge for the baby?	**Fate pagare per il bambino?**	faatay pahgaaray pair eel bahmbeenoa
That's too expensive.	**È troppo caro.**	ai troppoa kaaroa
Haven't you anything cheaper?	**Non ha nulla di meno caro?**	noan ah noollah dee mainoa kaaroa

How long *Quanto tempo?*

We'll be staying ...	**Resteremo ...**	raystayraymoa
overnight only	**una notte**	oonah nottay
a few days	**qualche giorno**	kwahlkay joarnoa
a week (at least)	**una settimana (come minimo)**	oonah saytteemaanah (koamay meeneemoa)
I don't know yet.	**Non ho ancora deciso.**	noan oa ahngkoarah daycheesoa

---

* Americans note: a type of sales tax in Italy.

NUMBERS, see page 147

Decision *Decisione*

May I see the room?	**Posso vedere la camera?**	possoa vaydayray lah kaamayrah
That's fine. I'll take it.	**Va bene, la prendo.**	vah bainay lah prehndoa
No, I don't like it.	**No, non mi piace.**	noa noan mee peeahchay
It's too ...	**È troppo ...**	ai troppoa
cold/hot	**fredda/calda**	frayddah/kahldah
dark/small	**buia/piccola**	booeeah/peekkoalah
noisy	**rumorosa**	roomoaroazah
I asked for a room with a bath.	**Ho chiesto una camera con bagno.**	oa keeehstoa oonah kaamayrah kon baañoa
Do you have anything ...?	**Ha qualcosa ...?**	ah kwahlkawsah
better	**migliore**	meelyoaray
bigger	**più grande**	peeoo grahnday
cheaper	**meno caro**	mainoa kaaroa
quieter	**più tranquillo**	peeoo trahngkooeelloa
Do you have a room with a better view?	**Ha una camera con una vista più bella?**	ah oonah kaamayrah kon oonah veestah peeoo baillah

Registration *Registrazione*

Upon arrival at a hotel or boarding house you'll be asked to fill in a registration form (*una scheda*—**oo**nah **skay**dah).

Cognome/Nome	Name/First name
Domicilio/Strada/N°	Home address/Street/Number
Cittadinanza/Professione	Nationality/Profession
Data/Luogo di nascita	Date/Place of birth
Proveniente da .../Diretto a ...	From .../To ...
Numero di passaporto	Passport number
Luogo/Data	Place/Date
Firma	Signature

| What does this mean? | **Cosa significa questo?** | kawsah seeñeefeekah kooaystoa |

👈	👉
Mi può mostrare il passaporto?	May I see your passport?
Vuol compilare la scheda, per cortesia?	Would you mind filling in this registration form?
Firmi qui, per favore.	Sign here, please.
Quanto tempo si trattiene?	How long will you be staying?

What's my room number?	**Qual è il numero della mia stanza?**	kwahl ai eel noomayroa dayllah meeah stahntsah
Will you have our luggage sent up?	**Può far portare su i nostri bagagli?**	pwo faar portaaray soo ee nostree bahgaalyee
Where can I park my car?	**Dove posso parcheggiare la macchina?**	doavay possoa pahrkaydjaaray lah mahkkeenah
Does the hotel have a garage?	**L'albergo ha il garage?**	lahlbayrgoa ah eel gahraazh
I'd like to leave this in your safe.	**Vorrei depositare questo nella vostra cassaforte.**	vorraiee daypozeetaaray kooaystoa nayllah vostrah kahssahfortay

Hotel staff *Personale d'albergo*

hall porter	**il portiere**	eel pawrteeayray
maid	**la cameriera (nelle camere)**	lah kahmayreeayrah (nayllay kaamayray)
manager	**il direttore**	eel deerehttoaray
page (bellboy)	**il fattorino**	eel fahttoreenoa
porter	**il facchino**	eel fahkkeenoa
receptionist	**il capo ricevimento**	eel kahpoa reechayveemayntoa
switchboard operator	**il (la) centralinista**	eel (lah) chayntrahleeneestah
waiter	**il cameriere**	eel kahmayreeayray
waitress	**la cameriera**	lah kahmayreeayrah

General requirements *Richieste generali*

The key, please.	**La chiave, per favore.**	lah keeaavay pair fahvoaray
Will you please wake me at ...?	**Potrebbe svegliarmi alle ...?**	poatrehbbay zvaylyaarmee ahllay

TELLING THE TIME, see page 153

Is there a bath on this floor?	C'è un bagno a questo piano?	chai oon baañoa ah kooaystoa peeaanoa
What's the voltage?	Qual è il voltaggio?	kwahl ai eel voaltahdjoa
Where's the socket (outlet) for the shaver?	Dov'è la presa per il rasoio?	doavai lah prayzah pair eel rahzoaeeoa
Can we have breakfast in our room?	Possiamo avere la colazione in camera?	posseeaamoa ahvayray lah koalahtseeoanay een kaamayrah
Can you find me a ...?	Può trovarmi ...?	pwo trawvahrmee
babysitter	una babysitter	oonah "babysitter"
secretary	una segretaria	oonah saygraytaareeah
typewriter	una macchina per scrivere	oonah mahkkeenah pair skreevayray
May I have a/an/ some ...?	Posso avere ...?	possoa ahvayray
ashtray	un portacenere	oon portahchaynayray
bath towel	un asciugamano	oon ahshoogahmaanoa
(extra) blanket	una coperta (in più)	oonah kopehrtah (een peeoo)
envelopes	delle buste	dayllay boostay
(more) hangers	degli attaccapanni (in più)	daylyee ahttahkkahpahnnee (een peeoo)
hot-water bottle	una borsa dell'acqua calda	oonah boarsah dehllahk-kwah kahldah
ice cubes	dei cubetti di ghiaccio	daiee koobehttee dee geeaahtchoa
needle and thread	un ago e del filo	oon aagoa ay dayl feeloa
(extra) pillow	un guanciale (in più)	oon gwahnchaalay (een peeoo)
reading-lamp	una lampada	oonah lahmpahdah
soap	una saponetta	oonah sahpoanehttah
writing-paper	della carta da lettere	dayllah kahrtah dah lehttayray
Where's the ...?	Dov'è ...?	doavai
bathroom	il bagno	eel baañoa
dining-room	la sala da pranzo	lah saalah dah prahndzoa
emergency exit	l'uscita di sicurezza	loosheetah dee seekoo-rehtsah
hairdresser's	il parrucchiere	eel pahrrookkeeayray
lift (elevator)	l'ascensore	lahshaynsoaray
Where are the toilets?	Dove sono i gabinetti?	doavay soanoa ee gahbee-nehttee

BREAKFAST, see page 38

Telephone—Post (mail) *Telefono—Posta*

Can you get me Rome 123-45-67?	**Può passarmi Roma 123-45-67?**	pwo pahssahrmee roamah 123-45-67
How much are my telephone charges?	**Quanto devo pagare per la telefonata?**	kwahntoa dayvoa pahgaaray pair lah taylayfoanaatah
Do you have stamps?	**Ha dei francobolli?**	ah daiee frahngkoaboallee
Would you please mail this for me?	**Può spedirmi questo, per favore?**	pwo spaydeermee kooaystoa pair fahvoaray
Are there any messages for me?	**Vi sono messaggi per me?**	vee soanoa mayssahdjee pair mai
Is there any mail for me?	**C'è posta per me?**	chai postah pair mai

Difficulties *Difficoltà*

The...doesn't work.	**...non funziona.**	...noan foontseeoanah
air conditioner	**il condizionatore d'aria**	eel koandeetseeoanahtoaray daareeah
fan	**il ventilatore**	eel vaynteelahtoaray
heating	**il riscaldamento**	eel reeskahldahmayntoa
light	**la luce**	lah loochay
radio	**la radio**	lah raadeeoa
television	**il televisore**	eel taylayveezoaray
The tap (faucet) is dripping.	**Il rubinetto sgocciola.**	eel roobeenehttoa zgotchoalah
There's no hot water.	**Non c'è acqua calda.**	noan chai ahkkwah kahldah
The wash-basin is blocked.	**Il lavabo è otturato.**	eel lahvaaboa ai ottooraatoa
The window is jammed.	**La finestra è incastrata.**	lah feenehstrah ai eengkahstraatah
The curtains are stuck.	**Le tende sono bloccate.**	lay taynday soanoa blokkaatay
The bulb is burned out.	**La lampadina è bruciata.**	lah lahmpahdeenah ai broochaatah
My room has not been made up.	**La mia camera non è stata rifatta.**	lah meeah kaamayrah noan ai staatah reefahttah

POST OFFICE AND TELEPHONE, see page 132

The ... is broken.	... è rotto(a).	... ai rottoa(ah)
blind	la persiana	lah pairseeaanah
lamp	la lampada	lah lahmpahdah
plug	la spina	lah speenah
shutter	l'imposta	leempoastah
switch	l'interruttore	leentayrroottoaray
Can you get it repaired?	Può ripararlo(la)?	pwo reepahrahrloa(lah)

Laundry—Dry cleaner's *Lavanderia—Lavanderia a secco*

I want these clothes ...	Voglio far ... questi abiti.	volyoa faar ... kooaystee aabeetee
cleaned	pulire	pooleeray
ironed	stirare	steeraaray
pressed	stirare a vapore	steeraaray ah vahpoaray
washed	lavare	lahvaaray
When will they be ready?	Quando saranno pronti?	kwahndoa sahrahnnoa proantee
I need them ...	Ne ho bisogno ...	nay oa beezoañoa
tonight	stasera	stahsayrah
tomorrow	domani	doamaanee
before Friday	prima di venerdì	preemah dee vaynayrdee
Can you ... this?	Mi può ... questo?	mee pwo ... kooaystoa
mend	rammendare	rahmmayndaaray
patch	rappezzare	rappehttsaaray
stitch	cucire	koocheeray
Can you sew on this button?	Può attaccare questo bottone?	pwo ahttahkkaaray kooaystoa boattoanay
Can you get this stain out?	Mi può togliere questa macchia?	mee pwo tolyayray kooaystah mahkkeeah
Can this be invisibly mended?	Mi può fare un rammendo invisibile?	mee pwo faaray oon rahmmayndoa eenveezeebeelay
Is my laundry ready?	È pronta la mia biancheria?	ai prontah lah meeah beeahngkayreeah
This isn't mine.	Questo non è mio.	kooaystoa noan ai meeoa
There's something missing.	Manca un capo.	mahngkah oon kaapoa
There's a hole in this.	C'è un buco in questo.	chai oon bookoa een kooaystoa

Albergo

Hairdresser—Barber   *Parrucchiere—Barbiere*

Is there a hairdresser/ beauty salon in the hotel?	C'è il parrucchiere/ l'istituto di bellezza nell'albergo?	chai eel pahrrookkeeayray/ leesteetootoa dee behllehttsah nayllahlbayrgoa
Can I make an appointment for Thursday?	Posso avere un appuntamento per giovedì?	possoa ahvayray oon ahppoontahmayntoa pair joavaydee
I'd like it cut and shaped.	Vorrei il taglio e la messa in piega.	vorraiee eel taalyoa ay lah mayssah een peeaygah
I want a haircut, please.	Voglio il taglio dei capelli, per favore.	volyoa eel taalyoa daiee kahpehllee pair fahvoaray
bleach	una decolorazione	oonah daykoaloaraht-seeooanay
blow-dry	l'asciugatura col fono	lashoogahtoorah kol fawno
colour rinse	un cachet	oon kahshay
dye	una tintura	oonah teentoorah
face-pack	la maschera di bellezza	lah mahskayrah dee behllehttsah
manicure	la manicure	lah mahneekoor
permanent wave	la permanente	lah pairmahnayntay
setting lotion	un fissatore	oon feessahtoaray
shampoo and set	shampoo e messa in piega	"shampoo" ay mayssah een peeaygah
with a fringe (bangs)	con la frangia	kon lah frahnjah
I'd like a shampoo for ... hair.	Vorrei uno shampoo per capelli ...	vorraiee oonoa "shampoo" pair kahpehllee
normal/dry/ greasy (oily)	normali/secchi/ grassi	noarmaalee/saykkee/ grahssee
Do you have a colour chart?	Avete una tabella dei colori?	ahvaytay oonah tahbayllah daiee koaloaree
Don't cut it too short.	Non li tagli troppo corti.	noan lee taalyee troppoa koartee
A little more off the ...	Ancora un po'...	ahngkoarah oon po
back	dietro	deeaytroa
neck	sul collo	sool kolloa
sides	ai lati	ahee laatee
top	in cima	een cheemah
I don't want any hairspray.	Non voglio lacca.	noan volyoa lahkkah

DAYS OF THE WEEK, see page 151

I'd like a shave.	**Vorrei che mi radesse.**	vorraiee kay mee rahdayssay
Would you please trim my ...?	**Per favore, vuole spuntarmi ...?**	pair fahvoaray vwawlay spoontahrmee
beard	**la barba**	lah bahrbah
moustache	**i baffi**	ee bahffee
sideboards (sideburns)	**le basette**	lay bahzayttay

Checking out   *Partenza*

May I please have my bill?	**Posso avere il conto, per favore?**	possoa ahvayray eel koantoa pair fahvoaray
I'm leaving early in the morning. Please have my bill ready.	**Partirò domani mattina presto. Mi prepari il conto, per favore.**	pahrteeroa doamaanee mahtteenah prehstoa. mee praypaaree eel koantoa pair fahvoaray
We'll be checking out around noon.	**Partiremo verso mezzogiorno.**	pahrteeraymoa vehrsoa mehdzoajoarnoa
I must leave at once.	**Devo partire immediatamente.**	dayvoa pahrteeray eemmaydeeahtahmayntay
Is everything included?	**È tutto incluso?**	ai toottoa eengkloozoa
Can I pay by credit card?	**Posso pagare con la carta di credito?**	possoa pahgaaray kon lah kahrtah dee kraydeetoa
You've made a mistake in this bill, I think.	**Ha fatto un errore nel conto, credo.**	ah fahttoa oon ehrroaray nayl koantoa kraydoa
Can you get us a taxi?	**Può chiamarci un taxi?**	pwo keeahmahrchee oon "taxi"
Would you send someone to bring down our luggage?	**Può mandare qualcuno a portare giù i nostri bagagli?**	pwo mahndaaray kwahl-koonoa ah portaaray joo ee nostree bahgaalyee
Here's the forwarding address.	**Ecco il mio prossimo indirizzo.**	ehkkoa eel meeoa prosseemoa eendeereettsoa
You have my home address.	**Avete il mio indirizzo abituale.**	ahvaytay eel meeoa eendeereettsoa ahbeetooaalay
It's been a very enjoyable stay.	**È stato un soggiorno molto piacevole.**	ai staatoa oon soadjoarnoa moaltoa peeahchayvoalay

TIPPING, see inside back-cover

Camping *Campeggio*

In Italy there are many authorized camping sites with excellent facilities. Most camp sites are equipped with water, electricity and toilets. You will find them listed in the telephone directory, under *Campeggio*. The local tourist office has a list of sites, tariffs and facilities available. The Touring Club Italiano also publish a list of campsites and touristic villages. It is on sale in bookshops.

Is there a camp site near here?	C'è un campeggio qui vicino?	chai oon kahmpaydjoa kooee veecheenoa
Can we camp here?	Possiamo campeggiare qui?	posseeaamoa kahmpaydjaaray kooee
Have you room for a tent/caravan (trailer)?	C'è posto per una tenda/una roulotte?	chai poastoa pair oonah taindah/oonah roolot
What's the charge ...?	Quanto si paga ...?	kwahntoa see paagah
per day	al giorno	ahl joarnoa
per person	per persona	pair payrsoanah
for a car	per una macchina	pair oonah mahkkeenah
for a tent	per una tenda	pair oonah taindah
for a caravan (trailer)	per una roulotte	pair oonah roolot
Is the tourist tax included?	È compresa la tassa di soggiorno?	ai koampraysah lah tahssah dee soadjoarnoa
Is there/Are there (a) ...?	C'è/Ci sono ...?	chai/chee soanoa
drinking water	l'acqua potabile	lahkkwah poataabeelay
electricity	l'elettricità	laylehttreecheetah
playground	il parco giochi	eel pahrkoa joakee
restaurant	il ristorante	eel reestoarahntay
shopping facilities	dei negozi	daiee naygotsee
swimming pool	la piscina	lah peesheenah
Where are the showers/toilets?	Dove sono le docce/i gabinetti?	doavay soanoa lay dotchay/ee gahbeenayttee
Where can I get butane gas?	Dove posso trovare del gas butano?	doavay possoa trovaaray dayl gahz bootaanoa
Is there a youth hostel near here?	C'è un ostello della gioventù qui vicino?	chai oon oastehlloa dayllah joavayntoo kooee veecheenoa

CAMPING EQUIPMENT, see page 106

Eating out

There are various types of places to eat and drink in Italy.
Here are some of them:

Autogrill (**ow**toagreel)	large restaurant on a motorway (express-way); usually table and cafeteria service available.
Bar (bahr)	bar; can be found on virtually every street corner; coffee and drinks served. In most of them you first have to get a ticket from the cashier. Then you go to the counter and order what you want. Only a few bars have tables and chairs. If you want to be served at a table, the charge for your drinks and food will be somewhat higher.
Caffè (kahf**fai**)	coffee shop; generally food isn't served there except for breakfast. If it offers *panini o toasts* you'll be able to get a snack. Coffee shops always serve alcoholic beverages.
Gelateria (jaylahtay**ree**ah)	ice-cream parlour; Italian ice-cream is very tasty, rich and creamy, often reminiscent of old-fashioned, homemade ice-cream.
Locanda (lo**kahn**dah)	simple restaurants serving local dishes.
Osteria (oastay**ree**ah)	inn; wine and simple food are served.
Paninoteca (pahneenoa**tay**kah)	a sort of coffee shop where you can find a great variety of sandwiches *(panini)* served hot or cold.
Pizzeria (peett**say**reeah)	pizza parlour; often other dishes are served, too.
Ristorante (reestoa**rahn**tay)	You'll encounter restaurants classified by stars, forks and knives and endorsed by everyone including travel agencies, auto-mobile associations and gastronomic guilds. Bear in mind that any form of classification is relative. Some restaurants are judged accord-ing to their fancy décor while others—linen and chandeliers aside—are rated merely by the quality of their cooking.

Rosticceria (roasteetchayreeah)	originally, it was a shop specializing in grilled meats, chicken and fish. But today *rosticcerie* often have tables where you eat grilled food on the premises.
Sala da tè (saalah dah tai)	serves ice-cream and pastries.
Taverna (tahvehrnah)	a more modest type of *trattoria*.
Tavola calda (taavoalah kahldah)	''hot table''; a cafeteria-style restaurant serving hot dishes at fairly low prices. They're usually crowded but quick; you may have to eat standing up.
Trattoria (trahttoareeah)	a medium-priced restaurant serving meals and drink. The food is simple but can be surprisingly good if you happen to hit upon the right place.

Most restaurants display a menu in the window. Many offer a tourist menu *(menù turistico),* a fixed-price three- or four-course meal with limited choice, or the speciality of the day *(piatto del giorno).*

All restaurants, no matter how modest, must now issue a formal bill *(la ricevuta fiscale)* with VAT, or sales tax *(I.V.A.).* A customer may actually be stopped outside the premises and fined if he cannot produce this receipt. The bill usually includes cover *(il coperto)* and service *(il servizio)* charges as well.

Meal times   *Orari dei pasti*

Breakfast *(la colazione*—lah kolahtseeoanay) at the hotel is normally served from 7 to 10 a.m. (See page 38 for a breakfast menu.)

Lunch *(il pranzo*—eel **prahn**dzoa) is served from 12.30 to 2 p.m.

Dinner *(la cena*—lah **chay**nah) begins at 7 or 8 p.m., but hotels tend to open their dining rooms earlier for the foreign tourists.

TIPPING, see inside back-cover

Note: The names of meals can be confusing. Lunch is sometimes called *colazione* and dinner *pranzo,* especially in towns. If you are invited out, make sure of the time, so you don't turn up at the wrong meal.

Italian cuisine   *Cucina italiana*

To many foreigners, Italian cooking means *spaghetti, macaroni, tagliatelle...* in other words, pasta. In fact, you will be amazed at the rich variety available: tasty hors d'œuvres, long-simmered soups, traditional meat dishes, fresh fish and shellfish, high-quality poultry, an incredible number of cheeses, not to mention the magnificent cakes and ice-cream.

Each region has its own speciality, never lacking in flavour or originality, inspired by sun-drenched fruit and vegetables. Italian cooking is like the country itself: colourful, happy, generous, exuberant.

Cosa desidera?	What would you like?
Le consiglio questo.	I recommend this.
Cosa desidera da bere?	What would you like to drink?
Non abbiamo ...	We haven't got ...
Vuole ...?	Do you want ...?

Hungry?   *Ha fame?*

I'm hungry/I'm thirsty	**Ho fame/Ho sete.**	oa faamay/oa saytay
Can you recommend a good restaurant?	**Può consigliarmi un buon ristorante?**	pwo koanseelyaarmee oon bwon reestoarahntay
Are there any inexpensive restaurants around here?	**Vi sono dei ristoranti economici qui vicino?**	vee soanoa daiee reestoarahntee aykoanawmeechee kooee veecheenoa

If you want to be sure of getting a table in a well-known restaurant, it may be better to telephone in advance.

I'd like to reserve a table for 4.	**Vorrei riservare un tavolo per 4.**	vorraiee reesehrvaaray oon taavoala pair 4
We'll come at 8.	**Verremo alle 8.**	vayrraymoa ahllay 8
Could we have a table ...?	**Potremmo avere un tavolo ...?**	poatraymmoa ahvayray oon taavoaloa
in the corner	**d'angolo**	dahnggoaloa
by the window	**vicino alla finestra**	veecheenoa ahllah feenaystrah
outside	**all'aperto**	ahllahpehrtoa
on the terrace	**sulla terrazza**	soollah tayrrahttsah
in a non-smoking area	**nel settore per non fumatori**	nayl sehttoaray pair noan foomahtoaree

Asking and ordering   *Chiedere e ordinare*

Waiter/Waitress!	**Cameriere/ Cameriera!**	kahmayreeairay/kahmay-reeairah
I'd like something to eat/drink.	**Vorrei mangiare/bere qualcosa.**	vorraiee mahnjaaray/bayray kwahlkawsah
May I have the menu, please?	**Posso avere il menù?**	possoa ahvayray eel maynoo
Do you have a set menu/local dishes?	**Avete un menù a prezzo fisso/dei piatti locali?**	ahvaytay oon maynoo ah prehttsoa feessoa/daiee peeahttee loakaalee
What do you recommend?	**Cosa consiglia?**	kawsah konseelyah
I'd like ...	**Vorrei ...**	vorraiee
Could we have a/ an ..., please?	**Potremmo avere ..., per favore?**	poatraymmoa ahvayray ... pair fahvoaray
ashtray	**un portacenere**	oon portahchaynayray
cup	**una tazza**	oonah tahttsah
extra chair	**una sedia in più**	oonah saideeah een peeoo
fork	**una forchetta**	oonah forkehttah
glass	**un bicchiere**	oon beekkeeairay
knife	**un coltello**	oon koaltehlloa
napkin (serviette)	**un tovagliolo**	oon toavahlyawloa
plate	**un piatto**	oon peeahttoa
spoon	**un cucchiaio**	oon kookkeeaaeeoa
May I have some ...?	**Potrei avere ...?**	poatraiee ahvayray
bread	**del pane**	dayl paanay
butter	**del burro**	dayl boorroa

NUMBERS, see page 147

lemon	**del limone**	dayl leemoanay
mustard	**della senape**	dayllah saynahpay
oil	**dell'olio**	dayllolyoa
pepper	**del pepe**	dayl paypay
salt	**del sale**	dayl saalay
seasoning	**del condimento**	dayl koandeemayntoa
sugar	**dello zucchero**	daylloa tsookkayroa
vinegar	**dell'aceto**	dayllah**chay**toa

Some useful expressions for dieters or those with special requirements:

I'm on a diet.	**Sono a dieta.**	soanoa ah deeaytah
I mustn't eat food containing ...	**Non devo mangiare cibi che contengono ...**	noan dayvoa mahnjaaray cheebee kay koantayng**g**oanoa
flour/fat	**farina/grasso**	fahreenah/grahssoa
salt/sugar	**sale/zucchero**	saalay/tsookkayroa
Do you have ... for diabetics?	**Avete ... per diabetici?**	ahvaytay ... pair deeahbaiteechee
cakes	**dei dolci**	daiee doalchee
fruit juice	**del succo di frutta**	dayl sookkoa dee froottah
special menu	**un menù speciale**	oon maynoo spaychaalay
Do you have vegetarian dishes?	**Avete dei piatti vegetariani?**	ahvaytay daiee peeahttee vayjaytahreeaanee
Could I have ... instead of the dessert?	**Potrei avere ... invece del dessert?**	potraiee ahvayray ... eenvaychay dayl dayssehr
Can I have an artificial sweetener?	**Posso avere del dolcificante?**	possoa ahvayray dayl doalcheefeekahntay

And ...

I'd like some more.	**Ne vorrei ancora.**	nai vorraiee ahngkoarah
Can I have more ..., please.	**Posso avere ancora un po' di ...?**	possoa ahvayray ahngkoarah oon po dee
Just a small portion.	**Una piccola porzione.**	oonah peekkoalah poartseeoanay
Nothing more, thanks.	**Nient'altro, grazie.**	neeayntahltroa graatseeay
Where are the toilets?	**Dove sono i gabinetti?**	doavay soanoa ee gahbeenayttee

Breakfast *Colazione*

Italians just have a *cappuccino* and a brioche for breakfast.
Hotels usually propose coffee or tea, bread, butter and jam.
You can ask for fruit juice, an egg and toast, if you like a
more copious breakfast.

I'd like breakfast, please.	**Vorrei fare colazione.**	vorraiee faaray kolah- tseeoanay
I'll have a/an/ some ...	**Desidero ...**	dayzeedayroa
bacon and eggs	**uova e pancetta**	wawvah ay pahnchehttah
boiled egg	**un uovo alla coque**	oon wawvoa ahllah kok
soft/hard	**molle/sodo**	mollay/sodoa
cereal	**dei cereali**	daiee chehrehaalee
eggs	**delle uova**	dayllay wawvah
fried eggs	**delle uova fritte**	dayllay wawvah freettay
scrambled eggs	**delle uova strapazzate**	dayllay wawvah strahpahttsaatay
fruit juice	**un succo di frutta**	oon sookkoa dee froottah
grapefruit	**pompelmo**	pompaylmoa
orange	**arancia**	ahrahnchah
ham and eggs	**uova e prosciutto**	wawvah ay proashoottoa
jam	**della marmellata**	dayllah mahrmayllaatah
marmalade	**della marmellata d'arance**	dayllah mahrmayllaatah dahrahnchay
toast	**del pane tostato**	dayl paanay tostaatoa
May I have some ...?	**Posso avere ...?**	possoa ahvayray
bread	**del pane**	dayl paanay
butter	**del burro**	dayl boorroa
(hot) chocolate	**una cioccolata (calda)**	oonah choakkoalaatah (kahldah)
coffee	**un caffè**	oon kahffai
decaffeinated	**decaffeinato**	daykahffeheenaatoa
black	**nero**	nayroa
with milk	**macchiato**	mahkkeeaatoa
honey	**del miele**	dayl meeaylay
milk	**del latte**	dayl lahttay
cold/hot	**freddo/caldo**	frayddoa/kahldoa
rolls	**dei panini**	daiee pahneenee
tea	**del tè**	dayl tai
with milk	**con latte**	kon lahttay
with lemon	**con limone**	kon leemoanay
(hot) water	**dell'acqua (calda)**	dayllahkkwah (kahldah)

What's on the menu?   *Che c'è sul menù?*

Under the headings below you'll find alphabetical lists of
dishes that might be offered on an Italian menu with their
English equivalent. You can simply show the book to the
waiter. If you want some cheese, for instance, let *him* point
to what's available on the appropriate list. Use pages 36 and
37 for ordering in general.

	page	
Starters (Appetizers)	41	**Antipasti**
Pizza	42	**Pizza**
Omelets	42	**Frittate**
Soups	43	**Minestre, zuppe**
Pasta	44	**Pasta**
Sauces	44	**Salse**
Rice	45	**Riso**
Fish and seafood	46	**Pesce e frutti di mare**
Meat	48	**Carne**
Game and poultry	50	**Cacciagione e pollame**
Vegetables and salads	52	**Verdure e insalate**
Spices and herbs	53	**Spezie e odori**
Cheese	53	**Formaggio**
Fruit	54	**Frutta**
Dessert	55	**Dolce**
Drinks	56	**Bevande**
Wine	56	**Vino**
Nonalcoholic drinks	60	**Bevande analcoliche**
Snacks—Picnic	63	**Spuntini—Picnic**

Note: Italian cooking remains essentially regional. Each of
the nation's 18 regions has its own specialities. There are, of
course, many well-known dishes that are common to all Italy.
But here again the terminology may vary from place to place.
(There are at least half a dozen names for octopus or squid!)
So in the lists that follow, be prepared for regional variations.

Ristorante

Reading the menu *Per leggere il menù*

Menù a prezzo fisso	Set menu
Piatto del giorno	Dish of the day
Lo chef consiglia ...	The chef recommends ...
Specialità della casa	Specialities of the house
Specialità locali	Local specialities
Contorno a scelta	Choice of vegetables
I nostri piatti di carne sono serviti con contorno	Our meat dishes are accompanied by vegetables
Su ordinazione	Made to order
Supplemento	Extra charge
Verdure di stagione	Vegetables in season
Attesa: 15 minuti	Waiting time: 15 minutes
Pane, grissini e coperto L. ...	Bread, *grissini* and cover L. ...
A scelta	Choice
Piatti freddi	Cold dishes

antipasti	ahnteepahstee	hors d'œuvres
bevande	bayvahnday	drinks
cacciagione	kahtchahjoanay	game
carne	kahrnay	meat
carne ai ferri	kahrnay ahee fehrree	grilled meat
crostacei	kroastahchayee	shellfish
dessert	dayssehr	dessert
formaggi	foarmahdjee	cheese
frutta	froottah	fruit
frutti di mare	froottee dee maaray	seafood
gelati	jaylaatee	ice-cream
insalate	eensahlaatay	salads
minestre	meenehstray	soups
pastasciutta	pahstahshoottah	pasta
pesci	payshee	fish
pollame	poallaamay	poultry
primi piatti	preemee peeahttee	first course
riso	reezoa	rice
secondi piatti	saykoandee peeahttee	second (main) course
verdure	vehrdooray	vegetables
vini	veenee	wines

Appetizers *Antipasti*

I'd like an appetizer.	**Vorrei un antipasto.**	vorraiee oon ahnteepahstoa
acciughe	ahtchoogay	anchovies
affettati misti	ahffayttaatee meestee	cold cuts of pork
antipasto assortito	ahnteepahtoa ahssoarteetoa	assorted appetizer
carciofi	kahrchofee	artichokes
caviale	kahveeaalay	caviar
coppa	koappah	cured pork shoulder
frutti di mare	froottee dee maaray	mixed seafood
gamberetti	gahmbayrayttee	shrimps
mortadella	moartahdehllah	Bologna sausage
olive	oleevay	olives
ostriche	ostreekay	oysters
prosciutto	proashoottoa	ham
cotto	kottoa	cooked ham
crudo di Parma	kroodoa dee pahrmah	cured ham from Parma
salame	sahlaamay	salami
salmone affumicato	sahlmoanay affoomeekaatoa	smoked salmon
sardine all'olio	sahrdeenay ahllolyoa	sardines in oil
sottaceti	soattahchaytee	pickled vegetables
tonno	tonnoa	tunny in oil

bagna cauda
(baañah kahoodah)
raw vegetables accompanied by a hot sauce made from anchovies, garlic, oil, butter and sometimes truffles (Northern Italy)

carciofini sottolio
(kahrchofeenee soattolyoa)
artichoke hearts in olive oil

insalata di frutti di mare
(eensahlaatah dee froottee dee maaray)
prawns and squid with lemon, pickles and olives

insalata di pollo
(eensahlaatah dee poalloa)
chicken salad with green salad, lemon, cream

insalata russa
(eensahlaatah roossah)
diced boiled vegetables in mayonnaise

mozzarella con pomodori
(motsahrayllah kon poamoadawree)
mozzarella cheese with tomatoes, basilic, pepper and olive oil

prosciutto crudo con melone
(proashoottoa kroodoa kon mayloanay)

sliced melon with cured ham from Parma

Pizza

Pizza (plural *pizze*) is surely one of Italy's best-known culinary exports. And the variety of toppings is endless, from simple cheese and tomato to assorted seafood. A *calzone* has basically the same ingredients, but the pastry forms a sort of sealed sandwich, with the filling inside.

Here are the best known variations on the theme:

capricciosa
(kahpreetchoasah)

the cook's speciality

margherita
(mahrgayreetah)

named after Italy's first queen, the *pizza* ingredients, tomato, cheese and basil, reflect the national colours

napoletana
(nahpoalaytaanah)

the classic *pizza* with anchovies, ham, capers, tomatoes, cheese and oregano

quattro stagioni
(kwahttroa stahjoanee)

"four seasons" – containing a variety of vegetables: tomatoes, artichoke, mushrooms, olives, plus cheese, ham and bacon

siciliana
(seecheeleeaanah)

with black olives, capers and cheese

Omelets *Frittate*

I'd like an omelet.	**Vorrei una frittata.**	vorraiee oonah freettaatah
frittata	freettaatah	omelet
di asparagi	dee ahspaarahjee	asparagus
di carciofi	dee kahrchofee	artichokes
di cipolle	dee cheepoallay	onions
di spinaci	dee speenaachee	spinach
di zucchine	dee tsookkeenay	dried baby marrow (zucchini)
frittata campagnola	freettaatah kahmpah-ñoalah	an omelet with onion, grated cheese, milk and cream
frittata primaverile	freettaatah preemah-vayreelay	omelet with vegetables

Soups *Minestre, zuppe*

In Italy, soup goes by many names, as the following list shows. Some of them are sufficient for a main course. An Italian meal always includes a soup or a dish of *pastasciutta*.

brodo	brawdoa	bouillon, broth, soup
di manzo	dee mahndzoa	meat broth
di pollo	dee poalloa	chicken broth
busecca	boozaykkah	thick tripe, vegetable and bean soup
cacciucco	kahtchookkoa	spicy seafood stew (chowder)
crema di legumi	krehmah dee laygoomee	vegetable cream soup
crema di pomodori	krehmah dee poamoa-dawree	tomato cream soup
minestra	meenehstrah	soup
in brodo	een brawdoa	bouillon with noodles or rice
di funghi	dee foonggee	cream of mushroom
minestrone	meenehstroanay	a thick vegetable soup (sometimes with noodles) sprinkled with parmesan cheese
passato di verdura	pahssaatoa dee vehr-doorah	mashed vegetable soup, generally with croutons
pasta e fagioli	pahstah ay fahjoalee	noodles and beans
pastina in brodo	pahsteenah een brawdoa	broth with little noodles
zuppa	tsooppah	soup
alla cacciatora	ahllah kahtchahtoarah	meat with mushrooms
alla marinara	ahllah mahreenaarah	spicy fish stew (chowder)
alla pavese	ahllah pahvayzay	consommé with poached egg, croutons and grated cheese
alla veneta	ahllah vaynaytah	vegetables with white wine and noodles
di datteri di mare	dee dahttayree dee maaray	sea dates (kind of mussel)
di frutti di mare	dee froottee dee maaray	seafood
di pesce	dee payshay	spicy fish stew (chowder)
di vongole	dee vonggoalay	clams and white wine

Pasta

Pasta (or *pastasciutta*), the generic name for a wide range of noodles and noodle-related dishes, constitutes the traditional Italian first course. In addition to the well-known *spaghetti,* pasta comes in a bewildering variety of sizes and shapes—ribbons, strings, tubes, shells or stars—known under as many different appellations. It can be served on its own, in broth, with butter or tomato sauce, stuffed with meat, cheese or vegetables, and is often accompanied by a highly flavoured sauce such as those described below.

agnolotti (ahñoalottee)	a round pasta parcel with a filling of chopped meat, vegetables and cheese
cannelloni (kahnnayllawnee)	tubular dough stuffed with meat, cheese or vegetables, covered with a white sauce and baked
cappelletti (kahppayllayttee)	small ravioli filled with meat, herbs, ham, cheese and eggs
fettuccine (fayttootcheenay)	narrow flat noodles
lasagne (lahzaañay)	thin layers of white or green *(lasagne verdi)* dough alternating with tomato sauce and sausage meat, white sauce and grated cheese; baked in the oven
rigatoni (reegahtawnee)	large macaroni, similar to *cannelloni* but smaller and ridged
tagliatelle (tahlyahtehllay)	flat noodles
tortellini (toartehlleenee)	rings of dough filled with seasoned minced meat and served in broth or with a sauce

Sauces *Salse*

It's the sauce that makes spaghetti and macaroni so delicious—Italian cooks are masters of the art.

aglio, olio, peperoncino (ahlyoa olyoa paypayroancheenoa)	garlic, olive oil, sweet peppers, anchovies and parmesan

al burro (ahl **boor**roa)	with butter and grated parmesan	
al sugo (ahl **soo**goa)	with tomato sauce and grated parmesan	
amatriciana (ahmahtree**chaa**nah)	tomatoes, red peppers, bacon, onions, garlic and white wine	
bolognese (boaloa**ñay**zay)	tomatoes, minced meat, onions and herbs	
carbonara (kahrboa**naa**rah)	smoked ham, cheese, eggs and olive oil	
carrettiera (kahrrayttee**ay**rah)	tuna, mushrooms, tomato purée, freshly ground pepper	
marinara (mahree**naa**rah)	tomatoes, olives, garlic, clams and mussels	
pesto (**pay**stoa)	basil leaves, garlic, cheese, and sometimes pine kernels and marjoram	
pommarola (poammah**raw**lah)	tomatoes, garlic, basil	
puttanesca (poottah**nay**skah)	capers, black olives, parsley, garlic, olive oil, black pepper	
ragù (rah**goo**)	like *bolognese*	
con le vongole (kon lay **voan**goalay)	clams, garlic, parsley, pepper, olive oil, sometimes tomatoes	

Rice *Riso*

In Northern Italy, a rice dish is often offered as a first course to replace pasta. Cooked on its own or together with vegetables, meat, herbs, fish and/or seafood, rice may also be served with a sauce.

risi e bisi	reesee ay **bee**see	rice with peas and bacon
riso in bianco	reesoa een bee**ahng**koa	boiled rice with butter and grated parmesan
risotto	ree**sot**toa	rice casserole
con fegatini	kon faygah**tee**nee	with chicken livers
con funghi	kon **foong**gee	with mushrooms
alla milanese	**ahl**lah meelah**nai**say	marrow, white wine, saffron and parmesan

46

Fish and seafood *Pesci e frutti di mare*

Don't miss the opportunity to sample some of the wide variety of fresh fish and seafood in coastal areas. Some inland regions offer special preparations of fish from their rivers, lakes and streams. Fish is most commonly baked or poached until just done, then dressed with a delicate sauce.

I'd like some fish.	**Vorrei del pesce.**	vorraiee dayl payshay
What kind of seafood do you have?	**Che genere di frutti di mare avete?**	kay jehnayray dee froottee dee maaray ahvaytay
acciughe	ahtchoogay	anchovies
aguglie	ahgoolyay	garfish
anguilla	ahnggooeellah	eel
aragosta	ahrahgoastah	lobster
aringa	ahreenggah	herring
arselle	ahrsehllay	scallops
baccalà	bahkkahlah	dried salt cod
bianchetti	beeahngkayttee	whitebait
branzino	brahndzeenoa	(sea) bass
calamaretti	kahlahmahrayttee	baby squid
calamari	kahlahmaaree	squid
carpa	kahrpah	carp
cozze	koatsay	mussels
dentice	dehnteechay	type of sea bream
eperlano	aypayrlaanoa	smelt
gamberetti	gahmbayrayttee	shrimps
gamberi	gahmbayree	crayfish
granchi	grahngkee	crabs
gronghi	groanggee	conger eel
lamprede	lahmprayday	lampreys
luccio	lootchoa	pike
lumache di mare	loomaakay dee maaray	sea snails
merlano	mayrlaanoa	whiting
merluzzo	mayrloottsoa	cod
nasello	nahsehlloa	coal-fish
orata	oaraatah	type of sea bream
ostriche	ostreekay	oysters
pesce persico	payshay pehrseekoa	perch
pesce spada	payshay spaadah	swordfish
polpo	poalpoa	octopus
razza	rahttsah	ray
ricci	reetchee	sea urchins
rombo	roamboa	turbot
salmone	sahlmoanay	salmon

sardine	sahrdeenay	sardines
scampi	skahmpee	prawns
scorfano	skoarfahnoa	sea-scorpion, sculpin
sgombro	zgoambroa	mackerel
seppia	sayppeeah	cuttlefish
sogliola	sawlyoalah	sole
spigola	speegoalah	sea bass
storione	stoareeoanay	sturgeon
tonno	toannoa	tunny (tuna)
triglie	treelyay	red mullet
trota	trawtah	trout
vongole	vonggoalay	clams

baked	**al forno**	ahl fornoa
boiled	**lesso**	layssoa
(deep) fried	**(ben) fritto**	(bain) freettoa
grilled	**alla griglia**	ahllah greelyah
marinated	**marinato**	mahreenaatoa
poached	**affogato**	ahffoagaatoa
smoked	**affumicato**	ahffoomeekaatoa
steamed	**cotto a vapore**	kottoa ah vahpoaray
stewed	**in umido**	een oomeedoa

Fish specialities *Specialità di pesce*

anguilla alla veneziana
(ahnggooeellah ahllah
vaynaytseeaanah)

eel cooked in sauce made from tunny
(tuna) and lemon

baccalà alla vicentina
(bahkkahlah ahllah
veechaynteenah)

cod cooked in milk with onion, garlic,
parsley, anchovies and cinnamon

fritto misto
(freettoa meestoa)

a fry of various small fish and shellfish

pesci in carpione
(payshee een kahrpeeoanay)

boiled fish, cooked in vinegar, served
cold with lemon

pesci al cartoccio
(payshee ahl kahrtotchoa)

baked in a parchment envelope with
onions, parsley and herbs

sgombri in umido
(zgoambree een oomeedoa)

stewed mackerel in white wine with
green peas

stoccafisso
(stoakkahfeessoa)

dried cod cooked with tomatoes,
olives and artichoke

sogliole alla mugnaia
(sawlyolay ahllah mooñaaeeah)

sole sautéed in butter, garnished with parsley and lemon

triglie alla livornese
(treelyay ahllah leevoarnaysay)

baked red mullet

Meat *Carne*

I'd like some ...   **Vorrei ...**   vorraiee

beef	**del manzo**	dayl **mahn**dzoa
lamb	**dell'agnello**	dayllah**ñeh**lloa
mutton	**del montone**	dayl moan**toa**nay
pork	**del maiale**	dayl maa**eeaa**lay
veal	**del vitello**	dayl vee**teh**lloa
animelle di vitello	ahnee**meh**llay dee vee**teh**lloa	sweetbreads
arrosto	ahr**roa**stoa	roast
bistecca	bees**tayk**kah	steak
di filetto	dee fee**leht**toa	rib steak
braciola	brah**choa**lah	chop
cosciotto	koa**shawt**toa	leg
costola	**kos**toalah	rib
costoletta	koastoa**layt**tah	cutlet
cervello	chayr**vehl**loa	brains
fegato	**fay**gahtoa	liver
fesa	**fay**sah	round cut from rump
filetto	fee**layt**toa	fillet
lingua	**leeng**gwah	tongue
lombata/lombo	loam**baa**tah/**loam**boa	loin
medaglioni	maydah**lyoa**nee	round fillet
midollo	mee**dol**loa	marrow
nodini	noa**dee**nee	veal chops
pancetta affumicata	pahn**cheht**tah ahffoo-mee**kaa**tah	bacon
polpette	poal**payt**tay	meatballs
polpettone	poalpayt**toa**nay	meat loaf of seasoned beef or veal
porcellino da latte/ porchetta	poarchayl**lee**noa dah **laht**tay/poar**kayt**tah	suck(l)ing pig
prosciutto	proa**shoot**toa	ham
rognoni	roa**ñoa**nee	kidneys
rosbif	**ros**beef	roast beef
salumi	sah**loo**mee	assorted pork products
salsicce	sahl**seet**chay	sausages

scaloppina	skahloappeenah	escalope	
spalla	spahllah	shoulder	
tripe	treeppay	tripe	

Meat dishes *Piatti di carne*

abbacchio (ahbbahkkeeoa)	roast lamb, often in a casserole with anchovies
bistecca alla fiorentina (beestaykkah ahllah feeoarayneenah)	a grilled steak flavoured with pepper, lemon juice and parsley
cima alla genovese (cheemah ahllah jaynoavaysay)	rolled veal stuffed with eggs, sausage and mushrooms
costata al prosciutto (koastaatah ahl proashoottoa)	a chop filled with ham, cheese and truffles; breaded and fried until golden brown
costoletta alla milanese (koastoalayttah ahllah meelahnaysay)	breaded veal cutlet, flavoured with cheese
fegato alla veneziana (faygahtoa ahllah vaynaytseeaanah)	thin slices of calf's liver fried with onions
involtini (eenvoalteenee)	thin slices of meat (beef, veal or pork) rolled and stuffed
ossi buchi (ossee bookee)	veal or beef knuckle braised and served in a highly flavoured sauce
piccata al marsala (peekkaatah ahl mahrsaalah)	thin veal escalope braised in marsala sauce
saltimbocca alla romana (sahlteemboakkah ahllah roamaanah)	veal escalope braised in marsala wine with ham and sage
scaloppina alla Valdostana (skahloappeenah ahllah vahldoastaanah)	veal escalope filled with cheese and ham
spezzatino (spaytsahteenoa)	meat or poultry stew
spiedino (speeaydeenoa)	pieces of meat grilled or roasted on a skewer

stracotto
(strahkottoa)

meat stew slowly cooked for several hours

trippe alla fiorentina
(treeppay ahllah feeoraynteenah)

tripe and beef braised in a tomato sauce, served with cheese

vitello tonnato
(veetaylloa toannaatoa)

cold veal with tuna fish sauce

zampone
(tsahmpoanay)

pig's trotter filled with seasoned pork, boiled and served in slices

How do you like your meat? *Come vuole la carne?*

baked	**al forno**	ahl fornoa
barbecued	**alla graticola/alla griglia**	ahllah grahteekoaliah/ ahllah greelyah
boiled	**lesso**	layssoa
braised	**brasato**	brahsaatoa
broiled	**allo spiedo**	ahlloa speeehdoa
casseroled	**in casseruola**	een kassayrwolah
fried	**fritto**	freettoa
grilled	**ai ferri**	ahee fehrree
roast(ed)	**arrosto**	ahrroastoa
spit-roasted	**allo spiedo**	ahlloa speeehdoa
stewed	**in umido**	een oomeedoa
stuffed	**farcito**	fahrcheetoa
underdone (rare)	**al sangue**	ahl sahnggooay
medium	**a puntino**	ah poonteenoa
well-done	**ben cotto**	bain kottoa

Game and poultry *Cacciagione e pollame*

Many small fowl not regarded as game birds in America or Britain are served as first or main courses in Italy. They're usually grilled or roasted. Among small fowl considered as gourmet dishes are lark, plover, thrush and ortolan.

I'd like some game.	**Vorrei della cacciagione.**	vorraiee dayllah kahtchahjoanay
What poultry dishes do you serve?	**Che piatti di pollame servite?**	kay peeahttee dee poallaamay sayrveetay

allodola	ahllodoalah	lark
anatra	aanahtrah	duck
beccaccia	baykkahtchah	woodcock
beccaccino	baykkahtcheenoa	snipe
camoscio	kahmoshoa	chamois
cappone	kahppoanay	capon
capretto	kahprayttoa	kid goat
capriolo	kahpreeoloa	roebuck
cervo	chehrvoa	deer
cinghiale	cheenggeeaalay	wild boar
coniglio	koaneelyoa	rabbit
fagiano	fahjaanoa	pheasant
faraona	fahrahoanah	guinea fowl
gallina	gahlleenah	stewing fowl
gallo cedrone	gahlloa chehdroanay	grouse
lepre	laipray	hare
oca	okah	goose
ortolano	oartoalaanoa	ortolan
pernice	payrneechay	partridge
piccione	peetchoanay	pigeon
piviere	peeveeehray	plover
pollo	poalloa	chicken
pollo novello	poalloa noavehlloa	spring chicken
quaglia	kwahlyah	quail
selvaggina	saylvahdjeenah	venison
tacchino	tahkkeenoa	turkey
tordo	toardoa	thrush

capretto ripieno al forno
(kahprayttoa reepeeaynoa ahl fornoa)

stuffed kid, oven-roasted

galletto amburghese
(gahllayttoa ahmboorgaysay)

young tender chicken, oven-roasted

palombacce allo spiedo
(pahloambahtchay ahlloa speeehdoa)

wood pigeon, spit-roasted

polenta e coniglio
(poalehntah ay koaneelyoa)

rabbit stew served with a mush made from maize flour (cornmeal mush)

polenta e uccelli
(poalehntah ay ootchehllee)

various small birds roasted on a spit and served with polenta (see immediately above)

pollo alla diavola
(poalloa ahllah deeaavoalah)

highly spiced and grilled chicken

Vegetables — Salads   *Verdure — Insalate*

What kind of vegetables have you got?	**Che genere di verdure avete?**	kay jehnayray dee vehrdooray ahvaytay
I'd like a (mixed) salad.	**Vorrei un'insalata (mista).**	vorraiee ooneensahlaatah (meestah)

asparagi	ahspaarahjee	asparagus
barbabietola	bahrbahbeeehtoalah	beetroot
broccoli	brokkolee	broccoli
carciofi	kahrchofee	artichokes
carote	kahrawtay	carrots
cavolfiore	kahvoalfeeoaray	cauliflower
cavolo	kaavoaloa	cabbage
cavolini di Bruxelles	kahvoaleenee dee broossayl	brussels sprouts
ceci	chaychee	chick-peas
cetriolini	chaytreeoaleenee	gherkins
cetriolo	chaytreeoloa	cucumber
cicoria	cheekoreeah	endive (Am. chicory)
cipolle	cheepollay	onions
fagioli	fahjoalee	haricot beans
fagiolini	fahjoaleenee	French (green) beans
fave	faavay	broad beans
finocchio	feenokkeeoa	fennel
funghi	foonggee	mushrooms
indivia	eendeeveeah	chicory (Am. endive)
insalata (verde)	eensahlaatah (vayrday)	(green) salad
lattuga	lahttoogah	lettuce
lenticchie	laynteekkeeay	lentils
melanzane	maylahntsaanay	aubergine (eggplant)
patate	pahtaatay	potatoes
peperoni	paypayroanee	sweet peppers
piselli	peesehllee	peas
pomodoro	poamoadawroa	tomato
porcini	poarcheenee	boletus mushrooms
porro	porroa	leeks
radicchio	rahdeekkeeoa	a kind of bitter, red and white lettuce
ravanelli	rahvahnehllee	radishes
sedano	sehdahnoa	celery
spinaci	speenaachee	spinach
tartufi	tahrtoofee	truffles
verdura mista	vehrdoorah meestah	mixed vegetables
verza	vehrdzah	green cabbage
zucca	tsookkah	pumpkin, gourd
zucchini	tsookkeenee	zucchini

Spices and herbs *Spezie e odori*

aglio	ahlyoa	garlic
basilico	bahzeeleekoa	basil
cannella	kahnnehllah	cinnamon
capperi	kahppehree	capers
chiodi di garofano	keeodee dee gahrofahnoa	cloves
cipollina	cheepoalleenah	chive
cumino	koomeenoa	cumin
lauro	lahooroa	bay
maggiorana	madjoaraanah	marjoram
menta	mayntah	mint
noce moscata	noachay moaskaatah	nutmeg
origano	oareegahnoa	origan
prezzemolo	prehttsaymoaloa	parsley
rosmarino	roazmahreenoa	rosemary
salvia	sahlveeah	sage
scalogno	skahloañoa	shallot
timo	teemoa	thyme
zafferano	dzahffehraanoa	saffron
zenzero	dzehndzehroa	ginger

Cheese *Formaggio*

Italy produces a great variety of cheese, many of them little known outside the locality in which they're made.

Bel Paese
(behl pahayzay)
smooth cheese with delicate taste

caciocavallo
(kahchoakahvahlloa)
firm, slightly sweet cheese from cow's or sheep's milk

gorgonzola
(goargoandzolah)
most famous of the Italian blue-veined cheese, rich with a tangy flavour

mozzarella
(motsahrehllah)
soft, unripened cheese with a bland, slightly sweet flavour, made from buffalo's milk in southern Italy, elsewhere with cow's milk

parmigiano (-reggiano)
(pahrmeejaanoa-raydjaanoa)
parmesan (also called *grana*), a hard cheese generally grated for use in hot dishes and pasta but also eaten alone

pecorino
(paykoareenoa)
a hard cheese made from sheep's milk

ricotta
(reekottah)
soft cow's or sheep's milk cheese

Fruit *Frutta*

Do you have fresh fruit?	**Avete della frutta fresca?**	ahvaytay dayllah froottah frayskah
I'd like a fresh fruit cocktail.	**Vorrei una macedonia di frutta.**	vorraiee oonah mahchaydo-neeah dee froottah

albicocca	ahlbeekokkah	apricot
ananas	ahnahnahss	pineapple
anguria	ahnggooreeah	watermelon
arachide	ahrahkeeday	peanuts
arancia	ahrahnchah	orange
banana	bahnaanah	banana
caco	kaakoa	persimmon
castagna	kahstaañah	chestnut
cedro	chaydroa	lime
ciliege	cheeleeayjay	cherries
cocomero	koakoamayroa	watermelon
cotogna	koatoañah	quince
datteri	dahttayree	dates
fico	feekoa	fig
fragole	fraagoalay	strawberries
lamponi	lahmpoanee	raspberries
limone	leemoanay	lemon
mandarino	mahndahreenoa	tangerine
mandorle	mahndoarlay	almonds
mela	maylah	apple
melone	mayloanay	melon
mirtilli	meerteellee	blueberries
more	moray	blackberries
nocciole	noatcholay	hazelnuts
noce di cocco	noachay dee kokkoa	coconut
noci	noachee	walnuts
pera	payrah	pear
pesca	pehskah	peach
pinoli	peenolee	pine kernels
pompelmo	poampaylmoa	grapefruit
prugna	prooñah	plum
prugna secca	prooñah saykkah	prune
ribes	reebays	redcurrants
ribes nero	reebays nayroa	blackcurrants
susina	soozeenah	plum
uva	oovah	grapes
bianca/nera	beeahngkah/nayrah	white/black
uva passa	oovah pahssah	raisins
uva spina	oovah speenah	gooseberries

Dessert *Dolce*

You'll find a profusion of cakes and tarts to round off the meal. Among the more interesting is the *zuppa inglese*—not a soup at all but a kind of trifle (see below). *Granita* is a partially frozen dessert made with coffee or fruit juice. Or try some of the delicious ice-cream for which Italy is renown.

I'd like a dessert, please.	**Vorrei un dessert, per favore.**	vorraiee oon dayssehr pair fahvoaray
What do you recommend?	**Cosa consiglia?**	kawsah koanseelyah
Something light, please.	**Qualcosa di leggero, per favore.**	kwahlkawsah dee laydjairoa pair fahvoaray
I'd like a slice of cake.	**Vorrei una fetta di torta.**	vorraiee oonah fehttah dee toartah
with/without (whipped) cream	**con/senza panna (montata)**	kon/sayntsah pahnnah (moantaatah)
budino	boodeenoa	pudding
crema	kraimah	custard
crostata di mele	kroastaatah dee maylay	apple pie
dolce	doalchay	cake
gelato	jaylaatoa	ice-cream
alla fragola	ahllah fraagoalah	strawberry
al limone	ahl leemoanay	lemon
alla vaniglia	ahllah vahneelyah	vanilla
misto	meestoa	mixed
tartufi di cioccolata	tahrtoofee dee choakkoalaatah	chocolate truffles
torta	toartah	cake
di cioccolata	dee choakkoalaatah	chocolate cake
di frutta	dee froottah	fruit cake

cassata (kassaatah)	ice cream with candied fruit (Am. spumoni)
cassata siciliana (kassaatah seecheeleeaanah)	sponge cake garnished with sweet cream cheese, chocolate and candied fruit
zabaglione (dzahbahlyoanay)	a mixture of eggyolks, sugar and Marsala wine; served warm
zuppa inglese (dzooppah eengglaysay)	sponge cake steeped in rum with candied fruit and custard or whipped cream

Drinks *Bevande*

Aperitifs *Aperitivi*

The average Italian is just as fond of his favourite *aperitivo* (ahpehree**tee**voa) as we are of our cocktail or highball. Often bittersweet, some aperitifs have a wine and brandy base with herbs and bitters while others may have a vegetable base. Here are some aperitifs you may want to try:

Americano (ahmayreekaanoa)	despite its name, one of the most popular Italian aperitifs; a vermouth to which bitters, brandy and lemon peel are added
Aperol (ahpayroal)	a non-alcoholic bitters
Campari (kahmpaaree)	reddish-brown bitters, flavoured with orange peel and herbs, it has a quinine taste
Cynar (cheenaar)	produced from artichoke
Martini (mahrteenee)	a brand-name vermouth not to be confused with a martini cocktail

neat (straight)	**liscio**	leeshoa
on the rocks	**con ghiaccio**	kon geeahtchoa
with (seltzer) water	**con acqua (di seltz)**	kon ahkkwah (dee sehltz)

> **SALUTE!/CIN-CIN!**
> (sahlootay/cheen cheen)
> YOUR HEALTH!/CHEERS!

Wine *Vino*

Italy is one of the most important wine producers in Europe. Vineyards are found all over the Italian peninsula and islands.

Some of the country's most reputed wines (like *Barbaresco, Barbera* and *Barolo*) come from the Piedmont in north-western Italy. But most other regions have noted wine, too. This is your opportunity to sample local wine, some of which is of surprisingly good quality.

Chianti is doubtless Italy's best-known wine outside of its borders. The best of it is produced between Florence and Siena. The term *Chianti classico* on the label indicates that the production of this wine has been carefully supervised. A *Chianti* of superior quality carries the term *riserva* on the label.

Some restaurants list their wines in a corner of the menu while others have them marked up on the wall. As much of the nation's wine doesn't travel well, don't expect a *trattoria* to offer more than a few types of wine. Most of the wine must be drunk young so don't look too hard for vintage labels. In smaller places you might get *vino aperto* (open wine) or *vino della casa* (house wine) at a moderate price, served in one-quarter, one-half or one-litre carafes.

May I have the wine list, please.	**Per favore, mi porti la lista dei vini.**	pair fahvoaray mee portee lah leestah daiee veenee
I'd like a bottle of white/red wine.	**Vorrei una bottiglia di vino bianco/ rosso.**	vorraiee oonah botteelyah dee veenoa beeahngkoa/ roassoa
half a bottle	**mezza bottiglia**	mehdzah botteelyah
a carafe	**una caraffa**	oonah kahrahffah
half a litre	**mezzo litro**	mehdzoa leetroa
a glass	**un bicchiere**	oon beekkeeairay
A bottle of champagne, please.	**Una bottiglia di champagne, per favore.**	oonah botteelyah dee shampahñ pair fahvoaray
Where does this wine come from?	**Da dove viene questo vino?**	dah doavay veeaynay kooaystoa veenoa

red	**rosso**	roassoa
white	**bianco**	beeahngkoa
rosé	**rosatello**	rawzahtehlloa
dry	**secco**	sehkkoa
full-bodied	**pieno**	peeaynoa
light	**leggero**	laydjairoa
sparkling	**spumante**	spoomahntay
sweet	**dolce**	doalchay

The following chart will help you to choose your wine if you want to do some serious wine-tasting.

Type of wine	Examples	Accompanies
sweet white wine	*Orvieto* from Umbria (the export variety is usually dry), *Aleatico* and *Vino Santo* from Tuscany and the famed *Marsala* from Sicily.	desserts, especially custard, pudding, cake
dry white wine	*Frascati* from Latium or *Verdicchio dei Castelli di Jesi* from the Adriatic Marches; local white wine generally falls into this category	fish, seafood, cold or boiled meat, fowl (the unconventional Romans enjoy drinking *Frascati* with a heavy meal)
rosé	*Lagrein* from Trentino-Alto Adige	goes with almost anything but especially cold dishes, eggs, pork and lamb
light-bodied red wine	*Bardolino* and *Valpolicella* from the Lake of Garda; local red wine, including Italian-Swiss *Merlot*, usually fits this category	roast chicken, turkey, veal, lamb, steaks, ham, liver, quail, pheasant, soft-textured cheeses, stews and pasta
full-bodied red wine	*Barolo, Barbera* and *Barbaresco* from Piedmont	duck, goose, kidneys, most game, tangy cheese like *gorgonzola*—in short, any strong-flavoured dishes
sparkling white wine	*Asti spumante* (Italians like to refer to it as champagne but it's slightly sweet)	goes nicely with dessert and pastry; if it's dry, you might try *spumante* as an aperitif or with shellfish, nuts or dried fruit

Beer *Birra*

Beer is always available and growing in popularity. Italian brands are weaker than northern European beers.

I'd like a beer, please.	**Vorrei una birra, per favore.**	vorraiee oonah beerrah pair fahvoaray
Do you have ... beer?	**Avete della birra ...?**	ahvaytay dayllah beerrah
bottled	**in bottiglia**	een botteelyah
draught	**alla spina**	ahllah speenah
foreign	**straniera**	strahneeayrah
light/dark	**bionda/scura**	beeoandah/skoorah

Other alcoholic drinks *Altre bevande alcoliche*

Coffee shops and bars usually have a good stock of foreign and domestic liquor—even some of your favourite brands.

aperitif	**un aperitivo**	oon ahpayreeteevoa
brandy	**un brandy**	oon "brandy"
cognac	**un cognac**	oon "cognac"
gin and tonic	**un gin e tonico**	oon "gin" ay toneekoa
liqueur	**un liquore**	oon lookwoaray
port	**un porto**	oon portoa
rum	**un rum**	oon room
vermouth	**un vermouth**	oon vehrmoot
vodka	**una vodka**	oonah vodkah
whisky (and soda)	**un whisky (e soda)**	oon "whisky" (ay sodah)

glass	**un bicchiere**	oon beekkeeairay
bottle	**una bottiglia**	oonah botteelyah
double (a double shot)	**doppio**	doappeeoa
neat (straight)	**liscio**	leeshoa
on the rocks	**con ghiaccio**	kon geeahtchoa

You'll certainly want to take the occasion to sip an after-dinner drink. If you'd like something which approaches French cognac try *Vecchia Romagna*. If you feel a digestive is called for ask for an *amaro* (bitter), or a glass of *Fernet-Branca* should fit the bill.

| I'd like to try a glass of ..., please. | **Vorrei assaggiare un bicchiere di ...** | vorraiee ahssahdjaaray oon beekkeeairay dee |
| Are there any local specialities? | **Avete specialità locali?** | ahvaytay spaychahleetah loakaalee |

Nonalcoholic drinks *Bevande analcoliche*

The Italian *caffè espresso* has a rich aroma and is excellent everywhere. Served in demi-tasses, it's stronger than what we're used to at home. However, if you'd like to try a more concentrated cup of espresso coffee, ask for a *ristretto* (reestray**t**toa). As against this, a *caffè lungo* (kahf**fay loong**-goa) is a slightly weaker cup of espresso coffee.

For breakfast don't miss the opportunity to drink a *cappuccino* (kahppoot**chee**noa), a delicious mixture of coffee and hot milk, dusted with cocoa. In summer, iced tea and coffee are popular.

I'd like a/an ...	**Vorrei ...**	vorraiee
chocolate	**un cioccolato**	oon choakkoalaatoa
coffee	**un caffè**	oon kahffai
with cream	**con panna**	kon pahnnah
iced coffee	**un caffè freddo**	oon kahffay frayddoa
fruit juice	**un succo di frutta**	oon sookkoa dee froottah
grapefruit	**di pompelmo**	dee poampaylmoa
lemon	**di limone**	dee leemoanay
orange	**d'arancia**	dahrahnchah
herb tea	**una tisana**	oonah teezaanah
lemonade	**una limonata**	oonah leemoanaatah
milk	**del latte**	dayl lahttay
milkshake	**un frullato di latte**	oon froollaatoa dee lahttay
mineral water	**dell'acqua minerale**	dayllahkkwah meenay-raalay
fizzy (carbonated)	**gasata**	gahzaatah
still	**naturale**	nahtooraalay
orangeade	**un'aranciata**	oonahrahnchaatah
tea	**un tè**	oon tai
with milk/lemon	**con latte/limone**	kon lahttay/leemoanay
iced tea	**un tè freddo**	oon tai frayddoa
tomato juice	**un succo di pomodoro**	oon sookkoa dee poamoadawroa
tonic water	**dell'acqua tonica**	dayllahkkwah toneekah

Complaints *Reclami*

There is a plate/glass missing.	**Manca un piatto/un bicchiere.**	mahngkah oon peeaht-toa/oon beekkeeairay
I have no knive/fork/spoon.	**Non ho il coltello/la forchetta/il cucchiaio.**	noan oa eel koltehlloa/lah forkehttah/eel kookkeeaaeeoa
That's not what I ordered.	**Non è ciò che avevo ordinato.**	noan ai cho kay ahvayvoa oardeenaatoa
I asked for ...	**Avevo chiesto ...**	ahvayvoa keeehstoa
There must be some mistake.	**Ci deve essere un errore.**	chee dayvay ehssayray oon ehrroaray
May I change this?	**Posso cambiare questo?**	possoa kahmbeeaaray kooaystoa
I asked for a small portion (for the child).	**Avevo chiesto una piccola porzione (per il bambino).**	ahvayvoa keeehstoa oonah peekkoalah poartseeoanay (pair eel bahmbeenoa)
The meat is ...	**La carne è ...**	lah kahrnay ai
overdone	**troppo cotta**	troppoa kottah
underdone	**poco cotta**	pokoa kottah
too rare	**troppo al sangue**	troppoa ahl sahnggooay
too tough	**troppo dura**	troppoa doorah
This is too ...	**Questo è troppo ...**	kooaystoa ai troppoa
bitter/salty	**amaro/salato**	ahmaaroa/sahlaatoa
sweet	**dolce**	doalchay
I don't like it.	**Non mi piace.**	noan mee peeaahchay
The food is cold.	**Il cibo è freddo.**	eel cheeboa ai frayddoa
This isn't fresh.	**Questo non è fresco.**	kooaystoa noan ai frayskoa
What's taking you so long?	**Perchè impiegate tanto tempo?**	pehrkai eempeeayaygaatay tahntoa tehmpoa
Have you forgotten our drinks?	**Ha dimenticato le nostre bevande?**	ah deemaynteekaatoa lay nostray bayvahnday
The wine tastes of cork.	**Il vino sa di tappo.**	eel veenoa sah dee tahppoa
This isn't clean.	**Questo non è pulito.**	kooaystoa noan ai pooleetoa
Would you ask the head waiter to come over?	**Vuole chiedere al capo cameriere di venire qui?**	vwolay keeaydayray ahl kaapoa kahmayreeehray dee vayneeray kooee

The bill (check) *Il conto*

Though the bill usually includes the service charge *(il servizio)*, it is customary to leave a tip *(la mancia)* for the waiter. Note that you will occasionally also find one or both of the following items added to your bill: *coperto* (cover charge), *supplemento* (surcharge).

I'd like to pay.	**Vorrei pagare.**	vorraiee pahgaaray
We'd like to pay separately.	**Vorremmo pagare separatamente.**	vorrehmmoa pahgaaray saypahrahtahmayntay
I think you've made a mistake in this bill.	**Penso che abbiate fatto un errore nel conto.**	pehnsoa kay ahbbeeaatay fahttoa oon ayrroaray nayl koantoa
What is this amount for?	**Per che cos'è questo importo?**	pair kay kozai kooaystoa eemportoa
Is service included?	**È compreso il servizio?**	ai koampraysoa eel sayrveetseeoa
Is the cover charge included?	**È compreso il coperto?**	ai koampraysoa eel kopairtoa
Is everything included?	**È tutto compreso?**	ai toottoa koampraysoa
Do you accept traveller's cheques?	**Accettate i traveller's cheques?**	ahtchayttaatay ee "traveller's cheques"
Can I pay with this credit card?	**Posso pagare con questa carta di credito?**	possoa pahgaaray kon kooaystah kahrtah dee kraydeetoa
Thank you, this is for you.	**Grazie, questo è per lei.**	graatseeay kooaystoa ai pair lehee
Keep the change.	**Tenga il resto.**	taynggah eel rehstoa
That was a delicious meal.	**È stato un pasto delizioso.**	ai staatoa oon paastoa dayleetseeoasoa
We enjoyed it, thank you.	**Ci è piaciuto, grazie.**	chee ai peeahchootoa graatseeay

```
SERVIZIO COMPRESO
SERVICE INCLUDED
```

TIPPING, see inside back-cover

Snacks—Picnic *Spuntini—Picnic*

Bars and snack bars stay open from early morning till late at night. Most have a selection of sandwiches *(panini imbottiti)* and pastries *(pasticcini)*, inexpensive if you eat at the counter. There are, of course, *pizzerie* for a sit-down pizza or, if you're in a hurry, places selling pizza by the slice. In a *paninoteca*, you can find all sorts of *panini* to eat on the spot or to bring away. The same in a *rosticceria*, plus a great variety of food ready to eat at home or in a picnic.

I'll have one of those, please.	**Per favore, vorrei uno di quelli.**	pair fahvoaray vorraiee oonoa dee kooayllee
Give me two of these and one of those.	**Mi dia due di questi e uno di quelli.**	mee deeah dooay dee kooaystee ay oonoa dee kooayllee
to the left/right	**a sinistra/a destra**	ah seeneestrah/a dehstrah
above/below	**sopra/sotto**	soaprah/soattoa
It's to take away.	**È da portare via.**	ai dah poartaaray veeah
How much is that?	**Quant'è?**	kwahntai
I'd like a/some ...	**Vorrei ...**	vorraiee
chicken	**un pollo**	oon poalloa
half a roasted chicken	**metà pollo arrosto**	maytah poalloa ahrroastoa
chips	**delle patatine fritte**	dayllay pahtahteenay freettay
(slice of) pizza	**una (fetta di) pizza**	oonah (fayttah dee) peettzah
sandwich	**un panino imbottito**	oon pahneenoa eembotteetoa
cheese	**al formaggio**	ahl foarmadjoa
ham	**al prosciutto cotto**	ahl proashoottoa kottoa
Parma ham	**al prosciutto crudo**	ahl proashoottoa kroodoa
salami	**al salame**	ahl sahlaamay

Here's a basic list of food and drink that might come in useful when shopping for a picnic.

Please give me a/an/ some ...	**Per favore, mi dia ...**	pair fahvoaray mee deeah
apples	**delle mele**	dayllay maylay
bananas	**delle banane**	dayllay bahnaanay

biscuits (Br.)	dei biscotti	daiee beeskoattee
beer	della birra	dayllah beerrah
bread	del pane	dayl paanay
butter	del burro	dayl boorroa
cake	una torta	oonah toartah
cheese	del formaggio	dayl foarmahdjoa
chips (Am.)	delle patatine fritte	dayllay pahtahteenay freettay
chocolate bar	una stecca di cioccolato	oonah staykkah dee chokkoalaatoa
coffee	del caffè	dayl kahffai
instant	solubile	soaloobeelay
cold cuts	degli affettati	daylyee ahffehttaatee
cookies	dei biscotti	daiee beeskoattee
crackers	dei cracker	daiee "cracker"
crisps	delle patatine fritte	dayllay pahtahteenay freettay
eggs	delle uova	dayllay wawvah
frankfurters	dei Würstel	daiee "würstel"
gherkins (pickles)	dei cetriolini	daiee chaytreeoaleenee
grapes	dell'uva	dayloovah
ham	del prosciutto	dayl proashoottoa
ice-cream	del gelato	dayl jaylaatoa
lemon	un limone	oon leemoanay
milk	del latte	dayl lahttay
mustard	della senape	dayllah saynahpay
(olive) oil	dell'olio (d'oliva)	dayllolyoa (doleevah)
oranges	delle arance	dayllay ahrahnchay
pastries	dei pasticcini	daiee pahsteetcheenee
peaches	delle pesche	dayllay payskay
peppers	dei peperoni	daiee paypayroanee
pickles	dei sottaceti	daiee soattahchaytee
plums	delle prugne	dayllay prooñay
rolls	dei panini	daiee pahneenee
salad	dell'insalata	daylleensahlaatah
salami	del salame	dayl sahlaamay
salt	del sale	dayl saalay
sausages	delle salsicce	dayllay sahlseetchay
soft drink	una bibita	oonah beebeetah
sugar	dello zucchero	daylloa tsookkayroa
tea	del tè	dayl tai
tomatoes	dei pomodori	daiee poamoadawree
vinegar	dell'aceto	dayllahchaytoa
(mineral) water	dell'acqua (minerale)	dayllahkkwah (meenayraalay)
wine	del vino	dayl veenoa
yoghurt	uno yogurt	oonoa eeoagoort

Travelling around

Plane *Aereo*

Is there a flight to Naples?	C'è un volo per Napoli?	chai oon **voa**loa pair **naa**poalee
Is it a direct flight?	È un volo diretto?	ai oon **voa**loa dee**rayt**toa
When's the next flight to Palermo?	A che ora è il prossimo volo per Palermo?	ah kay **oa**rah ai eel **prosseemoa voa**loa pair pah**lehr**moa
Do I have to change planes?	Devo cambiare aereo?	**day**voa kahmbee**aa**ray ah**ai**rayoa
Is there a connection to Venice?	C'è una coincidenza per Venezia?	chai **oo**nah koeenchee-**dehn**tsah pair vay**nay**tseeah
I'd like a ticket to Milan.	Vorrei un biglietto per Milano.	vor**raie** oon beel**yayt**toa pair mee**laa**noa
single (one-way) return (roundtrip)	andata andata e ritorno	ahn**daa**tah ahn**daa**tah ay ree**tor**noa
What time do we take off?	A che ora si parte?	ah kay **oa**rah see **pahr**tay
What time should I check in?	A che ora devo presentarmi?	ah kay **oa**rah **day**voa prayzehn**taar**mee
Is there a bus to the airport?	C'è un autobus per l'aeroporto?	chai oon **ow**toabooss pair lahayro**por**toa
What's the flight number?	Qual è il numero del volo?	kwahl ai eel **noo**mayroa dayl **voa**loa
What time do we arrive?	A che ora arriveremo?	ah kay **oa**rah ahrreevay**ray**moa
I'd like to ... my reservation on flight no ...	Vorrei ... la mia prenotazione sul volo ...	vor**raie** ... lah **mee**ah praynoatahtseeoanay sool **voa**loa
cancel change confirm	annullare cambiare confermare	ahnnool**laa**ray kahmbee**aa**ray koanfayr**maa**ray

ARRIVO ARRIVAL	**PARTENZA** DEPARTURE

Train *Treno*

Italian trains *try* to run on time as advertised. If you haven't booked, it's wise to arrive at the station at least 20 minutes before departure to be sure of a seat: Italy's trains are often very crowded.

The following list describes the various types of trains:

TEE (teh-eh-eh)	Trans Europ Express; a luxury, international service with first class only; additional fare and reservation required
Rapido (R) (raapeedoa)	Long-distance express train stopping at major cities only; first and second class
Intercity (IC) ("intercity")	Inter-city express with very few stops; a luxury, international service with first and second class
Espresso (EXP)/ Direttissimo (aysprehssoa/ deerehtteesseemoa)	Long-distance train, stopping at main stations
Diretto (D) (deerehttoa)	Slower than the *Espresso,* it makes a number of local stops
Locale (L) (loakaalay)	A local train which stops at almost every station
Accelerato (A) (ahtchaylayraatoa)	Same as a *Locale*
Littorina (leettoareenah)	Small diesel used on short runs

Here are some more useful terms which you may need.

Carrozza ristorante (kahrrottsah reestorahntay)	Dining-car
Vagone letto (vahgoanay lehttoa)	Sleeping-car with individual compartments and washing facilities
Carrozza cuccette (kahrrottsah kootchehttay)	A berth with blankets and pillows
Bagagliaio (bahgahlyaaeeoa)	Guard's van (baggage car): normally only registered luggage permitted

To the railway station *Per andare alla stazione*

Where's the railway station?	**Dove si trova la stazione (ferroviaria)?**	doavay see trawvah lah stahtseeoanay (fehrrovveeaareeah)
Taxi, please!	**Taxi, per favore!**	"taxi" pair fahvoaray
Take me to the railway station.	**Mi porti alla stazione.**	mee portee ahllah stahtseeoanay
What's the fare?	**Quant'è?**	kwahntai

ENTRATA	ENTRANCE
USCITA	EXIT
AI BINARI	TO THE PLATFORMS
INFORMAZIONI	INFORMATION

Where's the ...? *Dov'è ...?*

Where is/are the ...?	**Dov'è ...?**	doavai
bar	**il bar**	eel "bar"
booking office	**l'ufficio prenotazioni**	looffeechoa praynoatahtseeoanee
currency-exchange office	**l'ufficio cambio**	looffeechoa kahmbeeoa
left-luggage office (baggage check)	**il deposito bagagli**	eel daypawzeetoa bahgaalyee
lost property (lost-and-found) office	**l'ufficio oggetti smarriti**	looffeechoa odjehttee smahrreetee
luggage lockers	**la custodia automatica dei bagagli**	lah koostawdeeah owtoamaateekah daiee bahgaalyee
newsstand	**l'edicola**	laydeekoalah
platform 7	**il binario 7**	eel beenaareeoa 7
reservations office	**l'ufficio prenotazioni**	looffeechoa praynoatahtseeoanee
restaurant	**il ristorante**	eel reestorahntay
snack bar	**lo "snack bar"**	loa "snack bar"
ticket office	**la biglietteria**	lah beelyayttayreeah
waiting room	**la sala d'aspetto**	lah saalah dahspehttoa
Where are the toilets?	**Dove sono i gabinetti?**	doavay soanoa ee gahbeenayttee

TAXI, see page 21

Inquiries   *Informazioni*

When is the ... train to Rome?	Quando parte ... treno per Roma?	kwahndoa pahrtay ... traynoa pair roamah
first/last	il primo/l'ultimo	eel preemoa/loolteemoa
next	il prossimo	eel prosseemoa
What time does the train for Milan leave?	A che ora parte il treno per Milano?	ah kay oarah pahrtay eel traynoa pair meelaanoa
What's the fare to Ancona?	Quanto costa il biglietto per Ancona?	kwahntoa kostah eel beelyayttoa pair ahngkoanah
Is it a through train?	È un treno diretto?	ai oon traynoa deerehttoa
Is there a connection to ...?	C'è una coincidenza per ...?	chai oonah koaeenchee-dayntsah pair
Do I have to change trains?	Devo cambiare treno?	dayvoa kahmbeeaaray traynoa
How long will the train stop at ...?	Quanto tempo si fermerà il treno a ...?	kwahntoa tehmpoa see fayrmayrah eel traynoa ah
Is there sufficient time to change?	C'è il tempo per cambiare?	chai eel tehmpoa pair kahmbeeaaray
Will the train leave on time?	Partirà in orario il treno?	pahrteerah een oaraareeoa eel traynoa
What time does the train arrive at Florence?	A che ora arriverà a Firenze il treno?	ah kay oarah ahrreevayrah ah feerehntsay eel traynoa
Is there a dining-car/sleeping-car on the train?	C'è una carrozza ristorante/un vagone letto sul treno?	chai oonah kahrrottsah reestorahntay/oon vahgoa-nay lehttoa sool traynoa
Does the train stop at Lugano?	Il treno si fermerà a Lugano?	eel traynoa see fayrmayrah ah loogaanoa
What platform does the train for Verona leave from?	Da che binario parte il treno per Verona?	dah kay beenaareeoa pahrtay eel traynoa pair vayroanah
What platform does the train from Bari arrive at?	A che binario arriva il treno proveniente da Bari?	ah kay beenaareeoa ahrreevah eel traynoa pro-vayneeehntay dah baaree
I'd like to buy a timetable.	Vorrei comprare un orario ferroviario.	vorraie koampraaray oon oaraareeoa fehrro-veeaareeoa

È un treno diretto.	It's a through train.
Deve cambiare a ...	You have to change at ...
Cambi a ... e prenda un treno locale.	Change at ... and get a local train.
Il binario 7 è ...	Platform 7 is ...
laggiù/su dalle scale a sinistra/a destra	over there/upstairs on the left/on the right
C'è un treno per ... alle ...	There's a train to ... at ...
Il suo treno partirà dal binario 8.	Your train will leave from platform 8.
Ci sarà un ritardo di ... minuti.	There'll be a delay of ... minutes.
Prima classe in testa/ nel mezzo/in coda.	First class at the front/ in the middle/at the end.

Tickets *Biglietti*

I want a ticket to Rome.	**Desidero un biglietto per Roma.**	dayzeedayroa oon bee-lyayttoa pair roamah
single (one-way)	**andata**	ahndaatah
return (roundtrip)	**andata e ritorno**	ahndaatah ay reetornoa
first/second class	**prima/seconda classe**	preemah/saykoandah klahssay
half price	**metà tariffa**	maytah tahreeffah

Reservation *Prenotazione*

I want to book a ...	**Vorrei prenotare ...**	vorraie praynoataaray
seat (by the window)	**un posto (vicino al finestrino)**	oon postoa (veecheenoa ahl feenaystreenoa)
berth	**una cuccetta**	oonah kootchehttah
upper	**superiore**	soopayreeoaray
middle	**nel mezzo**	nayl mehdzoa
lower	**inferiore**	eenfayreeoaray
berth in the sleeping car	**un posto nel vagone letto**	oon postoa nayl vahgoanay lehttoa

70

All aboard *In vettura!*

Is this the right platform for the train to Bellinzona?	È il binario giusto per il treno che va a Bellinzona?	ai eel beenaareeo joostoa pair eel traynoa kay vah ah behlleendzoanah
Is this the right train to Genoa?	È il treno giusto per Genova?	ai eel traynoa joostoa pair jainoavah
Excuse me. May I get by?	Mi scusi. Posso passare?	mee skoozee. possoa pahssaaray
Is this seat taken?	È occupato questo posto?	ai oakkoopaatoa kooaystoa postoa

FUMATORI SMOKER	NON FUMATORI NONSMOKER

I think that's my seat.	Penso che questo sia il mio posto.	paynsoa kay kooaystoa seeah eel meeoa postoa
Would you let me know before we get to Milan?	Può avvisarmi prima di arrivare a Milano?	pwo ahvveezaarmee preemah dee ahrreevaaray ah meelaanoa
What station is this?	Che stazione è?	kay stahtseeoanay ai
How long does the train stop here?	Quanto tempo si ferma qui il treno?	kwahntoa tehmpoa see fayrmah kooee eel traynoa
When do we get to Pisa?	Quando arriveremo a Pisa?	kwahndoa ahrreevay-raymoa ah peezah

Sleeping *Nel vagone letto*

Are there any free compartments in the sleeping-car?	Ci sono degli scompartimenti liberi nel vagone letto?	chee soanoa dailyee skoampahrteemayntee leebayree nail vahgoanay lehttoa
Where's the sleeping-car?	Dov'è il vagone letto	doavai eel vahgoanay lehttoa
Where's my berth?	Dov'è la mia cuccetta?	doavai lah meeah kootchehttah
I'd like a lower berth.	Vorrei la cuccetta inferiore.	vorraie lah kootchehttah eenfayreeoaray

Would you make up our berths?	**Può preparare le nostre cuccette?**	pwo praypahraaray lay nostray kootchehttay
Would you call me at 7 o'clock?	**Può svegliarmi alle 7?**	pwo svaylyahrmee **ah**llay 7
Would you bring me some coffee in the morning?	**Può portarmi un caffè domani mattina?**	pwo portahrmee oon kahffai doamaanee mahtteenah

Eating *Nella carrozza ristorante*

You can get snacks and drinks in the buffet-car and in the dining-car when it isn't being used for main meals. On some trains an attendant comes around with snacks, tea, coffee and soft drinks.

| Where's the dining-car? | **Dov'è la carrozza ristorante?** | doavai lah kahrrottsah reestorahntay |

Baggage and porters *Bagagli e facchini*

Porter!	**Facchino!**	fahkkeenoa
Can you help me with my luggage?	**Può prendere il mio bagaglio?**	pwo prehndayray eel meeoa bahgaalyoa
Where are the luggage trolleys (carts)?	**Dove sono i carrelli portabagagli?**	doavay soanoa ee kahrrehllee portahbahgaalyee
Where are the luggage lockers?	**Dove sono le custodie automatiche dei bagagli?**	doavay soanoa lay koostawdeeay owtoamaateekay daiee bahgaalyee
Where's the left-luggage office (baggage check)?	**Dov'è il deposito bagagli?**	doavai eel daypawzeetoa bahgaalyee
I'd like to leave my luggage, please.	**Vorrei depositare i miei bagagli, per favore.**	vorraiee daypozeetaaray ee meeaiee bahgaalyee pair fahvoaray
I'd like to register (check) my luggage.	**Vorrei far registrare i miei bagagli.**	vorraiee fahr rayjeestraaray ee meeaiee bahgaalyee

---

REGISTRAZIONE BAGAGLI
REGISTERING (CHECKING) BAGGAGE

PORTERS, see also page 18

Coach (long-distance bus) *Pullman/Corriera*

You'll find information on destinations and timetables at the coach terminals, usually situated near railway stations. Many travel agencies offer coach tours.

When's the next coach to ...?	**A che ora parte il prossimo pullman per ...?**	ah kay oarah pahrtay eel prosseemoa poolmahn pair
Does this coach stop at ...?	**Questa corriera si ferma a ...?**	kooaystah korreeayrah see fayrmah ah
How long does the journey (trip) take?	**Quanto tempo dura il percorso?**	kwahntoa tehmpoa doorah eel payrkoarsoa

Note: Most of the phrases on the previous pages can be used or adapted for travelling on local transport.

Bus—Tram (streetcar) *Autobus—Tram*

Many cities have introduced an automatic system of fare-paying: either you insert the exact change into a ticket dispenser at the bus or tram stop or you punch your ticket in the machine.

If you're planning to get around a lot in one city by bus, tram, or *metropolitana* (see next page), enquire about a booklet of tickets or special runabout tickets, such as *biglietto giornaliero* (one-day ticket).

I'd like a booklet of tickets.	**Vorrei un blocchetto di biglietti.**	vorraiee oon blokkehttoa dee beelyayttee
Where can I get a bus to the Vatican?	**Dove posso prendere l'autobus per il Vaticano?**	doavay possoa prehndayray lowtoabooss pair eel vahteekaanoa
What bus do I take for the Colosseum?	**Quale autobus devo prendere per andare al Colosseo?**	kwaalay owtoabooss dayvoa prehndayray pair ahndaaray ahl koaloassaioa
Where's the bus stop?	**Dove si trova la fermata dell'autobus?**	doavay see trawvah lah fehrmaatah dayllowtoabooss

When is the ... bus to the Lido?	A che ora parte ... autobus per il Lido?	ah kay oarah pahrtay ... owtoabooss pair eel leedoa
first/last	il primo/l'ultimo	eel preemoa/loolteemoa
next	il prossimo	eel prosseemoa
How much is the fare to ...?	Quanto costa il biglietto per ...?	kwahntoa kostah eel beelyayttoa pair
Do I have to change buses?	Devo cambiare autobus?	dayvoa kahmbeeaaray owtoabooss
How many bus stops are there to ...?	Quante fermate ci sono fino a ...?	kwahntay fayrmaaty chee soanoa feenoa ah
Will you tell me when to get off?	Può dirmi quando devo scendere?	pwo deermee kwahndoa dayvoa shayndayray
I want to get off at Piazza di Spagna.	Voglio scendere a Piazza di Spagna.	volyoa shayndayray ah peeahtsah dee spahñah

| FERMATA D'AUTOBUS | REGULAR BUS STOP |
| FERMATA A RICHIESTA | STOPS ON REQUEST |

Underground (subway) *Metropolitana*

The *metropolitana* in Rome and Milan corresponds to the London underground or the New York subway. In both cities, the fare is always the same, irrespective of the distance you travel. Big maps in every *Metro* station make the system easy to use.

Where's the nearest underground station?	Dove si trova la più vicina stazione della metropolitana?	doavay see trawvah lah peeoo veecheenah stahtseeoanay dayllah maytroapoaleetaanah
Does this train go to ...?	Questo treno va a ...?	kooaystoa traynoa vah ah
Where do I change for ...?	Dove cambio per andare a ...?	doavay kahmbeeoa pair ahndaaray ah
Is the next station ...?	La prossima stazione è ...?	lah prosseemah stahtseeoanay ai
Which line should I take for ...?	Che linea devo prendere per ...?	kay leenayah dayvoa prehndayray pair

Boat service *Battello*

When does the next boat for … leave?	**A che ora parte il prossimo battello per …?**	ah kay oarah pahrtay eel prosseemoa bahttehlloa pair
Where's the embarkation point?	**Dove ci si imbarca?**	doavay chee see eembahrkah
How long does the crossing take?	**Quanto tempo dura la traversata?**	kwahntoa tehmpoa doorah lah trahvayrsaatah
At which ports do we stop?	**A che porti si ferma?**	ah kay portee see fayrmah
I'd like to take a cruise.	**Vorrei fare una crociera.**	vorraiee faaray oonah kroachayrah
boat	**il battello/la nave**	eel bahttehlloa/lah naavay
cabin	**la cabina**	lah kahbeenah
single/double	**a un letto/a due letti**	ah oon lehttoa/ah dooay lehttee
deck	**il ponte**	eel poantay
ferry	**il traghetto**	eel trahgehttoa
hydrofoil	**l'aliscafo**	lahleeskaafoa
life belt/boat	**la cintura/il canotto di salvataggio**	lah cheentoorah/eel kahnottoa dee sahlvahtahdjoa
ship	**la nave**	lah naavay

Bicycle hire *Noleggio biciclette*

In many cities of Italy there is the possibility to hire a bicycle. Ask any tourist office for the address of a rental firm.

I'd like to hire a bicycle.	**Vorrei noleggiare una bicicletta.**	vorraiee noalaydjaaray oonah beecheeklehttah

Other means of transport *Altri mezzi di trasporto*

cable car	**la funivia**	lah fooneeveeah
helicopter	**l'elicottero**	layleekottayroa
moped	**il motorino**	eel moatoareenoa
motorbike/scooter	**la moto/la motoretta**	lah motoa/lah motoarehttah

Or perhaps you prefer:

to hitchhike	**fare l'autostop**	faaray lowtoastop
to walk	**camminare**	kahmmeenaaray

Car *Macchina*

In general roads are good in Italy and Switzerland. Motorways (expressways) are subject to tolls *(il pedaggio)* in Italy. If you use the motorways in Switzerland you must purchase a sticker (valid for one year) to be displayed on the windscreen.

A red reflector warning triangle must be carried for use in case of a breakdown, and seat-belts *(le cinture di sicurezza)* are obligatory in Switzerland.

Where's the nearest filling station?	Dov'è la stazione di rifornimento più vicina?	doavai lah stahtseeoanay dee reeforneemayntoa peeoo veecheenah
Full tank, please.	Il pieno, per favore.	eel peeainoa pair fahvoaray
Give me ... litres of petrol (gasoline).	Mi dia ... litri di benzina.	mee deeah ... leetree dee bayndzeenah
super (premium)/ regular/unleaded/ diesel	super/normale/ senza piombo/ gasolio	soopayr/noarmaalay/ sayntsah peeoamboa/ gahzolyoa
Please check the ...	Per favore, controlli...	pair fahvoaray koantroallee
battery brake fluid oil/water	la batteria l'olio dei freni l'olio/l'acqua	lah bahttayreeah lolyoa daiee fraynee lolyoa/lahkkwah
Would you check the tyre pressure?	Può controllare la pressione delle gomme?	pwo koantroallaaray lah praysseeoanay dayllay goammay
1.6 front, 1.8 rear.	1,6 davanti, 1,8 dietro.	oonoa ay sehee dahvahntee oonoa ay ottoa deeehtroa
Please check the spare tyre, too.	Per favore, controlli anche la ruota di scorta.	pair fahvoaray koantroallee ahngkay lah rwawtah dee skortah
Can you mend this puncture (fix this flat)?	Può riparare questa foratura?	pwo reepahraaray kooaystah forahtoorah
Would you please change the ...?	Potrebbe cambiare ...	poatrehbbay kahmbeeaaray
bulb fan belt	la lampadina la cinghia del ventilatore	lah lahmpahdeenah lah cheenggeeah dayl vaynteelahtoaray

CAR HIRE, see page 20

spark(ing) plugs	le candele	lay kahndaylay
tyre	la gomma	lah goammah
wipers	i tergicristalli	ee tayrjeekreestahllee
Would you clean the windscreen (windshield)?	Mi pulisca il para-brezza, per favore.	mee pooleeskah eel pahrahbraydzah pair fahvooaray

Asking the way   *Per chiedere la strada*

Can you tell me the way to ...?	Può dirmi qual è la strada per ...?	pwo deermee kwahl ai lah straadah pair
How do I get to ...?	Come si va a ...?	koamay see vah ah
Are we on the right road for ...?	Siamo sulla strada giusta per ...?	seeaamoa soollah straadah joostah pair
How far is the next village?	Quanto dista il prossimo villaggio?	kwahntoa deestah eel prosseemoa veellahdjoa
How far is it to ... from here?	Quanto dista ... da qui?	kwahntoa deestah ... dah kooee
Is there a motorway (expressway)?	C'è un'autostrada?	chai oonowtoastraadah
Is there a road with little traffic?	C'è una strada con poco traffico?	chai oonah straadah kon pokoa trahffeekoa
How long does it take by car/on foot?	Quanto tempo ci vuole in macchina/a piedi?	kwahntoa tehmpoa chee vwolay een mahkkeenah/ah peeaydee
Can I drive to the centre of town?	Si può andare in macchina nel centro città?	see pwo ahndaaray een mahkkeenah nayl chayntroa cheettah
Can you tell me, where ... is?	Può dirmi dove si trova ...?	pwo deermee doavay see trawvah
How can I find this place?	Come posso trovare questo posto?	koamay possoa trovaaray kooaystoa poastoa
Where can I find this address?	Dove posso trovare questo indirizzo?	doavay possoa trovaaray kooaystoa eendeereettsoa
Where's this?	Dov'è questo?	doavai kooaystoa
Can you show me on the map where I am?	Può indicarmi sulla carta dove mi trovo?	pwo eendeekaarmee soollah kahrtah doavay mee trawvoa

Lei è sulla strada sbagliata.	You're on the wrong road.
Vada diritto.	Go straight ahead.
È laggiù a ...	It's down there on the ...
sinistra/destra	left/right
di fronte/dietro ...	opposite/behind ...
accanto a/dopo ...	next to/after ...
nord/sud	north/south
est/ovest	east/west
Vada fino al primo/ secondo incrocio.	Go to the first/second crossroad (intersection).
Al semaforo, giri a sinistra.	Turn left at the traffic lights.
Giri a destra al prossimo angolo.	Turn right at the next corner.
Prenda la strada per ...	Take the road for ...
Segua la direzione per Stresa.	Follow the sign for "Stresa".
Deve tornare indietro ...	You have to go back to ...

Parking *Parcheggio*

In town centres, most street parking is limited. The blue zones require the *disco di sosta* or parking disc (obtainable from petrol stations), which you set to show when you arrived and when you must leave.

Where can I park?	Dove posso parcheggiare?	doavay possoa pahrkayd-jaaray
Is there a car park nearby?	C'è un parcheggio qui vicino?	chai oon pahrkaydjoa kooee veecheenoa
May I park here?	Posso parcheggiare qui?	possoa pahrkaydjaaray kooee
How long can I park here?	Quanto tempo posso restare qui?	kwahntoa tehmpoa possoa raystaaray kooee
What's the charge per hour?	Quanto si paga all'ora?	kwahntoa see paagah ahl-loarah
Do you have some change for the parking meter?	Ha della moneta per il parchimetro?	ah dayllah moanaytah pair eel pahrkeemaytroa

Breakdown—Road assistance   *Guasti—Assistenza stradale*

Where's the nearest garage?	**Dov'è il garage più vicino?**	doavai eel gahraazh peeoo veecheenoa
Excuse me. My car has broken down.	**Mi scusi. Ho un guasto all'automobile.**	mee skoozee. oa oon **gwaa**stoa ahllowtoamawbeelay
May I use your phone?	**Posso usare il suo telefono?**	possoa oozaray eel **sooa** taylayfoanoa
I've had a breakdown at ...	**Ho avuto un guasto a ...**	oa ahvootoa oon **gwaa**stoa ah
Can you send a mechanic?	**Può mandare un meccanico?**	pwo mahn**daaray** oon maykkaaneekoa
My car won't start.	**La mia macchina non parte.**	lah meeah mahk**kee**nah noan **pahr**tay
The battery is dead.	**La batteria è scarica.**	lah bahttay**ree**ah ai **skaa**reekah
I've run out of petrol (gasoline).	**Sono rimasto(a) senza benzina.**	soanoa ree**mahs**toa(ah) sayntsah bayndzeenah
I have a flat tyre.	**Ho una gomma sgonfia.**	oa oonah **goam**mah sgoanfeeah
The engine is overheating.	**Il motore è surriscaldato.**	eel moatoaray ai soorree**skahl**daatoa
There is something wrong with ...	**Qualcosa non va con ...**	kwahl**kaw**sah noan vah kon
brakes	**i freni**	ee **fray**nee
carburettor	**il carburatore**	eel kahrboorah**toa**ray
exhaust pipe	**il tubo di scappamento**	eel **tooboa** dee skahppah**mayn**toa
radiator	**il radiatore**	eel rahdeeah**toa**ray
wheel	**la ruota**	lah **rwaw**tah
Can you send a breakdown van (tow truck)?	**Può mandare un carro attrezzi?**	pwo mahn**daaray** oon **kahr**roa attrehttsee
How long will you be?	**Quanto tempo impiegherete?**	**kwahn**toa tehmpoa eempeeaygay**ray**tay

Accident—Police   *Incidenti—Polizia*

| Please call the police. | **Per favore, chiami la polizia.** | pair fah**voa**ray kee**aa**mee lah poalee**tsee**ah |

There's been an accident.	C'è stato un incidente.	chai staatoa oon eencheedayntay
Where's the nearest telephone?	Dov'è il telefono più vicino?	doavai eel taylayfoanoa peeoo veecheenoa
Call a doctor/an ambulance quickly.	Chiami un medico/un'ambulanza, presto.	keeaamee oon maideekoa/oonahmboolahntsah prehstoa
There are people injured.	Ci sono dei feriti.	chee soanoa daiee fayreetee
What's your name and address?	Qual è il suo nome e indirizzo?	kwahl ai eel soooa noamay ay eendeereetsoa
What's your insurance company?	Qual è la sua assicurazione?	kwahl ai lah sooah ahsseekoorahtseeoanay

Road signs *Segnali stradali*

ACCENDERE I FARI IN GALLERIA	Switch on headlights before entering tunnel
ACCOSTARE A DESTRA (SINISTRA)	Keep right (left)
ALT	Stop
AREA DI SERVIZIO	Service area
CADUTA MASSI	Falling rocks
CARABINIERI	Police
CIRCONVALLAZIONE	Ring road (belt highway)
CORSIA D'EMERGENZA	Emergency parking zone
CURVE PER 5 KM.	Bends (curves) for 5 km.
DEVIAZIONE	Diversion/detour
DIVIETO DI SOSTA	No parking
DIVIETO DI SORPASSO	No overtaking (passing)
LAVORI IN CORSO	Road works ahead (men working)
PASSAGGIO A LIVELLO	Level (railroad) crossing
PERICOLO	Danger
POLIZIA STRADALE	Highway police
RALLENTARE	Reduce speed
SENSO UNICO	One way
SOCCORSO A.C.I.	A.C.I. emergency road service
STRADA DISSESTATA	Poor road surface
TRANSITO CON CATENE	Chains required
VICOLO CIECO	Dead end
VIETATO L'ACCESSO	No entry
VIGILI URBANI	City police
ZONA PEDONALE	Pedestrian zone

Sightseeing

Where's the tourist office?	Dov'è l'azienda di soggiorno e turismo (l'ufficio turistico)?	doavai lahdzeeayndah dee soadjoarnoa ay tooreezmoa (looffeechoa tooreesteekoa)
What are the main points of interest?	Quali sono i principali punti di interesse?	kwaalee soanoa ee preencheepaalee poontee dee eentayrayssay
We're here for …	Siamo qui per …	seeaamoa kooee pair
only a few hours	alcune ore soltanto	ahlkoonay oaray soltahntoa
a day	un giorno	oon joarnoa
a week	una settimana	oonah saytteemaanah
Can you recommend a sightseeing tour/an excursion?	Può consigliare un giro turistico/una gita?	pwo konseelyaaray oon jeeroa tooreesteekoa/oonah jeetah
What's the point of departure?	Da dove si parte?	dah doavay see pahrtay
Will the bus pick us up at the hotel?	Il pullman passerà a prenderci all'hotel?	eel poolmahn pahssayrah ah prehndehrchee ahllotehl
How much does the tour cost?	Quanto costa il giro?	kwahntoa koastah eel jeeroa
What time does the tour start?	A che ora inizia il giro?	ah kay oarah eeneetseeah eel jeeroa
Is lunch included?	Il pranzo è compreso?	eel prahndzoa ai koampraysoa
What time do we get back?	A che ora si ritorna?	ah kay oarah see reetoarnah
Do we have free time in …?	Avremo del tempo libero a …?	ahvraymoa dayl tehmpoa leebayroa ah
Is there an English-speaking guide?	C'è una guida che parla inglese?	chai oonah gooeedah kay pahrlah eengglaysay
I'd like to hire a private guide for …	Vorrei avere una guida privata per …	vorraiee ahvayray oonah gooeedah preevaatah pair
half a day	mezza giornata	mehddzah joarnaatah
a full day	una giornata intera	oonah joarnaatah eentayrah

Where is/Where are the ...?	Dove si trova/Dove si trovano ...?	doavay see trawvah/ doavay see trawvahnoa
abbey	l'abbazia	lahbbahtseeah
art gallery	la galleria d'arte	lah gahllayreeah dahrtay
artists' quarter	il quartiere degli artisti	eel kwahrteeayray daylee ahrteestee
botanical gardens	i giardini botanici	ee jahrdeenee botaaneechee
building	l'edificio	laydeefeechoa
business district	il quartiere degli affari	eel kwahrteeayray daylee ahffaaree
castle	il castello	eel kahstehlloa
catacombs	le catacombe	lay kahtahkombay
cathedral	la cattedrale	lah kahttaydraalay
cave	la grotta	lah grottah
cemetery	il cimitero	eel cheemeetairoa
city centre	il centro città	eel chayntroa cheettah
chapel	la cappella	lah kahppehllah
church	la chiesa	lah keeayzah
concert hall	la sala dei concerti	lah saalah daiee konchehrtee
convent	il convento	eel konvayntoa
court house	il palazzo di giustizia	eel pahlahttsoa dee joosteetseeah
downtown area	il centro (città)	eel chayntroa (cheettah)
exhibition	l'esposizione	layspozeetseeoanay
factory	la fabbrica	lah fahbbreekah
fair	la fiera	lah feeayrah
flea market	il mercato delle pulci	eel mehrkaatoa dayllay poolchee
fortress	la fortezza	lah fortehttsah
fountain	la fontana	lah foantaanah
gardens	i giardini	ee jahrdeenee
harbour	il porto	eel portoa
lake	il lago	eel laagoa
library	la biblioteca	lah beebleeotaikah
market	il mercato	eel mayrkaatoa
memorial	il memoriale	eel maymoareeaalay
monastery	il monastero	eel moanahstairoa
monument	il monumento	eel moanoomayntoa
museum	il museo	eel moozaioa
old town	la città vecchia	lah cheettah vehkkeeah
opera house	il teatro dell'opera	eel tayaatroa dayllopayrah
palace	il palazzo	eel pahlahttsoa
park	il parco	eel pahrkoa
parliament building	il Parlamento	eel pahrlahmayntoa

planetarium	**il planetario**	eel plahnaytaareeoa
royal palace	**il palazzo reale**	eel pahlahttsoa rayaalay
ruins	**le rovine**	lay roveenay
shopping area	**la zona dei negozi**	lah dzonah daiee naygotsee
square	**la piazza**	lah peeahtsah
stadium	**lo stadio**	loa staadeeoa
statue	**la statua**	lah staatooah
stock exchange	**la borsa valori**	lah borsah vahloaree
theatre	**il teatro**	eel tayaatroa
tomb	**la tomba**	lah toambah
tower	**la torre**	lah toarray
town hall	**il municipio**	eel mooneecheepeeoa
university	**l'università**	looneevayrseetah
zoo	**lo zoo**	loa dzoo

Admission   *All'entrata*

Is ... open on Sundays?	**È aperto la domenica il ...?**	ai ahpehrtoa lah doamay-neekah eel
When does it open?	**Quando apre?**	kwahndoa aapray
When does it close?	**Quando chiude?**	kwahndoa keeooday
How much is the entrance fee?	**Quanto costa l'entrata?**	kwahntoa kostah layntraatah
Is there any reduction for ...?	**C'è una riduzione per ...?**	chai oonah reedootseeoanay pair
children	**i bambini**	ee bahmbeenee
disabled	**gli andicappati**	lyee ahndeekahppaatee
groups	**i gruppi**	ee grooppee
pensioners	**i pensionati**	ee paynseeoanaatee
students	**gli studenti**	lyee stoodayntee
Have you a guide-book (in English)?	**Avete una guida turistica (in inglese)?**	ahvaytay oonah gooeedah tooreesteekah (een eengglaysay)
Can I buy a catalogue?	**Posso comprare un catalogo?**	possoa koampraaray oon kahtaaloagoa
Is it all right to take pictures?	**È permesso fare delle fotografie?**	ai pehrmayssoa faaray dayllay foatoagrahfeeay

ENTRATA LIBERA	ADMISSION FREE
VIETATO FOTOGRAFARE	NO CAMERAS ALLOWED

Who—What—When? *Chi—Cosa—Quando?*

What's that building?	**Che cos'è quest'edificio?**	kay kosai kooaystaydeefeechoa
Who was the ...?	**Chi è stato ...?**	kee ai staatoa
architect	**l'architetto**	lahrkeetehttoa
artist	**l'artista**	lahrteestah
painter	**il pittore**	eel peettoaray
sculptor	**lo scultore**	loa skooltoaray
Who built it?	**Chi lo costruì?**	kee loa koastrooee
Who painted that picture?	**Chi dipinse questo quadro?**	kee deepeensay kooaystoa kwaadroa
When did he live?	**Quando è vissuto?**	kwahndoa ai veessootoa
When was it built?	**Quando fu costruito?**	kwahndoa foo koastrooeetoa
Where's the house where ... lived?	**Dove si trova la casa in cui visse ...?**	doavay see trawvah lah kaasah een kooee veessay
We're interested in ...	**Ci interessiamo di ...**	chee eentayraysseeaamoa dee
antiques	**antichità**	ahnteekeetah
archaeology	**archeologia**	ahrkayoaloajeeah
art	**arte**	ahrtay
botany	**botanica**	botaaneekah
ceramics	**ceramiche**	chayraameekay
coins	**monete**	monaitay
fine arts	**belle arti**	behllay ahrtee
furniture	**mobilio**	mobeelyoa
geology	**geologia**	jayoaloajeeah
handicrafts	**artigianato**	ahrteejahnaatoa
history	**storia**	storeeah
medicine	**medicina**	maydeecheenah
music	**musica**	moozeekah
natural history	**storia naturale**	storeeah nahtooraalay
ornithology	**ornitologia**	oarneetoaloajeeah
painting	**pittura**	peettoorah
pottery	**terrecotte**	tehrraykottay
prehistory	**preistoria**	prayeestoreeah
religion	**religione**	rayleejoanay
sculpture	**scultura**	skooltoorah
zoology	**zoologia**	dzoaoaloajeeah
Where's the ... department?	**Dov'è il reparto di/del ...?**	doavai eel raypahrtoa dee/dayl

It's ...	È ...	ai
amazing	sorprendente	soarprayndehntay
awful	orribile	orreebeelay
beautiful	bello	behlloa
excellent	eccellente	ehtchehllayntay
gloomy	malinconico	mahleengkawneekoa
impressive	impressionante	eempraysseeoanahntay
interesting	interessante	eentayrayssahntay
magnificent	magnifico	mahñeefeekoa
nice	bello	behlloa
overwhelming	sbalorditivo	sbahloardeeteevoa
strange	strano	straanoa
superb	superbo	soopehrboa
terrifying	terrificante	tayrreefeekahntay
tremendous	fantastico	fahntahsteekoa
ugly	brutto	broottoa

Religious services *Funzioni religiose*

Most churches and cathedrals are open to the public, except, of course, during mass.

If you are interested in taking pictures, you should obtain permission first. Shorts and backless dresses are definitely out when visiting churches.

Is there a/an ... near here?	C'è una ... qui vicino?	chai oonah ... kooee veecheenoa
Catholic church	chiesa cattolica	keeayzah kahttoaleekah
Protestant church	chiesa protestante	keeayzah proataystahntay
synagogue	sinagoga	seenahgawgah
mosque	moschea	moaskaiah
At what time is ...?	A che ora è ...?	ah kay oarah ai
mass	la messa	lah mayssah
the service	la funzione	lah foontseeoanay
Where can I find a ... who speaks English?	Dove posso trovare un ... che parla inglese?	doavay possoa trovaaray oon ... kay pahrlah eengglaysay
priest/minister	prete/pastore	praitay/pahstoaray
rabbi	rabbino	rahbbeenoa
I'd like to visit the church.	Vorrei visitare la chiesa.	vorraiee veezeetaaray lah keeayzah

In the countryside   *In campagna*

Is there a scenic route to ...?	**C'è una strada panoramica per ...?**	chai oonah straadah pahnoaraameekah pair
How far is it to ...?	**Quanto dista ...?**	kwahntoa deestah
Can we walk?	**Possiamo andare a piedi?**	posseeaamoa ahndaaray ah peeaydee
How high is that mountain?	**Quanto è alta quella montagna?**	kwahntoa ai ahltah kooayllah moantaañah
What's the name of that ...?	**Come si chiama questo ...?**	koamay see keeaamah kooaystoa
animal/bird	**animale/uccello**	ahneemaalay/ootchehlloa
flower/tree	**fiore/albero**	feeoaray/ahlbayroa

Landmarks   *Punti di riferimento*

bridge	**il ponte**	eel poantay
cliff	**la scogliera**	lah skoalyayrah
farm	**la fattoria**	lah fahttoareeah
field	**il campo**	eel kahmpoa
footpath	**il sentiero**	eel saynteeayroa
forest	**la foresta**	lah fawrehstah
garden	**il giardino**	eel jahrdeenoa
hamlet	**il gruppo di casolari**	eel grooppoa dee kahsoalaaree
hill	**la collina**	lah koalleenah
house	**la casa**	lah kaasah
lake	**il lago**	eel laagoa
meadow	**il prato**	eel praatoa
mountain	**la montagna**	lah moantaañah
(mountain) pass	**il passo**	eel pahssoa
peak	**il picco**	eel peekkoa
pond	**lo stagno**	loa staañoa
river	**il fiume**	eel feeoomay
road	**la strada**	lah straadah
sea	**il mare**	eel maaray
spring	**la sorgente**	lah soarjayntay
valley	**la valle**	lah vahllay
village	**il villaggio/il paese**	eel veellahdjoa/eel pahayzay
vineyard	**la vigna**	lah veeñah
wall	**il muro**	eel mooroa
waterfall	**la cascata**	lah kahskaatah
well	**il pozzo**	eel poatsoa
wood	**il bosco**	eel boaskoa

ASKING THE WAY, see page 76

Relaxing

Cinema (movies) — Theatre   *Cinema — Teatro*

You can find out what's playing from newspapers and billboards. In Rome and in the main towns in Italy look for the weekly entertainment guides available at major newsstands, at the tourist office and the hotel reception.

What's showing at the cinema tonight?	**Cosa danno al cinema questa sera?**	kawsah dahnnoa ahl cheenaymah kooaystah sayrah
What's playing at the ... theatre?	**Che spettacolo c'è al teatro ...?**	kay spayttaakoaloa chai ahl tayaatroa
What sort of play is it?	**Che genere di commedia è?**	kay jainayray dee koammaideeah ai
Who's it by?	**Di chi è?**	dee kee ai
Can you recommend (a) ...?	**Può consigliarmi ...?**	pwo konseelyaarmee
good film	**un buon film**	oon bwawn "film"
comedy	**una commedia**	oonah koammaideeah
musical	**una commedia musicale**	oonah koammaideeah moozeekaalay
Where's that new film by ... being shown?	**In che cinema danno il nuovo film di ...?**	een kay cheenaymah dahnnoa eel nwovoa "film" dee
Who's in it?	**Chi sono gli attori?**	kee soanoa lyee ahttoaree
Who's playing the lead?	**Chi interpreta il ruolo principale?**	kee eentehrprehtah eel rwoloa preencheepaalay
Who's the director?	**Chi è il regista?**	kee ai eel rayjeestah
At what theatre is that new play by ... being performed?	**In quale teatro viene rappresentata la nuova commedia di ...?**	een kwaalay tayaatroa veeaynay rahppraysayntaatah lah nwovah koammaideeah dee
Is there a sound-and-light show on somewhere?	**C'è uno spettacolo suoni e luci da qualche parte?**	chai oonoa spayttaakoaloa swonee ay loochee dah kwahlkay paartay

What time does it begin?	A che ora incomincia?	ah kay oarah eengkoameenchah
Are there any seats for tonight?	Ci sono posti per questa sera?	chee soanoa postee pair kooaystah sayrah
How much are the seats?	Quanto costano i posti?	kwahntoa kostahnoa ee postee
I want to reserve 2 seats for the show on Friday evening.	Desidero prenotare 2 posti per lo spettacolo di venerdì sera.	dayzeedayroa praynoataaray 2 postee pair loa spayttaakoaloa dee vaynayrdee sayrah
Can I have a ticket for the matinée on Tuesday?	Posso avere un biglietto per lo spettacolo del pomeriggio di martedì?	possoa ahvayray oon beelyayttoa pair loa spayttaakoaloa dayl poamayreedjoa dee mahrtaydee
I want a seat in the stalls (orchestra).	Desidero una poltrona.	dayzeedayroa oonah poaltroanah
Not too far back.	Non troppo indietro.	noan troppoa eendeeaytroa
Somewhere in the middle.	A metà circa.	ah maytah cheerkah
How much are the seats in the circle (mezzanine)?	Quanto costano i posti in galleria?	kwahntoa kostahnoa ee postee een gahllayreeah
May I please have a programme?	Per favore, posso avere un programma?	pair fahvoaray possoa ahvayray oon prograhmmah
Where's the cloakroom?	Dov'è il guardaroba?	doavai eel gwahrdahrobah

☞   ☜

Sono spiacente, è tutto esaurito.	I'm sorry, we're sold out.
Vi sono solo alcuni posti in galleria.	There are only a few seats left in the circle (mezzanine).
Posso vedere il suo biglietto?	May I see your ticket?*
Questo è il suo posto.	This is your seat.

---

* It's customary to tip usherettes (la maschera) in most Italian theatres.

DAYS OF THE WEEK, see page 151

Opera—Ballet—Concert *Opera—Balletto—Concerto*

Can you recommend a ...?	**Può consigliarmi ...?**	pwo konseelyahrmee
ballet	**un balletto**	oon bahllehttoa
concert	**un concerto**	oon koanchehrtoa
opera	**un'opera**	oonopayrah
operetta	**un'operetta**	oonopayrayttah
Where's the opera house/the concert hall?	**Dov'è il teatro dell'opera/la sala dei concerti?**	doavai eel tayaatroa dayllopayrah/lah saalah daiee koanchehrtee
What's on at the opera tonight?	**Cosa danno all'Opera questa sera?**	kawsah dahnnoa ahllopayrah kooaystah sayrah
Who's singing/ dancing?	**Chi canta/balla?**	kee kahntah/bahllah
What orchestra is playing?	**Che orchestra suona?**	kay oarkaystrah swonah
What are they playing?	**Cosa suonano?**	kawsah swonahnoa
Who's the conductor/ soloist?	**Chi è il maestro/ il solista?**	kee ai eel mahehstroa/ eel soleestah

Nightclub *Night-club*

Can you recommend a good nightclub?	**Può consigliarmi un buon night-club?**	pwo konseelyahrmee oon bwon "night-club"
Is there a floor show?	**C'è il varietà?**	chai eel vahreeaytah
What time does the floor show start?	**A che ora inizia il varietà?**	ah kay oarah eeneetseeah eel vahreeaytah
Is evening dress necessary?	**È necessario l'abito da sera?**	ai naychayssaareeoa laabeetoa dah sayrah

Discos *Discoteche*

Where can we go dancing?	**Dove possiamo andare a ballare?**	doavay posseeaamoa ahndaaray ah bahllaaray
Is there a disco- theque in town?	**C'è una discoteca in città?**	chai oonah deeskoataykah een cheettah
Would you like to dance?	**Vuole ballare?**	vwolay bahllaaray

Sports *Sport*

Football (soccer), tennis, boxing, wrestling and bicycle, car and horse racing are among popular spectator sports. If you like sailing, fishing, horseback riding, golf, tennis, hiking, cycling, swimming, golf or trap shooting, you'll find plenty of opportunity to satisfy your recreational bent.

Is there a football (soccer) match anywhere this Saturday?	C'è una partita di calcio da qualche parte, sabato?	chai oonah pahrteetah dee kahlchoa dah kwahlkay pahrtay saabahtoa
Which teams are playing?	Che squadre giocano?	kay skwaadray joakahnoa
Can you get me a ticket?	Mi può procurare un biglietto?	mee pwo proakooraaray oon beelyayttoa

basketball	la pallacanestro	lah pahllahkahnehstroa
boxing	il pugilato	eel poojeelaatoa
car racing	la corsa automobilistica	lah koarsah owtoamoabeeleesteeka
cycling	il ciclismo	eel cheekleezmoa
football (soccer)	il calcio	eel kahlchoa
horse racing	la corsa di cavalli	lah koarsah dee kahvahllee
skiing	lo sci	loa shee
swimming	il nuoto	eel nwotoa
tennis	il tennis	eel "tennis"
volleyball	la pallavolo	lah pahllahvoaloa

I'd like to see a boxing match.	Vorrei vedere un incontro di pugilato.	vorraie vaydayray oon eengkoantroa dee poojeelaatoa
What's the admission charge?	Quanto costa l'entrata?	kwahntoa kostah layntraatah
Where's the nearest golf course?	Dove si trova il campo da golf più vicino?	doavay see trawvah eel kahmpoa dah golf peeoo veecheenoa
Where are the tennis courts?	Dove sono i campi da tennis?	doavay soanoa ee kahmpee dah "tennis"
What's the charge per ...?	Qual è il prezzo per ...?	kwahl ai eel prehttsoa pair
day/round/hour	un giorno/una partita/un'ora	oon joarnoa/oonah pahrteetah/oonoarah

Can I hire (rent) rackets?	Posso noleggiare le racchette?	possoa noalaydjaaray lay rahkkehttay
Where is the race course (track)?	Dov'è l'ippodromo?	doavai leeppoadrawmoa
Is there any good fishing around here?	Ci sono buone possibilità di pesca in questa zona?	chee soanoa bwawnay posseebeeleetah dee payskah een kooaystah dzoanah
Do I need a permit?	È necessario il permesso?	ai naychayssaareeoa eel payrmayssoa
Where can I get one?	Dove posso procurarmene uno?	doavay possoa proakoorahrmaynay oonoa
Can one swim in the lake/river?	Si può nuotare nel lago/fiume?	see pwo nwawtaaray nayl laagoa/feeoomay
Is there a swimming pool here?	C'è una piscina qui?	chai oonah peesheenah kooee
Is it open-air or indoor?	È una piscina all'aperto o coperta?	ai oonah peesheenah ahllahpehrtoa oa koapehrtah
Is it heated?	È riscaldata?	ai reeskahldaatah
What's the temperature of the water?	Qual è la temperatura dell'acqua?	kwahl ai lah taympayrahtoorah dayllahkkwah
Is there a sandy beach?	C'è una spiaggia di sabbia?	chai oonah speeahdjah dee sahbbeeah

On the beach *In spiaggia*

Is it safe for swimming?	Si può nuotare senza pericolo?	see pwo nwawtaaray sayntsah payreekoaloa
Is there a lifeguard?	C'è un bagnino?	chai oon bahñeenoa
There are some big waves.	Ci sono cavalloni.	chee soanoa kahvahlloanee
Is it safe for children?	È sicuro per i bambini?	ai seekooroa pair ee bahmbeenee
Are there any dangerous currents?	Vi sono correnti pericolose?	vee soanoa koarrayntee payreekoaloasay
What time is high tide/low tide?	A che ora è l'alta marea/la bassa marea?	ah kay oarah ai lahltah mahrayah/lah bahssah mahrayah

I want to hire a/an/ some ...	**Vorrei noleggiare ...**	vorraiee noalaydjaaray
bathing hut (cabana)	**una cabina**	oonah kahbeenah
deck-chair	**una sedia a sdraio**	oonah saydeeah ah sdraaeeoa
motorboat	**una barca a motore**	oonah bahrkah ah motoaray
rowing-boat	**una barca a remi**	oonah bahrkah ah raymee
sailboard	**una tavola a vela**	oonah taavolah ah vailah
sailing-boat	**una barca a vela**	oonah bahrkah ah vailah
sunshade (umbrella)	**un ombrellone**	oon oambraylloanay
surfboard	**un sandolino**	oon sahndoaleenoa
water-skis	**degli sci nautici**	daylyee shee nowteechee

SPIAGGIA PRIVATA	PRIVATE BEACH
DIVIETO DI BALNEAZIONE	NO SWIMMING

Winter sports *Sport invernali*

Is there a skating rink near here?	**C'è una pista di pattinaggio qui vicino?**	chai oonah peestah dee pahtteenadjoa kooee veecheenoa
I'd like to ski.	**Vorrei sciare.**	vorraiee sheeaaray
downhill/cross-country skiing	**sci di pista/sci di fondo**	shee dee peestah/shee dee foandoa
Are there any ski runs for ...?	**Vi sono delle piste per ...?**	vee soanoa dayllay peestay pair
beginners	**principianti**	preencheepeeahntee
average skiers	**sciatori medi**	sheeahtoaree maydee
good skiers	**buoni sciatori**	bwawnee sheeahtoaree
Can I take skiing lesson there?	**Posso prendere delle lezioni di sci?**	possoa prehndayray dayllay laytseeoaee dee shee
Are there ski lifts?	**Ci sono delle sciovie?**	chee soanoa dayllay sheeoveeai
I want to hire a/ some ...	**Vorrei noleggiare ...**	vorraiee noalaydjaaray
poles	**dei bastoni**	daiee bahstoanee
skates	**dei pattini**	daiee pahtteenee
ski boots	**degli scarponi da sci**	daylyee skahrpoanee dah shee
skiing equipment	**una tenuta da sci**	oonah taynootah dah shee
skis	**degli sci**	daylyee shee

Making friends

Introductions *Presentazioni*

May I introduce ...?	**Posso presentarle ...?**	possoa prayzayntaarlay
John, this is ...	**Giovanni, ti presento ...**	jovahnnee tee prayzayntoa
My name is ...	**Mi chiamo ...**	mee keeaamoa
Pleased to meet you.	**Piacere.**	peeahchayray
What's your name?	**Come si chiama?**	koamay see keeaamah
How are you?	**Come sta?**	koamay stah
Fine, thanks. And you?	**Bene, grazie. E lei?**	bainay graatseeay. ay laiee

Follow-up *Per rompere il ghiaccio*

How long have you been here?	**Da quanto tempo è qui?**	dah kwahntoa tehmpoa ai kooee
We've been here a week.	**Siamo qui da una settimana.**	seeaamoa kooee dah oonah saytteemaanah
Is this your first visit?	**È la prima volta che viene?**	ai lah preemah voltah kay veeaynay
No, we came here last year.	**No, siamo già venuti l'anno scorso.**	noa seeaamoa jah vaynootee lahnnoa skoarsoa
Are you enjoying your stay?	**Le piace il suo soggiorno?**	lay peeaachay eel sooo soadjoarnoa
Yes, I like it very much.	**Sì, mi piace molto.**	see mee peeaachay moaltoa
I like the landscape a lot.	**Mi piace molto il paesaggio.**	mee peeaachay moaltoa eel pahayzahdjoa
Do you travel a lot?	**Viaggia molto?**	veeahdjah moaltoa
Where do you come from?	**Da dove viene?**	dah doavay veeaynay
I'm from ...	**Sono di ...**	soanoa dee
What nationality are you?	**Di che nazionalità è?**	dee kai nahtseeoanahleetah ai

COUNTRIES, see page 146

I'm ...	Sono ...	soanoa
American	americano(a)	ahmayreekaanoa(ah)
British	britannico(a)	breetahnneekoa(ah)
Canadian	canadese	kahnahdaysay
English	inglese	eengglaysay
Irish	irlandese	eerlahndaysay
Scottish	scozzese	skotsaysay
Where are you staying?	Dove soggiorna?	doavay soadjoarnah
Are you on your own?	È solo(a)?	ai soaloa(ah)
I'm with my ...	Sono con ...	soanoa kon
wife	mia moglie	meeah moalyay
husband	mio marito	meeoa mahreetoa
family	la mia famiglia	lah meeah fahmeelyah
parents	i miei genitori	ee meeaiee jayneetoaree
boyfriend	il mio ragazzo	eel meeoa rahgahttsoa
girlfriend	la mia ragazza	lah meeah rahgahttsah

grandfather/ grandmother	il nonno/la nonna	eel nonnoa/la nonnah
father/mother	il padre/la madre	eel paadray/lah maadray
son/daughter	il figlio/la figlia	eel feelyoa/lah feelyah
brother/sister	il fratello/la sorella	eel frahtehlloa/lah sorehllah
uncle/aunt	lo zio/la zia	loa dzeeoa/lah dzeeah
nephew/niece	il nipote/la nipote	eel neepoatay/lah neepoatay
cousin	il cugino/la cugina	eel koojeenoa/lah koojeenah

Are you married/ single?	È sposato(a)/scapolo (nubile)?	ai spozaatoa(ah)/skaapoa-loa (noobeelay)
Do you have children?	Ha dei bambini?	ah daiee bahmbeenee
What do you think of the country/people?	Cosa pensa del paese/della gente?	kawsah paynsah dayl pahaysay/dayllah jayntay
What do you do?	Che lavoro fa?	kay lahvoaroa fah
I'm a student.	Sono studente.	soanoa stoodehntay
I'm here on a business trip.	Sono qui in viaggio d'affari.	soanoa kooee een veeahdjoa dahffaaree
Do you play cards/ chess?	Gioca a carte/a scacchi?	joakah ah kahrtay/ah skahkkee

The weather *Il tempo*

What a lovely day!	**Che bella giornata!**	kay behllah joarnaatah
What awful weather!	**Che tempo orribile!**	kay tehmpoa orreebeelay
Isn't it cold/hot today?	**Che freddo/caldo fa oggi!**	kay frehddoa/kahldoa fah odjee
Is it usually as warm as this?	**Fa sempre caldo così?**	fah sehmpray kahldoa kawsee
Do you think it's going to ... tomorrow?	**Pensa che domani ...?**	paynsah kay domaanee
be a nice day	**sarà una bella giornata**	sahrah oonah behllah joarnaatah
rain	**pioverà**	peeovayrah
snow	**nevicherà**	nayveekayrah
What is the weather forecast?	**Come sono le previsioni del tempo?**	koamay soanoa lay prehveezeeoanee dayl tehmpoa

cloud	**la nuvola**	lah noovolah
fog	**la nebbia**	lah nehbbeeah
frost	**il gelo**	eel jayloa
ice	**il ghiaccio**	eel geeahtchoa
lightning	**il lampo**	eel lahmpoa
moon	**la luna**	lah loonah
rain	**la pioggia**	lah peeodjah
sky	**il cielo**	eel chayloa
snow	**la neve**	lah nayvay
star	**la stella**	lah stayllah
sun	**il sole**	eel soalay
thunder	**il tuono**	eel twonoa
thunderstorm	**il temporale**	eel tehmpoaraalay
wind	**il vento**	eel vayntoa

Invitations *Inviti*

Would you like to have dinner with us on ...?	**Vorrebbe cenare con noi ...?**	vorrehbbay chaynaaray kon noaee
May I invite you for lunch?	**Posso invitarla a pranzo?**	possoa-eenveetaarlah ah prahndzoa

DAYS OF THE WEEK, see page 151

Can you come over for a drink this evening?	Può venire a bere un bicchiere da me questa sera?	pwo vayneeray ah bayray oon beekkeeayray dah mai kooaystah sayrah
There's a party. Are you coming?	C'è un ricevimento. Viene?	chai oon reechayvee-mayntoa. veeaynay
That's very kind of you.	È molto gentile da parte sua.	ai moaltoa jaynteelay dah pahrtay sooah
I'd love to come.	Verrò con piacere.	vayrro kon peeahchayray
What time shall we come?	A che ora dobbiamo venire?	ah kay oarah doab-beeaamoa vayneeray
May I bring a friend?	Posso portare un amico (un'amica)?	possoa portaaray oon ahmeekoa (oonahmeekah)
I'm afraid we've got to go now.	Mi dispiace, ma adesso dobbiamo andare.	mee deespeeaachay mah ahdehssoa doabbeeaamoa ahndaaray
Next time you must come to visit us.	La prossima volta dovete venire da noi.	lah prosseemah voltah doavaytay vayneeray dah noaee
Thanks for the evening. It was great.	Grazie per la serata. È stata splendida.	graatseeay pair la say-raatah. ai staatah splehndeedah

Dating *Appuntamento*

Do you mind if I smoke?	La disturbo se fumo?	lah deestoorboa say foomoa
Would you like a cigarette?	Posso offrirle una sigaretta?	possoa offreerlay oonah seegahrayttah
Do you have a light, please?	Ha un fiammifero, per favore?	ah oon feeahmmeefayroa pair fahvoaray
Why are you laughing?	Perchè ride?	payrkai reeday
Is my Italian that bad?	È così cattivo il mio italiano?	ai kosee kahtteevoa eel meeoa eetahleeaanoa
Do you mind if I sit down here?	Permette che mi sieda qui?	pehrmayttay kay mee seeaaydah kooee
Can I get you a drink?	Posso offrirle qualcosa da bere?	possoa offreerlay kwahlkawsah dah bayray
Are you waiting for someone?	Aspetta qualcuno?	ahspayttah kwahlkoonoa

Are you free this evening?	È libera stasera?	ai leebayrah stahsayrah
Would you like to go out with me tonight?	Uscirebbe con me stasera?	oosheerehbbay kon mai stahsayrah
Would you like to go dancing?	Le piacerebbe andare a ballare?	lay peeahchayrehbbay ahndaaray ah bahllaaray
I know a good discotheque.	Conosco una buona discoteca.	koanoaskoa oonah bwawnah deeskoataykah
Shall we go to the cinema (movies)?	Andiamo al cinema?	ahndeeaamoa ahl cheenaymah
Would you like to go for a drive?	Andiamo a fare un giro in macchina?	ahndeeaamoa ah faaray oon jeeroa een mahkkeenah
Where shall we meet?	Dove possiamo incontrarci?	doavay posseeaamoa eengkontraarchee
I'll pick you up at your hotel.	Passerò a prenderla all'albergo.	pahssayroa ah prayndayrlah ahllahlbehrgoa
I'll call for you at 8.	Passerò da lei alle 8.	pahssayroa dah laiee ahllay 8
May I take you home?	Posso accompagnarla a casa?	possoa ahkkoampahñaarlah ah kaasah
Can I see you again tomorrow?	Posso rivederla domani?	possoa reevaydayrlah doamaanee
What's your telephone number?	Qual è il suo numero di telefono?	kwahl ai eel soooa noomayroa dee taylaifoanoa

... and you might answer:

I'd love to, thank you.	Con piacere, grazie.	kon peeahchayray graatseeay
Thank you, but I'm busy.	Grazie, ma sono impegnato(a).	graatseeay mah soanoa eempayñaatoa(ah)
No, I'm not interested, thank you.	No, non mi interessa, grazie.	no noan mee eentayrehssah graatseeay
Leave me alone!	Mi lasci in pace!	mee lahshee een paachay
Thank you, it's been a wonderful evening.	Grazie, è stata una magnifica serata.	graatseeay ai staatah oonah mahñeefeekah sayraatah
I've enjoyed myself.	Mi sono divertito(a) molto.	mee soanoa deevayrteetoa(ah) moaltoa

Shopping guide

This shopping guide is designed to help you find what you want with ease, accuracy and speed. It features:

1. A list of all major shops, stores and services (p. 98);
2. Some general expressions required when shopping to allow you to be specific and selective (p. 100);
3. Full details of the shops and services most likely to concern you. Here you'll find advice, alphabetical lists of items and conversion charts listed under the headings below.

		Page
Bookshop/ Stationer's	books, magazines, newspapers, stationery	104
Camping equipment	all items required for camping	106
Chemist's (drugstore)	medicine, first-aid, cosmetics, toilet articles	108
Clothing	clothes, accessories, shoes	112
Electrical appliances	radios, cassette-recorders, shavers	119
Grocery	some general expressions, weights, measures and packaging	120
Jeweller's/ Watchmaker's	jewellery, watches, watch repairs	121
Optician	glasses, lenses, binoculars	123
Photography	cameras, films, developing accessories	124
Tobacconist's	smoker's supplies	126
Miscellaneous	souvenirs, records, cassettes, toys	127

LAUNDRY, see page 29 / HAIRDRESSER, see page 30

Shops, stores and services   *Negozi e servizi*

Shop hours in Italy differ from summer to winter. In winter the shops are generally open from 8 a.m. to 7 p.m. with a lunch break between 1 and 3 p.m. During the tourist season, shops open and close later in the afternoon (4 to 8 p.m.). Some remain open on Sundays but most close a half day during the week—often Monday morning or Thursday afternoon.

Swiss shops are open from 8 a.m. to noon or 12.30 p.m. and from 1.30 to 6.30 or 7 p.m. (Saturdays until 5 p.m.) with half-day closings similar to Italy.

Where's the nearest ...?	Dove si trova ... più vicino(a)?	doavay see trawvah ... peeoo veecheenoa(ah)
antique shop	l'antiquario	lahnteekwaareeoa
art gallery	la galleria d'arte	lah gahllayreeah dahrtay
baker's	la panetteria	lah pahnehttayreeah
bank	la banca	lah bahngkah
barber's	il barbiere	eel bahrbeeayray
beauty salon	l'istituto di bellezza	leesteetootoa dee behllehttsah
bookshop	la libreria	lah leebrayreeah
butcher's	la macelleria	lah mahchayllayreeah
cake shop	la pasticceria	lah pahsteetchayreeah
camera shop	il negozio d'apparecchi fotografici	eel naygotseeoa dahppah-rehkkee foatoagraafeechee
chemist's	la farmacia	lah fahrmahcheeah
confectioner's	la pasticceria	lah pahsteetchayreeah
dairy	la latteria	lah lahttayreeah
delicatessen	la salumeria	lah sahloomayreeah
department store	il grande magazzino	eel grahnday mahgah-dzeenoa
drugstore	la farmacia	lah fahrmahcheeah
dry cleaner's	la lavanderia a secco	lah lahvahndayreeah ah saykkoa
electrician	l'elettricista	laylehttreecheestah
fishmonger's	la pescheria	lah payskayreeah
flower shop	il fiorista	eel feeoareestah
furrier's	la pellicceria	lah paylleetchayreeah
greengrocer's	il negozio di frutta e verdura	eel naygotseeoa dee froottah ay vehrdoorah
grocery	il negozio di alimentari	eel naygotseeoa dee ahlee-mayntaaree
hairdresser's	il parrucchiere	eel pahrrookkeeayray

hardware store	il negozio di ferramenta	eel naygotseeoa dee fehrrahmayntah
health food shop	il negozio di cibi dietetici	eel naygotseeoa dee chee-beeh deeaytayteechee
ironmonger's	il negozio di ferramenta	eel naygotseeoa dee fehrrahmayntah
jeweller's	la gioielleria	lah joeeayllayreeah
launderette	la lavanderia automatica	lah lahvahndayreeah owtoamaateekah
laundry	la lavanderia	lah lahvahndayreeah
library	la biblioteca	lah beebleeoataykah
market	il mercato	eel mayrkaatoa
newsagent's	il giornalaio	eel joarnahlaaeeoa
newsstand	l'edicola	laydeekoalah
optician	l'ottico	lotteekoa
pastry shop	la pasticceria	lah pahsteetchayreeah
photographer	il fotografo	eel foatoagrahfoa
police station	il posto di polizia	eel poastoa dee poalee-tseeah
post office	l'ufficio postale	looffeechoa poastaalay
shoemaker's (repairs)	il calzolaio	eel kahltsoalaaeeoa
shoe shop	il negozio di scarpe	eel naygotseeoa dee skahrpay
souvenir shop	il negozio di ricordi	eel naygotseeoa dee reekordee
sporting goods shop	il negozio di articoli sportivi	eel naygotseeoa dee ahr-teekoalee sporteevee
stationer's	la cartoleria	lah kahrtoalayreeah
supermarket	il supermercato	eel soopairmayrkaatoa
tailor's	la sartoria	lah sahrtoreeah
tobacconist's	la tabaccheria	lah tahbahkkayreeah
toy shop	il negozio di giocattoli	eel naygotseeoa dee joakahttoalee
travel agency	l'agenzia di viaggi	lahjayntseeah dee veeaahdjee
vegetable store	il negozio di frutta e verdura	eel naygotseeoa dee froottah ay vehrdoorah
watchmaker's	l'orologiaio	loaroaloajaaeeoa
wine merchant	il vinaio	eel veenaaeeoa

ENTRATA	ENTRANCE
USCITA	EXIT
USCITA DI SICUREZZA	EMERGENCY EXIT

General expressions *Espressioni generali*

Where? *Dove?*

Where's a good ...?	**Dov'è un buon ...?**	doavai oon bwawn
Where can I find ...?	**Dove posso trovare ...?**	doavay possoa trovaaray
Where's the main shopping area?	**Dov'è la zona principale dei negozi?**	doavai lah dzoanah preencheepaalay daiee naygotsee
How far is from here?	**Quanto dista da qui?**	kwahntoa deestah dah kooee
How do I get there?	**Come ci si può arrivare?**	koamay chee see pwo ahrreevaaray

---

SALDI SALE

Service *Servizio*

Can you help me?	**Può aiutarmi?**	pwo aheeootaarmee
I'm just looking.	**Do soltanto un'occhiata.**	doa soaltahntoa oonokkeeaatah
I want ...	**Desidero ...**	dayzeedayroa
Can you show me some ...?	**Può mostrarmi dei ...?**	pwo moastraarmee daiee
Do you have any ...?	**Ha dei ...?**	ah daiee
Where is the ... department?	**Dove si trova il reparto ...?**	doavay see trawvah eel raypahrtoa
Where is the lift (elevator)/escalator?	**Dov'è l'ascensore/ la scala mobile?**	doavai lahshaynsoaray/ lah skahlah mobeelay
Where do I pay?	**Dov'è la cassa?**	doavai lah kahssah

That one *Quello là*

Can you show me ...?	**Mi può mostrare ...?**	mee pwo moastraaray
this/that	**questo/quello**	kooaystoa/kooaylloa
the one in the window/on the shelf	**quello in vetrina/ sullo scaffale**	kooaylloa een vaytreenah/ soolloa skahffaalay

Defining the article *Descrizione dell'articolo*

I'd like a ... one.	Ne vorrei un ...	nay vorraiee oon
big	grande	grahnday
cheap	economico	aykoanawmeekoa
dark	scuro	skooroa
good	buono	bwawnoa
heavy	pesante	paysahntay
large	grande	grahnday
light (weight)	leggero	laydjairoa
light (colour)	chiaro	keeaaroa
oval	ovale	ovaalay
rectangular	rettangolare	rehttahngolaaray
round	rotondo	rotoandoa
small	piccolo	peekkoaloa
square	quadrato	kwahdraatoa
sturdy	solido	soaleedoa

I don't want anything too expensive.	Non voglio qualcosa di troppo caro.	noan voglyoa kwahlkawsah dee troppoa kaaroa

Preference *Preferenze*

Can you show me some more?	Me ne può mostrare degli altri?	may nay pwo moastraaray daylyee ahltree
Haven't you anything ...?	Non ha qualcosa ...?	noan ah kwahlkawsah
better	migliore	meelyoaray
cheaper	meno caro	maynoa kaaroa
larger	più grande	peeoo grahnday
smaller	più piccolo	peeoo peekkoaloa

How much? *Quanto?*

How much is this?	Quanto costa questo?	kwahntoa kostah kooaystoa
How much are they?	Quanto costano?	kwahntoa kostahnoa
I don't understand.	Non capisco.	noan kahpeeskoa
Please write it down.	Per favore, me lo scriva.	pair fahvoaray may loa skreevah
I don't want to spend more than ... lire.	Non voglio spendere più di ... lire.	noan voglyoa spehndayray peeoo dee ... leeray

COLOURS, see page 113

Decision *Decisione*

It's not quite what I want.	**Non è ciò che volevo.**	noan ai choa kay voalayvoa
No, I don't like it.	**No, non mi piace.**	noa noan mee peeaachay
I'll take it.	**Lo prendo.**	loa **prayn**doa

Ordering *Ordinazione*

Can you order it for me?	**Può ordinarmelo?**	pwo oardeenaarmayloa
How long will it take?	**Quanto tempo ci sarà da aspettare?**	kwahntoa tehmpoa chee sahrah dah ahspehttaaray

Delivery *Consegna*

I'll take it with me.	**Lo porto via.**	loa **poar**toa veeah
Deliver it to the ... Hotel.	**Lo consegni all'Albergo ...**	loa konsaynee ahllahl-bayrgoa
Please send it to this address.	**Per favore, lo mandi a questo indirizzo.**	pair fahvoaray loa mahndee ah kooaystoa eendeereettsoa
Will I have any difficulty with the customs?	**Avrò delle difficoltà alla dogana?**	ahvroa dayllay deeffee-koaltah ahllah doagaanah

Paying *Pagamento*

How much is it?	**Quant'è?**	kwahntai
Can I pay by traveller's cheque?	**Accettate i traveller's cheque?**	ahtchehttaatay ee "traveller's cheque"
Do you accept dollars/pounds?	**Accettate dei dollari/delle sterline?**	ahtchehttaatay daiee dollahree/dayllay stayrleenay
Do you accept credit cards?	**Accettate carte di credito?**	ahtchehttaatay kahrtay dee kraydeetoa
Do I have to pay the VAT (sales tax)?	**Devo pagare l'I.V.A.?**	dayvoa pahgaaray leevah
Haven't you made a mistake in the bill?	**Non vi siete sbagliati nel fare il conto?**	noan vee seeaytay sbah-lyaatee nayl faaray eel koantoa

Anything else? *Qualcos'altro?*

No, thanks, that's all.	**No, grazie, è tutto.**	no graatseeay ai toottoa
Yes. I want ...	**Sì, desidero ...**	see dayzeedayroa
Show me ...	**Mi mostri ...**	mee moastree
May I have a bag, please?	**Può darmi un sacchetto, per favore?**	pwo daarmee oon sahkkehttoa pair fahvoaray

Dissatisfied *Scontento*

Can you please exchange this?	**Può cambiare questo, per favore?**	pwo kahmbeeaaray kooaystoa pair fahvoaray
I want to return this.	**Desidero rendere questo.**	dayzeedayroa rayndayray kooaystoa
I'd like a refund. Here's the receipt.	**Desidero essere rimborsato. Ecco la ricevuta.**	dayzeedayroa ehssayray reemboarsaatoa. ehkkoa lah reechayvootah

Posso aiutarla?	Can I help you?
Cosa desidera?	What would you like?
Che ... desidera?	What ... would you like?
colore/forma qualità/quantità	colour/shape quality/quantity
Mi dispiace, non ne abbiamo.	I'm sorry, we haven't any.
L'abbiamo esaurito.	We're out of stock.
Dobbiamo ordinarglielo?	Shall we order it for you?
Lo porta via o dobbiamo mandarglielo?	Will you take it with you or shall we send it?
Qualcos'altro?	Anything else?
Sono ... lire, per favore.	That's ... lire, please.
La cassa è laggiù.	The cashier's over there.

Bookshop—Stationer's   *Libreria—Cartoleria*

In Italy, bookshops and stationer's are usually separate shops, though the latter will often sell paperbacks. Newspapers and magazines are sold at newsstands.

Where's the nearest ...?	Dov'è ... più vicina?	doavai ... peeoo veecheenah
bookshop	la libreria	lah leebrayreeah
stationer's	la cartoleria	lah kahrtoalayreeah
newsstand	l'edicola	laydeekoalah
Where can I buy an English-language newspaper?	Dove posso comprare un giornale in inglese?	doavay possoa kompraaray oon joarnaalay een eengglaysay
Where's the guide-book section?	Dov'è il reparto delle guide turistiche?	doavai eel raypahrtoa dayllay gooeeday tooreesteekay
Where do you keep the English books?	Dov'è il reparto dei libri inglesi?	doavai eel raypahrtoa daiee leebree eengglaysee
Do you have second-hand books?	Avete libri d'occasione?	ahvaytay leebree dokkahzeeoanay
I'd like a/an/some ...	Vorrei ...	vorraiee
address book	un'agenda per gli indirizzi	oonahjayndah pair lyee eendeereettsee
ball-point pen	una biro	oonah beeroa
book	un libro	oon leebroa
calendar	un calendario	oon kahlayndaareeoa
carbon paper	della carta carbone	dayllah kahrtah kahrboanay
cellophane tape	del nastro adesivo	dayl nahstroa ahdayzeevoa
crayons	dei pastelli	daiee pahstehllee
dictionary	un dizionario	oon deetseeoanaareeoa
Italian-English	italiano-inglese	eetahleeaanoa/eengglaysay
pocket	tascabile	tahskaabeelay
drawing paper	della carta da disegno	dayllah kahrtah dah deesayñoa
drawing pins	delle puntine	dayllay poonteenay
envelopes	delle buste	dayllay boostay
eraser	una gomma	oonah goammah
exercise book	un quaderno	oon kwahdairnoa
felt-tip pen	un pennarello	oon paynnahrehlloa
fountain pen	una penna stilografica	oonah paynnah steeloagraafeekah

glue	della colla	dayllah kollah
grammar book	una grammatica	oonah grahmmahteekah
guidebook	una guida turistica	oonah gooeedah tooreesteekah
ink	dell'inchiostro	daylleengkeeostroa
(adhesive) labels	delle etichette (adesive)	dayllay ayteekehttay (ahdayzeevay)
magazine	una rivista	oonah reeveestah
map	una carta geografica	oonah kahrtah jayoagraafeekah
map of the town	una pianta della città	oonah peeahntah dayllah cheettah
road map of ...	una carta stradale di ...	oonah kahrtah strahdaalay dee
mechanical pencil	un portamine	oon poartahmeenay
newspaper	un giornale	oon joarnaalay
notebook	un taccuino	oon tahkkooeenoa
note paper	della carta da lettere	dayllah kahrtah dah lehttayray
paintbox	una scatola di colori	oonah skaatoalah dee koaloaree
paper	della carta	dayllah kahrtah
paperback	un libro tascabile	oon leebroa tahskaabeelay
paperclips	dei fermagli	daiee fayrmahlyee
paste	della colla	dayllah kollah
pen	una penna	oonah paynnah
pencil	una matita	oonah mahteetah
pencil sharpener	un temperamatite	oon taympayrahmahteetay
playing cards	delle carte da gioco	dayllay kahrtay dah jokoa
pocket calculator	una calcolatrice tascabile	oonah kahlkoalahtreechay tahskaabeelay
postcard	una cartolina	oonah kahrtoaleenah
propelling pencil	un portamine	oon poartahmeenay
refill (for a pen)	un ricambio (per biro)	oon reekahmbeeoa (pair beeroa)
rubber	una gomma	oonah goammah
ruler	una riga	oonah reegah
staples	delle graffette	dayllay grahffehttay
string	dello spago	daylloa spaagoa
thumbtacks	delle puntine	dayllay poonteenay
tissue paper	della carta velina	dayllah kahrtah vayleenah
typewriter ribbon	un nastro per macchina da scrivere	oon nahstroa pair mahkkeenah dah skreevayray
typing paper	della carta per macchina da scrivere	dayllah kahrtah pair mahkkeenah dah skreevayray
writing pad	un blocco per appunti	oon blokkoa pair appoontee

COLOURS, see page 113

Camping equipment *Materiale da campeggio*

I'd like a/an/some ...	Vorrei ...	vorraiee
bottle-opener	un apribottiglia	oon ahpreebotteelyah
bucket	un secchio	oon saykkeeoa
butane gas	del gas butano	dayl gahz bootaanoa
campbed	un letto da campo	oon lehttoa dah kahmpoa
can opener	un apriscatole	oon ahpreeskaatoalay
candles	delle candele	dayllay kahndaylay
(folding) chair	una sedia (pieghevole)	oonah saydeeah (peeaygayvoalay)
charcoal	della carbonella	dayllah kahrboanayllah
clothes pegs	delle mollette da bucato	dayllay mollehttay dah bookaatoa
compass	una bussola	oonah boossoalah
cool box	una ghiacciaia	oonah geeahtchaaeeah
corkscrew	un cavatappi	oon kahvahtahppee
dishwashing detergent	del detersivo per lavare i piatti	dayl dehtehrseevoa pair lahvaaray ee peeahttee
first-aid kit	una cassetta del pronto soccorso	oonah kahssehttah dayl proantoa soakkoarsoa
fishing tackle	degli arnesi da pesca	daylyee ahrnayzee dah payskah
flashlight	una lampadina tascabile	oonah lahmpahdeenah tahskaabeelay
food box	un contenitore per il cibo	oon koantayneetoaray pair eel cheeboa
frying-pan	una padella	oonah pahdehllah
groundsheet	un telo per il terreno	oon tayloa pair eel tayrraynoa
hammer	un martello	oon mahrtehlloa
hammock	un'amaca	oonaamahkah
ice-pack	un elemento refrigerante	oon aylaymayntoa rayfreejayrahntay
kerosene	del petrolio	dayl paytrolyo
knapsack	uno zaino	oonoa dzaaeenoa
lamp	una lampada	oonah lahmpahdah
lantern	una lanterna	oonah lahntehrnah
matches	dei fiammiferi	daiee feeahmmeefayree
mattress	un materasso	oon mahtayrahssoa
methylated spirits	dell'alcool metilico	dayllahlkoal mayteeleekoa
mosquito net	una zanzariera	oonah dzahndzahreeayrah
pail	un secchio	oon saykkeeoa
paper napkins	dei tovagliolo di carta	daiee toavahlyoalee dee kahrtah
paraffin	del petrolio	dayl paytrolyo

penknife	un temperino	oon taympayreenoa
picnic basket	un cestino da picnic	oon chaysteenoa dah "picnic"
plastic bag	un sacchetto di plastica	oon sahkkehttoa dee plahsteekah
rope	della corda	dayllah koardah
rucksack	uno zaino	oonoa dzaaeenoa
saucepan	una casseruola	oonah kahssayrwoalah
scissors	un paio di forbici	oon paaeeoa dee foarbeechee
screwdriver	un cacciavite	oon kahtchahveetay
sleeping bag	un sacco a pelo	oon sahkkoa ah payloa
(folding) table	una tavola (pieghevole)	oonah taavoalah (peeaygayvoalay)
tent	una tenda	oonah tayndah
tent pegs	dei picchetti per tenda	daiee peekkehttee pair tayndah
tent pole	un palo per tenda	oon paaloa pair tayndah
tinfoil	un foglio di alluminio	oon foalyoa dee ahlloomeeneeoa
tin opener	un apriscatole	oon ahpreeskaatoalay
tongs	un paio di tenaglie	oon paaeeoa dee taynaalyay
torch	una lampadina tascabile	oonah lahmpahdeenah tahskaabeelay
vacuum flask	un thermos	oon tairmoas
washing powder	del detersivo	dayl daytehrseevoa
water flask	una borraccia	oonah boarratchah
wood alcohol	dell'alcool metilico	dayllahlkoal mayteeleekoa

Crockery *Stoviglie*

cups	delle tazze	dayllay tahttsay
mugs	dei boccali	daiee boakkaalee
plates	dei piatti	daiee peeahttee
saucers	dei piattini	daiee peeahtteenee
tumblers	dei bicchieri	daiee beekeeayree

Cutlery *Posate*

forks	delle forchette	dayllay forkehttay
knives	dei coltelli	daiee koaltehllee
spoons	dei cucchiai	daiee kookkeeaaee
teaspoons	dei cucchiaini	daiee kookkeeaaheenee
(made of) plastic	(di) plastica	(dee) plahsteekah
(made of) stainless steel	(di) acciaio inossidabile	(dee) ahtchaaeeoa eenosseedaabeelay

Chemist's (drugstore) *Farmacia*

The Italian chemists' normally don't stock the great range of goods that you'll find in England or in the U.S. For example, they don't sell photographic equipment or books. For perfume, make-up, etc., you can also go to a *profumeria* (proafoomay**ree**ah).

You can recognize a chemist's by the sign outside—a green or red cross, illuminated at night. In the window you'll see a notice telling where the nearest all-night chemist's is.

This section is divided into two parts:

1. Pharmaceutical—medicine, first-aid, etc.
2. Toiletry—toilet articles, cosmetics

General *Generalità*

Where's the nearest (all-night) chemist's?	**Dov'è la farmacia (di turno) più vicina?**	doavai lah fahrmah**cheeah** (dee **toor**noa) peeoo veecheenah
What time does the chemist's open/ close?	**A che ora apre/ chiude la farmacia?**	ah kay oarah aapray/ keeooday lah fahrmahcheeah

1—Pharmaceutical *Medicine, primi soccorsi, ecc.*

I want something for a ...	**Desidero qualcosa per ...**	dayzeedayroa kwahl**kaw**sah pair
cold	**il raffreddore**	eel rahffrayd**doa**ray
cough	**la tosse**	lah toassay
hay fever	**la febbre del fieno**	lah **fayb**bray dayl feeaynoa
insect bites	**le punture d'insetti**	lay poontooray deen**seht**tee
hangover	**il mal di testa**	eel mahl dee **teh**stah
sunburn	**una scottatura solare**	oonah skoattah**too**rah soa**laa**ray
travel sickness	**il mal d'auto**	eel mahl **dow**toa
upset stomach	**il mal di stomaco**	eel mahl dee **sto**mahkoa
Can you make up this prescription for me?	**Può prepararmi questa ricetta?**	pwo praypah**raar**mee **koo**aystah ree**cheht**tah
Can I get it without a prescription?	**Può darmi questa medicina senza ricetta?**	pwo **daar**mee **koo**aystah maydee**chee**nah **sayn**tsah ree**cheht**tah

DOCTOR, see page 137

Can I have a/an/some ...?	Mi può dare ...?	mee pwo daaray
analgesic	un analgesico	oon ahnahljaizeekoa
antiseptic cream	della crema antisettica	dayllah kraimah ahntee-sehtteekah
aspirin	delle aspirine	dayllay ahspeereenay
bandage	una benda	oonah bayndah
elastic bandage	una benda elastica	oonah bayndah aylahsteekah
Band-Aids	dei cerotti	daiee chayrottee
contraceptives	degli antifecondativi	daylyee ahnteefaykoandahteevee
corn plasters	dei cerotti callifughi	daiee chayrottee kahhleefoogee
cotton wool (absorbent cotton)	del cotone idrofilo	dayl koatoanay eedroafeeloa
cough drops	delle pasticche per la tosse	dayllay pahsteekkay pair lah toassay
disinfectant	del disinfettante	dayl deeseenfehttahntay
ear drops	delle gocce per le orecchie	dayllay goatchay pair lay oraykkeeay
Elastoplast	dei cerotti	daiee chayrottee
eye drops	delle gocce per gli occhi	dayllay goatchay pair lyee okkee
gauze	della garza	dayllah gahrdzah
insect repellent/spray	una crema contro gli insetti/uno spray insetticida	oonah kraimah koantroa lyee eensehttee/oonoa "spray" eensehtteecheedah
iodine	della tintura di iodio	dayllah teentoorah dee eeodeeoa
laxative	un lassativo	oon lahssahteevoa
mouthwash	un gargarismo	oon gahrgahreezmoa
nose drops	delle gocce nasali	dayllay goatchay naasaalee
sanitary towels (napkins)	degli assorbenti igienici	daylyee ahssoarbayntee eejayneechee
sleeping pills	dei sonniferi	daiee soanneefayree
suppositories	delle supposte	dayllay soappostay
... tablets	delle pastiglie ...	dayllay pahsteelyay
tampons	dei tamponi igienici	daiee tahmpoanee eejayneechee
thermometer	un termometro	oon tayrmoamaytroa
throat lozenges	delle pasticche per la gola	dayllay pahsteekkay pair lah goalah
tranquillizers	dei tranquillanti	daiee trahnkooeellahntee
vitamin pills	delle vitamine	dayllay veetahmeenay

SHOPPING GUIDE

2—Toiletry *Articoli da toilette*

I'd like a/an/some ...	Desidero ...	dayzeedayroa
after-shave lotion	una lozione dopobarba	oonah loatseeoanay dawpoabahrbah
bath salts	dei sali da bagno	daiee saalee dah baañoa
bubble bath	un bagnoschiuma	oon baañoaskeeoomah
cream	una crema	oonah kraimah
cleansing cream	una crema detergente	oonah kraimah daytehrjayntay
foundation cream	un fondo tinta	oon foandoa teentah
moisturizing cream	una crema idratante	oonah kraimah eedrahtahntay
night cream	una crema da notte	oonah kraimah dah nottay
cuticle remover	un prodotto per togliere le pellicine	oon proadoattoa pair tolyay-ray lay pehlleecheenay
deodorant	un deodorante	oon dayoadoarahntay
emery board	una limetta per unghie	oonah leemehttah pair oonggeeay
eye liner	un eye-liner	oon "eye-liner"
eye pencil	una matita per occhi	oonah mahteetah pair okkee
eye shadow	un ombretto	oon oambrayttoa
face powder	della cipria	dayllah cheepreeah
foot cream	una crema per i piedi	oonah kraimah pair ee peeaydee
hand cream	una crema per le mani	oonah kraimah pair lay maanee
lipsalve	un burro cacao	oon boorroa kahkaaoa
lipstick	un rossetto	oon roassehttoa
make-up remover pads	dei tamponi per togliere il trucco	daiee tahmpoanee pair tolyayray eel trookkoa
nail brush	uno spazzolino da unghie	oonoa spahtsoaleenoa dah oonggeeay
nail file	una lima da unghie	oonah leemah dah oonggeeay
nail polish	uno smalto	oonoa smahltoa
nail polish remover	un solvente per le unghie	oon soalvayntay pair lay oonggeeay
nail scissors	un paio di forbicine per le unghie	oon paaeeoa dee forbee-cheenay pair lay oonggeeay
perfume	un profumo	oon proafoomoa
powder	della cipria	dayllah cheepreeah
razor	un rasoio	oon rahsoaeeoa
razor blades	delle lamette	dayllay lahmayttay
rouge	del fard	dayl "fard"

Guida degli acquisti

safety pins	**delle spille di sicurezza**	dayllay speellay dee seekoorayttsah
shaving cream	**una crema da barba**	oonah kraimah dah bahrbah
soap	**una saponetta**	oonah sahpoanayttah
sun-tan cream	**una crema solare**	oonah kraimah soalaaray
sun-tan oil	**un olio solare**	oon olyoa soalaaray
talcum powder	**del talco**	dayl tahlkoa
tissues	**dei fazzolettini di carta**	daiee fahttsoalehtteenee dee kahrtah
toilet paper	**della carta igienica**	dayllah kahrtah eejayneekah
toilet water	**dell'acqua di colonia**	dayllahkkwah dee koaloneeah
toothbrush	**uno spazzolino da denti**	oonoa spahttsoaleenoa dah dehntee
toothpaste	**un dentifricio**	oon daynteefreechoa
tweezers	**delle pinzette**	dayllay peentsehttay

For your hair *Per i vostri capelli*

bobby pins	**delle mollette**	dayllay mollayttay
colour shampoo	**uno shampoo colorante**	oonoa shahmpoa koaloarahntay
comb	**un pettine**	oon paytteenay
dry shampoo	**uno shampo secco**	oonoa shahmpoa sehkkoa
hairbrush	**una spazzola per capelli**	oonah spahttsoalah pair kahpayllee
hair slide	**un fermaglio**	oon fayrmaalyoa
hairgrips	**delle mollette**	dayllay mollayttay
hair lotion	**una lozione per capelli**	oonah loatseeoanay pair kahpehllee
hairspray	**della lacca**	dayllah lahkkah
setting lotion	**una lozione fissativa**	oonah loatseeoanay feessahteevah
shampoo for dry/greasy (oily) hair	**dello shampoo per capelli secchi/grassi**	daylloa shahmpoa pair kahpehllee saykkee/grahssee

For the baby *Per il vostro bambino*

baby food	**degli alimenti per bebè**	daylyee ahleemaintee pair baybay
dummy (pacifier)	**un succhiotto**	oon sookkeeottoa
feeding bottle	**un biberon**	oon beebayroan
nappies (diapers)	**dei pannolini**	daiee pahnnoaleenee

Clothing *Abbigliamento*

If you want to buy something specific, prepare yourself in advance. Look at the list of clothing on page 116. Get some idea of the colour, material and size you want. They're all listed on the next few pages.

General *Generalità*

I'd like ...	Vorrei ...	vorraiee
I want ... for a 10-year-old boy/girl.	Desidero ... per un bambino/una bambina di 10 anni.	dayzeedayroa ... pair oon bahmbeenoa/oonah bahmbeenah dee 10 ahnnee
I want something like this.	Voglio qualcosa come questo.	volyoa kwahlkawsah koamay kooaystoa
I like the one in the window.	Mi piace quello in vetrina.	mee peeaachay kooaylloa een vaytreenah
How much is that per metre?	Quanto costa al metro?	kwahntoa kostah ahl maytroa

1 centimetre (cm.)	= 0.39 in.	1 inch	= 2.54 cm.
1 metre (m.)	= 39.37 in.	1 foot	= 30.5 cm.
10 metres	= 32.81 ft.	1 yard	= 0.91 m.

Colour *Colore*

I want something in ...	Voglio qualcosa di colore ...	volyoa kwahlkawsah dee koaloaray
I'd like a darker/lighter shade.	Desidero una tonalità più scura/più chiara.	dayzeedayroa oonah toanahleetah peeoo skoorah/peeoo keeaarah
I want something to match this.	Voglio qualcosa per ravvivare questo.	volyoa kwahlkawsah pair rahvveevaaray kooaystoa
I'd like the same colour as ...	Vorrei lo stesso colore che ...	vorraiee loa stayssoa koaloaray kai
I don't like the colour.	Non mi piace il colore.	noan mee peeaachay eel koaloaray

beige	**beige**	baizh
black	**nero**	nayroa
blue	**blu**	bloo
light blue	**azzurro**	ahdzoorroa
brown	**marrone**	mahrroanay
golden	**dorato**	doaraatoa
green	**verde**	vayrday
grey	**grigio**	greejoa
mauve	**lilla**	leellah
orange	**arancio**	ahrahnchoa
pink	**rosa**	rawzah
purple	**viola**	veeolah
red	**rosso**	roassoa
silver	**argentato**	ahrjayntaatoa
turquoise	**turchese**	toorkayzay
white	**bianco**	beeahngkoa
yellow	**giallo**	jahlloa
light ...	**... chiaro**	keeaaroa
dark ...	**... scuro**	skooroa

tinta unita	**a righe**	**a pallini**	**a quadri**	**fantasia**
(teentah ooneetah)	(ah reegay)	(ah pahlleenee)	(ah kwaadree)	(fahntahzeeah)

Material *Tessuto*

Do you have anything in ...?	**Ha qualcosa in ...?**	ah kwahlkawsah een
I want a cotton blouse.	**Voglio una blusa di cotone.**	volyoa oonah bloosah dee koatoanay
Is that ...?	**È un prodotto ...?**	ai oon proadoattoa
handmade	**fatto a mano**	fahttoa ah maanoa
imported	**importato**	eempoartaatoa
made here	**nazionale**	nahtseeoanaalay
I want something thinner.	**Desidero qualcosa di più fine.**	dayzeedayroa kwahlkawsah dee peeoo feenay
Do you have any better quality?	**Ha una qualità migliore?**	ah oonah kwahleetah meelyoaray
What's it made of?	**Di che cos'è?**	dee kay kosai

cambric	**la tela battista**	lah **taylah** bah**tteesta**h
camel-hair	**il pelo di cammello**	eel **payloa** dee kahm-**mehlloa**
chiffon	**lo chiffon**	loa sheef**foan**
corduroy	**il velluto a coste**	eel vayl**lootoa** ah **koasta**y
cotton	**il cotone**	eel koa**toana**y
crepe	**il crespo**	eel **krayspoa**
denim	**la tela di cotone**	lah **taylah** dee koa**toana**y
felt	**il feltro**	eel **fayltroa**
flannel	**la flanella**	lah flah**nehlla**h
gabardine	**il gabardine**	eel gahbahr**deen**
lace	**il pizzo**	eel **peettsoa**
leather	**la pelle**	lah **pehllay**
linen	**il lino**	eel **leenoa**
poplin	**il popeline**	eel poa**paylee**n
satin	**il raso**	eel **raasoa**
silk	**la seta**	lah **sayta**h
suede	**la renna**	lah **rehnna**h
towelling	**il tessuto di spugna**	eel tays**sootoa** dee
(terrycloth)		**spooña**h
velvet	**il velluto**	eel vayl**lootoa**
velveteen	**il velluto di cotone**	eel vayl**lootoa** dee
		koa**toana**y
wool	**la lana**	lah **laana**h
worsted	**il pettinato**	eel payt**teenaatoa**

Is it ...?	**È ...?**	ai
pure cotton/wool	**puro cotone/pura lana**	**pooroa** koa**toana**y/**poorah laana**h
synthetic	**sintetico**	seen**tayteekoa**
colourfast	**di colore solido**	dee koa**loaray soleedoa**
wrinkle resistant	**ingualcibile**	eengwahl**cheebeelay**
Is it hand washable/ machine washable?	**Si può lavare a mano/ in lavatrice?**	see pwo lah**vaara**y ah **maa-noa**/een lahvah**treecha**y
Will it shrink?	**Si restringe al lavaggio?**	see ray**streenja**y ahl lah**vahdjoa**

Size *Taglia*

I take size 38.	**La mia taglia è il 38.**	lah **meeah tahlyah** ai eel 38
Could you measure me?	**Può prendermi le misure?**	pwo **prehndayrmee** lay mee**zoora**y
I don't know the Italian sizes.	**Non conosco le misure italiane.**	noan koa**noaskoa** lay mee**zoora**y eetah**leeaana**y

Sizes can vary somewhat from one manufacturer to another, so be sure to try on shoes and clothing before you buy.

Women   *Donne*

Dresses/Suits						
American	8	10	12	14	16	18
British	10	12	14	16	18	20
Continental	36	38	40	42	44	46

Stockings							Shoes			
American	} 8	8½	9	9½	10	10½	6	7	8	9
British							4½	5½	6½	7½
Continental	0	1	2	3		4	5	37	38	40	41

Men   *Uomini*

Suits/Overcoats							Shirts			
American	} 36	38	40	42	44	46	15	16	17	18
British										
Continental	46	48	50	52	54	56	38	41	43	45

Shoes									
American	} 5	6	7	8	8½	9	9½	10	11
British									
Continental	38	39	41	42	43	43	44	44	45

A good fit?   *Una buona prova?*

Can I try it on?	**Posso provarlo?**	possoa provahrloa
Where's the fitting room?	**Dov'è la cabina di prova?**	doavai lah kahbeenah dee prawvah
Is there a mirror?	**C'è uno specchio?**	chai oonoa spaykkeeoa
It fits very well.	**Va molto bene.**	vah moaltoa bainay
It doesn't fit.	**Non va bene.**	noan vah bainay
It's too ...	**È troppo ...**	ai troppoa
short/long	**corto/lungo**	koartoa/loonggoa
tight/loose	**stretto/largo**	strayttoa/lahrgoa

NUMBERS, see page 147

| How long will it take to alter? | Quanto tempo ci vuole per le modifiche? | kwahntoa tehmpoa chee vwolay pair lay moadeefeekay |

Clothes and accessories *Indumenti e accessori*

I'd like a/an/some ...	Vorrei ...	vorraiee
anorak	una giacca a vento	oonah jahkkah ah vayntoa
bathing cap	una cuffia da bagno	oonah kooffeeah dah baañoa
bathing suit	un costume da bagno	oon koastoomay dah baañoa
bathrobe	un accappatoio	oon ahkkahppahtoaeeoa
blouse	una blusa	oonah bloozah
bow tie	una cravatta a farfalla	oonah krahvahttah ah fahrfahllah
bra	un reggiseno	oon raydjeesaynoa
braces	delle bretelle	dayllay braytehllay
briefs	uno slip	oonoa "slip"
cap	un berretto	oon bayrrayttoa
cardigan	un cardigan	oon "cardigan"
coat	un cappotto	oon kahppottoa
dress	un abito	oon aabeetoa
dressing gown	una vestaglia	oonah vehstahlyah
evening dress (woman's)	un abito da sera	oon aabeetoa dah sayrah
frock	un abito	oon aabeetoa
garter belt	un reggicalze	oon raydjeekahltsay
girdle	un busto	oon boostoa
gloves	dei guanti	daiee gwahntee
handbag	una borsetta	oonah boarsayttah
handkerchief	un fazzoletto	oon fahtsoalehttoa
hat	un cappello	oon kahppehlloa
jacket	una giacca	oonah jahkkah
jeans	dei jeans	daiee "jeans"
jersey	una maglietta	oonah mahlyehttah
jumper (Br.)	un maglione	oon mahlyoanay
kneesocks	dei calzettoni	daiee kahltsehttoanee
nightdress	una camicia da notte	oonah kahmeechah dah nottay
overalls	una tuta	oonah tootah
pair of ...	un paio di ...	oon paaeeoa dee
panties	uno slip	oonoa "slip"
pants (Am.)	dei pantaloni	daiee pahntahloanee
panty girdle	una guaina	oonah gwaaeenah
panty hose	dei collant	daiee kollahnt

pullover	un pullover	oon "pullover"
roll-neck (turtle-neck)	a collo alto	ah kolloa ahltoa
round	a girocollo	ah jeeroakolloa
V-neck	con scollatura a punta	kon skollahtoorah ah poontah
pyjamas	un pigiama	oon peejaamah
raincoat	un impermeabile	oon eempayrmayaabeelay
scarf	una sciarpa	oonah shahrpah
shirt	una camicia	oonah kahmeechah
shorts	uno short	oonoa "short"
skirt	una gonna	oonah goannah
slip	una sottoveste	oonah soattoavehstay
socks	dei calzini	daiee kahltseenee
stockings	delle calze da donna	dayllay kahltsay dah donnah
suit (man's)	un completo	oon koamplaytoa
suit (woman's)	un tailleur	oon "tailleur"
suspenders (Am.)	delle bretelle	dayllay braytehllay
sweater	un maglione	oon mahlyoanay
sweatshirt	una blusa	oonah bloozah
swimming trunks/swimsuit	un costume da bagno	oon koastoomay dah baañoa
T-shirt	una maglietta di cotone	oonah mahlyehttah dee koatoanay
tie	una cravatta	oonah krahvahttah
tights	dei collant	daiee kollahnt
tracksuit	una tuta sportiva	oonah tootah sporteevah
trousers	dei pantaloni	daiee pahntahloanee
umbrella	un ombrello	oon oambrehlloa
underpants	delle mutande/uno slip	dayllay mootahnday/oonoa "slip"
undershirt	una canottiera	oonah kahnotteeayrah
vest (Am.)	un panciotto	oon pahnchottoa
vest (Br.)	una canottiera	oonah kahnotteeayrah
waistcoat	un panciotto	oon pahnchottoa

belt	la cintura	lah cheentoorah
button	il bottone	eel boattoanay
pocket	la tasca	lah tahskah
press stud (snap fastener)	il bottone a pressione	eel boattoanay ah praysseeoanay
sleeve	la manica	lah maaneekah
zip (zipper)	la cerniera	lah chehrneeayrah

Shoes *Scarpe*

I'd like a pair of ...	Vorrei un paio di ...	vorraiee oon paaeeoa dee
boots	stivali	steevaalee
moccasins	mocassini	moakahsseenee
plimsolls (sneakers)	scarpe da tennis	skahrpay dah tainnees
sandals	sandali	sahndahlee
shoes	scarpe	skahrpay
flat	basse	bahssay
with a heel	con i tacchi	koan ee tahkkee
slippers	pantofole	pahntofoalay
These are too ...	Queste sono troppo ...	kwaystay soanoa troppoa
narrow/wide	strette/larghe	strayttay/lahrgay
large/small	grandi/piccole	grahndee/peekkoalay
Do you have a larger/ smaller size?	Ha un numero più grande/più piccolo?	ah oon noomayroa peeoo grahnday/peeoo peekkoaloa
Do you have the same in black?	Ha le stesse in nero?	ah lay stehssay een nayroa
cloth/leather/ rubber/suede	in tela/pelle/ gomma/camoscio	een taylah/pehllay/ goammah/kahmoshoa
Is it genuine leather?	È vera pelle?	ai vayrah pehllay
I need some shoe polish/shoelaces.	Mi serve del lucido/ dei lacci.	mee sairvay dayl loocheedoa/daiee lahtchee

Shoes worn out? Here's the key to getting them fixed again:

Can you repair these shoes?	Mi può riparare queste scarpe?	mee pwo reepahraaray kooaystay skahrpay
Can you stitch this?	Può attaccare questo?	pwo ahttahkkaaray kooaystoa
I want new soles and heels.	Desidero suole e tacchi nuovi.	dayzeedayroa swolay ay tahkkee nwawvee
When will they be ready?	Quando saranno pronte?	kwahndoa sahrahnnoa proantay
I need them ...	Ne ho bisogno ...	nay oa beezoañoa
as soon as possible	il più presto possibile	eel peeoo prehstoa posseebeelay
tomorrow	domani	doamaanee

COLOURS, see page 113

Electrical appliances   *Apparecchi elettrici*

In Italy you will usually find 220-volt current, though some older buildings, particularly in Rome, have 125-volt outlets.

What's the voltage?	**Qual è il voltaggio?**	kwahl ai eel voaltahdjoa
Do you have a battery for this?	**Ha una pila per questo?**	ah oonah peelah pair kooaystoa
This is broken. Can you repair it?	**È rotto. Me lo può riparare?**	ai roattoa. may loa pwo reepahraaray
Can you show me how it works?	**Può mostrarmi come funziona?**	pwo moastraarmee koamay foontseeoanah
I'd like (to hire) a video cassette.	**Vorrei (noleggiare) una video cassetta.**	vorraiee (noalaydjaaray) oonah veedayoa kahssehttah
I'd like a/an/some …	**Vorrei …**	vorraiee
adaptor	**una presa multipla**	oonah prayzah moolteeplah
amplifier	**un amplificatore**	oon ahmpleefeekahtoaray
bulb	**una lampadina**	oonah lahmpahdeenah
clock-radio	**una radio-sveglia**	oonah raadeeoa-svaylyah
electric toothbrush	**uno spazzolino da denti elettrico**	oonoa spatsoaleenoa dah dayntee aylehttreekoa
extension lead (cord)	**una prolunga**	oonah proaloonggah
hair dryer	**un asciugacapelli**	oon ashoogahkahpayllee
headphones	**una cuffia (d'ascolto)**	oonah kooffeeah (dahskoaltoa)
(travelling) iron	**un ferro da stiro (da viaggio)**	oon fehrroa dah steeroa (dah veeahdjoa)
lamp	**una lampada**	oonah lahmpahdah
plug	**una spina**	oonah speenah
portable …	**… portatile**	… poartaateelay
radio	**una radio**	oonah raadeeoa
car radio	**un'autoradio**	oonowtoaraadeeoa
record player	**un giradischi**	oon jeerahdeeskee
shaver	**un rasoio elettrico**	oon rahsoaeeoa aylehttreekoa
speakers	**degli altoparlanti**	daylyee ahltoapahrlahntee
(cassette) tape recorder	**un registratore (a cassette)**	oon rayjeestrahtoaray (ah kassehttay)
(colour) television	**un televisore (a colori)**	oon taylayveezoaray (ah koaloaree)
transformer	**un trasformatore**	oon trahsfoarmahtoaray
video-recorder	**un video registratore**	oon veedayoa rayjeestrahtoaray

SHOPPING GUIDE

Grocery *Negozio di alimentari*

I'd like some bread, please.	**Vorrei del pane, per favore.**	vorraiee dayl paanay pair fahvoaray
What sort of cheese do you have?	**Che formaggi avete?**	kay foarmahdjee ahvaytay
A piece of that one/ the one on the shelf.	**Un pezzo di quello/ quello sullo scaffale.**	oon pehtsoa dee kooaylloa/ kooaylloa soolloa skahf-faalay
I'll have one of those, please.	**Vorrei uno di quelli, per favore.**	vorraiee oonoa dee kooayllee pair fahvoaray
May I help myself?	**Posso servirmi?**	possoa sayrveermee
I'd like ...	**Vorrei ...**	vorraiee
a kilo of apples	**un chilo di mele**	oon keeloa dee maylay
half a kilo of tomatoes	**mezzo chilo di pomodori**	mehdzoa keeloa dee pomodawree
100 grams of butter	**100 grammi (un etto) di burro**	chehntoa grahmmee (oon ehttoa) dee boorroa
a litre of milk	**un litro di latte**	oon leetroa dee lahttay
half a dozen eggs	**mezza dozzina di uova**	mehdzah doadzeenah dee wawvah
4 slices of ham	**4 fette di prosciutto**	4 fehttay dee proashoottoa
a packet of tea	**un pacchetto di tè**	oon pahkkehttoa dee tai
a jar of jam	**un vasetto di marmellata**	oon vahzehttoa dee marmehllaatah
a tin (can) of peaches	**una scatola di pesche**	oonah skaatoalah dee payskay
a tube of mustard	**un tubetto di mostarda**	oon toobehttoa dee moastahrdah
a box of chocolates	**una scatola di cioccolatini**	oonah skaatoalah dee chokkoalahteenee

---

1 kilogram or kilo (kg.) = 1000 grams (g.)	
100 g. = 3.5 oz.	½ kg. = 1.1 lbs.
200 g. = 7.0 oz.	1 kg. = 2.2 lbs.
1 oz. = 28.35 g.	
1 lb. = 453.60 g.	

---

1 litre (l.) = 0.88 imp. quarts = 1.06 U.S. quarts	
1 imp. quart = 1.14 l.	1 U.S. quart = 0.95 l.
1 imp. gallon = 4.55 l.	1 U.S. gallon = 3.8 l.

Guida degli acquisti

FOOD, see also page 63

Jeweller's—Watchmaker's *Gioielleria—Orologeria*

Could I please see that?	Potrei vedere quello, per favore?	potraiee vaydayray kooayl-loa pair fahvoaray
Do you have anything in gold?	Avete qualcosa in oro?	ahvaytay kwahlkawsah een oroa
How many carats is this?	Di quanti carati è?	dee kwahntee kahraatee ai
Is this real silver?	È vero argento?	ai vayroa ahrjayntoa
Can you repair this watch?	Può riparare questo orologio?	pwo reepahraaray kooay-stoa oaroalojoa
I'd like a/an/some ...	Vorrei ...	vorraiee
alarm clock	una sveglia	oonah svaylyah
bangle	un braccialetto	oon brahtchahlehttoa
battery	una pila	oonah peelah
bracelet	un braccialetto	oon brahtchahlehttoa
chain bracelet	un braccialetto a catena	oon brahtchahlehttoa ah kahtaynah
charm bracelet	un braccialetto a ciondoli	oon brahtchahlehttoa ah choandoalee
brooch	una spilla	oonah speellah
chain	una catenina	oonah kahtayneenah
charm	un ciondolo	oon choandoaloa
cigarette case	un portasigarette	oon portahseegahrayttay
cigarette lighter	un accendino	oon ahtchayndeenoa
clip	un fermaglio	oon fayrmaalyoa
clock	un orologio	oon oaroalojoa
cross	una croce	oonah kroachay
cuckoo clock	un orologio a cucù	oon oaroalojoa ah kookoo
cuff links	dei gemelli	daiee jaymehllee
cutlery	delle posate	dayllay poasaatay
earrings	degli orecchini	daylyee oaraykkeenee
gem	una pietra preziosa	oonah peeaytrah pray-tseeoasah
jewel box	un portagioielli	oon portahjoeeehllee
music box	un carillon	oon kahreeyon
necklace	una collana	oonah koallaanah
pendant	un pendente	oon payndayntay
pocket watch	un orologio da tasca	oon oaroalojoa dah tahskah
powder compact	un portacipria	oon portahcheepreeah
ring	un anello	oon ahnehlloa
engagement ring	un anello di fidanzamento	oon ahnehlloa dee feedahntsahmayntoa

signet ring	**un anello con stemma**	oon ahnehlloa kon stehmmah
wedding ring	**una fede nuziale**	oonah fayday nootseeaalay
rosary	**un rosario**	oon rawzaareeoa
silverware	**dell'argenteria**	dayllahrjayntayreeah
tie clip	**un fermacravatte**	oon fayrmahkrahvahttay
tie pin	**uno spillo per cravatta**	oonoa speelloa pair krahvahttah
watch	**un orologio**	oon oaroalojoa
automatic	**automatico**	owtoamaateekoa
digital	**digitale**	deejeetaalay
quartz	**al quarzo**	ahl kwahrtsoa
with a second hand	**con lancetta dei secondi**	kon lahnchehttah daiee saykoandee
watchstrap	**un cinturino per orologio**	oon cheentooreenoa pair oaroaloajoa
wristwatch	**un orologio braccia-letto**	oon oaroaloajoa brahtchah-lehttoa

alabaster	**l'alabastro**	lahlahbahstroa
amber	**l'ambra**	lahmbrah
amethyst	**l'ametista**	lahmayteestah
copper	**il rame**	eel raamay
coral	**il corallo**	eel koarahlloa
crystal	**il cristallo**	eel kreestahlloa
cut glass	**il vetro tagliato**	eel vaytroa tahlyaatoa
diamond	**il diamante**	eel deeahmahntay
emerald	**lo smeraldo**	loa smayrahldoa
enamel	**lo smalto**	loa smahltoa
gold	**l'oro**	loroa
gold plate	**placcato d'oro**	plahkkaatoa doroa
ivory	**l'avorio**	lahvoreeoa
jade	**la giada**	lah jaadah
onyx	**l'onice**	loneechay
pearl	**la perla**	lah pehrlah
pewter	**il peltro**	eel payltroa
platinum	**il platino**	eel plaateenoa
ruby	**il rubino**	eel roobeenoa
sapphire	**lo zaffiro**	loa dzahffeeroa
silver	**l'argento**	lahrjayntoa
silver plate	**placcato d'argento**	plahkkaatoa dahrjayntoa
stainless steel	**l'acciaio inossida-bile**	lahtchaaeeoa eenoas-seedaabeelay
topaz	**il topazio**	eel toapaatseeoa
turquoise	**il turchese**	eel toorkayzay

Optician *Ottico*

I've broken my glasses.	Ho rotto gli occhiali.	oa **roa**ttoa lyee okkee**aa**lee
Can you repair them for me?	Può ripararmeli?	pwo reepahr**aar**maylee
When will they be ready?	Quando saranno pronti?	**kwah**ndoa sah**rahn**noa **proa**ntee
Can you change the lenses?	Può cambiare le lenti?	pwo kahm**bee**aaray lay **lehn**tee
I want tinted lenses.	Desidero delle lenti colorate.	day**zee**dayroa **day**llay **lehn**tee koaloa**raa**tay
The frame is broken.	La montatura è rotta.	lah moantah**too**rah ai **roa**ttah
I'd like a spectacle case.	Vorrei un astuccio per occhiali.	vor**raie** oon ah**stoot**choa pair okkee**aa**lee
I'd like to have my eyesight checked.	Vorrei farmi controllare la vista.	vor**raie fahr**mee koan-troal**laa**ray lah **vee**stah
I'm short-sighted/long-sighted.	Sono miope/presbite.	**soa**noa **mee**oapay/**preh**zbeetay
I want some contact lenses.	Desidero delle lenti a contatto.	day**zee**dayroa **day**llay **lehn**tee ah koan**taht**toa
I've lost one of my contact lenses.	Ho perso una lente a contatto.	oa **pehr**soa **oo**nah **lehn**tay ah koan**taht**toa
Could you give me another one?	Può darmene un'altra?	pwo **daar**mehneh oon**ahl**trah
I have hard/soft lenses.	Ho delle lenti a contatto dure/morbide.	oa **day**llay **lehn**tee ah koan**taht**toa **doo**ray/**mor**beeday
Have you any contact-lens liquid?	Avete del liquido per lenti a contatto?	ah**vay**tay dayl lee**kooee**doa pair **lehn**tee ah koan**taht**toa
I'd like to buy a pair of sunglasses.	Vorrei degli occhiali da sole.	vor**raie day**lyee okkee**aa**lee dah **soa**lay
May I look in a mirror?	Posso guardarmi in uno specchio?	**poss**oa gwahr**daar**mee een **oo**noa **spehk**keeoa
I'd like to buy a pair of binoculars.	Vorrei acquistare un binocolo.	vor**raie** akkooee**staa**ray oon bee**noa**koaloa

Photography *Fotografia*

I want a(n) ... camera.	Voglio una macchina fotografica ...	volyoa oonah **mahk**keenah foatoagraafeekah
automatic	automatica	owtoa**maat**eekah
inexpensive	economica	aykoanoa**mee**kah
simple	semplice	saym**plee**chay
Show me some cine (movie) cameras, please.	Per favore, mi faccia vedere alcune cineprese.	pair fah**voa**ray mee **faht**chah vay**day**ray ahl**koo**nay cheenay**pray**zay
I'd like to have some passport photos taken.	Vorrei che mi facesse delle fotografie d'identità.	vor**raie** kay mee faht**chayss**ay **day**llay foatoa**graf**feeay deedaynteetah

Film *Pellicola*

I'd like a film for this camera.	Vorrei una pellicola per questa macchina fotografica.	vor**raie** oonah pehlee**koa**lah pair **kooays**tah **mahk**keenah foatoagraafeekah
black and white	in bianco e nero	een bee**ahng**koa ay **nay**roa
colour	a colori	ah koa**loa**ree
colour negative	per negativo a colori	pair naygah**tee**voa ah koa**loa**ree
colour slide	per diapositive	pair deeahpoa**zee**teevay
cartridge	un rotolo	oon **roa**toaloa
roll film	una bobina	oonah boa**bee**nah
video cassette	una video cassetta	oonah **vee**dayoa kahss**saytt**ah
24/36 exposures	ventiquattro/trentasei pose	vaynteek**waht**troa/trayn**tah**sehee **poa**zay
this size	questo formato	kooaystoa foar**maat**oa
this ASA/DIN number	questo numero ASA/DIN	kooaystoa **noo**mayroa aasah/deen
artificial light type	per luce artificiale	pair **loo**chay ahrteefee**chaal**ay
daylight type	par luce naturale	pair **loo**chay nahtoo**raal**ay
fast (high-speed)	rapido	**raa**peedoa
fine grain	a grana fine	ah **graan**ah **feen**ay

Processing *Sviluppo*

How much do you charge for developing?	Quanto fate pagare per lo sviluppo?	**kwahn**toa **faat**ay pah**gaa**ray pair loa svee**loopp**oa

NUMBERS, see page 147

I want ... prints of each negative.	Voglio ... stampe per ogni negativa.	volyoa ... stahmpay pair oañee naygahteevah
with a mat finish	su carta opaca	soo kahrtah oapaakah
with a glossy finish	su carta lucida	soo kahrtah loocheedah
Will you please enlarge this?	Mi può ingrandire questo, per favore?	mee pwo eenggrahndeeray kooaystoa pair fahvoaray
When will the photos be ready?	Quando saranno pronte le fotografie?	kwahndoa sahrahnnoa prontay lay foatoagrahfeeay

Accessories and repairs *Accessori e riparazioni*

I want a/an/some ...	Vorrei ...	vorraiee
battery	una pila	oonah peelah
cable release	uno scatto	oonoa skahttoa
camera case	un astuccio (per macchina fotografica)	oon ahstootchoa (pair mahkkeenah foatoagraafeekah)
(electronic) flash	un flash (elettronico)	oon "flash" (aylayttroneekoa)
filter	un filtro	oon feeltroa
for black and white	per bianco e nero	pair beeahngkoa ay nayroa
for colour	per foto a colori	pair foatoa ah koaloaree
lens	un obiettivo	oon oabeeaytteevoa
telephoto lens	un teleobiettivo	oon taylayoabeeaytteevoa
wide-angle lens	un grandangolare	oon grahndahngoalaaray
lens cap	un cappuccio (per obiettivo)	oon kahppootchoa (pair oabeeaytteevoa)
Can you repair this camera?	Può riparare questa macchina fotografica?	pwo reepahraaray kooaystah mahkkeenah foatoagraafeekah
The film is jammed.	La pellicola è bloccata.	lah pehlleekoalah ai bloakkaatah
There's something wrong with the ...	... non funziona.	noan foontseeoanah
exposure counter	il contatore di esposizioni	eel koantahtoaray dee ayspoazeetseeoanee
film winder	la leva d'avanzamento della pellicola	lah layvah dahvahntsahmayntoa dayllah pehlleekoalah
flash attachment	l'attaccatura del flash	lahttahkkahtoorah dayl "flash"
light meter	l'esposimetro	layspoazeemaytroa
rangefinder	il telemetro	eel taylaymaytroa
shutter	l'otturatore	loattoorahtoaray

Tobacconist's *Tabaccheria*

Tobacco is a state monopoly in Italy. You recognize licensed tobacconist's by a large white "T" on a black background. Cigarettes are also sold in some cafés and newsstands.

A packet of cigarettes, please.	**Un pacchetto di sigarette, per favore.**	oon pahkkayttoa dee seegahrayttay pair fahvoaray
Do you have any American/English cigarettes?	**Avete sigarette americane/inglesi?**	ahvaytay seegahrayttay ahmayreekaanay/eengglaysee
I'd like a carton.	**Ne vorrei una stecca.**	nay vorraiee oonah staykkah
Give me a/some ..., please.	**Per favore, mi dia ...**	pair fahvoaray mee deeah
candy	**delle caramelle**	dayllay kahrahmaillay
chewing gum	**della gomma da masticare**	dayllah goammah dah mahsteekaaray
chocolate	**del cioccolato**	dayl choakkoalaatoa
cigarette case	**un portasigarette**	oon portahseegahrayttay
cigarette holder	**un bocchino**	oon boakkeenoa
cigarettes	**delle sigarette**	dayllay seegahrayttay
filter-tipped/	**con filtro/**	kon feeltroa/
without filter	**senza filtro**	sayntsah feeltroa
light/dark tobacco	**tabacco chiaro/scuro**	tahbahkkoa keeaaroa/skooroa
mild/strong	**leggere/forti**	laydjayray/fortee
menthol	**al mentolo**	ahl mayntoaloa
king-size	**formato lungo**	foarmaatoa loonggoa
cigars	**dei sigari**	daiee seegahree
lighter	**un accendino**	oon ahtchayndeenoa
lighter fluid/gas	**della benzina/del gas per accendino**	dayllah bayndzeenah/dayl gahz pair ahtchayndeenoa
matches	**dei fiammiferi**	daiee feeahmmeefayree
pipe	**una pipa**	oonah peepah
pipe cleaners	**dei nettapipe**	daiee nayttahpeepay
pipe tobacco	**del tabacco da pipa**	dayl tahbahkkoa dah peepah
pipe tool	**un curapipe**	oon koorahpeepay
postcard	**una cartolina**	oonah kahrtoaleenah
stamps	**dei francobolli**	daiee frahngkoaboallee
sweets	**delle caramelle**	dayllay karahmillay
wick	**uno stoppino**	oonoa stoppeenoa

Miscellaneous *Diversi*

Souvenirs *Oggetti ricordo*

Here are some suggestions for articles you might like to bring back as a souvenir or a gift. Italy is particularly noted for its top fashions for men and women, for articles made of silk, leather, olive wood and alabaster, for pottery and embroidered clothes and accessories. Hand-made jewellery of amber, gold and silver are particularly appreciated.

antiques	**l'antichità**	lahnteekeeitah
ceramics	**la ceramica**	lah chayraameekah
doll	**la bambola**	lah bahmboalah
flask of Chianti	**il fiasco di Chianti**	eel feeaaskoa dee keeahntee
glassware	**gli articoli di vetro**	lyee ahrteekoalee dee vehtroa
jewellery	**i gioielli**	ee joeeehllee
knitwear	**la maglieria**	lah mahlyayreeah
leather work	**la pelletteria**	lah payllayttayreeah
needlework	**il ricamo**	eel reekaamoa
porcelain	**la porcellana**	lah poarchayllaanah
silk	**la seta**	lah saitah
woodwork	**il lavoro in legno**	eel lahvoaroa een lehñoa

Some typical products of Switzerland are:

chocolate	**il cioccolato**	eel choakkoalaatoa
cuckoo clock	**l'orologio a cucù**	loaroalojoa ah kookoo
fondue forks/pot	**le forchette/il pentolino per la fonduta**	lay foarkayttay/eel payntoaleenoa pair lah foandootah
watch	**l'orologio**	loaroalojoa

Records—Cassettes *Dischi—Cassette*

Do you have any records by …?	**Avete dischi di …?**	ahvaytay deeskee dee
I'd like a …	**Vorrei …**	vorraie
cassette	**una cassetta**	oonah kahssayttah
video cassette	**una video cassetta**	oonah veedayoa kahssayttah
compact disc	**un disco compatto**	oon deeskoa koampahttoa

| Have you any songs by ...? | Avete delle canzoni di ...? | ahvaytay dayllay kahntsoanee dee |
| Can I listen to this record? | Posso ascoltare questo disco? | possoa ahskoaltaaray kooaystoa deeskoa |

L.P. (33 rpm)	33 giri	trayntahtray jeeree
E.P. (45 rpm)	super 45 giri	soopair kwahrahntahcheengkooay jeeree
single	45 giri	kwahrahntahcheengkooay jeeree

chamber music	musica da camera	moozeekah dah kaamayrah
classical music	musica classica	moozeekah klahsseekah
folk music	musica folcloristica	moozeekah folkloreesteekah
instrumental music	musica strumentale	moozeekah stroomayntaalay
jazz	jazz	"jazz"
light music	musica leggera	moozeekah laydjairah
orchestral music	musica sinfonica	moozeekah seenfoneekah
pop music	musica pop	moozeekah pop

Toys *Giocattoli*

I'd like a toy/ game ...	Vorrei un giocattolo/ un gioco ...	vorraiee oon joakahttoaloa/oon joakoa
for a boy	per un bambino	pair oon bahmbeenoa
for a 5-year-old girl	per una bambina di 5 anni	pair oonah bahmbeenah dee 5 ahnnee
beach ball	un pallone (da spiaggia)	oon pahlloanay (dah speeahdjah)
bucket and spade (pail and shovel)	un secchiello e una paletta	oon saykkeeaylloa ay oonah pahlayttah
building blocks (bricks)	un gioco di costruzioni	oon joakoa dee koastrootseeoanee
card game	delle carte da gioco	dayllay kahrtay dah joakoa
chess set	degli scacchi	daylyee skahkkee
doll	una bambola	oonah bahmboalah
electronic game	un gioco elettronico	oon joakoa aylayttroneekoa
flippers	delle pinne	dayllay peennay
roller skates	dei pattini a rotelle	daiee pahtteenee ah rotehllay
snorkel	la maschera da subacqueo	lah mahskayrah dah soobahkkooayoa

Your money: banks—currency

Italy's monetary unit is the *lira* (**lee**rah), plural *lire* (**lee**ray), abbreviated to *L.* or *Lit.* There are coins of 10, 20, 50, 100, 200 and 500 lire. Banknotes come in denomination of 500, 1,000, 2,000, 5,000, 10,000, 50,000 and 100,000 lire.

In Switzerland, the basic unit currency is the *franco* (**frahng**koa) divided into 100 *centesimi* (chayn**tay**zeemee). There are coins of 5, 10, 20 and 50 centimes and of 1, 2 and 5 francs. There are banknotes of 10, 20, 50, 100, 500 and 1,000 francs.

Though hours can vary, banks in Italy are generally open from 8.30 to 1 p.m. and from 2.30 to 3.30 p.m., Monday to Friday.

In Switzerland banks are generally open from 8.30 or 9 a.m. to noon and from 1.30 or 2 to 4.30 or 5 p.m., Monday to Friday. Main branches often remain open during the lunch hours.

In both countries you will find currency-exchange offices *(uffici cambio)* which are often open outside regular banking hours.

Credit cards may be used in an increasing number of hotels, restaurants, shops, etc. Signs are posted indicating which cards are accepted.

Traveller's cheques are accepted by hotels, travel agents and many shops, although the exchange rate is invariably better at a bank. Don't forget to take your passport when going to cash a traveller's cheque. Eurocheques are also accepted.

Where's the nearest bank?	**Dov'è la banca più vicina?**	doavai lah bahngkah peeoo veecheenah
Where is the currency exchange office?	**Dov'è l'ufficio cambio?**	doavai looffeechoa kahmbeeoa

130

At the bank   *In banca*

I want to change some dollars/pounds.	**Desidero cambiare dei dollari/delle sterline.**	dayzeedayroa kahmbeeaaray daiee dollahree/dayllay stayrleenay
I want to cash a traveller's cheque/Eurocheque.	**Voglio incassare un traveller's cheque/un eurocheque.**	volyoa eengkahssaaray oon "traveller's cheque"/oon "eurocheque"
What's the exchange rate?	**Qual è il corso del cambio?**	kwahl ai eel koarsoa dayl kahmbeeoa
How much commission do you charge?	**Quanto trattiene di commissione?**	kwahntoa trahtteeaynay dee koammeesseeooanay
Can you cash a personal cheque?	**Può cambiare un assegno personale?**	pwo kahmbeeaaray oon ahssayñoa payrsoanaalay
Can you telex my bank in London?	**Può mandare un telex alla mia banca a Londra?**	pwo mahndaaray oon "telex" ahllah meeah bahngkah ah loandrah
I have a/an/some ...	**Ho ...**	oa
bank card	**una carta d'identità bancaria**	oonah kahrtah deedaynteetah bahngkaareeah
credit card	**una carta di credito**	oonah kahrtah dee kraydeetoa
introduction from ...	**una lettera di presentazione di ...**	oonah lehttayrah dee prayzayntahtseeooanay dee
letter of credit	**una lettera di credito**	oonah lehttayrah dee kraydeetoa
I'm expecting some money from New York. Has it arrived?	**Aspetto del denaro da New York. È arrivato?**	ahspehttoa dayl daynaaroa dah "New York". ai ahrreevaatoa
Please give me ... notes (bills) and some small change.	**Per favore, mi dia ... banconote e della moneta.**	pair fahvoaray mee deeah ... bahngkoanotay ay dayllah moanaytah

Depositing—Withdrawing   *Depositi—Prelevamenti*

I want to credit this to my account.	**Desidero accreditare questo sul mio conto.**	dayzeedayroa ahkkraydeetaaray kooaystoa sool meeoa koantoa
I want to ...	**Desidero ...**	dayzeedayroa
open an account	**aprire un conto**	ahpreeray oon koantoa
withdraw ... lire	**prelevare ... lire**	praylayvaaray ... leeray

NUMBERS, see page 147

| I want to credit this to Mr...'s account. | **Desidero accreditare questo sul conto del signor ...** | dayzeedayroa ahkkraydee-taaray kooaystoa sool koantoa dayl seeñoar |
| Where should I sign? | **Dove devo firmare?** | doavay dayvoa feermaaray |

Business terms *Termini d'affari*

My name is ...	**Mi chiamo ...**	mee keeaamoa
Here's my card.	**Ecco il mio biglietto.**	ehkkoa eel meeoa beelyayt-teenoa
I have an appointment with ...	**Ho un appuntamento con ...**	oa oon appoontahmayntoa kon
Can you give me an estimate of the cost?	**Può farmi un preventivo?**	pwo faarmee oon prayvayn-teevoa
What's the rate of inflation?	**Qual è il tasso di inflazione?**	kwahl ai eel tahssoa dee eenflahtseeooanay
Can you provide me with an interpreter/ a secretary?	**Può procurarmi un interprete/una segretaria?**	pwo prokooraarmee oon eentehrprehtay/oonah saygraytaareeah
Where can I make photocopies?	**Dove posso fare delle fotocopie?**	doavay possoa faaray dayllay fotokawpeeay

amount	l'importo	leempoartoa
balance	il bilancio	eel beelahnchoa
capital	il capitale	eel kahpeetaalay
cheque book	il libretto d'assegni	eel leebrehttoa dahssayñee
contract	il contratto	eel koantrahttoa
expenses	le spese	lay spaysay
interest	l'interesse	leentayrehssay
investment	l'investimento	leenvaysteemayntoa
invoice	la fattura	lah fahttoorah
loss	la perdita	lah payrdeetah
mortgage	l'ipoteca	leepoataykah
payment	il pagamento	eel pahgahmayntoa
percentage	la percentuale	lah payrchayntooaalay
profit	il profitto	eel proafeettoa
purchase	l'acquisto	lahkooeestoa
sale	la vendita	lah vayndeetah
share	l'azione	lahtseeoanay
transfer	il trasferimento	eel trahsfayreemayntoa
value	il valore	eel vahloaray

At the post office

Post offices in Italy bear the sign *PT* and are normally open from 8.15 a.m. to 1 or 2 p.m., Monday to Friday, Saturday till 12 noon or 1 p.m. Offices in major towns and tourist resorts stay open longer, but often for urgent matters only. Stamps are also sold at tobacconist's *(tabaccaio)* and at some hotel desks. Letter boxes (mailboxes) are red in Italy, and yellow in Switzerland.

Swiss post offices are recognized by a *PTT* sign and are open from 7.30 a.m. to noon and from 1.45 to 6.30 p.m., Monday to Friday, Saturday till 11 a.m.

Note that telephone service in Italy is generally separated from the post office.

Where's the nearest post office?	**Dov'è l'ufficio postale più vicino?**	doavai looffeechoa poastaalay peeoo veecheenoa
What time does the post office open/ close?	**A che ora apre/ chiude l'ufficio postale?**	ah kay oarah aapray/ keeooday looffeechoa poastaalay
A stamp for this letter/postcard, please.	**Un francobollo per questa lettera/cartolina, per favore.**	oon frahngkoaboalloa pair kooaystah lehttayrah/kahrtoaleenah pair fahvoaray
I want 2 ... -lire stamps.	**Vorrei 2 francobolli da ... lire.**	vorraiee 2 frahngkoaboallee dah ... leeray
What's the postage for a letter to London?	**Qual è l'affrancatura per una lettera per Londra?**	kwahl ai lahffrahngkahtoorah pair oonah lehttayrah pair loandrah
What's the postage for a postcard to Los Angeles?	**Qual è l'affrancatura per una cartolina per Los Angeles?**	kwahl ai lahffrahngkahtoorah pair oonah kahrtoaleenah pair "Los Angeles"
Where's the letter box (mailbox)?	**Dov'è la cassetta delle lettere?**	doavai lah kahssehttah dayllay lehttayray
I want to send this parcel.	**Vorrei spedire questo pacco.**	vorraiee spaydeeray kooaystoa pahkkoa

I want to send this by ...	Desidero inviare questo per ...	dayzeedayroa eenveeaaray kooaystoa pair
airmail	via aerea	veeah ahayrayah
express (special delivery)	espresso	aysprehssoa
registered mail	raccomandata	rahkkoamahndaatah
At which counter can I cash an international money order?	A quale sportello posso riscuotere un vaglia internazionale?	ah kwaalay sportehlloa possoa reeskwotayray oon vaalyah eentayrnahtseeoanaalay
Where's the poste restante (general delivery)?	Dov'è lo sportello del fermo posta?	doavai loa spoartehlloa dayl fayrmoa postah
Is there any mail for me? My name is ...	C'è della posta per me? Mi chiamo ...	chai dayllah postah pair may? mee keeaamoa

FRANCOBOLLI	STAMPS
PACCHI	PARCELS
VAGLIA POSTALI	MONEY ORDERS

Telegrams *Telegrammi*

In Italy and Switzerland, you can either go directly to the post-office to send a telegram or phone it in. Some telegraph offices are open 24 hours a day.

I want to send a telegram/telex.	Vorrei inviare un telegramma/telex.	vorraiee eenveeaaray oon taylaygrahmmah/"telex"
May I please have a form?	Può darmi un modulo?	pwo daarmee oon modooloa
How much is it per word?	Quanto costa ogni parola?	kwahntoa kostah oñee pahrolah
How long will a cable to Boston take?	Quanto tempo ci vorrà per inviare un telegramma a Boston?	kwahntoa tehmpoa chee vorrah pair eenveeaaray oon taylaygrahmmah ah boston
How much will this telex cost?	Quanto costerà questo telex?	kwahntoa koastayrah kooaystoa "telex"

Telephoning *Per telefonare*

The telephone system in Italy and Switzerland is virtually entirely automatic. International or long-distance calls can be made from phone boxes, or ask at your hotel. Local calls in Italy can also be made from cafés, where you might have to pay after the call or to buy a *gettone* (token) to put into the phone.

Telephone numbers are given in pairs in Italy so that 12 34 56 would be expressed in Italian, twelve, thirty-four, fifty-six.

Where's the telephone?	**Dov'è il telefono?**	doavai eel taylayfoanoa
I'd like a telephone token.	**Vorrei un gettone (telefonico).**	vorraiee oon jayttoanay (taylayfoneekoa)
Where's the nearest telephone booth?	**Dov'è la cabina te- lefonica più vicina?**	doavai lah kahbeenah tay- layfoneekah peeoo veecheenah
May I use your phone?	**Posso usare il suo telefono?**	possoa oozaaray eel soooa taylayfoanoa
Do you have a telephone directory for Rome?	**Ha un elenco telefonico di Roma?**	ah oon aylayngkoa taylay- foneekoa dee roamah
What's the dialling (area) code for ...?	**Qual è il prefisso di ...?**	kwahl ai eel prayfeessoa dee
How do I get the international operator?	**Come si ottiene il servizio inter- nazionale?**	koamay see otteeaynay eel sayrveetseeoa eentayr- nahtseeoanaalay

Operator *Centralinista*

Good morning, I want Venice 12 34 56.	**Buon giorno. Desi- dero il 12 34 56 di Venezia.**	bwon joarnoa. dayzee- dayroa eel 12 34 56 dee vaynaitseeah
Can you help me get this number?	**Mi può aiutare a ottenere questo numero?**	mee pwo aheeootaaray ah oattaynayray kooaystoa noomayroa

NUMBERS, see page 147

I want to place a ...	**Vorrei fare ...**	vorraiee faaray
personal (person-to-person) call	**una telefonata con preavviso**	oonah taylayfoanaatah kon prayahvveezoa
reversed charge (collect) call	**una telefonata a carico del destinatario**	oonah taylayfoanaatah ah kaareekoa dayl daysteenahtaareeoa

Speaking   *Al telefono*

Hello. This is ... speaking.	**Pronto. Qui parla ...**	prontoa. kooee pahrlah
I want to speak to ...	**Vorrei parlare a ...**	vorraiee pahrlaaray ah
I want extension ...	**Mi dia la linea interna ...**	mee deeah lah leenayah eentehrnah
Speak louder/more slowly, please.	**Parli più forte/più lentamente, per favore.**	pahrlee peeoo fortay/peeoo layntahmayntay pair fahvoaray

Bad luck   *Sfortuna*

Would you please try again later?	**Per favore, vuol provare di nuovo più tardi?**	pair fahvoaray vwawl proavaaray dee nwawvoa peeoo tahrdee
Operator, you gave me the wrong number.	**Signorina, mi ha dato il numero sbagliato.**	seeñoareenah mee ah daatoa eel noomayroa zbahlyaatoa
Operator, we were cut off.	**Signorina, la comunicazione si è interrotta.**	seeñoareenah lah komooneekahtseeoanay see ai eentehrroattah

---

Telephone alphabet

A	**Ancona**	ahngkoanah	N	**Napoli**	naapoalee
B	**Bari**	baaree	O	**Otranto**	oatrahntoa
C	**Catania**	kahtaaneeah	P	**Palermo**	pahlehrmoa
D	**Domodossola**	doamoadossoalah	Q	**Quarto**	kwahrtoa
E	**Empoli**	aympoalee	R	**Roma**	roamah
F	**Firenze**	feerehntsay	S	**Sassari**	sahssahree
G	**Genova**	jainoavah	T	**Torino**	tawreenoa
H	**Hotel**	oatehl	U	**Udine**	oodeenay
I	**Imperia**	eempayreeah	V	**Venezia**	vaynaitseeah
J	**i lunga**	ee loonggah	W	**v doppia**	vee doappeeah
K	**kappa**	kahppah	X	**ix**	eekss
L	**Livorno**	leevoarnoa	Y	**i greca**	ee graykah
M	**Milano**	meelaanoa	Z	**zeta**	dzaitah

Not there *La persona è assente*

When will he/she be back?	**Quando ritornerà?**	kwahndoa reetoarnehrah
Will you tell him/her I called? My name is ...	**Vuol dirgli/dirle che ho telefonato? Mi chiamo ...**	vwawl deerlyee/deerlay kay oa taylayfoanaatoa. mee keeaamoa
Would you ask him/her to call me?	**Può chiedergli/ chiederle di telefonarmi?**	pwo keeaidayrlyee/ keeaidayrlay dee taylay-foanaarmee
Would you please take a message?	**Per favore, può trasmettere un messaggio?**	pair fahvoaray pwo trahzmayttayray oon mayssahdjoa

Charges *Costo della telefonata*

What was the cost of that call?	**Quanto è costata la telefonata?**	kwahntoa ai kostaatah lah taylayfoanaatah
I want to pay for the call.	**Desidero pagare la telefonata.**	dayzeedayroa pahgaaray lah taylayfoanaatah

---

C'è una telefonata per lei.	There's a telephone call for you.
Che numero chiama?	What number are you calling?
La linea è occupata.	The line's engaged.
Non risponde.	There's no answer.
Ha chiamato il numero sbagliato.	You've got the wrong number.
Il telefono non funziona.	The phone is out of order.
Un momento!	Just a moment.
Resti in linea.	Hold on, please.
Egli/Ella è fuori in questo momento.	He's/She's out at the moment.

Doctor

To be at ease, make sure your health insurance policy covers any illness or accident while on holiday. If not, ask your insurance representative, automobile association or travel agent for details of special health insurance.

General *Generalità*

Can you get me a doctor?	**Può chiamarmi un medico?**	pwo keeahmaarmee oon maideekoa
Is there a doctor here?	**C'è un medico qui?**	chai oon maideekoa kooee
I need a doctor, quickly!	**Mi serve un medico—presto!**	mee sayrvay oon maideekoa—prehstoa
Where can I find a doctor who speaks English?	**Dove posso trovare un medico che parla inglese?**	doavay possoa troavaaray oon maideekoa kay pahrlah eengglaysay
Where's the surgery (doctor's office)?	**Dov'è l'ambulatorio del medico?**	doavai lahmboolahtoreeoa dayl maideekoa
What are the surgery (office) hours?	**Quali sono le ore di consultazione?**	kwahlee soanoa lay oaray dee koansooltahtseeoanay
Could the doctor come to see me here?	**Il medico può venire a visitarmi qui?**	eel maideekoa pwo vayneeray ah veezeetaarmee kooee
What time can the doctor come?	**Quando può venire il medico?**	kwahndoa pwo vayneeray eel maideekoa
Can you recommend a/an ...?	**Può consigliarmi ...?**	pwo koanseelyaarmee
general practitioner	**un medico generico**	oon maideekoa jehnayreekoa
children's doctor	**un pediatra**	oon paydeeaatrah
eye specialist	**un oculista**	oon okooleestah
gynaecologist	**un ginecologo**	oon jeenaykoloagoa
Can I have an appointment ...?	**Può fissarmi un appuntamento ...?**	pwo feessaarmee oon ahppoontahmayntoa
right now	**subito**	soobeetoa
tomorrow	**domani**	doamaanee
as soon as possible	**il più presto possibile**	eel peeoo prehstoa posseebeelay

CHEMIST'S (PHARMACY), see page 108

Parts of the body *Parti del corpo*

appendix	l'appendice	lahppayndeechay
arm	il braccio	eel brahtchoa
artery	l'arteria	lahrtaireeah
back	la schiena	lah skeeainah
bladder	la vescica	lah vaysheekah
bone	l'osso	lossoa
bowels	l'intestino	leentaysteenoa
breast	il petto	eel pehttoa
chest	il torace	eel toaraachay
ear	l'orecchio	loaraykkeeoa
eye(s)	l'occhio (gli occhi)	lokkeeoa (lyee okkee)
face	il viso	eel veezoa
finger	il dito della mano	eel deetoa dayllah maanoa
foot	il piede	eel peeayday
genitals	i genitali	ee jayneetaalee
gland	la ghiandola	lah geeahndoalah
hand	la mano	lah maanoa
head	la testa	lah tehstah
heart	il cuore	eel kworay
intestines	l'intestino	leentaysteenoa
jaw	la mascella	lah mahshehllah
joint	l'articolazione	lahrteekoalahtseeoanay
kidney	il rene	eel rainay
knee	il ginocchio	eel jeenokkeeoa
leg	la gamba	lah gahmbah
lip	il labbro	eel lahbbroa
liver	il fegato	eel faygahtoa
lung	il polmone	eel poalmoanay
mouth	la bocca	lah boakkah
muscle	il muscolo	eel mooskoaloa
neck	il collo	eel kolloa
nerve	il nervo	eel nehrvoa
nervous system	il sistema nervoso	eel seestaimah nehrvoasoa
nose	il naso	eel naasoa
rib	la costola	lah kostoalah
shoulder	la spalla	lah spahllah
skin	la pelle	lah pehllay
spine	la spina dorsale	lah speenah doarsaalay
stomach	lo stomaco	loa stomahkoa
tendon	il tendine	eel tehndeenay
throat	la gola	lah goalah
toe	il dito del piede	eel deetoa dayl peeayday
tongue	la lingua	lah leenggwah
tonsils	le tonsille	lay toanseellay
vein	la vena	lah vaynah

Accident—Injury   *Incidente—Ferita*

There has been an accident.	**C'è stato un incidente.**	chai staatoa oon eencheedayntay
My child has had a fall.	**Il mio bambino/ la mia bambina è caduto(a).**	eel meeoa bahmbeenoa/ lah meeah bahmbeenah ai kahdootoa(ah)
He/She has hurt his/ her head.	**Lui/Lei si è fatto(a) male alla testa.**	looee/layee see ai fahttoa(ah) maalay ahllah tehstah
He's/She's uncon- scious.	**È svenuto(a).**	ai zvaynootoa(ah)
He's/She's bleeding heavily.	**Perde molto sangue.**	payrday moaltoa sahnggooay
He's/She's (seriously) injured.	**È (gravemente) ferito(a).**	ai (grahvaimayntay) fayreetoa(ah)
His/Her arm is broken.	**Si è rotto(a) il braccio.**	see ai rottoa(ah) eel brahtchoa
His/Her ankle is swollen.	**Ha la caviglia gonfia.**	ah lah kahveelyah goanfeeah
I've been stung.	**Sono stato punto.**	soanoa staatoa poontoa
I've got something in my eye.	**Ho qualcosa nell'occhio.**	oa kwahlkawsah nehllokkeeoa
I've got a/an ...	**Ho ...**	oa
blister	**una vescica**	oonah vaysheekah
boil	**un foruncolo**	oon foaroongkoaloa
bruise	**una contusione**	oonah koantoozeeooanay
burn	**una scottatura**	oonah skottahtoorah
cut	**un taglio**	oon taalyoa
graze	**un'escoriazione**	oonayskoareeoahtseeoanay
insect bite	**una puntura d'insetto**	oonah poontoorah deensehttoa
lump	**un bernoccolo**	oon bayrnokkoaloa
rash	**un esantema**	oon ayzahntehmah
sting	**una puntura**	oonah poontoorah
swelling	**un gonfiore**	oon goanfeeoaray
wound	**una ferita**	oonah fayreetah
Could you have a look at it?	**Può esaminarlo?**	pwo ayzaheemeenaarloa
I can't move my ...	**Non posso muo- vere ...**	noan possoa mwovayray
It hurts.	**Mi fa male.**	mee fah maalay

Dove fa male?	Where does it hurt?
Che genere di dolore è?	What kind of pain is it?
debole/acuto/lancinante costante/a intervalli	dull/sharp/throbbing constant/on and off
È ...	It's ...
rotto/distorto slogato/lacerato	broken/sprained dislocated/torn
Voglio che faccia una radiografia.	I want you to have an X-ray taken.
Sarà ingessato.	You'll get a plaster.
Ha fatto infezione.	It's infected.
È stato vaccinato(a) contro il tetano?	Have you been vaccinated against tetanus?
Le darò un antisettico/ un antinevralgico.	I'll give you an antiseptic/ a painkiller.

Illness *Malattia*

I'm not feeling well.	**Non mi sento bene.**	noan mee **sayn**toa **bai**nay
I'm ill.	**Mi sento male.**	mee **sayn**toa **maa**lay
I feel ...	**Mi sento ...**	mee **sayn**toa
dizzy	**stordito(a)**	stoar**dee**toa(ah)
nauseous	**la nausea**	lah **now**zayah
shivery	**rabbrividire**	rahbbreevee**dee**ray
I've got a fever.	**Ho la febbre.**	oa lah **fehb**bray
My temperature is 38 degrees.	**Ho la febbre a 38.**	oa lah **fehb**bray ah 38
I've been vomiting.	**Ho vomitato.**	oa voamee**taa**toa
I'm constipated/ I've got diarrhoea.	**Sono costipato(a)/ Ho la diarrea.**	**soa**noa koastee**paa**toa(ah)/ oa lah deeah**rray**ah
My ... hurt(s).	**Ho male al/alla ...**	oa **maa**lay ahl/**ahl**lah
I have a nosebleed.	**Mi sanguina il naso.**	mee sahng**gooee**nah eel **naa**soa

NUMBERS, see page 147

I've got (a/an) ...	**Ho ...**	oa
asthma	**l'asma**	lahzmah
backache	**il mal di schiena**	eel mahl dee skeeainah
cold	**il raffreddore**	eel rahffrayddoaray
cough	**la tosse**	lah tossay
cramps	**i crampi**	ee krahmpee
earache	**il mal d'orecchi**	eel mahl doaraykkee
hay fever	**la febbre del fieno**	lah fehbbray dayl feeehnoa
headache	**il mal di testa**	eel mahl dee tehstah
indigestion	**un'indigestione**	ooneendeejaysteeoanay
palpitations	**delle palpitazioni**	dayllay pahlpeetahtsee-oanee
rheumatism	**i reumatismi**	ee rayoomahteezmee
sore throat	**il mal di gola**	eel mahl dee goalah
stiff neck	**il torcicollo**	eel torcheekolloa
stomach ache	**il mal di stomaco**	eel mahl dee stomahkoa
sunstroke	**un colpo di sole**	oon koalpoa dee soalay

I have difficulties breathing.	**Ho difficoltà a respirare.**	oa deeffeekoltah ah rayspeeraaray
I have a pain in my chest.	**Ho un dolore nel torace.**	oa oon doaloaray nehl toaraachay
I had a heart attack ... years ago.	**Ho avuto un attacco cardiaco ... anni fa.**	oa ahvootoa oon ahttahkkoa kahrdeeahkoa ... ahnnee fah
My blood pressure is too high/too low.	**La mia pressione è troppo alta/troppo bassa.**	lah meeah prehsseeoanay ai troppoa ahltah/troppoa bahssah
I'm allergic to ...	**Sono allergico a ...**	soanoa ahllayrjeekoa ah
I'm a diabetic.	**Ho il diabete.**	oa eel deeahbehtay

Women's section *Sezione femminile*

I have period pains.	**Ho delle mestruazioni dolorose.**	oa dayllay maystrooah-tseeoanee doaloarawsay
I have a vaginal infection.	**Ho un'infezione vaginale.**	oa ooneenfaytseeoanay vahjeenaalay
I'm on the pill.	**Prendo la pillola.**	prehndoa lah peelloalah
I haven't had my period for 2 months.	**Non ho avuto le mestruazioni per 2 mesi.**	noan oa ahvootoa lay maystrooahtseeoanee pair 2 maisee
I'm (3 months) pregnant.	**Sono incinta (di 3 mesi).**	soanoa eencheentah (dee 3 maisee)

Da quanto tempo si sente così?	How long have you been feeling like this?
È la prima volta che ha questo disturbo?	Is this the first time you've had this?
Le misuro la pressione/ la febbre.	I'll take your blood pressure/ temperature.
Tiri su la manica.	Roll up your sleeve, please.
Si spogli (fino alla vita).	Please undress (down to the waist).
Per favore, si sdrai qui.	Please lie down over there.
Apra la bocca.	Open your mouth.
Respiri profondamente.	Breathe deeply.
Tossisca, prego.	Cough, please.
Dove sente il dolore?	Where do you feel the pain?
Lei ha ...	You've got (a/an) ...
l'appendicite	appendicitis
un avvelenamento da cibi	food poisoning
una cistite	cystitis
la gastrite	gastritis
un'infiammazione a ...	inflammation of ...
l'influenza	flu
l'itterizia	jaundice
una malattia venerea	venereal disease
il morbillo	measles
la polmonite	pneumonia
Le farò un'iniezione.	I'll give you an injection.
Desidero un campione del sangue/dell'urina/delle feci.	I want a specimen of your blood/urine/stools.
Deve restare a letto per ... giorni.	You must stay in bed for ... days.
Deve consultare uno specialista.	I want you to see a specialist.
Deve andare all'ospedale per un controllo generale.	I want you to go to the hospital for a general check-up.
Deve essere operato(a).	You'll have to have an operation.

Prescription — Treatment *Ricetta — Cura*

This is my usual medicine.	**Questa è la mia medicina abituale.**	kooaystah ai lah meeah maydeecheenah ahbeetooaalay
Can you give me a prescription for this?	**Può farmi una ricetta per questo?**	pwo faarmee oonah reechayttah pair kooaystoa
Can you prescribe a/an/some ...?	**Può prescrivermi ...?**	pwo prayskreevayrmee
antidepressant	**un antidepressivo**	oon ahnteedayprehsseevoa
sleeping pills	**dei sonniferi**	daiee soanneefayree
tranquillizer	**un tranquillante**	oon trahngkooeellahntay
I'm allergic to antibiotics/penicillin.	**Sono allergico(a) agli antibiotici/alla penicillina.**	soanoa ahllayrjeekoa(ah) ahlyee ahnteebeeoateechee/ahllah paineecheelleenah
I don't want anything too strong.	**Non voglio qualcosa troppo forte.**	noan volyoa kwahlkawsah troppoa foartay
How many times a day should I take it?	**Quante volte al giorno devo prenderla?**	kwahntay voltay ahl joarnoa dayvoa prehndayrlah
Must I swallow them whole?	**Devo inghiottirle intere?**	dayvoa eenggeeoatteerlay eentayray

---

Che cura fa?	What treatment are you having?
Che medicine prende?	What medicine are you taking?
Per iniezioni o via orale?	By injection or orally?
Prenda ... cucchiaini di questa medicina ...	Take ... teaspoons of this medicine ...
Prenda una compressa con un bicchiere d'acqua ...	Take one pill with a glass of water ...
ogni ... ore	every ... hours
... volte al giorno	... times a day
prima/dopo ogni pasto	before/after each meal
al mattino/alla sera	in the morning/at night
in caso di dolore	if there is any pain
per ... giorni	for ... days

CHEMIST'S (PHARMACY), see page 108

Fee *Onorario*

How much do I owe you?	**Quanto le devo?**	kwahntoa lay dayvoa
May I have a receipt for my health insurance?	**Posso avere una ricevuta per la mia assicurazione malattia?**	possoa ahvayray oonah reechayvootah pair lah meeah asseekoorahtseeoanay mahlahtteeah
Can I have a medical certificate?	**Posso avere un certificato medico?**	possoa ahvayray oon chayrteefeekaatoa maideekoa
Would you fill in this health insurance form, please?	**Potrebbe compilare questo modulo per l'assicurazione malattie, per favore?**	potrehbbay koampeelaaray kooaystoa moadooloa pair lasseekoorahtseeoanay mahlahtteeay pair fahvoaray

Hospital *Ospedale*

What are the visiting hours?	**Quali sono gli orari di visita?**	kwahlee soanoa lyee oraaree dee veezeetah
When can I get up?	**Quando posso alzarmi?**	kwahndoa possoa ahltsaarmee
When will the doctor come?	**Quando verrà il dottore?**	kwahndoa vayrrah eel dottawray
I'm in pain.	**Ho male.**	oa maalay
I can't eat/I can't sleep.	**Non ho appetito/ Non riesco a dormire.**	noan oa ahppayteetoa/ noan reeehskoa ah doarmeeray
Can I have a painkiller/some sleeping pills?	**Posso avere un calmante/dei sonniferi?**	possoa ahvayray oon kahlmahntay/daiee soanneefayree
Where is the bell?	**Dov'è il campanello?**	doavai eel kahmpahnehlloa

nurse	l'infermiera	leenfayrmeeayrah
patient	il/la paziente	eel/lah pahtseeaintay
anaesthetic	l'anestetico	lahnaystaiteekoa
blood transfusion	la trasfusione di sangue	lah trahsfoozeeoanay dee sahnggooay
injection	l'iniezione	leeneeaaytseeoanay
operation	l'operazione	loapayrahtseeoanay
bed	il letto	eel lehttoa
bedpan	la padella	lah pahdehllah
thermometer	il termometro	eel tayrmomaytroa

Dentist *Dentista*

Can you recommend a good dentist?	**Può consigliarmi un buon dentista?**	pwo koanseelyahrmee oon bwawn daynteestah
Can I make an (urgent) appointment to see Dr ...?	**Desidero un appuntamento (urgente) con il dottor/la dottoressa ...**	dayzeedayroa oon ahppoontahmayntoa (oorjehntay) kon eel doattoar/lah doatoarehssah
Can't you possibly make it earlier than that?	**Non è possibile prima?**	noan ai poasseebeelay preemah
I have a broken tooth.	**Mi sono rotto un dente.**	mee soanoa rottoa oon dehntay
I have a toothache.	**Ho mal di denti.**	oa mahl dee dehntee
I have an abscess.	**Ho un ascesso.**	oa oon ahshehssoa
This tooth hurts.	**Mi fa male questo dente.**	mee fah maalay kooaystoa dehntay
at the top	**in alto**	een ahltoa
at the bottom	**in basso**	een bahssoa
in the front	**davanti**	dahvahntee
at the back	**dietro**	deeehtroa
Can you fix it temporarily?	**Può curarlo provvisoriamente?**	pwo kooraarloa proavveezoareeahmayntay
I don't want it extracted.	**Non voglio un'estrazione.**	noan volyoa oonaystrahtseeoanay
Could you give me an anaesthetic?	**Potrebbe farmi l'anestesia?**	potrehbbay faarmee lahnaystayzeeah
I've lost a filling.	**L'otturazione si è staccata.**	loattoorahtseeoanay see ai stahkkaatah
The gum ...	**La gengiva ...**	lah jaynjeevah
is very sore	**è infiammata**	ai eenfeeahmmaatah
is bleeding	**sanguina**	sahnggooeenah
I've broken this denture.	**Ho rotto questa dentiera.**	oa roattoa kooaystah daynteeehrah
Can you repair this denture?	**Può ripararmi questa dentiera?**	pwo reepahraarmee kooaystah daynteeehrah
When will it be ready?	**Quando sarà pronta?**	kwahndoa sahrah proantah

Reference section

Where do you come from? *Da dove viene?*

Africa	l'Africa	laafreekah
Asia	l'Asia	laazeeah
Australia	l'Australia	lowstraaleeah
Europe	l'Europa	layooropah
North America	l'America del Nord	lahmaireekah dayl nord
South America	l'America del Sud	lahmaireekah dayl sood
Algeria	l'Algeria	lahljayreeah
Austria	l'Austria	lowstreeah
Belgium	il Belgio	eel behljoa
Canada	il Canada	eel kahnahdah
China	la Cina	lah cheenah
Denmark	la Danimarca	lah dahneemahrkah
England	l'Inghilterra	leengeeltehrrah
Finland	la Finlandia	lah feenlahndeeah
France	la Francia	lah frahnchah
Germany	la Germania	lah jayrmaaneeah
Great Britain	la Gran Bretagna	lah grahn braytaañah
Greece	la Grecia	lah graichah
India	l'India	leendeeah
Ireland	l'Irlanda	leerlahndah
Israel	Israele	eesrahaylay
Italy	l'Italia	leetaaleeah
Japan	il Giappone	eel jahppoanay
Luxembourg	il Lussemburgo	eel loossaymboorgoa
Morocco	il Marocco	eel mahrokkoa
Netherlands	l'Olanda	lolahndah
New Zealand	la Nuova Zelanda	lah nwawvah dzaylahndah
Norway	la Norvegia	lah norvayjah
Portugal	il Portogallo	eel portogahlloa
Scotland	la Scozia	lah skotseeah
South Africa	il Sudafrica	eel soodaafreekah
Soviet Union	l'Unione Sovietica	looneeoanay soaveeeeh-teekah
Spain	la Spagna	lah spaañah
Sweden	la Svezia	lah svehtseeah
Switzerland	la Svizzera	lah sveettsayrah
Tunisia	la Tunisia	lah tooneezeeah
Turkey	la Turchia	lah toorkeeah
United States	gli Stati Uniti	lyee staatee ooneetee
Wales	il Galles	eel gahllayss
Yugoslavia	la Iugoslavia	lah eeoogoaslaaveeah

Numbers *Numeri*

0	**zero**	**dzeh**roa
1	**uno**	**oon**oa
2	**due**	**doo**ay
3	**tre**	tray
4	**quattro**	**kwaht**troa
5	**cinque**	**cheeng**kooay
6	**sei**	sehee
7	**sette**	**seht**tay
8	**otto**	**ot**toa
9	**nove**	**naw**vay
10	**dieci**	**dee**aichee
11	**undici**	**oon**deechee
12	**dodici**	**doa**deechee
13	**tredici**	**tray**deechee
14	**quattordici**	kwaht**tor**deechee
15	**quindici**	**kooeen**deechee
16	**sedici**	**say**deechee
17	**diciassette**	deechahs**seht**tay
18	**diciotto**	dee**chot**toa
19	**diciannove**	deechahn**naw**vay
20	**venti**	**vayn**tee
21	**ventuno**	vayn**toon**oa
22	**ventidue**	vayntee**doo**ay
23	**ventitre**	vayntee**tray**
24	**ventiquattro**	vayntee**kwaht**troa
25	**venticinque**	vayntee**cheeng**kooay
26	**ventisei**	vayntee**seh**ee
27	**ventisette**	vayntee**seht**tay
28	**ventotto**	vayn**tot**toa
29	**ventinove**	vayntee**naw**vay
30	**trenta**	**trayn**tah
31	**trentuno**	trayn**toon**oa
32	**trentadue**	trayntah**doo**ay
33	**trentatre**	trayntah**tray**
40	**quaranta**	kwah**rahn**tah
41	**quarantuno**	kwahrahn**toon**oa
42	**quarantadue**	kwahrahntah**doo**ay
43	**quarantatre**	kwahrahntah**tray**
50	**cinquanta**	cheengk**wahn**tah
51	**cinquantuno**	cheengkwahn**toon**oa
52	**cinquantadue**	cheengkwahntah**doo**ay
53	**cinquantatre**	cheengkwahntah**tray**
60	**sessanta**	says**sahn**tah
61	**sessantuno**	sayssahn**toon**oa
62	**sessantadue**	sayssahntah**doo**ay

63	sessantatre	sayssahntahtray
70	settanta	sayttahntah
71	settantuno	sayttahntoonoa
72	settantadue	sayttahntahdooay
73	settantatre	sayttahntahtray
80	ottanta	ottahntah
81	ottantuno	ottahntoonoa
82	ottantadue	ottahntahdooay
83	ottantatre	ottahntahtray
90	novanta	noavahntah
91	novantuno	noavahntoonoa
92	novantadue	noavahntahdooay
93	novantatre	noavahntahtray
100	cento	chehntoa
101	centouno	chehntoaoonoa
102	centodue	chehntoadooay
110	centodieci	chehntoadeeaichee
120	centoventi	chehntoavayntee
130	centotrenta	chehntoatrayntah
140	centoquaranta	chehntoakwahrahntah
150	centocinquanta	chehntoacheengkwahntah
160	centosessanta	chehntoasayssahntah
170	centosettanta	chehntoasayttahntah
180	centottanta	chehntottahntah
190	centonovanta	chehntoanoavahntah
200	duecento	dooaychehntoa
300	trecento	traychehntoa
400	quattrocento	kwahttroachehntoa
500	cinquecento	cheengkooaychehntoa
600	seicento	seheechehntoa
700	settecento	sehttaychehntoa
800	ottocento	ottochehntoa
900	novecento	noavaychehntoa
1000	mille	meellay
1100	millecento	meellaychehntoa
1200	milleduecento	meellaydooaychehntoa
2000	duemila	dooaymeelah
5000	cinquemila	cheengkooaymeelah
10,000	diecimila	deeaicheemeelah
50,000	cinquantamila	cheengkwahntahmeelah
100,000	centomila	chehntoameelah
1,000,000	un milione	oon meelyoanay
1,000,000,000	un miliardo	oon meelyahrdoa

first/second	**primo/secondo**	preemoa/saykoandoa
third/fourth	**terzo/quarto**	tehrtsoa/kwahrtoa
fifth/sixth	**quinto/sesto**	kooeentoa/sehstoa
seventh/eighth	**settimo/ottavo**	sehtteemoa/ottaavoa
ninth/tenth	**nono/decimo**	nonoa/dehcheemoa
once	**una volta**	oonah voltah
twice	**due volte**	dooay voltay
three times	**tre volte**	tray voltay
a half	**un mezzo**	oon mehddzoa
half a ...	**mezzo ...**	mehddzoa
half of ...	**metà di ...**	maytah dee
half (adj.)	**mezzo**	mehddzoa
a quarter	**un quarto**	oon kwahrtoa
one third	**un terzo**	oon tehrtsoa
a pair of	**un paio di**	oon paaeeoa dee
a dozen	**una dozzina**	oonah doaddzeenah
one per cent	**uno per cento**	oonoa pair chehntoa
3.4%	**3,4%**	tray **veer**goalah **kwaht**troa pair chehntoa
1981	**millenovecentottantuno**	meellay-noavaychehntottahntoonoa
1992	**millenovecentonovantadue**	meellay-noavaychehntoanoavahntahdooay
2003	**duemilatre**	dooaymeelahtray

Year and age *Anno ed età*

year	**l'anno**	lahnnoa
leap year	**l'anno bisestile**	lahnnoa beesaysteelay
decade	**il decennio**	eel dehchehnneeoa
century	**il secolo**	eel saikoloa
this year	**quest'anno**	kooaystahnnoa
last year	**l'anno scorso**	lahnnoa skoarsoa
next year	**l'anno prossimo**	lahnnoa prosseemoa
each year	**ogni anno**	oñee ahnnoa
2 years ago	**2 anni fa**	2 ahnnee fah
in one year	**in un anno**	een oon ahnnoa
in the eighties	**negli anni ottanta**	naylyee ahnnee ottahntah
the 16th century	**il sedicesimo secolo**	eel sehdeechayzeemoa saikoloa
in the 20th century	**nel ventesimo secolo**	nayl vayntayzeemoa saikoloa

REFERENCE SECTION

How old are you?	**Quanti anni ha?**	kwahntee ahnnee ah
I'm 30 years old.	**Ho trent'anni.**	oa trayntahnnee
He/She was born in 1960.	**Lui/Lei è nato(a) nel millenovecento-sessanta.**	looee/laiee ai nahtoa(ah) nayl meellay-noavaychehn-toa-sayssahntah
What is his/her age?	**Quanti anni ha?**	kwahntee ahnnee ah
Children under 16 are not admitted.	**Vietato ai minori di sedici anni.**	veeaytaatoa ahee meenoa-ree dee saydeechee ahnnee

Seasons *Stagioni*

spring/summer	**la primavera/l'estate**	lah preemahvayrah/laystaatay
autumn/winter	**l'autunno/l'inverno**	lowtoonnoa/leenvehrnoa
in spring	**in primavera**	een preemahvayrah
during the summer	**durante l'estate**	doorahntay laystaatay
in autumn	**in autunno**	een owtoonnoa
during the winter	**durante l'inverno**	doorahntay leenvehrnoa
high season	**alta stagione**	ahltah stahjoanay
low season	**bassa stagione**	bahssah stahjoanay

Months *Mesi*

January	**gennaio***	jehnnaaeeoa
February	**febbraio**	fehbbraaeeoa
March	**marzo**	mahrtsoa
April	**aprile**	ahpreelay
May	**maggio**	mahdjoa
June	**giugno**	jooñoa
July	**luglio**	loolyoa
August	**agosto**	ahgoastoa
September	**settembre**	sayttehmbray
October	**ottobre**	oattoabray
November	**novembre**	noavehmbray
December	**dicembre**	deechehmbray
in September	**in settembre**	een sayttehmbray
since October	**da ottobre**	dah oattoabray
the beginning of January	**l'inizio di gennaio**	leeneetseeoa dee jehnnaaeeoa
the middle of February	**la metà di febbraio**	lah maytah dee fehbbraaeeoa
the end of March	**la fine di marzo**	lah feenay dee mahrtsoa

---

* The names of months aren't capitalized in Italian.

Days and Date   *Giorni e data*

What day is it today?	**Che giorno è oggi?**	kay **joar**noa ai **o**djee
Sunday	**domenica***	doa**may**neekah
Monday	**lunedì**	loo**nay**dee
Tuesday	**martedì**	mahr**tay**dee
Wednesday	**mercoledì**	mehrkoa**lay**dee
Thursday	**giovedì**	joa**vay**dee
Friday	**venerdì**	vay**nayr**dee
Saturday	**sabato**	**saa**bahtoa
It's ...	**È ...**	ai
July 1	**il primo luglio**	eel **pree**moa **loo**lyoa
March 10	**il 10 marzo**	eel **dee**aichee **mahr**tsoa
in the morning	**al mattino**	ahl mah**tee**noa
during the day	**durante il giorno**	doo**rahn**tay eel **joar**noa
in the afternoon	**nel pomeriggio**	nayl poamay**reed**joa
in the evening	**alla sera**	**ahl**lah **say**rah
at night	**la notte**	lah **not**tay
the day before yesterday	**ieri l'altro**	ee**ai**ree **lahl**troa
yesterday	**ieri**	ee**ai**ree
today	**oggi**	**o**djee
tomorrow	**domani**	doa**maa**nee
the day after tomorrow	**dopodomani**	dopoadoa**maa**nee
the day before	**il giorno prima**	eel **joar**noa **pree**mah
the next day	**il giorno seguente**	eel **joar**noa saygoo**ayn**tay
two days ago	**due giorni fa**	**doo**ay **joar**nee fah
in three days' time	**fra tre giorni**	frah tray **joar**nee
last week	**la settimana scorsa**	lah saytteemaanah **skoar**sah
next week	**la settimana prossima**	lah saytteemaanah **pros**seemah
for a fortnight (two weeks)	**per quindici giorni**	pair kooeen**dee**chee **joar**nee
birthday	**il compleanno**	eel koamplay**ah**nnoa
day off	**il giorno di riposo**	eel **joar**noa dee ree**po**soa
holiday	**il giorno festivo**	eel **joar**noa fay**stee**voa
holidays/vacation	**le vacanze**	lay vah**kahn**tsay
week	**la settimana**	lah saytteemaanah
weekend	**il fine settimana**	eel **fee**nay saytteemaanah
working day	**il giorno feriale**	eel **joar**noa fayree**aa**lay

---

* The names of days aren't capitalized in Italian.

Public holidays   *Giorni festivi*

While there may be additional regional holidays in Italy, only national holidays are cited below.

January 1	**Capodanno** or **Primo dell'Anno**	New Year's Day
April 25	**Anniversario della Liberazione (1945)**	Liberation Day
May 1	**Festa del Lavoro**	Labour Day
August 15	**Ferragosto**	Assumption Day
November 1	**Ognissanti**	All Saints' Day
December 8	**L'Immacolata Concezione**	Immaculate Conception
December 25	**Natale**	Christmas Day
December 26	**Santo Stefano**	St. Stephen's Day
Movable date:	**Lunedì di Pasqua (Pasquetta)**	Easter Monday

Except for the 25th April, all the Italian holidays are celebrated in the Ticino, as well as the 19th March *(San Giuseppe)*, 1st August (National Holiday), and the usual holidays *Ascensione* (Ascension Day), *Lunedì di Pentecoste* (Whit Monday) and *Corpus Domini*.

Greetings and wishes   *Saluti e auguri*

Merry Christmas!	**Buon Natale!**	bwawn nahtaalay
Happy New Year!	**Buon anno!**	bwawn ahnnoa
Happy Easter!	**Buona Pasqua!**	bwawnah pahskwah
Happy birthday!	**Buon compleanno!**	bwawn koamplayahnnoa
Best wishes!	**Tanti auguri!**	tahntee ahoogooree
Congratulations!	**Congratulazioni!**	koangrahtoolahtseeoanee
Good luck/All the best!	**Buona fortuna!**	bwawnah foartoonah
Have a good trip!	**Buon viaggio!**	bwawn veeahdjoa
Have a good holiday!	**Buone vacanze!**	bwawnay vahkahntsay
Best regards from ...	**I migliori saluti da ...**	ee meelyoaree sahlootee dah
My regards to ...	**I miei saluti a ...**	ee meeaiee sahlootee ah

What time is it? *Che ore sono?*

Excuse me. Can you tell me the time?	Mi scusi. Può dirmi che ore sono?	mee skoozee. pwo deermee kay oaray soanoa
It's five past one.	È l'una e cinque.	ai loonah ay cheengkooay
It's ...	Sono le ...	soanoa lay
ten past two	due e dieci	dooay ay deeaichee
a quarter past three	tre e un quarto	tray ay oon kwahrtoa
twenty past four	quattro e venti	kwahttroa ay vayntee
twenty-five past five	cinque e venticinque	cheengkooay ay vaynteecheengkooay
half past six	sei e mezza	sehee ay mehddzah
twenty-five to eight	sette e trentacinque	sehttay ay trayntahcheengkooay
twenty to eight	otto meno venti	ottoa mainoa vayntee
a quarter to nine	nove meno un quarto	nawvay mainoa oon kwahrtoa
ten to ten	dieci meno dieci	deeaichee mainoa deeaichee
five to eleven	undici meno cinque	oondeechee mainoa cheengkooay
twelve o'clock (noon/midnight)	dodici (mezzogiorno/ mezzanotte)	doadeechee (mehdzoajoarnoa/ mehdzahnottay)
in the morning	del mattino	dayl mahtteenoa
in the afternoon	del pomeriggio	dayl poamayreedjoa
in the evening	della sera	dayllah sayrah
The train leaves at ...	Il treno parte alle ...	eel traynoa pahrtay ahllay
13.04 (1.04 p.m.)	tredici e quattro*	traydeechee ay kwahttroa
0.40 (0.40 a.m.)	zero e quaranta	dzehroa ay kwahrahntah
in five minutes	fra cinque minuti	frah cheengkooay meenootee
in a quarter of an hour	fra un quarto d'ora	frah oon kwahrtoa doarah
half an hour ago	mezz'ora fa	mehdzoarah fah
about two hours	circa due ore	cheerkah dooay oaray
more than 10 minutes	più di dieci minuti	peeoo dee deeaichee meenootee
less than 30 seconds	meno di trenta secondi	mainoa dee trayntah saykoandee
The clock is fast/ slow.	L'orologio è avanti/ indietro.	loaroalojoa ai ahvahntee/ eendeeaytroa

---

* In ordinary conversation, time is expressed as shown above. However, official time uses a 24-hour clock which means that after noon hours are counted from 13 to 24.

Common abbreviations *Abbreviazioni correnti*

A.A.T.	**Azienda Autonoma di Soggiorno, Cura e Turismo**	local tourist board
a.	**arrivo**	arrival
ab.	**abitanti**	inhabitants, population
a.C.	**avanti Cristo**	B.C.
A.C.I.	**Automobile Club d'Italia**	Italian Automobile Association
a.D.	**anno Domini**	A.D.
A.G.I.P.	**Azienda Generale Italiana Petroli**	Italian National Oil Company
alt.	**altitudine**	altitude
C.I.T.	**Compagnia Italiana Turismo**	Italian Travel Agency
c.m.	**corrente mese**	of this month
C.P.	**casella postale**	post office box
C.so	**Corso**	avenue
d.C.	**dopo Cristo**	A.D.
ecc.	**eccetera**	etc.
E.N.I.T.	**Ente Nazionale italiano per il Turismo**	National Tourist Organization
F.F.S.	**Ferrovie Federali Svizzere**	Swiss Federal Railways
F.S.	**Ferrovie dello Stato**	Italian State Railways
I.V.A.	**Imposta sul Valore Aggiunto**	value added tax (sales tax)
Mil.	**militare**	military
p.	**partenza; pagina**	departure; page
P.T.	**Poste & Telecomunicazioni**	Post & Telecommunications
P.za	**Piazza**	square
R.A.I.	**Radio Audizioni Italiane**	Italian Broadcasting Company
Rep.	**Repubblica**	republic
sec.	**secolo**	century
Sig.	**Signor**	Mr.
Sig.a	**Signora**	Mrs.
Sig.na	**Signorina**	Miss
S.p.a.	**Società per azioni**	Ltd., Inc.
S.P.Q.R.	**Senatus Populusque Romanus**	The Senate and the People of Rome (Latin)
S.r.l.	**Società a responsabilità limitata**	limited liability company
S./S.ta	**San(to)/Santa**	Saint
S.S.	**Sua Santità**	His Holiness
T.C.I.	**Touring Club Italiano**	Italian Touring Association
V.le	**Viale**	avenue
V.U.	**Vigili Urbani**	city police

Signs and notices *Cartelli*

Affittasi	To let, for hire
Al completo	Full/No vacancies
Aperto da ... a ...	Open from ... to ...
Ascensore	Lift (elevator)
Attenti al cane	Beware of the dog
Caldo	Hot
Cassa	Cash desk
Chiudere la porta	Close the door
Chiuso	Closed
Chiuso per ferie/per riposo settimanale	Closed for holiday/Weekly closing day
Entrare senza bussare	Enter without knocking
Entrata	Entrance
Entrata libera	Free entrance
Freddo	Cold
Fuori servizio	Out of order
I trasgressori saranno puniti a norma di legge	Trespassers will be prosecuted
Informazioni	Information
In sciopero	On strike
In vendita	For sale
Libero	Vacant
Non disturbare	Do not disturb
Non toccare	Do not touch
Occupato	Occupied
Pericolo (di morte)	Danger (of death)
Pista per ciclisti	Path for cyclists
Pittura fresca	Wet paint
Privato	Private
Prudenza	Caution
Riservato	Reserved
Saldi	Sales
Signore	Ladies
Signori	Gentlemen
Spingere	Push
Strada privata	Private road
Suonare, per favore	Please ring
Svendita	Sales
Tirare	Pull
Uscita	Exit
Uscita di sicurezza	Emergency exit
Vietato ...	... forbidden
Vietato fumare	No smoking
Vietato l'ingresso	No entrance
Vietato toccare	Do not touch

Emergency *Emergenza*

Call the police	**Chiami la polizia**	keeaamee lah poaleetseeah
DANGER	**PERICOLO**	payreekoaloa
FIRE	**AL FUOCO**	ahl **fwaw**koa
Gas	**Gas**	gaz
Get a doctor	**Chiami un medico**	keeaamee oon **mai**deekoa
Go away	**Se ne vada**	say nay **vaa**dah
HELP	**AIUTO**	aheeootoa
Get help quickly	**Chiami aiuti, presto**	keeaamee aheeootee **preh**stoa
I'm ill	**Mi sento male**	mee **sayn**toa maalay
I'm lost	**Mi sono perso(a)**	mee soanoa **pehr**soa(ah)
Leave me alone	**Mi lasci in pace**	mee laashee een **paa**chay
LOOK OUT	**ATTENZIONE**	ahttayntseeoanay
Poison	**Veleno**	vaylaynoa
POLICE	**POLIZIA**	poaleetseeah
Quick	**Presto**	**preh**stoa
STOP	**FERMATEVI**	fayrmaatayvee
Stop that man/ woman	**Fermate quell'uomo/ quella donna**	fayrmaatay kooa**yll**womoa/ kooayllah **don**nah
STOP THIEF	**AL LADRO**	ahl **laa**droa

Emergency telephone numbers *Chiamate di emergenza*

Italy:	Police, all-purpose emergency number	113
	Road assistance (Automobile Club d'Italia)	116
Switzerland:	Police, all-purpose emergency number	117
	Fire	118

Lost! *In caso di perdite o di furti*

Where's the ...?	Dov'è ...?	doavai
lost-property (lost and found) office	**l'ufficio oggetti smarriti**	looffeechoa oadjehttee zmahrreetee
police station	**il posto di polizia**	eel poastoa dee poaleetseeah
I want to report a theft.	**Devo denunciare un furto.**	dayvoa daynoonchaaray oon foortoa
My ... has been stolen.	**Mi hanno rubato ...**	mee ahnnoa roobaatoa
I've lost my ...	**Ho perso ...**	oa **pehr**soa
handbag	**la mia borsetta**	lah meeah boarsayttah
passport	**il mio passaporto**	eel meeoa pahssahpoartoa
wallet	**il mio portafogli**	eel meeoa portahfoalyee

CAR ACCIDENTS, see page 78

Informazioni varie

Conversion tables

Centimetres and inches

To change centimetres into inches, multiply by .39.

To change inches into centimetres, multiply by 2.54.

	in.	feet	yards
1 mm.	0.039	0.003	0.001
1 cm.	0.39	0.03	0.01
1 dm.	3.94	0.32	0.10
1 m.	39.40	3.28	1.09

	mm.	cm.	m.
1 in.	25.4	2.54	0.025
1 ft.	304.8	30.48	0.305
1 yd.	914.4	91.44	0.914

(32 metres = 35 yards)

Temperature

To convert centigrade into degrees Fahrenheit, multiply centigrade by 1.8 and add 32.

To convert degrees Fahrenheit into centigrade, subtract 32 from Fahrenheit and divide by 1.8.

Kilometres into miles

1 kilometre (km.) = 0.62 miles

km.	10	20	30	40	50	60	70	80	90	100	110	120	130
miles	6	12	19	25	31	37	44	50	56	62	68	75	81

Miles into kilometres

1 mile = 1.609 kilometres (km.)

miles	10	20	30	40	50	60	70	80	90	100
km.	16	32	48	64	80	97	113	129	145	161

Fluid measures

1 litre (l.) = 0.88 imp. quart or = 1.06 U.S. quart

1 imp. quart = 1.14 l.   1 U.S. quart = 0.95 l.
1 imp. gallon = 4.55 l.   1 U.S. gallon = 3.8 l.

litres	5	10	15	20	25	30	35	40	45	50
imp. gal.	1.1	2.2	3.3	4.4	5.5	6.6	7.7	8.8	9.9	11.0
U.S. gal.	1.3	2.6	3.9	5.2	6.5	7.8	9.1	10.4	11.7	13.0

Weights and measures

1 kilogram or kilo (kg.) = 1000 grams (g.)

100 g. = 3.5 oz.   ½ kg. = 1.1 lb.
200 g. = 7.0 oz.   1 kg. = 2.2 lb.

1 oz. = 28.35 g.
1 lb. = 453.60 g.

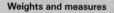

CLOTHING SIZES, see page 115/YARDS AND INCHES, see page 112

A very basic grammar

Articles

There are two genders in Italian—masculine (masc.) and feminine (fem.).

1. Definite article (the):

	singular	plural
masc.	l' before a vowel	gli
	lo before z or s + consonant	gli
	il before all other consonants	i
	l'amico (the friend)	gli amici (the friends)
	lo studente (the student)	gli studenti (the students)
	il treno (the train)	i treni (the trains)
fem.	l' before a vowel	le
	la before a consonant	le
	l'arancia (the orange)	le arance (the oranges)
	la casa (the house)	le case (the houses)

2. Indefinite article (a/an):

masc. **un** (**uno** before z or s + consonant*)

    un piatto (a plate)
    uno specchio (a mirror)

fem. **una** (**un'** before a vowel)

    una strada (a street)
    un'amica (a girl friend)

3. Partitive (some/any)

In affirmative sentences and some interrogatives, **some** and **any** are expressed by **di + definite article**, which has the following contracted forms:

masc.	dell' before a vowel	degli
	dello before z or s + consonant	degli
	del before other consonants	dei
fem.	dell' before a vowel	delle
	della before a consonant	delle

*When s is followed by a vowel, the masculine articles are il/i (definite) and un (indefinite).

For other contractions of preposition + definite article, see page 163.

Desidero del vino	I want some wine.
Vorrei delle sigarette.	I'd like some cigarettes.
Ha degli amici a Roma?	Have you any friends in Rome?

Nouns

Nouns ending in **o** are generally masculine. To form the plural, change **o** to **i**.

il tavolo (the table)   **i tavoli** (the tables)

Nouns ending in **a** are usually feminine. To form the plural, change **a** to **e**.

la casa (the house)   **le case** (the houses)

Nouns ending in **e**—no rule as to gender. Learn each noun individually. Plurals are formed by changing the **e** to **i**.

il piede (the foot)	**i piedi** (the feet)
la notte (the night)	**le notti** (the nights)

Adjectives

They agree with the noun they modify in number and gender. There are two basic types—ending in **o** and ending in **e**.

	singular	plural
masc.	**leggero** light (in weight)	**leggeri**
	grande big	**grandi**
fem.	**leggera**	**leggere**
	grande	**grandi**

They usually follow the noun but certain common adjectives precede the noun.

un caro amico (a dear friend)
una strada lunga (a long street)

Demonstratives

this	**questo/questa** (contracted to **quest'** before a vowel)
these	**questi/queste** (no contraction)
that	**quell', quello, quel** (masc.)/**quell', quella*** (fem.)
those	**quegli, quei** (masc.)/ **quelle** (fem.)

Possessive adjectives and pronouns

These agree in number and gender *with the nouns they modify* (or replace). They are almost always used with the definite article.

	masculine		feminine	
	singular	plural	singular	plural
my, mine	**il mio**	**i miei**	**la mia**	**le mie**
your, yours	**il tuo**	**i tuoi**	**la tua**	**le tue**
his, her, hers, its	**il suo**	**i suoi**	**la sua**	**le sue**
our, ours	**il nostro**	**i nostri**	**la nostra**	**le nostre**
your, yours	**il vostro**	**i vostri**	**la vostra**	**le vostre**
their, theirs	**il loro**	**i loro**	**la loro**	**le loro**
** your, yours (sing.)	**il suo**	**i suoi**	**la sua**	**le sue**
** your, yours (plur.)	**il loro**	**i loro**	**la loro**	**le loro**

Thus, depending on the context, **il suo cane** can mean *his, her* or *your dog*, **la sua casa,** *his, her* or *your house*.

Personal pronouns

	Subject	Direct Object	Indirect Object	After a Preposition
I	**io**	**mi**	**mi**	**me**
you	**tu**	**ti**	**ti**	**te**
he, it (masc.)	**lui/egli**	**lo**	**gli**	**lui**
she, it (fem.)	**lei/ella**	**la**	**le**	**lei**
we	**noi**	**ci**	**ci**	**noi**
you	**voi**	**vi**	**vi**	**voi**
they (masc.)	**loro/essi**	**li**	**loro**	**loro**
they (fem.)	**loro/esse**	**le**	**loro**	**loro**

* These forms follow the same system as **dell'/dello/della**, etc. (see p. 163).
** This is the formal form—used in addressing people you do not know well.

Note: There are two forms for "you" in Italian: **tu** (singular) is used when talking to relatives, close friends and children (and between young people); the plural of **tu** is **voi**. **Lei** (singular) and **Loro** (plural) are used in all other cases (with the 3rd person singular/plural of the verb).

Verbs

Here we are concerned only with the infinitive and the present tense.

Learn these two **auxiliary verbs**:

essere (to be)	avere (to have)
io* sono (I am)	io* ho (I have)
tu sei (you are)	tu hai (you have)
lui, lei è (he, she, it is)	lui, lei ha (he, she, it has)
lei è (you are)	lei ha (you have)
noi siamo (we are)	noi abbiamo (we have)
voi siete (you are)	voi avete (you have)
essi/esse sono (they are)	essi/esse hanno (they have)

C'è/Ci sono are equivalent to "there is/there are":

C'è una lettera per Lei.	There's a letter for you.
Ci sono due pacchi per lui.	There are two parcels for him.

Regular verbs follow one of three patterns (conjugations) depending on the ending of the infinitive.

	ends in -**are**	ends in -**ere**	ends in -**ire**
Infinitive:	amare (to love)	vendere (to sell)	partire (to leave)
io*	amo	vendo	parto
tu	ami	vendi	parti
lui, lei	ama	vende	parte
noi	amiamo	vendiamo	partiamo
voi	amate	vendete	partite
essi/esse	amano	vendono	partono

* The subject pronouns are seldom used except for emphasis.

Irregular verbs: As in all languages, these have to be learned. Here are four you'll find useful.

Infinitive:	andare (to go)	potere (to be able)	volere (to want)	fare (to make)
io	vado	posso	voglio	faccio
tu	vai	puoi	vuoi	fai
lui/lei	va	può	vuole	fa
noi	andiamo	possiamo	vogliamo	facciamo
voi	andate	potete	volete	fate
essi/esse	vanno	possono	vogliono	fanno

Negatives

Negatives are formed by putting **non** before the verb.

Non vado a Roma.   I am not going to Rome.

Questions

In Italian, questions are often formed by simply changing the inflexion of your voice. Remember that the personal pronoun is rarely used, either in affirmative sentences or in questions.

Parlo italiano.   I speak Italian.
Parla italiano?   Do you speak Italian?

Prepositions

There is a list of prepositions on page 14. Note the following contractions:

Definite Article	a at, to	da by, from	di of	in in	su on	con with
+ il	al	dal	del	nel	sul	col
+ l'	all'	dall'	dell'	nell'	sull'	coll'
+ lo	allo	dallo	dello	nello	sullo	con lo
+ la	alla	dalla	della	nella	sulla	con la
+ i	ai	dai	dei	nei	sui	coi/con i
+ gli	agli	dagli	degli	negli	sugli	con gli
+ le	alle	dalle	delle	nelle	sulle	con le

Dictionary
and alphabetical index

English–Italian

f feminine   *m* masculine   *pl* plural

a un(a) 159
abbey abbazia *f* 81
abbreviation abbreviazione *f* 154
able, to be potere 163
about *(approximately)* circa 153
above sopra 15, 63
absces ascesso *m* 145
absorbent cotton cotone idrofilo *m* 109
accept, to accettare 62, 102
accessories accessori *m/pl* 116, 125
accident incidente *m* 78, 79, 139
accommodation alloggio *m* 22
account conto *m* 130, 131
ache dolore *m*, male *m* 141
adaptor presa multipla *f* 119
address indirizzo *m* 21, 31, 76, 79, 102
address book agenda per gli indirizzi *f* 104
adhesive adesivo(a) 105
admission entrata *f* 82, 89, 155
Africa Africa *f* 146
after dopo 14, 77
afternoon pomeriggio *m* 151, 153
after-shave lotion lozione dopobarba *f* 110
age età *f* 149; anni *m* 150
ago fa 149, 151
air conditioner condizionatore d'aria *m* 28
air conditioning aria condizionata *f* 23
airmail via aerea 133
airplane aereo *m* 65
airport aeroporto *m* 16, 21, 65

alabaster alabastro *m* 122
alarm clock sveglia *f* 121
alcohol alcool *m* 107
alcoholic alcolico(a) 59
Algeria Algeria *f* 146
allergic allergico(a) 141, 143
almond mandorla *f* 54
alphabet alfabeto *m* 8
also anche 15
amazing sorprendente 84
amber ambra *f* 122
ambulance ambulanza *f* 79
American americano(a) 93, 126
American plan pensione completa *f* 24
amethyst ametista *f* 122
amount importo *m* 62, 131
amplifier amplificatore *m* 119
anaesthetic anestetico *m* 144
analgesic analgesico *m* 109
anchovy acciuga *f* 41, 46
and e 15
animal animale *m* 85
ankle caviglia *f* 139
anorak giacca a vento *f* 116
another un(') altro(a) 123
answer, to rispondere 136
antibiotic antibiotico *m* 143
antidepressant antidepressivo *m* 143
antiques antichità *f/pl* 83
antique shop antiquario *m* 98
antiseptic antisettico(a) 109
antiseptic antisettico *m* 140
any del, della 14
anyone qualcuno(a) 11
anything qualcosa 17, 25, 113

aperitif aperitivo m 56
appendicitis appendicite f 142
appendix appendice f 138
appetizer antipasto m 41
apple mela f 54, 63
appliance apparecchio m 119
appointment appuntamento m 30, 131, 137, 145
apricot albicocca f 54
April aprile m 150
archaeology archeologia f 83
architect architetto m 83
area code prefisso m 134
arm braccio m 138, 139
arrival arrivo m 16, 65
arrive, to arrivare 65, 68, 130
art arte f 83
artery arteria f 138
art gallery galleria d'arte f 81, 98
artichoke carciofo m 41, 52
artificial artificiale 124
artist artista m/f 81, 83
ashtray portacenere m 27, 36
Asia Asia f 146
ask for, to chiedere 25, 61, 136
asparagus asparago m 52
aspirin aspirina f 109
assorted assortito(a) 41
asthma asma f 141
at a 14, 163
at least come minimo 24
at once subito 15; immediatamente 31
aubergine melanzana f 52
August agosto m 150
aunt zia f 93
Australia Australia f 146
Austria Austria f 146
automatic automatico(a) 20, 122, 124
autumn autunno m 150
average medio(a) 91
awful orribile 84

B

baby bambino m 24, 111; bebè m 111
baby food alimenti per bebè m/pl 111
babysitter babysitter f 27
back schiena f 138
backache mal di schiena m 141
bacon pancetta f 38
bacon and eggs uova e pancetta m/pl 38
bad cattivo(a) 13, 95

bag borsa f 18; sacchetto m 103
baggage bagagli m/pl 18, 26, 31, 71
baggage cart carrello portabagagli m 18, 71
baggage check deposito bagagli m 67, 71
baggage locker custodia automatica dei bagagli f 18, 67, 71
baked al forno 47, 50
baker's panetteria f 98
balance (account) bilancio m 131
balcony balcone m 23
ball (inflated) pallone m 128
ballet balletto m 88
ball-point pen biro f 104
banana banana f 54, 63
bandage benda f 109
Band-Aid cerotto m 109
bangle braccialetto m 121
bangs frangia f 30
bank (finance) banca f 98, 129
bank card carta d'identità bancaria f 130
banknote banconota f 130
bar bar m 33, 67; (chocolate) stecca f 64
barbecued alla graticola, alla griglia 50
barber's barbiere m 30, 98
basil basilico m 53
basketball pallacanestro f 89
bath (hotel) bagno m 23, 25, 27
bathing cap cuffia da bagno f 116
bathing hut cabina f 91
bathing suit costume da bagno m 116
bathrobe accappatoio m 116
bathroom bagno m 27
bath salts sali da bagno m/pl 110
bath towel asciugamano m 27
battery pila f 119, 121, 125; (car) batteria f 75, 78
be, to essere 162; trovarsi 11
beach spiaggia f 90
bean fagiolo m 52
beard barba f 31
beautiful bello(a) 13, 84
beauty salon istituto di bellezza m 30, 98
bed letto m 24, 144
bed and breakfast camera e colazione f 24
bedpan padella f 144
beef manzo m 48

beer birra *f* 59, 64
beet(root) barbabietola *f* 52
before *(place)* davanti a 14; *(time)* prima di 14, 151
begin, to iniziare 80, 88; incominciare 87
beginner principiante *m/f* 91
beginning inizio *m* 150
behind dietro 14, 77
beige beige 113
Belgium Belgio *m* 146
bell *(electric)* campanello *m* 144
bellboy fattorino *m* 26
below al di sotto 15; sotto 63
belt cintura *f* 117
bend *(road)* curva *f* 79
berth cuccetta *f* 69, 70, 71
best migliore 152
better migliore 13, 25, 101, 113
beware attento(a) 155
between tra, fra 15
bicycle bicicletta *f* 74
big grande 13, 101
bill conto *m* 31, 62, 102; *(banknote)* banconota *f* 130
billion *(Am.)* miliardo *m* 148
binoculars binocolo *m* 123
bird uccello *m* 85
birth nascita *f* 150
birthday compleanno *m* 151, 152
biscuit *(Br.)* biscotto *m* 64
bitter amaro(a) 61
black nero(a) 113
black and white bianco e nero 124, 125
blackberry mora *f* 54
blackcurrant ribes nero *m* 54
bladder vescica *f* 138
blanket coperta *f* 27
bleed, to perdere sangue 139; sanguinare 145
blind *(window)* persiana *f* 29
blister vescica *f* 139
block, to otturare 28
blood sangue *m* 142
blood pressure pressione *f* 141
blood transfusion trasfusione di sangue *f* 144
blouse blusa *f* 116
blow-dry asciugatura col fono *f* 30
blue blu, azzurro(a) 113
blueberry mirtillo *m* 54
boar *(wild)* cinghiale *m* 51
boarding house pensione *f* 19, 22

boat battello *m* 74
bobby pin molletta *f* 111
body corpo *m* 138
boil foruncolo *m* 139
boiled lesso(a) 47, 50
boiled egg uovo alla coque *m* 38
bone osso *m* 138
book libro *m* 11, 104
book, to prenotare 69
booking office ufficio prenotazioni *m* 19, 67
booklet blocchetto *m* 72
bookshop libreria *f* 98, 104
boot stivale *m* 118
born nato(a) 150
botanical gardens giardino botanico *m* 81
botany botanica *f* 83
bottle bottiglia *f* 17, 57
bottle-opener apribottiglia *m* 106
bottom basso *m* 145
bowels intestino *m* 138
bow tie cravatta a farfalla *f* 116
box scatola *f* 120
boxing pugilato *m* 89
boy *(child)* bambino *m* 112, 128
boyfriend ragazzo *m* 93
bra reggiseno *m* 116
bracelet braccialetto *m* 121
braces *(suspenders)* bretelle *f/pl* 116
braised brasato(a) 50
brake freno *m* 78
brake fluid olio dei freni *m* 75
brandy brandy *m* 59
bread pane *m* 36, 38, 64
break, to rompere 29, 119, 123, 145; rompersi 139, 145
break down, to avere un guasto 78
breakdown guasto *m* 78
breakdown van carro attrezzi *m* 78
breakfast colazione *f* 24, 34, 38
breast petto *m* 138
breathe, to respirare 141
bridge ponte *m* 85
briefs slip *m* 116
bring, to portare 12
bring down, to portare giù 31
British britannico(a) 93
broken rotto(a) 29, 119, 140
brooch spilla *f* 121
brother fratello *m* 93
brown marrone 113
bruise contusione *f* 139
brush spazzola *f* 111

Brussels sprouts cavolini di Bruxelles *m/pl* 52
bubble bath bagnoschiuma *m* 110
bucket secchio *m* 106; secchiello *m* 128
build, to costruire 83
building edificio *m* 81, 83
building blocks/bricks gioco di costruzioni *m* 128
bulb lampadina *f* 28, 75, 119
burn scottatura *f* 139
burn out, to *(bulb)* bruciare 28
bus autobus *m* 18, 19, 65, 72, 73; pullman *m* 72, 80
business affari *m/pl* 16, 131
business trip viaggio d'affari *m* 93
bus stop fermata dell'autobus *f* 72, 73
busy impegnato(a) 96
but ma, però 15
butane gas gas butano *m* 32, 106
butcher's macelleria *f* 98
butter burro *m* 36, 38, 64
button bottone *m* 29, 117
buy, to comprare 82, 104; acquistare 123

C

cabana cabina *f* 91
cabbage cavolo *m* 52
cabin *(ship)* cabina *f* 74
cable telegramma *m* 133
cable car funivia *f* 74
cable release scatto *m* 125
café caffè *m* 33
caffein-free decaffeinato 38, 60
cake dolce *m* 55; torta *f* 55, 64
cake shop pasticceria *f* 98
calculator calcolatrice *f* 105
calendar calendario *m* 104
call *(phone)* telefonata *f* 135, 136
call, to chiamare 11, 78, 156; telefonare 136
cambric tela battista *f* 114
camel-hair pelo di cammello *m* 114
camera macchina fotografica *f* 124, 125
camera case astuccio (per macchina fotografica) *m* 125
camera shop negozio di apparecchi fotografici *m*
camp, to campeggiare 32
campbed letto da campo *m* 106
camping campeggio *m* 32

camping equipment materiale da campeggio *m* 106
camp site campeggio *m* 32
can *(of peaches)* scatola *f* 120
can *(to be able)* potere 11, 12, 163
Canada Canada *m* 146
cancel, to annullare 65
candle candela *f* 106
candy caramella *f* 126
can opener apriscatole *m* 106
cap berretto *m* 116
caper cappero *m* 53
capital *(finance)* capitale *m* 131
car macchina *f* 19, 20, 75, 76, 78; automobile *f* 78
carafe caraffa *f* 57
carat carato *m* 121
caravan roulotte *f* 32
caraway cumino *m* 53
carbon paper carta carbone *f* 104
carburettor carburatore *m* 78
card carta *f* 93; *(visiting)* bigliettino *m* 131
card game carte da gioco *f/pl* 128
cardigan cardigan *m* 116
car hire autonoleggio *m* 19, 20
car park parcheggio *m* 77
car racing corsa automobilistica *f* 89
car radio autoradio *f* 119
car rental autonoleggio *m* 20
carrot carota *f* 52
carry, to portare 21
cart carrello *m* 18
carton *(of cigarettes)* stecca (di sigarette) *f* 17
cartridge *(camera)* rotolo *m* 124
case *(instance)* caso *m* 143; *(cigarettes etc)* astuccio *m* 123, 125
cash, to incassare 130; riscuotere 133
cash desk cassa *f* 103, 155
cashier cassiere(a) *m/f* 103
cassette cassetta *f* 119, 127
castle castello *m* 81
catacomb catacomba *f* 81
catalogue catalogo *m* 82
cathedral cattedrale *f* 81
Catholic cattolico(a) 84
cauliflower cavolfiore *m* 52
caution prudenza *f* 155
cave grotta *f* 81
celery sedano *m* 52
cellophane tape nastro adesivo *m* 104

cemetery cimitero m 81

centimetre centimetro m 112

centre centro m 19, 21, 76, 81

century secolo m 149

ceramics ceramica f 83, 127

cereal cereali m/pl 38

certificate certificato m 144

chain catena f 79

chain (jewellery) catenina f 121

chain bracelet braccialetto a catena m 121

chair sedia f 36, 106

chamber music musica da camera f 128

change (money) moneta f 77, 130; resto m 62

change, to cambiare 61, 65, 68, 73, 75, 123; (money) 18, 130

chapel cappella f 81

charcoal carbonella f 106

charge tariffa f 20; prezzo m 89; costo m 136

charge, to fare pagare 24; (commission) trattenere 130

charm (trinket) ciondolo m 121

charm bracelet braccialetto a ciondoli m 121

cheap buon mercato 13; economico(a) 101

check assegno m 130; (restaurant) conto m 62

check, to controllare 75, 123; (luggage) far registrare 71

check book libretto d'assegni m 131

check in, to (airport) presentarsi 65

check out, to partire 31

checkup (medical) controllo m 142

cheers! salute! cin-cin! 56

cheese formaggio m 53, 63, 64

chef chef m 40

chemist's farmacia f 98, 108

cheque assegno m 130

cheque book libretto d'assegni m 131

cherry ciliegia f 54

chess scacchi m/pl 93, 128

chest torace m 138, 141

chestnut castagna f 54

chewing gum gomma da masticare f 126

chicken pollo m 51, 63

chick-pea cece m 52

chicory indivia f 52; (Am.) cicoria f 52

chiffon chiffon m 114

child bambino(a) m/f 24, 61, 82, 93, 139

children's doctor pediatra m/f 137

China Cina f 146

chips patatine fritte f/pl 63, 64

chives cipollina f 53

chocolate cioccolato m 126, 127; (hot) cioccolata (calda) f 38, 60

chocolate bar stecca di cioccolato f 64

choice scelta f 40

chop braciola f 48

Christmas Natale m 152

church chiesa f 81, 84

cigar sigaro m 126

cigarette sigaretta f 17, 95, 126

cigarette case portasigarette m 121, 126

cigarette lighter accendino m 121

cine camera cinepresa f 124

cinema cinema m 86, 96

cinnamon cannella f 53

circle (theatre) galleria f 87

city città f 81

clam vongola f 45, 47

classical classico(a) 128

clean pulito(a) 61

clean, to pulire 29, 76

cleansing cream crema detergente f 110

cliff scogliera f 85

clip fermaglio m 121

clock orologio m 121, 153

clock-radio radio-sveglia f 119

close (near) vicino(a) 78, 98

close, to chiudere 11, 82, 108, 132

closed chiuso(a) 155

clothes abiti m/pl 29; indumenti m/pl 116

clothes peg molletta da bucato f 106

clothing abbigliamento m 112

cloud nuvola f 94

clove chiodo di garofano m 53

coach (bus) pullman m 72

coat cappotto m 116

coconut noce di cocco f 54

cod baccalà m 46, 47; (fresh) merluzzo m 46

coffee caffè m 38, 60, 64

coin moneta f 83

cold freddo(a) 13, 25, 61, 94, 155

cold (illness) raffreddore m 108, 141

cold cuts affettati m/pl 64

colour colore m 103, 112, 124, 125

colour chart tabella dei colori f 30
colour negative negativo a colori m 124
colour shampoo shampoo colorante m 111
colour slide diapositiva f 124
colour television *(set)* televisore a colori m 119
comb pettine m 111
come, to venire 36, 92, 95, 137, 146
comedy commedia f 86
commission commissione f 130
common *(frequent)* corrente 154
compact disc disco compatto m 127
compartment scompartimento m 70
compass bussola f 106
complaint reclamo m 61
concert concerto m 88
concert hall sala dei concerti f 81, 88
conductor *(orchestra)* maestro m 88
confectioner's pasticceria f 98
confirm, to confermare 65
confirmation conferma f 23
congratulations congratulazioni f/pl 152
connection *(train)* coincidenza f 65, 68
constant costante 140
constipated costipato(a) 140
contact lens lente a contatto f 123
contain, to contenere 37
contraceptive antifecondativo m 109
contract contratto m 131
control controllo m 16
convent convento m 81
cookie biscotto m 64
cool box ghiacciaia f 106
copper rame m 122
coral corallo m 122
corduroy velluto a coste m 114
cork tappo m 61
corkscrew cavatappi m 106
corner angolo m 21, 36, 77
corn plaster cerotto callifugo m 109
cost preventivo m 131
cost, to costare 10, 80, 133, 136
cotton cotone m 114
cotton wool cotone idrofilo m 109
cough tosse f 108, 141
cough, to tossire 142
cough drops pasticche per la tosse f/pl 109
counter sportello m 133
countryside campagna f 85

court house palazzo di giustizia m 81
cousin cugino(a) m/f 93
cover charge coperto m 62
crab granchio m 46
cramp crampo m 141
crayfish gambero m 46
crayon pastello m 104
cream panna f 55, 60; *(toiletry)* crema f 110
credit credito m 130
credit, to accreditare 130, 131
credit card carta di credito f 20, 31, 62, 102, 130
crockery stoviglie f/pl 107
crisps patatine fritte f/pl 64
cross croce f 121
crossing *(by sea)* traversata f 74
crossroads incrocio m 77
cruise crociera f 74
crystal cristallo m 122
cuckoo clock orologio a cucù m 121
cucumber cetriolo m 52
cuff link gemelli m/pl 121
cuisine cucina f 35
cup tazza f 36, 107
currency valuta f 129
currency exchange office ufficio cambio m 18, 67, 129
current corrente m 90
curtain tenda f 28
curve *(road)* curva f 79
custard crema f 55
customs dogana f 16, 122
cut *(wound)* taglio m 139
cut off, to *(phone)* interrompere 135
cut glass vetro tagliato m 122
cuticle remover prodotto per togliere le pellicine m 110
cutlery posate f/pl 107, 121
cuttlefish seppia f 47
cycling ciclismo m 89
cystitis cistite f 142

D

dairy latteria f 98
dance, to ballare 88, 96
danger pericolo m 155, 156
dangerous pericoloso(a) 90
dark buio(a) 25; scuro(a) 101, 112, 113
date data f 25, 151; *(fruit)* dattero m 54
daughter figlia f 93
day giorno m 16, 20, 24, 32, 80, 151

daylight luce naturale f 124
day off giorno di riposo m 151
death morte f 155
decade decennio m 149
December dicembre m 150
decision decisione f 25, 102
deck (ship) ponte m 74
deck-chair sedia a sdraio f 91
declare, to dichiarare 16, 17
deer cervo m 51
delay ritardo m 69
delicatessen salumeria f 98
delicious delizioso(a) 62
deliver, to consegnare 102
delivery consegna f 102
denim tela di cotone f 114
dentist dentista m/f 145
denture dentiera f 145
deodorant deodorante m 110
department (museum, shop) reparto m 83, 100
department store grande magazzino m 98
departure partenza f 65
deposit (car hire) cauzione f 20; (bank) deposito m 130
deposit, to (bank) depositare 130
dessert dessert m 40, 55; dolce m 39, 55
detour (traffic) deviazione f 79
develop, to sviluppare 124
diabetes diabete m 141
diabetic diabetico(a) m/f 37
dialling code prefisso m 134
diamond diamante m 122
diaper pannolino m 111
diarrhoea diarrea f 140
dictionary dizionario m 104
diet dieta f 37
difficult difficile 13
difficulty difficoltà f 28, 102, 141
digital digitale 122
dine, to cenare 94
dining-car carrozza ristorante f 66, 68, 71
dining-room sala da pranzo f 27
dinner cena f 34
direct diretto(a) 65
direct, to indicare 12
direction direzione f 76
director(theatre) regista m 86
directory (phone) elenco m 134
disabled andicappato(a) 82
disc disco m 77, 127

discotheque discoteca f 88, 96
disease malattia f 142
dish piatto m 36, 37, 40
dishwashing detergent detersivo per lavare i piatti m 106
disinfectant disinfettante m 109
dislocate, to slogare 140
dissatisfied scontento(a) 103
district (town) quartiere m 81
disturb, to disturbare 155
diversion (traffic) deviazione f 79
dizzy stordito(a) 140
do, to fare 163
doctor medico m 79, 137; dottore m (dottoressa f) 144, 145
doctor's office ambulatorio m 137
dog cane m 155
doll bambola f 127, 128
dollar dollaro m 18, 130
door porta f 155
double doppio(a) 59
double bed letto matrimoniale m 23
double room camera doppia f 19, 23
down giù 15
downstairs di sotto 15
down there laggiù 77
downtown centro m 81
dozen dozzina f 120, 149
draught beer birra alla spina f 59
drawing paper carta da disegno f 104
drawing pin puntina f 104
dress abito m 116
dressing gown vestaglia f 116
drink bevanda f 40, 56, 59, 60, 61; bicchiere m 95
drink, to bere 35, 36
drinking water acqua potabile f 32
drip, to (tap) sgocciolare 28
drive, to guidare, andare 21, 76
driving licence patente f 20
drop (liquid) goccia f 109
drugstore farmacia f 98, 108
dry secco(a) 30, 57, 111
dry cleaner's lavanderia a secco f 29, 98; tintoria f 38
dry shampoo shampoo secco m 111
duck anatra f 48
dull (pain) debole 140
dummy succhiotto m 111
during durante 14, 150, 151
duty (customs) dazio m 17
duty-free shop negozio duty-free m 19
dye tintura f 30, 111

E

each ogni 149
ear orecchio m 138
earache mal d'orecchi m 141
ear drops gocce per le orecchie f/pl 109
early presto 13, 31
earring orecchino m 121
east est m 77
Easter Pasqua f 152
easy facile 13
eat, to mangiare 36
eel anguilla f 44
egg uovo m (pl uova f) 38, 64
eggplant melanzana f 52
eight otto 147
eighteen diciotto 147
eighth ottavo(a) 149
eighty ottanta 148
elastic elastico(a) 109
elastic bandage benda elastica f 109
Elastoplast cerotto m 109
electrical elettrico(a) 119
electrical appliance apparecchio elettrico m 119
electrician elettricista m 98
electricity elettricità f 32
electronic elettronico(a) 125, 128
elevator ascensore m 27, 100
eleven undici 147
embark, to imbarcare 74
emerald smeraldo m 122
emergency emergenza f 156
emergency exit uscita di sicurezza f 27, 99, 155
emery board limetta per unghie f 110
empty vuoto(a) 13
enamel smalto m 122
end fine f 150
endive cicoria f 52; (Am.) indivia f 52
engagement ring anello di fidanzamento m 121
engine (car) motore m 78
England Inghilterra f 146
English inglese 11, 80, 82, 84, 104, 105, 126, 137
enjoyable piacevole 31
enjoy oneself, to divertirsi 96
enlarge, to ingrandire 125
enough abbastanza 14
enquiry informazione f 68
enter, to entrare 155
entrance entrata f 67, 99, 155
entrance fee entrata f 82

envelope busta f 27, 104
equipment equipaggiamento m, tenuta f 91; materiale m 106
eraser gomma f 104
escalator scala mobile f 100
escalope scaloppina f 49
Europe Europa f 146
evening sera f 87, 96, 151, 153; serata f 95, 96
evening dress abito da sera m 88, 116
everything tutto 31
examine, to esaminare 139
excellent eccellente 84
exchange, to cambiare 103
exchange rate corso del cambio m 18, 130
excursion gita f 80
excuse, to scusare 10
exercise book quaderno m 104
exhaust pipe tubo di scappamento m 78
exhibition esposizione f 81
exit uscita f 67, 99, 155
expect, to aspettare 130
expense spesa f 131
expensive caro(a) 13, 19, 24, 101
exposure (photography) posa f 124
exposure counter contatore di esposizioni m 125
express espresso 133
expression espressione f 9
expressway autostrada f 76
extension cord/lead prolunga f 119
extra supplemento m 40
extract, to (tooth) estrarre 145
eye occhio m (pl occhi) 138, 139
eye drops gocce per gli occhi f/pl 109
eye pencil matita per occhi f 110
eye shadow ombretto m 110
eyesight vista f 123
eye specialist oculista m/f 137

F

face viso m 138
face-pack maschera di bellezza f 30
face powder cipria f 110
factory fabbrica f 81
fair fiera f 81
fall caduta f 139; (autumn) autunno m 150
family famiglia f 93
fan ventilatore m 28

DICTIONARY

fan belt cinghia del ventilatore f 75
far lontano(a) 13
fare prezzo m 21
farm fattoria f 85
fast rapido(a) 124
fat *(meat)* grasso m 37
father padre m 93
faucet rubinetto m 28
February febbraio m 150
fee *(doctor)* onorario m 144
feeding bottle biberon m 111
feel, to *(physical state)* sentirsi 140
felt feltro m 114
felt-tip pen pennarello m 104
fennel finocchio m 52
ferry traghetto m 74
fever febbre f 140
few pochi(e) 14; *(a)* alcuni(e) 14
field campo m 85
fifteen quindici 147
fifth quinto(a) 149
fifty cinquanta 147
fig fico m 54
file *(tool)* lima f 110
fill in, to compilare 26, 144
fillet filetto m 48
filling *(tooth)* otturazione f 145
filling station stazione di rifornimento
f 75
film *(movie)* film m 86; *(camera)*
pellicola f 124, 125
filter filtro m 125
filter-tipped con filtro 126
find, to trovare 10, 11, 100, 137
fine *(OK)* bene 25
fine arts belle arti f/pl 83
finger dito m 138
fire fuoco m 156
first primo(a) 68, 73, 149
first-aid kit cassetta del pronto soccorso f 106
first class prima classe f 69
first course primo piatto m 40
first name nome m 25
fish pesce m 46
fish, to pescare 90
fishing pesca f 90
fishing tackle arnese da pesca m 106
fishmonger's pescheria f 98
fit, to andare bene 115
fitting room cabina di prova f 115
five cinque 147
fix, to riparare 75; curare 145
fizzy *(mineral water)* gasato(a) 60

flannel flanella f 114
flash *(photography)* flash m 125
flash attachment attaccatura del
flash f 125
flashlight lampadina tascabile f 106
flask fiasco m 127
flat basso(a) 118
flat *(apartment)* appartamento m 22
flat tyre foratura f 75; gomma sgon-
fia f 78
flea market mercato delle pulci m 81
flight volo m 65
flight number numero del volo m 65
flippers pinne f/pl 128
floor piano m 27
floor show varietà m 88
florist's fiorista m/f 98
flour farina f 37
flower fiore m 85
flu influenza f 142
fog nebbia f 94
folding chair sedia pieghevole f 107
folding table tavola pieghevole f 107
folk music musica folcloristica f 128
food cibo m 37, 61; alimento m 111
food box contenitore per il cibo m
142
food poisoning avvelenamento da
cibo m 142
foot piede m 138
football calcio m 89
foot cream crema per i piedi f 110
footpath sentiero m 85
for per 15, 143
forbid, to vietare 155
forecast previsione f 94
foreign straniero(a) 59
forest foresta f 85
fork forchetta f 36, 61, 107, 127
form *(document)* modulo m 133;
scheda f 25, 26
fortnight quindici giorni m/pl 151
fortress fortezza f 81
forty quaranta 147
foundation cream fondo tinta m 110
fountain fontana f 81
fountain pen penna stilografica f
104
four quattro 147
fourteen quattordici 147
fourth quarto(a) 149
frame *(glasses)* montatura f 123
France Francia f 146
free libero(a) 13, 70, 82, 96, 155

Dizionario

French bean fagiolino *m* 52
French fries patatine fritte *f/pl* 63
fresh fresco(a) 54, 61
Friday venerdì *m* 151
fried fritto(a) 47, 50
fried egg uovo fritto *m* 38
friend amico *m/f* 95
fringe frangia *f* 30
frock abito *m* 116
from da 14, 163
front davanti 75
fruit frutta *f* 54
fruit cocktail macedonia di frutta *f* 54
fruit juice succo di frutta *m* 38, 60
frying-pan padella *f* 106
full pieno(a) 13; completo(a) 155; intero(a) 80
full board pensione completa *f* 20
full insurance assicurazione completa *f* 20
furniture mobilio *m* 83
furrier's pellicceria *f* 98

G

gabardine gabardine *m* 114
gallery galleria *f* 81, 98
game gioco *m* 128; *(food)* cacciagione *f* 50
garage garage *m* 26, 78
garden giardino *m* 81, 85
garlic aglio *m* 53
gas gas *m* 156
gasoline benzina *f* 75, 78
gastritis gastrite *f* 142
gauze garza *f* 109
general generale 26, 100
general delivery fermo posta *m* 133
general practitioner medico generico *m* 137
genitals genitali *m/pl* 138
gentleman signore *m* 155
genuine vero(a) 118
geology geologia *f* 83
Germany Germania *f* 146
get, to *(find)* trovare 10, 21, 32; *(call)* chiamare 31, 137; *(obtain)* ottenere 134; procurarsi 89, 90
get back, to ritornare 80
get off, to scendere 73
get to, to andare a 19; arrivare a 70
get up, to alzarsi 144
gherkin cetriolino *m* 52, 64
gin and tonic gin e tonico *m* 60

girdle busto *m* 116
girl *(child)* bambina *f* 112, 128
girlfriend ragazza *f* 93
give, to dare 12, 123, 135
glad *(to know you)* piacere 92
gland ghiandola *f* 138
glass bicchiere *m* 36, 57, 60, 61, 143
glasses occhiali *m/pl* 123
glassware articolo di vetro *m* 127
gloomy malinconico(a) 84
glossy *(finish)* lucido(a) 125
glove guanto *m* 116
glue colla *f* 105
go, to andare 95, 96, 163
go away, to andarsene 156
glad dorato(a) 113
gold oro *m* 121, 122
golden dorato(a) 113
gold plate placcato d'oro *m* 122
golf golf *m* 89
good buono(a) 13, 101
good-bye arrivederci 9
goods merci *f/pl* 16
goose oca *f* 51
gooseberry uva spina *f* 54
go out, to uscire 96
gram grammo *m* 120
grammar book grammatica *f* 105
grandfather nonno *m* 93
grandmother nonna *f* 93
grape uva *f* 54, 64
grapefruit pompelmo *m* 54
grapefruit juice succo di pompelmo *m* 38, 60
gray grigio(a) 113
graze escoriazione *f* 139
greasy grasso(a) 30, 111
Great Britain Gran Bretagna *f* 146
Greece Grecia *f* 146
green verde 113
green bean fagiolino *m* 52
greengrocer's negozio di frutta e verdura *m* 98
green salad insalata verde *f* 52
greeting saluto *m* 9, 152
grey grigio(a) 113
grilled alla griglia 47; ai ferri 50
grocery negozio di alimentari *m* 98, 120
group gruppo *m* 82
guide guida *f* 80
guidebook guida turistica *f* 82, 104, 105
gum *(teeth)* gengiva *f* 145
gynaecologist ginecologo(a) *m/f* 137

H

hair capelli m/pl 30, 111
hairbrush spazzola per capelli f 111
haircut taglio dei capelli m 30
hairdresser's parrucchiere m 27, 30, 98
hair dryer asciugacapelli m 119
hair lotion lozione per capelli f 111
hair slide fermaglio m 111
hairspray lacca f 30, 111
half metà f, mezzo m 149
half a day mezza giornata f 80
half a dozen mezza dozzina f 120
half an hour mezz'ora f 153
half board mezza pensione f 24
half price (ticket) metà tariffa f 69
hall (large room) sala f 81, 88
ham prosciutto m 41, 48, 63, 64
hammer martello m 106
hammock amaca f 106
hand mano f 138
handbag borsetta f 116, 156
hand cream crema per le mani f 110
handicrafts artigianato m 83
handkerchief fazzoletto m 116
handmade fatto(a) a mano 113
hanger attaccapanni m 27
hangover mal di testa m 108
happy felice, buon(a) 152
harbour porto m 81
hard duro(a) 123
hard-boiled egg uovo sodo m 38
hardware shop negozio di ferramenta m 99
hare lepre f 51
hat cappello m 116
have, to avere 12
hay fever febbre del fieno f 108, 141
hazelnut nocciola f 54
he egli, lui 161
head testa f 138, 139
headache mal di testa m 141
headlight faro m 79
headphones cuffia (d'ascolto) f 119
health salute f 56
health food shop negozio di cibi dietetici m 99
health insurance assicurazione malattie f 144
heart cuore m 138
heart attack attacco cardiaco m 141
heating riscaldamento m 23, 28
heavy pesante 13, 101
heel tacco m 118

height altitudine f 85
helicopter elicottero m 74
hello! (phone) pronto 135
help aiuto m 156
help, to aiutare 13, 21, 100, 134; (oneself) servirsi 120
her suo, sua (pl suoi, sue) 161
herbs odori m/pl 53
herb tea tisana f 60
here qui, ecco 13
herring aringa f 46
high alto(a) 90, 141
high season alta stagione f 150
high tide alta marea f 90
hill collina f 85
hire noleggio m 20, 74
hire, to noleggiare 19, 20, 74, 90, 91, 119; affittare 155
his suo, sua (pl suoi, sue) 161
history storia f 83
hitchhike, to fare l'autostop 74
hold on! (phone) resti in linea! 136
hole buco m 29
holiday giorno festivo m 151
holidays vacanze f/pl 151; ferie f/pl 155
home address domicilio m 25
honey miele m 38
hors d'oeuvre antipasto m 41
horse riding corsa di cavalli f 89
hospital ospedale m 144
hot caldo(a) 14, 25, 38, 94
hotel albergo m 19, 21, 22; hotel m 22, 80
hotel guide guida degli alberghi f 19
hotel reservation prenotazione d'albergo f 19
hot water acqua calda f 23, 28
hot-water bottle borsa dell'acqua calda f 27
hour ora f 153
house casa f 83, 85
how come 10
how far quanto dista 10, 76, 85, 100
how long quanto tempo 10, 24
how many quanti 10
how much quanto 10, 24
hundred cento 148
hungry, to be aver fame 12, 35
hurry (to be in a) avere fretta 21
hurt, to fare male 139, 145; (oneself) farsi male 139
husband marito m 93
hydrofoil aliscafo m 74

I

I io 161
ice ghiaccio *m* 94
ice-cream gelato *m* 55, 64
ice-cream parlour gelateria *f* 33
ice cube cubetto di ghiaccio *m* 27
iced coffee caffè freddo *m* 60
ice pack elemento refrigerante *m* 106
iced tea tè freddo *m* 60
ill malato(a) 140
illness malattia *f* 160
important importante 12
impressive impressionante 84
in in 13, 163
include, to comprendere 20, 24, 32, 62, 80; includere 31
India India *f* 146
indigestion indigestione *f* 141
indoor *(swimming pool)* coperto(a) 90
inexpensive economico(a) 35, 124
infection infezione *f* 141
inflammation infiammazione *f* 142
inflation inflazione *f* 131
inflation rate tasso d'inflazione *m* 131
influenza influenza *f* 142
information informazione *f* 67, 155
injection iniezione *f* 142, 144
injure, to ferire 139
injured ferito(a) 79, 139
injury ferita *f* 139
ink inchiostro *m* 105
inn locanda *f* 22, 33; osteria *f* 33
inquiry informazione *f* 68
insect bite puntura d'insetto *f* 108, 139
insect repellent crema contro gli insetti *f* 109
insect spray spray insetticida *m* 109
inside dentro 15
instead invece 37
instrumental *(music)* strumentale 128
insurance assicurazione *f* 20, 79, 144
interest interesse *m* 80, 131
interested, to be interessarsi 83, 96
interesting interessante 84
international internazionale 133, 134
interpreter interprete *m/f* 131
intersection incrocio *m* 77
introduce, to presentare 92
introduction presentazione *f* 92, 130
investment investimento *m* 131
invitation invito *m* 94
invite, to invitare 94

invoice fattura *f* 131
iodine tintura di iodio *f* 109
Ireland Irlanda *f* 146
iron *(laundry)* ferro da stiro *m* 119
iron, to stirare 29
ironmonger's negozio di ferramenta *m* 99
Israel Israele *m* 146
Italian italiano(a) 10, 11, 95, 104, 114
Italy Italia *f* 146
its suo, sua *(pl* suoi, sue) 161
ivory avorio *m* 122

J

jacket giacca *f* 116
jade giada *f* 122
jam marmellata *f* 38
jam, to incastrare 28; bloccare 125
January gennaio *m* 150
Japan Giappone *m* 146
jar vasetto *m* 120
jaundice itterizia *f* 142
jaw mascella *f* 138
jeans jeans *m/pl* 116
jersey maglietta *f* 116
jewel gioiello *m* 121
jeweller's gioielleria *f* 99, 121
jewellery gioielli *m/pl* 127
joint articolazione *f* 138
journey percorso *m* 72
juice succo *m* 38, 60
July luglio *m* 150
jumper *(sweater)* maglione *m* 116
June giugno *m* 116
just *(only)* soltanto 100

K

keep, to tenere 62
kerosene petrolio *m* 106
key chiave *f* 26
kidney rognone *m* 48; rene *m* 138
kilogram chilogrammo *m* 120
kilometre chilometro *m* 20
kind gentile 95
kind *(type)* genere *m* 140
knapsack zaino *m* 106
knee ginocchio *m* 138
kneesocks calzettoni *m/pl* 116
knife coltello *m* 36, 61, 107
knitwear maglieria *f* 127
knock, to bussare 155
know, to sapere 16; conoscere 96, 114

DICTIONARY

Dizionario

L

label etichetta f 105
lace pizzo m 114
lady signora f 155
lake lago m 81, 85, 90
lamb agnello m 48
lamp lampada f 46
landmark punto di riferimento m 85
landscape paesaggio m 92
lantern lanterna f 106
large grande 101, 118
lark allodola f 51
last ultimo(a) 13, 68, 73; scorso(a) 149, 151
last name cognome m 25
late tardi 13
later più tardi 135
laugh, to ridere 95
launderette lavanderia automatica f 99
laundry (place) lavanderia f 29, 99; (clothes) biancheria f 29
laundry service servizio di lavanderia m 23
laxative lassativo m 109
lead (theatre) ruolo principale m 86
lead piombo m 75
leap year anno bisestile m 149
leather pelle f 114, 118
leather goods pelletteria f 127
leave, to partire 31, 68, 74, 162; lasciare 156; (deposit) depositare 26, 71
leek porro m 52
left sinistro(a) 21, 63, 69, 77
left-luggage office deposito bagagli m 67, 71
leg gamba f 138
lemon limone m 37, 38, 54, 55, 60, 64
lemonade limonata f 60
lemon juice succo di limone m 60
lens (glasses) lente f 123; (camera) obiettivo m 125
lens cap cappuccio per obiettivo m 125
lentil lenticchia f 52
less meno 14
lesson lezione f 91
let, to (hire out) affittare 155
letter lettera f 132
letter box cassetta delle lettere f 132
letter of credit lettera di credito f 130
lettuce lattuga f 52

level crossing passaggio a livello m 79
library biblioteca f 81, 99
lie down, to sdraiarsi 142
life belt cintura di salvataggio f 74
life boat canotto di salvataggio m 74
lifeguard bagnino m 90
lift ascensore m 27, 100
light leggero(a) 13, 55, 57, 101, 128; (colour) chiaro(a) 101, 112, 112
light luce f 28, 124; (cigarette) fiammifero m 95
lighter accendino m 126
lighter fluid benzina per accendino f 126
lighter gas gas per accendino m 126
light meter esposimetro m 125
like, to volere 12, 20, 23; desiderare 103; piacere 25, 61, 92, 96, 102, 112
lime cedro m 54
line linea f 73, 136
linen (cloth) lino m 114
lip labbro m 138
lipsalve burro cacao m 110
lipstick rossetto m 110
liqueur liquore m 59
liquid liquido m 123
listen, to ascoltare 128
litre litro m 57, 75, 120
little (a) un po' 14
live, to vivere 83
liver fegato m 48, 138
lobster aragosta f 46
local locale 36, 60
London Londra f 130
long lungo(a) 115
long-sighted presbite 123
look, to guardare 123
look for, to cercare 12
look out! attenzione! 156
loose (clothes) largo(a) 115
lose, to perdere 123, 156
loss perdita f 131
lost perduto(a) 12; perso(a) 156
lost and found office ufficio oggetti smarriti m 67, 156
lost property office ufficio oggetti smarriti m 67, 156
lot (a) molto 14
lotion lozione f 110
loud (voice) forte 135
love, to amare 162

lovely bello(a) 94
low basso(a) 90, 141
lower inferiore 69, 70
low season bassa stagione f 150
low tide bassa marea f 90
luck fortuna f 152
luggage bagagli m/pl 18, 26, 31, 71
luggage locker custodia automatica
   dei bagagli f 18, 67, 71
luggage trolley carrello portabagagli
   m 18, 71
lump *(bump)* bernoccolo m 139
lunch pranzo m 34, 80, 94
lung polmone m 138

M

mackerel sgombro m 47
magazine rivista f 105
magnificent magnifico(a) 84
maid cameriera f 26
mail, to spedire 28
mail posta f 28, 133
mailbox cassetta delle lettere f 132
main principale 80
make, to fare 131, 163
make up, to rifare 28; preparare 108
make-up remover pad tampone per
   togliere il trucco m 110
man uomo m *(pl* uomini) 115
manager direttore m 26
manicure manicure f 30
many molti(e) 14
map carta geografica f 76, 105;
   pianta f 105
March marzo m 150
marinated marinato(a) 47
marjoram maggiorana f 63
market mercato m 81, 99
marmalade marmellata d'arance f
   38
married sposato(a) 93
marrow midollo m 48
mass *(church)* messa f 84
mat *(finish)* opaco(a) 125
match fiammifero m 106, 126;
   (sport) partita f, incontro m 89
match, to *(colour)* ravvivare 112
material *(cloth)* tessuto m 113
matinée spettacolo del pomeriggio
   m 87
mattress materasso m 106
mauve lilla 113
May maggio m 150
may *(can)* potere 11, 12, 163

meadow prato m 85
meal pasto m 24, 34, 62, 143
mean, to significare 10, 25
means mezzo m 74
measles morbillo m 142
measure, to prendere le misure 114
meat carne f 48, 49, 61
meatball polpetta f 48
mechanic meccanico m 78
mechanical pencil portamine m 105
medical medico(a) 144
medicine medicina f 83, 143
medium *(meat)* a puntino 50
meet, to incontrare 96
melon melone m 54
mend, to riparare 75; *(clothes)* ram-
   mendare 29
menthol *(cigarettes)* mentolo m 126
menu menù m 36, 39, 40
message messaggio m 28, 136
methylated spirits alcool metilico m
   106
metre metro m 112
mezzanine *(theatre)* galleria f 87
middle mezzo m 69; metà f 87, 150
midnight mezzanotte f 153
mileage chilometraggio m 20
milk latte m 38, 60, 64
milkshake frullato di latte m 60
million milione m 148
mineral water acqua minerale f 60
minister *(religion)* pastore m 84
minute minuto m 153
mirror specchio m 115, 123
miscellaneous diverso(a) 127
Miss Signorina f 9
miss, to mancare 18, 29, 61
mistake errore m 31, 61, 62
mixed misto(a) 55
moccasin mocassino m 118
modified American plan mezza pensione f 24
moisturizing cream crema idratante f
   110
moment momento m 136
monastery monastero m 81
Monday lunedì m 151
money denaro m 129, 130
money order vaglia m 133
month mese m 16, 150
monument monumento m 81
moon luna f 94
moped motorino m 74
more più 14

morning mattino *m* 151, 153
mortgage ipoteca *f* 131
mosque moschea *f* 84
mosquito net zanzariera *f* 106
motel motel *m* 22
mother madre *f* 93
motorbike moto *f* 74
motorboat barca a motore *f* 91
motorway autostrada *f* 76
mountain montagna *f* 85
moustache baffi *m/pl* 31
mouth bocca *f* 138
mouthwash gargarismo *m* 109
move, to muovere 139
movie film *m* 86
movie camera cinepresa *f* 124
movies cinema *m* 86, 96
Mr. Signor *m* 9
Mrs. Signora *f* 9
much molto(a) 14
mug boccale *m* 107
muscle muscolo *m* 138
museum museo *m* 81
mushroom fungo *m* 52
music musica *f* 83, 128
musical commedia musicale *f* 86
mussel cozza *f* 46
must, to dovere 23, 31, 37, 61, 95
mustard senape *f* 37, 64
my mio, mia (*pl* miei, mie) 161

N

nail *(human)* unghia *f* 110
nail file lima da unghie *f* 110
nail polish smalto *m* 110
nail polish remover solvente per le unghie *m* 110
nail scissors forbicine per le unghie *f/pl* 110
name nome *m* 23, 25, 79; cognome *m* 25
napkin tovagliolo *m* 36, 105, 106
nappy pannolino *m* 111
narrow stretto(a) 118
nationality cittadinanza *f* 25; nazionalità *f* 92
natural naturale 83
natural history storia naturale *f* 83
nausea nausea *f* 140
near vicino(a) 13; vicino a 14
nearby qui vicino 77, 84
nearest il (la) più vicino(a) 78, 98
neat *(drink)* liscio(a) 56, 59
neck collo *m* 30, 138

necklace collana *f* 121
need, to aver bisogno 29, 118; essere necessario 90; servire 118
needle ago *m* 27
needlework ricamo *m* 127
negative negativo *m* 125
nephew nipote *m* 93
nerve nervo *m* 138
nervous nervoso(a) 138
never mai 15
new nuovo(a) 13
newsagent's giornalaio *m* 99
newspaper giornale *m* 104, 105
newsstand edicola *f* 19, 67, 99, 104
New Year Capodanno *m* 152
New Zealand Nuova Zelanda *f* 146
next prossimo(a) 65, 68, 73, 76, 149; seguente 151
next to accanto a 14, 77
niece nipote *f* 93
night notte *f* 24, 151
nightclub night-club *m* 88
night cream crema da notte *f* 110
nightdress camicia da notte *f* 116
nine nove 147
nineteen diciannove 147
ninety novanta 148
ninth nono(a) 149
no no 9
noisy rumoroso(a) 25
nonalcoholic analcolico(a) 60
none nessuno(a) 15
nonsmoker non fumatori *m/pl* 36, 70
noon mezzogiorno *m* 31, 153
normal normale 30
north nord *m* 77
North America America del Nord *f* 140
nose naso *m* 138
nosebleed emorragia nasale *f* 140
nose drops gocce nasali *f/pl* 109
not non 15, 163
note *(banknote)* banconota *f* 130
notebook taccuino *m* 105
note paper carta da lettere *m* 105
nothing nulla 15, 17; niente 15
notice *(sign)* cartello *m* 155
November novembre *m* 150
now adesso 15
number numero *m* 26, 65, 135, 136, 147
nurse infermiera *f* 144
nutmeg noce moscata *f* 53

O

occupied occupato(a) 13, 155
October ottobre *m* 150
octopus polpo *m* 46
offer, to offrire 95
office ufficio *m* 19, 67, 99, 132, 133, 156
oil olio *m* 37, 64, 75, 111
oily grasso(a) 30, 111
old vecchio(a), anziano(a) 13
old town città vecchia *f* 81
olive oliva *f* 41
omelet frittata *f* 42
on su 14, 163
once una volta 149
one uno(a) 147
one-way *(ticket)* andata *f* 69
on foot a piedi 76
onion cipolla *f* 52
only soltanto 15, 80
on request a richiesta 73
on time in orario 68
onyx onice *m* 122
open aperto(a) 13, 82, 155
open, to aprire 10, 17, 82, 108, 131, 132, 142
open-air all'aperto 90
opera opera *f* 88
opera house teatro dell'opera *m* 81, 88
operation operazione *f* 144
operator centralinista *m/f* 134
operetta operetta *f* 88
opposite di fronte 77
optician ottico *m* 99, 123
or o 15
oral orale 143
orange arancio 113
orange arancia *f* 54, 64
orange juice succo d'arancia *m* 38, 60
orangeade aranciata *f* 60
orchestra orchestra *f* 88; *(seats)* poltrona *f* 87
orchestral music musica sinfonica *f* 128
order *(goods, meal)* ordinazione *f* 40, 102
order, to *(goods, meal)* ordinare 61, 102, 103
oregano origano *m* 53
ornithology ornitologia *f* 83
our nostro(a) 161
out of order fuori servizio 155

out of stock esaurito(a) 103
outlet *(electric)* presa *f* 27
outside fuori 15; all'aperto 36
oval ovale 101
over there laggiù 69
overalls tuta *f* 116
overdone troppo cotto(a) 61
overheat, to *(engine)* surriscaldare 78
overtake, to sorpassare 79
owe, to dovere 144
overwhelming sbalorditivo(a) 84
oyster ostrica *f* 41, 46

P

pacifier succhiotto *m* 111
packet pacchetto *m* 120, 126
page pagina *f* 77
page *(hotel)* fattorino *m* 26
pail secchio *m* 106; secchiello *m* 128
pain dolore *m* 140, 141; male *m* 144
painkiller antinevralgico *m* 140; calmante *m* 144
paint pittura *f* 155
paint, to dipingere 83
paintbox scatola di colori *f* 105
painter pittore *m* 83
painting pittura *f* 83
pair paio *m* 116, 118, 149
pajamas pigiama *m* 117
palace palazzo *m* 81
palpitation palpitazione *f* 141
panties slip *m* 116
pants *(trousers)* pantaloni *m/pl* 116
panty girdle guaina *f* 116
panty hose collant *m* 116
paper carta *f* 105
paperback libro tascabile *m* 105
paper napkin tovagliolo di carta *m* 107
paraffin *(fuel)* petrolio *m* 106
parcel pacco *m* 132
pardon? prego? 10
parents genitori *m/pl* 93
park parco *m* 81
park, to parcheggiare 26, 77
parking parcheggio *m* 77, 79
parking disc disco di sosta *m* 77
parking meter parchimetro *m* 77
parliament parlamento *m* 81
parsley prezzemolo *m* 53
part parte *f* 138
partridge pernice *f* 51

party *(social gathering)* ricevimento m 95

pass *(mountain)* passo m 85

pass, to *(car)* sorpassare 79

passport passaporto m 16, 17, 25, 26, 156

passport photo fotografia d'identità f 124

pass through, to essere di passaggio 16

pasta pasta f 44

paste *(glue)* colla f 105

pastry pasticcino m 64

pastry shop pasticceria f 99

patch, to *(clothes)* rappezzare 29

path sentiero m 85; pista f 155

patient paziente m/f 144

pay, to pagare 31, 62, 102

payment pagamento m 102, 131

pea pisello m 52

peach pesca f 54

peak picco m 85

peanut arachide f 54

pear pera f 54

pearl perla f 122

pedestrian pedonale 79

peg *(tent)* picchetto m 107

pen penna f 105

pencil matita f 105

pencil sharpener temperamatite m 105

pendant pendente m 121

penicillin penicillina f 143

penknife temperino m 107

pensioner pensionato m 82

people gente f 93

pepper pepe m 37; *(sweet)* peperone m 52

per cent per cento 149

percentage percentuale f 131

perch pesce persico m 46

per day per un giorno 20, 89; al giorno 32

perform, to *(theatre)* rappresentare 86

perfume profumo m 110

perfume shop profumeria f 108

perhaps forse 15

per hour all'ora 77; per un'ora 89

period *(monthly)* mestruazioni f/pl 141

period pains mestruazioni dolorose f/pl 141

permanent wave permanente f 30

permit permesso m 90

per night per una notte 24

per person per persona 32

person persona f 32

personal personale 17

personal call telefonata con preavviso f 135

personal cheque assegno personale m 130

person-to-person call telefonata con preavviso f 135

per week per una settimana 20, 24

petrol benzina f 75, 78

pewter peltro m 122

pheasant fagiano m 51

photo fotografia f 82, 124, 125

photocopy fotocopia f 131

photograph, to fotografare, fare delle fotografie 82

photographer fotografo m 99

photography fotografia f 124

phrase espressione f 11

pick up, to prendere 80, 96

pickles sottaceti m/pl 41, 64

picnic picnic m 63

picnic basket cestino da picnic m 107

picture quadro m 83; *(photo)* fotografia f 82

piece pezzo m 120

pig porcellino m, porchetta f 46

pigeon piccione m 51

pill pillola f 141; compressa f 143

pillow guanciale m 27

pin spillo m 111, 122

pineapple ananas m 54

pink rosa 113

pipe pipa f 126

pipe cleaner nettapipe m 126

pipe tobacco tabacco da pipa m 126

pipe tool curapipe m 126

pizza pizza f 42, 63

pizza parlour pizzeria f 33

place luogo m 25; posto m 76

place of birth luogo di nascita m 25

plane aereo m 65

planetarium planetario m 82

plaster, to ingessare 140

plastic plastica f 107

plastic bag sacchetto di plastica m 107

plate piatto m 36, 61, 107

platform *(station)* binario m 67, 68, 69, 70

platinum platino m 122

play *(theatre)* commedia f 86
play, to interpretare 86; suonare 88; giocare 89, 93
playground parco giochi m 32
playing card carte da gioco f/pl 105
please per favore, per piacere 9
plimsolls scarpe da tennis f/pl 118
plug *(electric)* spina f 28
plum prugna f 54, 64
pneumonia polmonite f 142
poached affogato(a) 47
pocket tasca f 117
pocket watch orologio da tasca m 121
point punto m 80
point, to *(show)* indicare 11
poison veleno m 156
poisoning avvelenamento m 142
pole *(ski)* bastone m 91
police polizia f 78, 156
police station posto di polizia m 99, 156
polish *(nails)* smalto m 110
pond stagno m 85
pop music musica pop f 28
poplin popeline m 114
porcelain porcellana f 127
pork maiale m 48
port porto m 74; *(wine)* porto m 59
portable portatile 119
porter facchino m 18, 26, 71
portion porzione f 37, 61
Portugal Portogallo m 146
possible possibile 137
post *(letters)* posta f 28, 133
post, to spedire 28
postage affrancatura f 132
postage stamp francobollo m 28, 126, 132
postcard cartolina f 105, 126, 132
poste restante fermo posta m 133
post office ufficio postale m 99, 132
potato patata f 52
pottery terracotta f 83
poultry pollame m 50
pound *(money)* sterlina f 18, 130; *(weight)* libbra f 120
powder cipria f 110
powder compact portacipria m 121
prawns scampi m/pl 47
preference preferenza f 101
pregnant incinta 141
premium *(gasoline)* super 75
prescribe, to prescrivere 143

prescription ricetta f 108, 143
press, to *(iron)* stirare a vapore 29
press stud bottone a pressione m 117
pressure pressione f 75, 142
price prezzo m 24
priest prete m 84
print *(photo)* stampa f 125
private privato(a) 80, 91, 155
processing *(photo)* sviluppo m 124
profession professione f 25
profit profitto m 131
programme programma m 87
prohibit, to vietare 79, 91, 155
pronunciation pronuncia f 6
propelling pencil portamine m 105
Protestant protestante 84
provide, to procurare 131
prune prugna secca f 54
public holiday giorno festivo m 152
pull, to tirare 155
pullover pullover m 117
pumpkin zucca f 52
puncture foratura f 75
purchase acquisto m 131
pure puro(a) 114
purple viola 113
push, to spingere 155
put, to mettere 24
pyjamas pigiama m 117

Q

quail quaglia f 51
quality qualità f 103, 113
quantity quantità f 14, 103
quarter quarto m 149; *(part of town)* quartiere m 81
quarter of an hour quarto d'ora m 153
quartz quarzo m 122
question domanda f 10, 163
quick rapido(a) 13; presto 156
quickly presto 137, 156
quiet tranquillo(a) 23, 25
quince cotogna f 54

R

rabbi rabbino m 84
rabbit coniglio m 51
race course/track ippodromo m 90
racket *(sport)* racchetta f 90
radiator radiatore m 78
radio *(set)* radio f 23, 28, 119
radish ravanello m 52

railroad crossing passaggio a livello m 79

railway ferrovia f 154

railway station stazione f 19, 21, 67, 70

rain pioggia f 94

rain, to piovere 94

raincoat impermeabile m 117

raisin uva passa f 54

rangefinder telemetro m 125

rare (meat) al sangue 50, 61

rash esantema m 139

raspberry lampone m 54

rate tariffa f 20; tasso m 131

razor rasoio m 110

razor blade lametta f 110

reading-lamp lampada f 27

ready pronto(a) 29, 118, 123, 125, 145

real vero(a) 121

rear dietro 75

receipt ricevuta f 103, 144

reception ricevimento m 23

receptionist capo ricevimento m 26

recommend, to consigliare 35, 36, 40, 80, 86, 88, 137, 145

record (disc) disco m 127, 128

record player giradischi m 119

rectangular rettangolare 101

red rosso(a) 57, 113

redcurrant ribes m 54

red mullet triglia f 46

reduction riduzione f 24, 82

refill ricambio m 105

refund, to rimborsare 103

regards saluti m/pl 152

register, to (luggage) far registrare 71

registered mail raccomandato(a) 133

registration registrazione f 25

registration form scheda f 25, 26

regular (petrol) normale 75

religion religione f 83

religious service funzione religiosa f 84

rent, to noleggiare 19, 20, 74, 89, 91, 119; affittare 155

rental noleggio m 20, 74

repair riparazione f 125

repair, to riparare 29, 118, 119, 121, 123, 125, 145

repeat, to ripetere 11

report, to denunciare 156

reservation prenotazione f 19, 23, 65, 69

reservations office ufficio prenotazioni m 19, 67

reserve, to prenotare 19, 23, 87; riservare 36

restaurant ristorante m 19, 32, 33, 35, 67

return (ticket) andata e ritorno 69

return, to (give back) rendere 103

reverse the charges, to telefonare a carico del destinatario 135

rheumatism reumatismo m 141

rib costola f 48, 138

ribbon nastro m 105

rice riso m 45

right destro(a) 63, 69, 77; (correct) giusto 63, 70

ring (on finger) anello m 121

ring, to suonare 155

river fiume m 85, 90

road strada f 76, 77, 85

road assistance assistenza stradale f 78

road map carta stradale f 105

road sign segnale stradale m 79

roast arrosto 48, 50

roast beef rosbif m 48

rock masso m 79

roll (bread) panino m 38, 64

roller skates pattini a rotelle m/pl 128

roll film bobina f 124

roll-neck a collo alto 117

room camera f 19, 23, 24, 25, 28; (space) posto m 32

room number numero della stanza m 26

room service servizio nella stanza m 23

rope corda f 107

rosary rosario m 122

rosé rosatello 57

rosemary rosmarino m 53

rouge fard m 110

round rotondo(a) 101

round-neck a girocollo 117

roundtrip (ticket) andata e ritorno 69

rowing-boat barca a remi f 91

royal reale 82

rubber gomma f 105, 118

ruby rubino m 122

rucksack zaino m 107

ruin rovina f 82

ruler (for measuring) riga f 105

rum rum m 60

running water acqua corrente f 23

S

safe (not dangerous) sicuro(a), senza pericolo 90
safe cassaforte f 26
safety pin spillo di sicurezza m 111
saffron zafferano m 53
sage salvia f 53
sailing-boat barca a vela f 91
salad insalata f 52, 64
salami salame m 41, 63, 64
sale vendita f 131; (bargains) saldi m/pl 100, svendita f 155
sales tax I.V.A. f 24, 102
salmon salmone m 41, 46
salt sale m 37, 64
salty salato(a) 61
sand sabbia f 90
sandal sandalo m 118
sandwich panino imbottito m 63
sanitary towel/napkin assorbente igienico m 109
sardine sardina f 41, 47
satin raso m 114
Saturday sabato m 151
sauce salsa f 44
saucepan casseruola f 107
saucer piattino m 107
sausage salsiccia f 48, 64
scallop arsella f 46
scarf sciarpa f 117
scenic route strada panoramica f 85
scissors forbici f/pl 107; forbicine f/pl 110
scooter motoretta f 74
Scotland Scozia f 146
Scottish scozzese 93
scrambled eggs uova strapazzate f/pl 38
screwdriver cacciavite m 107
sculptor scultore m 83
sculpture scultura f 83
sea mare m 23, 85,
sea bass spigola f 47
sea bream orata f 46
seafood frutti di mare m/pl 46
season stagione f 40, 150
seasoning condimento m 37
seat posto m 69, 70, 87
seat belt cintura di sicurezza f 75
second secondo 149
second secondo m 153
second class seconda classe f 69
second hand lancetta dei secondi f 122

second-hand d'occasione 104
secretary segretaria f 27, 131
see, to guardare 11
sell, to vendere 162
send, to mandare 31, 78, 102, 103; spedire 132; inviare 133
send up, to portare su 26
separately separatamente 62
September settembre m 150
seriously (wounded) gravemente 139
service servizio m 24, 62, 98, 100; (religion) funzione f 84
serviette tovagliolo m 36
set (hair) messa in piega f 30
set menu menù (a prezzo fisso) m 36, 40
setting lotion fissatore m 30; lozione fissativa f 111
seven sette 147
seventeen diciassette 147
seventh settimo 149
seventy settanta 148
sew, to attaccare 29
shade (colour) tonalità f 112
shampoo shampoo m 30, 111
shape forma f 103
share (finance) azione f 131
sharp (pain) acuto(a) 140
shave, to radere 31
shaver rasoio (elettrico) m 27, 119
shaving cream crema da barba f 111
she ella, lei 161
shelf scaffale m 100, 120
ship nave f 74
shirt camicia f 117
shiver, to rabbrividire 140
shoe scarpa f 118
shoelace laccio m 118
shoemaker's calzolaio m 99
shoe polish lucido m 118
shoe shop negozio di scarpe m 99
shop negozio m 98
shopping acquisti m/pl 97
shopping area zona dei negozi f 19, 82, 100
short corto(a) 30, 115,
shorts short m 117
short-sighted miope 123
shoulder spalla f 138
shovel paletta f 49, 128
show spettacolo m 86, 87
show, to mostrare 11, 12, 100, 101, 103, 119

shower doccia f 23, 32
shrimp gamberetto m 41, 46
shrink, to restringersi 114
shut chiuso(a) 13
shutter *(window)* imposta f 29; *(camera)* otturatore m 125
sick, to be *(ill)* sentirsi male 140, 156
sickness *(illness)* malattia f 140
side lato m 30
sideboards/burns basette f/pl 31
sightseeing visita turistica f 80
sightseeing tour giro turistico m 80
sign *(notice)* cartello m 155; *(road)* segnale m 79
sign, to firmare 26, 131
signature firma f 25
signet ring anello con stemma m 122
silk seta f 114, 127
silver argentato(a) 113
silver argento m 121, 122
silver plate placcato d'argento 122
silverware argenteria f 122
simple semplice 124
since da 15, 150
sing, to cantare 88
single scapolo m, nubile f 93
single *(ticket)* andata 69
single room camera singola f 19, 23
sister sorella f 93
sit down, to sedersi 95
six sei 147
sixteen sedici 147
sixth sesto 149
sixty sessanta 147
size formato m 124; *(clothes)* taglia f, misura f 114, 115; *(shoes)* numero m 118
skates pattini m/pl 91
skating rink pista di pattinaggio f 91
ski sci m 91
ski, to sciare 91
ski boot scarpone da sci m 91
skier sciatore m (sciatrice f) 91
skiing sci m 89, 91
ski lift sciovia m 91
skin pelle f 138
skirt gonna f 117
ski run pista di sci f 91
sky cielo m 94
sled slitta f 91
sleep, to dormire 144
sleeping bag sacco a pelo m 107
sleeping-car vagone letto m 66, 68, 69, 70

sleeping pill sonnifero m 109, 143, 144
sleeve manica f 117
slice fetta f 55, 63, 120
slide *(photo)* diapositiva f 124
slip sottoveste f 117
slipper pantofola f 118
slow lento(a) 13
slow down, to rallentare 79
slowly lentamente 11, 21, 135
small piccolo(a) 13, 25, 101, 118
smoke, to fumare 95
smoked affumicato(a) 41, 47
smoker *(compartment)* fumatori m/pl 70
snack spuntino m 63
snack bar snack bar m 67
snail lumaca f 46
snap fastener bottone a pressione m 117
sneakers scarpe da tennis f/pl 118
snorkel maschera da subacqueo f 128
snow neve f 94
snow, to nevicare 94
soap saponetta f 27, 111
soccer calcio m 89
sock calzino m 117
socket *(outlet)* presa f 27
soft morbido(a) 123
soft drink bibita f 64
soft-boiled *(egg)* molle 38
sold out *(theatre)* esaurito 87
sole suola f 118; *(fish)* sogliola f 47
soloist solista m/f 88
some del, della *(pl* dei, delle) 14
someone qualcuno 95
something qualcosa 36, 55, 108, 112, 113, 139
son figlio m 93
song canzone f 128
soon presto 15
sore *(painful)* infiammato(a) 145
sore throat mal di gola m 141
sorry *(I'm)* mi dispiace 11, 16
sort genere m 86
sound-and-light show spettacolo suoni e luci m 86
soup minestra f, zuppa f 43
south sud m 77
South Africa Sudafrica m 146
South America America del Sud f 146
souvenir oggetto ricordo m 127
souvenir shop negozio di ricordi m 99
Soviet Union Unione Sovietica f 146

spade paletta f 128
Spain Spagna f 146
spare tyre ruota di scorta f 75
spark(ing) plug candela f 76
sparkling (wine) spumante 57
speak, to parlare 11, 135
speaker (loudspeaker) altoparlante f
specialist specialista m/f 142
speciality specialità f 40, 60
specimen (medical) campione m
142
spectacle case astuccio per occhiali
m 123
spell, to sillabare 11
spend, to spendere 101
spice spezia f 53
spinach spinacio m 52
spine spina dorsale f 138
spiny lobster aragosta f 46
spit-roasted allo spiedo 50
spoon cucchiaio m 36, 61, 107
sport sport m 89
sporting goods shop negozio di articoli sportivi m 99
sprain, to distorcere 140
spring (season) primavera f 150;
(water) sorgente f 85
square piazza f 82
squid calamaro m 46
stadium stadio m 82
staff personale m 26
stain macchia f 29
stainless steel acciaio inossidabile m
107, 122
stalls (theatre) poltrona f 87
stamp (postage) francobollo m 28,
126, 132
staple graffetta f 105
star stella f 94
start, to iniziare 80, 88; (car) partire
78
starter antipasto m 41
station stazione f 19, 21, 67, 70, 73
stationer's cartoleria f 99, 104
statue statua f 82
stay soggiorno m 31, 92
stay, to restare 16, 24; trattenersi
26; soggiornare 93
steak bistecca f 48
steal, to rubare 156
steamed cotto(a) a vapore 47
stew spezzatino m 49
stewed in umido 50
stiff neck torcicollo m 141

still (mineral water) naturale 60
sting puntura f 139
sting, to pungere 139
stitch, to (clothes) cucire 29; (shoes)
attaccare 118
stock exchange borsa valori f 82
stocking calza da donna f 117
stomach stomaco m 138
stomach ache mal di stomaco m
141
stools feci f/pl 142
stop (bus) fermata f 72, 73
stop! fermatevi! 156
stop, to fermarsi 21, 68, 70, 72
stop thief! al ladro! 156
store negozio m 98
straight (drink) liscio 56, 59
straight ahead diritto 21, 77
strange strano 84
strawberry fragola f 54, 55
street strada f 25
streetcar tram m 72
street map pianta della città f 19, 105
strike sciopero m 155
string spago m 105
strong forte 143
student studente(essa) m 82, 93
stuffed farcito(a) 50
subway (railway) metropolitana f 73
suede renna f 114; camoscio m 118
sugar zucchero m 37, 64
suit (man) completo m 117;
(woman) tailleur m 117
suitcase valigia f 18
summer estate f 150
sun sole m 94
sunburn scottatura solare f 108
Sunday domenica f 151
sunglasses occhiali da sole m/pl 123
sunshade (beach) ombrellone m 91
sunstroke colpo di sole m 141
sun-tan cream crema solare f 111
sun-tan oil olio solare m 111
super (petrol) super 75
superb superbo 84
supermarket supermercato m 99
suppository supposta f 109
surfboard sandolino m 91
surgery (consulting room) ambulatorio m 137
surname cognome m 25
suspenders (Am.) bretelle f/pl 117
swallow, to inghiottire 143
sweater maglione m 117

sweatshirt blusa *f* 117
Sweden Svezia *f* 146
sweet dolce 57, 61
sweet caramella *f* 126
sweetener dolcificante *m* 37
swell, to gonfiare 139
swelling gonfiore *m* 139
swim, to nuotare 90
swimming nuoto *m* 89; balneazione *f* 91
swimming pool piscina *f* 32, 90
swimming trunks costume da bagno *m* 117
swimsuit costume da bagno *m* 117
Swiss svizzero(a) 18
switch interruttore *m* 29
switchboard operator centralinista *m/f* 26
switch on, to *(light)* accendere 79
Switzerland Svizzera *f* 146
swollen gonfio(a) 139
swordfish pesce spada *m* 46
synagogue sinagoga *f* 84
synthetic sintetico 114
system sistema *m* 138

T

table tavolo *m* 36; tavola *f* 107
tablet pastiglia *f* 109
tailor's sartoria *f* 99
take, to prendere 18, 25, 73, 102; durare 72; portare 114
take away, to *(carry)* portare via 63, 102
talcum powder talco *m* 111
tampon tampone igienico *m* 109
tangerine mandarino *m* 54
tap *(water)* rubinetto *m* 28
tape recorder registratore *m* 119
tax tassa *f* 32; I.V.A. *f* 24, 102
taxi taxi *m* 19, 21, 31
tea tè *m* 38, 60, 64
tearoom sala da tè *f* 34
teaspoon cucchiaino *m* 107, 143
telegram telegramma *m* 133
telegraph office ufficio telegrafico *m* 133
telephone telefono *m* 28, 78, 79, 134
telephone, to telefonare 134
telephone booth cabina telefonica *f* 134
telephone call telefonata *f* 135, 136

telephone directory elenco telefonico *m* 134
telephone number numero di telefono *m* 96, 135, 136
telephoto lens teleobiettivo *m* 125
television *(set)* televisore *m* 23, 28, 119
telex telex *m* 133
telex, to mandare un telex 130
tell, to dire 12, 73, 76, 136, 153
temperature temperatura *f* 90; *(fever)* febbre *f* 140, 142
temporary provvisoriamente 145
ten dieci 147
tendon tendine *m* 138
tennis tennis *m* 89
tennis court campo da tennis *m* 89
tennis racket racchetta da tennis *f* 89
tent tenda *f* 32, 107
tenth decimo 149
tent peg picchetto per tenda *m* 107
tent pole palo per tenda *m* 107
term *(word)* termine *m* 131
terrace terrazza *f* 36
terrifying terrificante 84
terrycloth tessuto di spugna *m* 114
tetanus tetano *m* 140
than di 14
thank you grazie 9
that quello, quella 10, 100, 161
the il, lo, la *(pl* i, gli, le) 159
theatre teatro *m* 82, 86
theft furto *m* 156
their il, la loro *(pl* i, le loro) 161
then poi, in seguito 15
there là 13; ecco 13
thermometer termometro *m* 109, 144
these questi, queste 63, 160
they essi, loro 161
thief ladro *m* 156
thin fine 113
think, to pensare 62, 94
third terzo 149
third terzo *m* 149
thirsty, to be aver sete 12
thirteen tredici 147
thirty trenta 147
this questo, questa 10, 100, 160
those quegli, quei, quelle 160; quelli, quelle 63, 120
thousand mille 148
thread filo *m* 27

three tre 147
throat gola f 138, 141
throat lozenge pasticca per la gola f 109
through train treno diretto m 68, 69
thumbtack puntina f 105
thunder tuono m 94
thunderstorm temporale m 94
Thursday giovedì m 151
thyme timo m 53
ticket biglietto m 65, 69, 72, 87, 89
ticket office biglietteria f 67
tide marea f 90
tie cravatta f 117
tie clip fermacravatte m 122
tie pin spillo per cravatta m 122
tight *(clothes)* stretto(a) 115
tights collant m 117
time tempo m 80; *(clock)* ora f 137, 153; *(occasion)* volta f 143
timetable orario ferroviario m 68
tin *(can)* scatola f 120
tinfoil foglio d'alluminio m 107
tin opener apriscatole m 107
tint sfumatura f 111
tinted colorato(a) 123
tip mancia f 62
tire ruota f 75; gomma f 76
tired stanco(a) 12
tissue *(handkerchief)* fazzoletto di carta m 111
to a 14, 163
toast pane tostato m 38
tobacco tabacco m 126
tobacconist's tabaccheria f 99, 126
today oggi 29, 151
toe dito del piede m 138
toilet paper carta igienica f 111
toiletry articoli da toilette m/pl 110
toilets gabinetti m/pl 27, 32, 37, 67
token *(telephone)* gettone m 134
toll pedaggio m 75
tomato pomodoro m 52
tomato juice succo di pomodoro m 60
tomb tomba f 82
tomorrow domani 29, 151
tongue lingua f 48, 138
tonic water acqua tonica f 60
tonight stasera 29, 96; questa sera 86, 87
tonsil tonsilla f 138
too troppo(a) 14; *(also)* anche 15
tooth dente m 145
toothache mal di denti m 145

toothbrush spazzolino da denti m 111, 119
toothpaste dentifricio m 111
top cima f 30; alto m 145
topaz topazio m 122
torch *(flashlight)* lampadina tascabile f 107
torn lacerato(a) 140
touch, to toccare 155
tough duro(a) 61
tourist office azienda di soggiorno e turismo f, ufficio turistico m 22, 80
tourist tax tassa di soggiorno f 32
towards verso 14
towel asciugamano m 27
towelling tessuto di spugna m 114
town hall municipio m 82
tow truck carro attrezzi m 78
toy giocattolo m 128
toy shop negozio di giocattoli m 99
tracksuit tuta sportiva f 117
traffic traffico m 76
traffic light semaforo m 77
trailer roulotte f 32
train treno m 66, 68, 69, 70, 73
tram tram m 72
tranquillizer tranquillante m 109, 143
transfer *(bank)* trasferimento m 131
transformer trasformatore m 119
translate, to tradurre 11
transport trasporto m 74
travel, to viaggiare 92
travel agency agenzia di viaggi f 99
travel guide guida turistica f 105
traveller's cheque traveller's cheque m 18, 62, 102, 130
travel sickness mal d'auto m 108
treatment cura f 143
tree albero m 85
tremendous fantastico(a) 84
trim, to *(beard)* spuntare 31
trip viaggio m 93, 152; percorso m 72
tripe trippe f/pl 49
trolley carrello m 18, 71
trousers pantaloni m/pl 117
trout trota f 47
truffle tartufo m 52
try, to provare 115; *(sample)* assaggiare 60
T-shirt maglietta di cotone f 117
tube tubetto m 120
Tuesday martedì m 151
tumbler bicchiere m 107
tuna tonno m 41, 47

Tunisia Tunisia f 146
tunnel galleria f 79
tunny tonno m 41, 47
turbot rombo m 46
Turkey Turchia f 146
turkey tacchino m 51
turn, to (change direction) girare 21, 77
turquoise turchese 113
turquoise turchese m 122
turtleneck a collo alto 117
tweezers pinzette f/pl 111
twelve dodici 147
twenty venti 147
twice due volte 149
twin bed due letti m/pl 23
two due 147
typewriter macchina per scrivere f 27, 105
typewriter ribbon nastro per macchina da scrivere m 105
typing paper carta per macchina da scrivere f 105
tyre ruota f 75; gomma f 76

U

ugly brutto(a) 13, 84
umbrella ombrello m 117; (beach) ombrellone m 91
uncle zio m 93
unconscious svenuto(a) 139
under sotto 15
underdone (meat) al sangue 50; poco cotto(a) 61
underground (railway) metropolitana f 73
underpants mutande f/pl, slip m 117
undershirt canottiera f 117
understand, to capire 11, 16
undress, to spogliare 142
United States Stati Uniti m/pl 146
university università 82
unleaded senza piombo 75
until fino a 14
up su, in alto 15
upper superiore 69
upset stomach mal di stomaco m 108
upstairs di sopra 15
urgent urgente 12, 145
urine urina f 142
use uso m 17
use, to usare 78, 134
useful utile 15
usual abituale 143

V

vacancy camera libera f 23
vacant libero 13, 155
vacation vacanze f/pl 151
vaccinate, to vaccinare 140
vacuum flask thermos m 107
vaginal vaginale 141
valley valle f 85
value valore m 131
value-added tax I.V.A. f 24, 102, 154
vanilla vaniglia f 55
VAT (sales tax) I.V.A. f 24, 102, 154
veal vitello m 48
vegetable verdura f 52
vegetable store negozio di frutta e verdura m 99
vegetarian vegetariano m 37
vein vena f 138
velvet velluto m 114
velveteen velluto di cotone m 114
venereal disease malattia venerea f 142
venison selvaggina f 51
vermouth vermouth m 59
very molto 15
vest canottiera f 117; (Am.) panciotto m 117
video cassette video cassetta f 119, 124, 127
video recorder video registratore m 119
view vista f 23, 25
village villaggio m 76, 85; paese m 85
vinegar aceto m 37
vineyard vigna f 85
visit, to visitare 84
visiting hours orari di visita m/pl 144
vitamin pills vitamine f/pl 109
V-neck con scollatura a punta 117
volleyball pallavolo f 89
voltage voltaggio m 27, 119
vomit, to vomitare 140

W

waistcoat panciotto m 117
wait, to aspettare 21, 95
waiter cameriere m 26, 36
waiting-room sala d'aspetto f 67
waitress cameriera f 26, 36
wake, to svegliare 26
Wales Galles m 146
walk, to camminare 74; andare a piedi 85
wall muro m 85

DICTIONARY

wallet portafogli *m* 156
walnut noce *f* 54
want, to volere 18, 35, 163; *(wish)* desiderare 12
warm caldo(a) 94
wash, to lavare 29, 114
wash-basin lavabo *m* 28
washing powder detersivo *m* 107
watch orologio *m* 121
watchmaker's orologiaio *m* 99; orologeria *f* 121
watchstrap cinturino per orologio *m* 122
water acqua *f* 23, 28, 32, 38, 75, 90
waterfall cascata *f* 85
water flask borraccia *f* 107
watermelon anguria *f* 54, cocomero *m* 54
water-ski sci nautico *m* 91
way strada *f* 76
we noi 161
weather tempo *m* 93
weather forecast previsioni del tempo *f/pl* 94
wedding ring fede nuziale *f* 122
Wednesday mercoledì *m* 151
week settimana *f* 16, 24, 80, 151
weekend fine settimana *m* 151
well pozzo 85; *(healthy)* bene 9, 140
well-done *(meat)* ben cotto(a) 50
west ovest *m* 77
what che cosa 10, 12; quanto 20; quale 20, 21
wheel ruota *f* 78
when quando, a che ora 10
where dove 10
which quale 10
whipped cream panna montata *f* 55
whisky whisky *m* 17, 59
white bianco(a) 57, 113
whiting merlano *m* 46
who chi 10
why perchè 10
wick stoppino *m* 126
wide largo(a) 118
wide-angle lens grandangolare *m* 125
wife moglie *f* 93
wild boar cinghiale *m* 51
wind vento *m* 94
window finestra *f* 28, 36; *(train)* finestrino *m* 69; *(shop)* vetrina *f* 100, 112
windscreen/shield parabrezza *m* 76
wine vino *m* 56, 57, 61

wine list lista dei vini *f* 57
wine merchant vinaio *m* 99
winter inverno *m* 150
winter sports sport invernali *m/pl* 91
wipers tergicristalli *m/pl* 76
wish augurio *m* 152
with con 14, 163
withdraw, to *(bank)* prelevare 131
without senza 14
woman donna *f* 115
wonderful magnifico(a) 96
wood bosco *m* 85
wood alcohol alcool metilico *m* 107
woodwork lavoro in legno *m* 127
woodcock beccaccia *f* 51
wool lana *f* 114
word parola *f* 11, 15, 133
work lavoro *m* 79
work, to *(function)* funzionare 28, 119
working day giorno feriale *m* 151
worse peggiore 13
wound ferita *f* 139
wrinkle resistant ingualcibile 114
wristwatch orologio braccialetto *m* 122
write, to scrivere 11, 101
writing pad blocco per appunti *m* 105
writing-paper carta da lettere *f* 27
wrong sbagliato(a) 13, 135

X

X-ray *(photo)* radiografia *f* 140

Y

year anno *m* 149
yellow giallo 113
yes sì 9
yesterday ieri 151
yet ancora 15
yoghurt yogurt *m* 64
you tu, voi 161
young giovane 13
your tuo(a) *(pl* tuoi, tue) 161; vostro(a) *(pl* vostri(e)) 161
youth hostel ostello della gioventù *m* 22, 32
Yugoslavia Iugoslavia *f* 146

Z

zero zero *m* 147
zip(per) cerniera *f* 117
zoo zoo *m* 82
zoology zoologia *f* 83

Dizionario

Indice italiano

Abbigliamento	112	Cartoleria	104
Abbreviazioni	154	Cassette	127
Acquisti, guida degli	97	Chiedere la strada	76
Aereo	65	Chiesa	84
Aeroporto	16, 65	Cinema	86
Affari, termini d'	131	Colazione	38
Albergo	22	Colori	113
difficoltà	28	Concerto	88
partenza	31	Conoscenze	92
posta	28	Conversione, tavole di	
prenotazione	19	capacità	158
ricevimento	23	miglia in km	158
Alfabeto	8	pesi	158
Alimentari	63, 120	taglie	115
Alloggio	22	temperatura	157
Anni	149	Corpo, parti del	138
Aperitivi	56	Corriera	72
Apparecchi elettrici	119		
Appuntamento	95	Data	151
Articoli da toilette	110	Denaro	18, 129
Auguri	152	Dentista	145
Autobus	72	Diabetici	37, 141
		Direzioni	76
Bagagli	18, 71	Dischi	127
Balletto	88	Discoteche	88
Banca	129	Distrazioni	86
Barbiere	30	Dogana	16
Battello	74		
Bevande	56	Elettricista	119
analcoliche	60	Emergenze	156
Biciclette, noleggio	74	Escursioni	65
Biglietti		Espressioni correnti	9
calcio	89	Età	150
concerto	87		
museo	82	Famiglia	93
treno	69	Ferite	139
Birra	59	Formaggio	53
		Fotografia	124
Cacciagione	50	Francobolli	132
Cambio	18, 129	Frittate	42
Campagna	85	Frutta	54
Campeggio	32	Frutti di mare	46
Carne	48	Funzioni religiose	84
Cartelli	155	Furto	156

Giocattoli	128
Gioielleria	121
Giornali	104
Grammatica	159
Incidenti	78, 139
Insalate	52
Inviti	94
Lavanderia	29
Lavanderia a secco	29
Libreria	104
Macchina	75
guasti	78
incidenti	78
noleggio	20
parcheggio	77
Malattia	140
Medico	137
Menù	39
Mesi	150
Metropolitana	73
Minestre	43
Musica	88, 128
Negozi, elenco dei	98
Nightclub	88
Numeri	147
Oggetti smarriti	156
Opera	88
Ora	153
Orologeria	121
Ospedale	144
Ottico	123
Paesi, nomi di	146
Parrucchiere	30
Passaporto	16
Pasta	44
Personale d'albergo	26
Pesca	90
Pesci	46
Picnic	63,120
Pizza	42
Polizia	78, 156
Pollame	50

Posate	107
Presentazioni	92
Pullman	72
Ristorante	33
conto	62
menù	39
ordinazione	36
reclami	61
Salse	44
Scarpe	118
Segnali stradali	79
Spezie	53
Spiaggia	90
Sport	89
Sport invernali	91
Stagioni	150
Stazione	67
Stazione di rifornimento	75
Stoviglie	107
Tabaccheria	126
Taglie	115
Taxi	21
Teatro	86
Telefono	134
Telegrammi, telex	133
Tempo	94
Tessuti	114
Toilette, articoli da	110
Trasporti	
aereo	65
autobus	73
battello	74
biglietti	69
informazioni	68
tram	72
treno	66
Ufficio postale	132
Ufficio turistico	80
Vegetariani	37
Verdure	52
Vino	56
Visite turistiche	80